A New Imperial History of Northern Eurasia, 600–1700

A New Imperial History of Northern Eurasia, 600–1700

From Russian to Global History

Volume 1

Edited by Ilya Gerasimov
Authored by Ilya Gerasimov, Marina Mogilner,
and Sergey Glebov

With the collaboration of Alexander Semyonov

BLOOMSBURY ACADEMIC
LONDON • NEW YORK • OXFORD • NEW DELHI • SYDNEY

BLOOMSBURY ACADEMIC
Bloomsbury Publishing Plc
50 Bedford Square, London, WC1B 3DP, UK
1385 Broadway, New York, NY 10018, USA
29 Earlsfort Terrace, Dublin 2, Ireland

BLOOMSBURY, BLOOMSBURY ACADEMIC and the Diana logo are trademarks of
Bloomsbury Publishing Plc

First published in Great Britain 2024

Copyright © Ilya Gerasimov, Marina Mogilner, and Sergey Glebov 2024

Ilya Gerasimov, Marina Mogilner, and Sergey Glebov have asserted their right under the
Copyright, Designs and Patents Act, 1988, to be identified as authors of this work.

Cover image: design by Bloomsbury; image used https://commons.wikimedia.org/wiki/File:
CEM-15-Asia-Mercator-1595-Tartaria-2532.jpg (Asia ex magna Orbis terrae descriptione
Gerardi Mercatoris desumpta, studio & industria G.M. Iunioris)

Bloomsbury Publishing Plc does not have any control over, or responsibility for, any third-
party websites referred to or in this book. All internet addresses given in this book were
correct at the time of going to press. The author and publisher regret any inconvenience
caused if addresses have changed or sites have ceased to exist, but can accept no
responsibility for any such changes.

Every effort has been made to trace the copyright holders and obtain permission to
reproduce the copyright material. Please do get in touch with any enquiries or any
information relating to such material or the rights holder. We would be pleased to rectify
any omissions in subsequent editions of this publication should they be drawn to our
attention.

A catalogue record for this book is available from the British Library.

A catalog record for this book is available from the Library of Congress.

ISBN: HB: 978-1-3501-9679-7
PB: 978-1-3501-9680-3
ePDF: 978-1-3501-9681-0
eBook: 978-1-3501-9682-7

Typeset by Deanta Global Publishing Services, Chennai, India

To find out more about our authors and books visit www.bloomsbury.com and
sign up for our newsletters.

Contents

Note on the Text	vi
Introduction	1
1 Political Ecology: The Formation of the Northern Eurasia Region	5
2 Mechanisms of Political and Cultural Self-Organization of Northern Eurasia's First Polities: The Formation of the Rous' Lands	37
3 Consolidation of New Political Systems: State-Building in Northern Eurasia (Eleventh–Thirteenth Centuries)	93
4 From Local Polities to Hierarchical Statehood: Interaction and Entanglement of Competing Scenarios of Power (Thirteenth–Fourteenth Centuries)	143
5 New Times: The Problem of Substantiating Sovereignty and Its Boundaries in the Grand Principality of Moscow (Fifteenth–Sixteenth Centuries)	179
6 The Transformation of Social Imagination: The Seventeenth Century	219
7 The Tsardom of Muscovy in Search of an "Assembly Point"	245
Index	291

Note on the Text

All translations of original documents are the authors' unless otherwise stated.

In general, transliterations of proper names follow their direct rendering in English from the original language, unless there is an established historiographical tradition standardizing a particular spelling. One methodological decision that was essential for the project concerns the usage of the original categories from the primary sources synchronous with the historical events discussed in this book. The most obvious example here would be the now conventional rendering of medieval Rous' as Russia/Russian, which the authors consciously reconsider. Such retrospective alterations in spelling in latter-day national historiographies often project nationalizing claims onto the past, thus distorting it and imposing counterfactual historical genealogies. The authors have made every effort to avoid both traditional Russification and retrospective nationalization of historical actors, by working with historical terms as concepts in need of contextualization and exploration. In many cases, we cite several renderings of the same name.

Illustrations to this volume are accessible online at [https://bloomsbury.pub/history-northern-eurasia]. Reference numbers in the text correspond to illustration numbers on the website.

Introduction

Developing a Synthetic Narrative beyond Russian History

Since the breakup of the Soviet Union in 1991, the single field of Russian history has disintegrated into autonomous national histories and the corresponding area studies. This process has restored the centrality of hitherto marginalized peoples, cultures, and regions and discarded the hegemonic historical narrative that framed events in the past by referring to the evolution of Russian centralized statehood and Russian-language culture. The proverbial Russocentrism of this approach resulted not only from a political penchant but also from the inability to structure a synthetic history covering a period of many centuries by any other narrative.[1] The only working alternative to national history was Orthodox Marxist class analysis, but this profoundly structuralist framework rendered history in the sense of storytelling virtually impossible. Even the most radical Marxist historians of the 1920s, anti-imperialist, anticolonial, and explicitly anti-Russian in their views, had to rely on national markers to differentiate one group of "feudals" and peasants from another and account for intraclass conflicts and interclass alliances.[2] Another shortcoming of Marxist methodology as an alternative to a nationalizing view of history was its blindness to human diversity other than class differentiation or imperialist exploitation. Hence, "Russia" and "the state" remained umbrella concepts for tracing the development of complex sociopolitical entities within the borders of the Russian Empire and later the Soviet Union. Given the prevalence of national history as a mode of history writing, Russia was interpreted, implicitly or deliberately, as the country of the Russian ethnocultural nation. The state was understood as the Russian nation-state; Russian culture—as a national culture. To this day, the course in "Russian literature" is usually limited to the Russian national literary canon as representing the entire scene of literary creativity in a multicultural society. Accordingly, the dominant version of Russian history was Russian national history, and its use as an envelope for multiple other national histories was inherently restrictive politically and increasingly outdated methodologically. When the old Russian history was separated into individual national histories, they all benefited from the initial emancipatory impact that released them from the constraints of Russocentrism.

The strategic compartmentalization of the previously single Russian history had one major unforeseen result. The demise of the obsolete, repressive "Russian" framework left a void in place of a perspective and a conceptual language capable of framing a broader historical context for the emerging separate histories. The political sovereignty and cultural autonomy of post-Soviet countries are indisputable, and so is the need to develop historical narratives of their emerging political bodies and societies. However, this task is unattainable beyond the most immediate historical horizon. All the post-Soviet countries were shaped as national republics of the USSR in the 1920s, when their boundaries as well as demographic, economic, and cultural outlooks were determined. Even during the Soviet era, these processes were intertwined with more general developments—those persisting from the imperial period and those emerging within the Soviet Union and internationally. As to the pre-Soviet period, no "national" history can be properly reconstructed without taking into consideration the general historical context of the Russian Empire and its neighbors, and before the empire—of the entangled developments on the loosely defined landmass between northern China and western Europe. New national histories greatly weaken their explanatory potential when developing in isolation from each other and ignoring the findings in "adjacent" fields. There is a practical need for a broader perspective and a narrative capable of reconstructing that entangled historical context without imposing a normative scenario of some eternal entity evolving through centuries on the same territory, be it "Russia" or "the state."

Clearly, no single, all-embracing narrative is capable of equally serving every national, regional, or thematic historical perspective. The relevant broader context will be different for a history of the Tatars in the Russian Empire and the Tatar Autonomous Republic in the USSR, for an early modern history of Ukrainian lands, or a history of professions in late imperial Russia. Each case study needs to reconstruct its own historical context, both diachronously and synchronously. The old Russian history provided a rigidly normative general background that allowed some level of entangled history writing. New national historiographies can cooperate to sustain a more complex and multifaceted common historical context through a productive dialogue, which requires the development of a conceptual language that enables a postnational and globalized historical narrative. This two-volume history course, *A New Imperial History of Northern Eurasia: From Russian to Global History*, which covers the years 600–1918, takes a step in this direction in terms of both conceptual work and the production of a coherent narrative that defies the canonical "scheme of Russian history."

The task was carried out by the four editors of the journal *Ab Imperio*, which for more than two decades has been exploring the possibilities of a postimperial and postnational history of the post-Soviet space. Hundreds of the journal's authors, who represent the global community of specialists on the region, have produced innovative studies on a vast array of subjects. Their work—to which we are indebted—at some point produced a critical mass that allowed a reorganization of the history of the vast space between the Carpathian Mountains and the Far East within a new narrative. This new narrative focuses on the clashing local processes of self-organization and organization from above, and on the social and natural diversity in various societies. As a result, a new possibility emerges: a historical narrative that decenters rulers and the structures behind them as demiurgic historical forces. Viewing diversity as a fundamental social condition that permeates even the most authoritarian regimes striving to impose the hegemony of a single culture or social group turns the still dominant "scheme of Russian history" upside down. If anything unites this narrative, it is not the geographic space, a national framework, or a view of the past of the currently

Introduction 3

existing state. Rather, it is the working assumption that human diversity is constitutive of the historical process that shapes our project.

We have thoroughly explored vast bodies of international historiographies in several languages, including studies published in *Ab Imperio*. Our greatest challenge was to produce a new analytical language and a coherent historical narrative that can withstand the criticism of different national historians in the region and resonate with the most productive critical and analytical approaches in the global historiography of imperial formations. We started writing *A New Imperial History of Northern Eurasia: From Russian to Global History* in Russian and published chapters in *Ab Imperio* in serial form to invite professional feedback from our peers in different parts of the world, but especially in post-Soviet Eurasia. After incorporating their criticisms and recommendations, the final version was published separately in 2017 for a general audience. The book was included in the top-ten Russian publications at the 2017 Frankfurt Book Fair and it quickly sold out at bookstores. It is used as the primary textbook by lecturers at a number of Russian universities, including the Moscow State Institute of International Relations, the Higher School of Economics in St. Petersburg, and Kazan Federal University in the Tatar republic. The book was also positively received in Ukraine, despite the explosive sensibility of "the common past" trope in the present political climate.

Now we make the upgraded version of this history course available in English. The general reader can expect to find in the book a comprehensive history of the region inscribed in a broader historical context, from China and the Ottoman Empire to Britain and the United States, discussing the same problems and mentioning many of the same events as other modern regional and global imperial histories. As is the case with any synthetic work, professional historians will recognize familiar material in the sections related to their respective fields of expertise but can find inspiration in the ways this material is connected with other cases that may be unfamiliar to them or unexpected. This is what a novel historical narrative can do by presenting familiar facts in a new light, allowing one to see previously unseen connections, exposing the complexities and inequalities of human interactions, and problematizing key notions such as "state," "Russia," "nation," and "empire." Today's graduate students rarely receive equally comprehensive training in all periods and parts of the vast region's history. This book will save them much time and effort by offering a model, a language of analysis, a comparative perspective, and the most up-to-date historical narrative of the region's entangled past.

It should be added that *A New Imperial History of Northern Eurasia: From Russian to Global History* was written with an eye toward the college classroom and has been successfully tested in teaching—particularly of students who had zero knowledge of the region of the former Soviet Union or even family ties to it. Besides use in traditional Russian history courses, the book or its individual chapters will be valuable in any special course at the undergraduate or graduate level that requires background information on the history of the region. It helps to situate Turkestan or the Baltic region in the broader historical context of the nineteenth and early twentieth centuries, and to provide a more informative take on Russia's role in Polish history or on the changing place of Siberia in the imperial political imagination. Constantly keeping an eye on synchronous processes in the world, our history course consistently renders Northern Eurasian history as a hitherto neglected part of the global history of comparisons, connections, and contestations. It can be productively used in courses on global history, comparative empires, colonialisms, and nation-building. Volume 1 covers the period 600–1700 CE, when the perception of the region as a single geographical and social entity had been forged through the interactions and conflicts of local self-organization projects. Volume 2 covers the imperial period of 1700–1918, when the diverse spaces of Northern Eurasia became an arena of empire-building from above and self-organization and competition—within the framework of the Russian imperial formation—from below.

As the authors of this alternative historical narrative of a vast region with fluid boundaries, we identify with the modern international historical profession rather than with any of its national chapters. We have written this book in dialogue with colleagues across the globe. Our goal is to sustain this global conversation about human diversity and show how the field formerly known as Russian history can be productive and important in the twenty-first century.

Notes

1 For a detailed discussion of this problem, see Ilya Gerasimov, "Narrating Russian History after the Imperial Turn," *Ab Imperio* 21, no. 4 (2020): 21–61.
2 See Korine Amacher, "Mikhail N. Pokrovsky and Ukraine: A Normative Marxist between History and Politics," *Ab Imperio* 19, no. 1 (2018): 101–32.

1

Political Ecology

The Formation of the Northern Eurasia Region

The Region's Borders

Three basic concepts frame our modern perception of society—the spatial cohesion of the populated landmass, the synchronicity of world history, and common chronology. All three are of a comparatively recent genesis. To be sure, since the days of antiquity, individuals and whole peoples regularly came into contact with the inhabitants of even very remote lands. However, these contacts did not produce some common "position of an observer," whether actual or collective, that would have made it possible to envision different spaces and societies in universal terms. Each local culture had its own names for the same rivers and mountains, and even had differing perceptions of where one mountain range ended and another began. Different observers not only had different names to describe neighboring peoples but also disagreed on which groups made up a certain people and which did not. The great literate civilizations of antiquity—whether Ancient Egypt, the Middle Kingdom (China), or Ancient Greek poleis—considered themselves to be unique oases within the surrounding space that was populated by "barbarians." Their practical knowledge of neighboring lands and peoples may have been quite extensive at times, but this did not lead them to think of their own culture as a constitutive part of a global whole. Does this mean that modern generalizing terms such as "Northern Eurasia" are not applicable in describing the organization of populations and the comprehension of space in antiquity?

Yes, and no. It is indeed impossible to imagine the position of an observer in the past who would have perceived the colossal expanses of the Eurasian continent north of the Himalayas and the Mongolian and Central Asian deserts as one whole. Where is such an observer to obtain the knowledge needed for such a generalization, and to what purpose would it have been necessary, overall, to conceive of this space as a unified whole? Yet, despite its not being perceived as a unified whole either from outside or from within, this territory nevertheless turned out to be delineated by rather precise borders, at first by natural borders and, gradually, by sociocultural ones.

An Imaginary Bird's-Eye View of Ecoregions

Let us imagine being an observer, moving southward from the North Pole and along the Ural ridge sometime in the mid-first millennium CE, at a height sufficient to survey the breadth of the continent from Kamchatka to Scandinavia. From the northern seas to the Arctic Circle these lands are practically unpeopled, both to the east and west. The few inhabitants of the tundra and the forest-tundra live by hunting Arctic foxes and reindeer, obliged to constantly migrate tracking their prey: the reindeer cover a few thousand miles each summer in search of feed. The Arctic reindeer would be domesticated only toward the end of the first millennium, which allowed northern peoples to establish more permanent and better-populated settlements. But at this time, their social organization is wholly dependent on the conditions of the harsh climate and the populations of wild game. [1]

The wide belt of the taiga spreads farther to the south and covers nearly the whole Scandinavian Peninsula, the territories of present-day Finland and European Russia to the north of St. Petersburg and Moscow and, beyond Urals, to the north of Novosibirsk in Siberia and Khabarovsk in the Far East. The sparse inhabitants of the taiga are true forest people: the forest provides everything they require, even grain. They hunt and, until the end of the nineteenth century, the dominant form of agriculture was slash-and-burn. This means that they burn out a tract of the forest and sow the seeds directly into the ash. Such a tract will remain fertile for a few years, and then it becomes necessary to clear another. The population density in the taiga is never above three people per square mile and it is usually much less. Both hunting and slash-and-burn agriculture demand enormous spaces (at least seventeen acres per household). There are no roads through the woods and mass migrations are rare and difficult, so the intensity of intergroup contacts is very low.

In the west and east of the continent, the taiga turns to mixed and temperate deciduous forest, and closer to the Urals, from the Volga River to the Altai Mountains, to forest steppe. The biome of mixed forest (practically all of western Europe to the Pyrenees, and all of central Europe) is characterized by a more temperate climate. These forests are easier to clear, they provide the population with abundant firewood and materials for construction, and are rich in game. This natural biome presents an obstacle to the expansion of nomads—or, more precisely, it is of little interest due to the absence of broad pastures—and is open for the spreading of sedentary settlers and the establishment of more thorough and permanent social ties.

Farther south, the forest steppe stretches onto the continent in a belt from the eastern foothills of the Carpathian Mountains (in today's Ukraine and Moldova), across what is now Russia (to the south from Kursk and Kazan) and to the Altai Mountains. Woods alternate with open spaces, which, with their fertile chernozem, had attracted farmers since ancient times.

The steppe is a vast grassland almost completely devoid of trees. In an unbroken, undulating belt, widening and narrowing, the steppe stretches from the northern foothills of the Caucasus and the north of the Black Sea coast, across the south of the Eastern European plain (reaching Belgorod), along the Volga (up to Saratov in the north), across northern Kazakhstan and into Western Siberia and Inner Mongolia. Here the imagined observer will find a thinly distributed population of nomads (the population density is akin to that in the taiga, fewer than three people per square mile), unequally dispersed: separate nomadic extended families may at times unify to form steppe confederacies. The invisible borders of pastures and permanent migratory routes divide the distinct groups of nomads on the steppes. Certain events, such as the onset of drought, an invasion by powerful enemies, or the will of a charismatic leader, are capable of gathering nomadic tribes into a single mass and displacing them across many hundreds and thousands of miles of open steppe, sweeping weaker or less organized communities out of the way. [2]

The observer continues to move south, noticing that the steppe regions are also found beyond the ridge of the Caucasus in the southwest—in Central Anatolia—and the mixed and deciduous temperate forests in the southeast begin in Inner Mongolia. However, descending south to approximately forty degrees latitude, our observer encounters a wholly new situation: the role of the natural landscape in the organization of people's lives declines, giving way to the social landscape as the primary influence. In reality, there is no marked and unmovable line between the two, and the reshuffling of the "nature–human" ecological binary occurs hundreds and even thousands of miles farther north or south. This reshuffling no longer depends on climate or soil, but on the development of complex social formations.

Social Landscapes and Collective Observers

In the southeast, the Middle Kingdom led by the Sui imperial dynasty spreads from the Pacific Ocean to Tian-Shan. Military and economic conquest of vast territories, each with differing climate and population, occurs alongside their intellectual exploration by the empire. The educated of ancient China reconceptualize the countless fragments of "local knowledge" wielded by local tribes, warriors, merchants, and civil servants, and create a synthesized understanding of their own civilization and the surrounding world. China became a distinct and independent corner of the world not because it is definitively delineated by mountains or rivers (in fact, the political borders of China and even the meaning of the concept changed radically from era to era), but because China was understood as being its own world by inhabitants who have acknowledged their own cultural and political unity—the multitribal "Chinese." The Chinese can observe only a portion of the Eurasian continent, but they certainly make for a real, not imaginary, collective observer who offers a coherent version of a cognitive structuring of space. Therefore, their cultural model of the inhabited ("civilized") world seeks authority and superiority over that imagined by their northern nomadic neighbor: the Chinese have established a harmonious picture of the world and of culture, whereas the nomads, for the time being, do not see the need for such globalized presentations, which are, moreover, impossible to concretize in all their nuances without the aid of writing. [3]

Farther to the west, across a string of buffer political units—whether codependent or warring ones—the vast Persian Empire of the Sasanian dynasty spread from what is present-day Pakistan, across Central Asia and the Southern Caucasus to eastern Turkey, running likewise along the southern edge of the Mediterranean until Egypt. From the perspective of an enlightened inhabitant of this Persian Empire, the Caucasus Mountains were not seen as an "objective" natural frontier. To the contrary, Central Asia and the Caucasus were counted as being part of the general space that was the Middle Eastern world. This space was delineated and structured by culture to a much greater extent than the specific conditions of climate and landscape affected culture. As in the case of China, the unity of the Sasanian holdings was based in developed social institutions and a shared cultural space, which united diverse tribes and political entities. The dominant religion of Zoroastrianism and the large class of literate people, alongside the single political organization of society into social estates, lent stability to this "Persian world" with its own geographical conceptions and a "mental map" of the peoples inhabiting the empire and adjoining territories. [4]

Even farther west lay the Christian Eastern Roman Empire (Byzantium), the political opponent and trading partner of the Sasanians, and yet an additional powerful and original center of culture that provided still another alternate view structuring the Eurasian space. At this time the territory of Byzantium nearly wholly encircled the shores of the Mediterranean Sea (with the exception of the Iberian Peninsula), which itself acted as an enormous "internal lake" for the empire. The diversity of the local population and the variety of climate and topographical terrain did not pose obstacles to politically and culturally mastering the broadest of spaces. Christianity provided a common cultural context, stimulating the proliferation of writing and literacy including in vernacular tongues: Armenian and Georgian, Slavonic and Gothic. This manifoldly intensified the intellectual contacts as well as the development and propagation of Byzantium's version of the general "map of the world." [5]

West of Byzantium, beyond the Alps and the Carpathian Mountains, Europe presented itself more as the "north" than the "south": it was a politically fragmented, culturally segmented space with a migrating population. Waves of nomads arrived from Asia by way of the steppe "corridor," traveled to the valley of the Danube and stopped there, having come upon the ancient Hercynian Forest (Hercynia silva)—a train of mountain ridges covered with thick woods, behind the wall of which the borders of the first Germanic kingdoms were being drawn and redrawn. Only a few of the Germanic tribes had adopted Christianity at this point, but even their level of literacy was negligible and their "vision of the world" was fragmented and limited. The future "Western Europe" existed as a remote outskirt of the Christian Greco-Roman (at the time predominantly Byzantine) world. [6]

Thus, "Northern Eurasia" emerges as a multitude of spaces, a hypothetical entity which can be defined only negatively, as the blind spot in the perspective of actually existing "collective observers" of the time: ancient China, Persia, and Byzantium. It is not only that written sources from precisely these cultures have been passed down to us—and not sources from, say, forest Finno-Ugric or nomadic Turkic tribes that had lived farther north—but also that these sources reflect the imaginings of the most numerous "collective observers." Despite all the difficulty and circumstantiality of retrospective demographic censuses, the population ruled by the Sui dynasty is estimated at 46 million people at the beginning of the seventh century; the Sasanians united around 25 million people in the middle of the same century; and the population of the Byzantine Empire, the territory of which had been gradually decreasing in size, had shrunk to 10.5 million by the mid-seventh century, as opposed to the 26 million counted a century earlier. These numbers may seem modest, given that the population of Hindustan numbered around 100 million people. Nevertheless, these three great cultural-political entities together represented nearly half of the world's population at the time, and the results of these cultures' spatial imagination carried significant weight even statistically. At the time, the combined population of western Europe, including Britain and Scandinavia, was about 5.5 million people, and of central and eastern Europe, 3.5 million. The most populous confederacies of nomads in Asia that had created powerful empires (the Xiongnu in the second and third centuries BCE, the Mongols at the beginning of the thirteenth century CE) numbered no more than 700,000–800,000 people. Accordingly, while occupying separate socioecological niches, the nomads of the steppes, the farmers of the forest steppe and forest biomes, the hunters in the taiga and the tundra, all scattered across a great territory from the Pacific Ocean to the Baltic Sea, to the north of what were then the centers of accumulated written knowledge, amounted to a total of a few million people. They lacked the structural capacity as well as the cultural need to unify local and regional knowledge and thus to synthesize some alternate version of the "collective observer."

However, toward the end of the first millennium CE, the situation entirely changes. Upon the sweeps of Northern Eurasia, heretofore unified by nothing except their common absence from existing "visions of the world," there appeared political entities that now mastered spaces rather than adapted to them. The territory, unknown to the external observer, began to be understood, described, and structured from within. Becoming a part of culture, the territory gained the foundations of internal subdivisions and external borders and was made part of a shared history.

The Phenomenon of Early Statehood

The way we conceptualize social relations and structures today is not fully applicable to the societies of antiquity. The terms and concepts that we now use were elaborated over just the past century or two, and therefore bear the imprint of a particular type of culture. Thus, contemporary society and contemporary social sciences clearly separate the private sphere (e.g., familial relations) from the public (e.g., the holding of an office). We know that the economy entails the production and redistribution of material goods. Politics is the realm of power relations, decision making, and governing of society. Culture and science conceptualize and describe the world in the language of an artistic imagination or of a systematically organized knowledge, which is consistently being checked for objectivity and faults. Military action is performed in defense of one's own country or as an attack on a neighbor, and war is not compatible with peace. We also tend to describe large unions of people, who, as a rule, speak the same language, practice the same religion, and populate one state—as nations. Groups that are smaller in size but share a culture and history although without having their own state or being scattered across multiple states are more likely to be characterized as ethnic communities. Peoples that are less developed or fewer in number can be called tribes.

It is necessary to correct all these concepts with respect to society at the end of the first millennium CE. The overwhelming majority of organized human collectives (with the exception of those few that unified hundreds of thousands or even millions of people) rested on a hierarchy and network of familial ties. One's position in a family tree turned out to be a key social category. The relatives of a ruler were appointed as his delegates in subordinate tribes that were either unrelated or of an entirely different culture. Rituals such as joint celebrations, the exchange of gifts, and marriages were the most important elements that supported power: the family was a fundamental political category. War was not only an important and, for some, the basic element of economic activity but also a crucial form of interaction, within the scope of which death and destruction coexisted with the transfer of knowledge and the borrowing of social institutions. Territorial expansion was synonymous with cultural exploration and the study of space; religious views, political theory, and scientific knowledge were all inextricably intertwined. Contemporary researchers put forth various hypotheses about the "ethnicity" of one group or another, often partially based only on archaeological excavation; given the absence of written evidence, however, all such suppositions are extremely hypothetical. These particulars regarding the "germination" of early forms of statehood explain much in the history of the region.

Nomads as the First Eurasian Unifiers

Examining the time period and territories as surveyed by our imaginary observer of the northern part of the Eurasian continent, it is obvious that attempts to organize complex societies were bound to meet major obstacles. To begin with, the very need for the populations of Northern Eurasia to unify is questionable. The inhabitants of the tundra, the hunters and fishermen of the taiga, and even the farmers of the regions where deciduous forests permitted slash-and-burn agriculture, were all limited in the expansion of their social organization by precisely those same ecological niches that they inhabited and on which they depended entirely. Settling too close to each other threatened to deplete available game and made it more difficult to find a new plot of forest to sow that was also not too far from the previous one—so there was no economic need to unify. With the existing negligible population density, the greatest external threat would have come only from another, nonnumerous group of hunters or farmers: a large family or a small tribe, in other words, the same kind of elementary social group. A more sizable attack on a small settlement half-lost in the woods would have been unlikely. The low intensity of contact even between friendly and related groups, and the lack of economic and military stimuli for interaction slowed the process of complexifying society.

Political Ecology   11

Nomads have gone down in history in the guise of enormous hordes sowing death and destruction in their wake. In fact, population density in the steppes, and even more so in semideserts and deserts, is negligible and inextensible, as opposed to a sedentary population, with a density that is capable of exponentially multiplying. The number of nomads had always been comparatively small, but they possessed a high degree of mobility. In contrast to the inhabitants of forest biomes, nomads are capable of gathering together in large numbers for prolonged periods of time, providing such collective nomadism is organized and communal, thus permitting a smooth transfer to untouched pasture ground. It was precisely nomads who created the first sizable political entities in the northern part of Eurasia: the Scythian kingdom north of the Black Sea (seventh century BCE), the Xiongnu "empire" in the northern frontiers of China (third and second centuries BCE), the Turkic Khaganate, which, in the sixth century CE, established its influence across the entire steppe belt from Manchuria to the Northern Caucasus. Such steppe confederacies could arise for internal reasons, as a result of confrontations among various nomadic groups, whether over a redistribution of pastures or an attempt to subjugate neighbors. However, according to researchers of nomadic societies, the stability of large nomad confederacies enduring decades and even centuries was only made possible by the proximity of developed sedentary cultures, with which the confederacies enter into a type of symbiosis.

The nomad-herdsmen of the Northern Eurasian steppes are a relatively recent phenomenon. Nomadism is a late stage in the evolution of agrarian societies and has no connection to the prehistoric wandering hunters and gatherers. Only with the domestication of the dog, and, later, the horse (4000–3000 BCE) did the mobile pasturing of herds become, in principle, possible. The widespread nomadic form of production, and thus the organization of society, occurred even later. The dependence of nomads on sedentary neighbors was the consequence of their high economic-ecological specialization of production. The nomads' entire way of life became oriented toward the yearly cycle of transferring herds between summer and winter pastures, which could be achieved only at the price of losing economic self-sufficiency. Alongside meat, milk, and hides, which were produced in abundance, the nomads likewise required bread, silk, silver, and iron. Therefore, they turned out to be the main driving force of establishing intracontinental connections and exchanges, frequently in the form of wars and conquests. Precisely the possibility of regularly acquiring products that could not be produced in the steppes—through trade, raids, and collection of tributes—explains the endurance of a rigid hierarchy of authority and discipline in the nomadic army and the "nomadic empire" built around it. Therefore, the most important factor for the consolidation of the nomads came in the form of powerful farming neighbors in the south—China, Persia, and Byzantium.

The nomadic inhabitants of the steppe belt had similar interests regarding their sedentary neighbors in the north, in those forest steppes and deciduous forests so ideally suited for farming. A moderate climate, highly fertile soil, and sufficient water resources permitted the development there of a high-yielding grain economy, without incurring those additional technical and organizational expenditures that the nomads' southern neighbors were forced to resort to, such as irrigation systems, laboring slave armies, or strict regulation of communes' freemen. But the absence of their own

12   *New Imperial History of Northern Eurasia*

state made these farmers on the northern border of the steppes entirely dependent on their nomadic neighbors. Moreover, the absence of economic incentives to unify and the extremely low population density even further slowed the process of political organization. As a result, the development of agriculture and sedentary societies in these regions became circumscribed by the political situation in the steppes. The consolidation of nomadic alliances within the framework of another steppe "empire" created conditions for the agroeconomic colonization of the forest steppe, when relations between steppe dwellers and farmers began to be built on a long-term basis. Paying regular tribute as a substitute for ruinous raids and trade were beneficial for both sides.

At that time, "tribute" was more than a synonym for forceful extortion. Tribute served as the main institutional form of acknowledgment of one's political subjecthood. The English term "tribute" originated from the Latin *tribus*, "tribe", whereas the Russian word for subjecthood, *poddanstvo*, means "subjected to tribute." Paying tribute entailed reciprocal obligations: the ruler who received the tribute was obliged to provide protection and patronage in return. The destabilization of steppe politics as a result of the disintegration of nomadic confederacies, mass migration, and war hit the agrarian neighbors hard: in these periods, the sedentary societies dwindled in population and receded to the protection of thick forests, so archaeologists discover only burned-out remains in the places of old settlements.

The Khazar Khaganate and the Revolutionary Transformation of Nomadic Society

The borders between the sedentary civilizations of the south, the nomads of the steppes, and the inhabitants of the northern forest zones had never been impregnable. Byzantium, Persia, and China each entered into temporary alliances with particular groups of nomads in order to defend themselves against yet other groups or to pitch them against each other to prevent their consolidation. But even the Migration Period in the fourth and fifth centuries and the consequent fall of the Western Roman Empire to barbarian assaults did not destroy the structural isolation of the southern sedentary civilizations from the nomadic world of the steppes. A radical change occurred in the seventh century CE, when Northern Eurasia encountered an enemy whose goal was not merely looting and domination but also the spread of a specific universal culture: the triumphant Arab Caliphate. Even though it crumbled into separate kingdoms at the beginning of the ninth century, the caliphate left in its wake the unified space of the Islamic world, which itself presented something more than religious unity: a common field of written knowledge and a collective imagination. [7]

By the mid-seventh century, the Arabs conquered the Persian Sasanian Empire and significant portions of Byzantium's territory. By 661, all of the Southern Caucasus was conquered by the Arabs, who definitively cemented their dominance in the Caucasus at the beginning of the eighth century, taking over a significant portion of Central

Asia and progressing until the Indian Punjab. The further northward expansion had been blocked for the Arabs by the Khazar Khaganate, which served as a sort of bridge between the remote forest societies of the north and Byzantium, stretching north to south along the Volga and the Don Rivers, from the northernmost border of the forest steppes to the South Caucasus.

The Beginning of a New Political Cycle in the Steppes

The beginning period in the history of the Khazars is typical of nomadic societies in the Eurasian steppes. It is likely they were one of the nomadic tribes that had arrived from Asia during the Migration Period and had been part of the tribal confederacy known as the Turkic Khaganate. The earliest mentions of the Khazars date to the mid-sixth century, when they participated in raids on Sasanian lands. The Khazars became strategic allies of Byzantium and participated in Byzantium's war with the Sasanians between 602 and 628. The war delivered rich rewards: the Khazars plundered Caucasian Albania in 627 and, together with the Byzantines, captured Tbilisi. Soon enough the Turkic Khaganate fully disintegrated and, in its southern lands, two nomadic confederacies emerged: Great Bulgaria, founded by Khan Kurbat in 632 near the Black Sea, and Khazaria, in the steppes of the Caspian Sea. A generation later, following the death of Kurbat, Bulgaria itself fells apart into five hordes under the leadership of Kurbat's sons. Under the pressure of the Khazars, the Bulgar hordes migrated to other shores: one went to the lower reaches of the Danube and founded the Bulgar kingdom, another went into the steppes of the Don River. A portion of the Bulgars moved to Italy (to Campagna), and another portion to central Europe, where at that moment the Avar Khaganate reigned. The rest remained in place, having acknowledged the authority of the Khazars. As a result, in the last third of the seventh century, Khazaria controlled the steppe to the west of the Volga, and its leader adopted the title of khagan—the highest title possible among Eurasian nomads. [8]

A new cycle of stability began for the steppes of Eastern Eurasia: the Khazars stopped the inflow of new groups of nomads from Asia and established secure ties with their sedentary neighbors. The Khazars traded with Byzantine holdings in Crimea and partially adopted the sedentary mode of life in nearby Taman and in Dagestan, where they developed viticulture. Still, the chief occupation of the Khazars was nomadic pastoralism, and for war bounty—an important element of the nomads' economy— they set off on raids in the South Caucasus. [9]

Nomad Politics

Despite the existence of complex hierarchies of kinship, nomad society was fundamentally egalitarian: every grown man was an armed warrior who could put up resistance to attempts at coercion or, at the very least, fled with his own family. Therefore, the power of the leader resided in his authority as the eldest, but also in his ability to lead victorious campaigns that brought home bounty. Researchers of various nomadic societies underline the key role of the chief's charisma in securing the obedience of the other members of society. The Khazars were no exception in this regard. They were so awed by the magnitude of power at the disposal of the khagan that perceived it as a sacred apparition. The khagan was thought to be not the source, but the channel of this superhuman power. Great honor was shown to him for this, but only as the executor of a holy function. As a result, the almighty ruler of the Khazars turned out to be a hostage, or even a slave, of his own power. It was said that the main part of the ceremony marking the khagan's ascent to the throne entailed strangling the khagan with a silk thread. Before losing consciousness, he had to state the duration of his reign. When the designated number of years was up, he was killed and his heir in the "royal" line became the next khagan. If the new khagan "reserved" too long a reign, he was killed all the same on reaching the age forty, for it was deemed that as the ruler grew older, the godly power *kut* gradually left him. It is possible that these stories are merely the fruit of fantasies of Arab travelers, who were renowned for their thirst for exoticism and rumors. Such stories nevertheless attest that power began to be understood as an independent phenomenon distinct from kinship relations. Instead of becoming embodied in a certain political institution such as the state, the idea of power and the great degree of responsibility that comes with it were conceptualized within the framework of religious rituals.

Kinship continued to play a key role even during the appointing of a new khagan, as he could only belong to the "royal" line. Adhering to the rota ("ladder") line of succession, adopted in the steppes (at least by the Turks), power passed from the eldest to the youngest brother, then to the sons of the elder brother, then to the sons of the younger, and so on. This principle facilitated the maintaining of horizontal ties between families, who, after two or three generations, in these steppe conditions could forever part ways and scatter, thereby consolidating nomadic society. This principle of succession would later become a barrier to political consolidation, when it was borrowed by sedentary populations (for instance, Eastern Slavs) and imposed within the context of the "immovable" property of territory, as opposed to that of the mobile herds that grazed on the broad steppe.

But this would happen a few centuries later. Back in the seventh century CE, the Khazars were a middle link in the chain of steppe confederacies between the Avar Khaganate in Pannonia in what is present-day Hungary, Slovakia, and Romania beyond the Carpathian Mountains and the Eastern-Turkic Khaganate beyond the Ural Mountains. In time, they should have repeated the fate of their predecessors and, on disbanding, entered the ranks of a new confederacy, once again leaving researchers to argue about whether this new confederacy should be considered Turkic, Iranian, or Mongolian, given the absence of reliable written evidence as well as the constant mixing of different nomadic groups. But the Arabs' invasion of Dagestan at the beginning of the eighth century and their obvious intention to keep moving farther north created a principally new threat to the Khazars. The Arabs could not be included in the confederacy of subordinate tribes, and the Khazars, as they were, could not enter into the Arabs' political union while retaining the rights of a lesser partner. These traditional strategies of steppe politics facilitated the succession of steppe confederacies, largely rendering meaningless the question of the "ethnicity" of a given union of nomads—always a motley crew of various groups. They did not work with the zealously Muslim Arab polity.

Toward a Nomad "State": The Impact of the Arab Neighbor-Enemy

Continuing the tradition of partnering with Byzantium, the Khazars helped contain the Arabs in Asia Minor. They contributed to the failure of a siege of Constantinople by caliphate troops in 716–18, having routinely attacked Caucasian Albania and mowed down a portion of the Arab army (and having looted the region to boot). In 730–1, the Khazars penetrated so far into Arab territory that, having routed a 25,000-strong army, they reached Mosul in northern Iraq. But the future caliph Marwan II (Marwan the Deaf), an experienced military commander, organized a punitive expedition against the Khazar Khaganate in 737. He drew on the forces of a large army (some sources set its size at 120,000). The Arabs captured the capital of the khaganate, Semender somewhere in northern Dagestan, near the Caspian Sea, and continued to pursue the khagan, who fled into the steppes. Somewhere between the Volga and the Don, the Arabs smashed the khagan's forces, and the condition for peace was the khagan's promise to convert to Islam. [10]

The Arab threat passed: Marwan returned south, and from then on the caliphate made no attempts on the Northern Caucasus. The khagan did not become Muslim, but the consequences of the Arab invasion did turn out to be very important to the Khazars. The Khazars left the Northern Caucasus, moving northeast, advancing farther and farther north along the Don and the Volga Rivers. At the Volga's delta, Atil becomes the new capital, and the previous capital, Semender, is left on what becomes the southern frontier of Khazaria. Parallel to the geographical displacement, a gradual socioeconomic reorientation of the khaganate's population occurs: retaining nomadic pastoralism in the steppes north of the Black Sea and the region between the Volga and Don rivers, the khaganate's southern territories (Crimea, Taman, Northern Dagestan) and northern territories (in the Middle Volga and the region surrounding the River Kama) witness the transition to sedentary agriculture. What is more, by controlling the Volga's flow from the forested regions and into the Caspian Sea, the Khazars gain control over a crucial trading artery that links north and south. The Volga's importance radically increased, precisely thanks to the unprecedented expansion of the Arab Caliphate, which had created a common trading space and a market for northern furs, honey, wax, and linen that stretched from the Caucasus and Central Asia to the Indian Ocean. As some historians hypothesize, the Volga trade gradually became the main source of income for the khaganate, which then transformed from a typical nomadic steppe confederacy into an early state, having become a type of bridge that for the first time linked the isolated societies of the northern reaches with the highly integrated societies in the south of Eurasia. [11]

Of no less importance was the Arabs' attempt to convert the Khazars to Islam. As did most nomads of the Eurasian steppes in the first millennium CE irrespective of their "ethnic" or linguistic association, the Khazars practiced Tengrism. They believed in the almighty God Eternal Blue Sky (Tengri), the holy Earth-Water, and other lesser deities that embodied the forces of nature. Tengrism permitted different groups of nomads to find a common language, both literally and figuratively, but it did not present a cultural system as rigid and finely developed as the monotheistic religions did. As society became more complex, monotheism appeared to be a more attractive

Adopting Judaism

The defeat of the khagan's forces at the hands of the Arabs in the heart of the khagan's own territory transformed religion from an issue of culture and worldview into a crucial political factor. The Khazars did not adopt Islam in 737, but, around 740, one of the Khazar top military commanders and the head of a senior clan, Bulan, publicly adopted Judaism. As with many other circumstances in Khazar history, there is no full agreement among historians as to the precise date of this event; however, the direct connection between Bulan's decision and the political situation of the khaganate seems obvious. Khazaria was increasingly evolving into a centralized, early state entity. This new political organization required a vision of the world that not only would be common to all the tribes wishing to enter into the nomadic confederacy but also would draw a sharp border between it and the social world outside. This vision of the world must be infused with the idea of a clear hierarchy and unquestionable higher authority, both within the universe and within the khaganate as the universe in miniature. Islam was the religion of the primary foe, and Christianity the religion of the primary ally: for this reason, these religions of direct neighbors were not suitable to be the "official" religions of the khaganate. To adopt either would have created the threat of gradual loss of the Khazars' political independence (sovereignty) and cultural distinctiveness. The selection of Judaism by a high-ranking chief was an unorthodox decision: for one, Judaism did not prescribe proselytism. Still, it appeared to be a logical choice from the perspective of Khazaria's external relationships.

Relying on the highly fragmented evidence at our disposal, some historians suggest that the selection of Judaism by a fraction of the Khazar clan aristocracy can likewise be analyzed as indirect confirmation of the increased role of trade in the economy of the Khazar Khaganate. In the eighth century the transcontinental caravan trade in Eurasia, which stretched from China to the banks of the Rhône in France, was practiced by Jewish merchants. Some sources name these merchants Radhanites: this may be of Persian origin, from a phrase meaning "those who know the way," or perhaps the name stems from a place in northern Iran or even in France (the Rhône valley in Latin being *Rhodanus*). As is always the case with social groups of antiquity, it is difficult to correlate the Radhanites with a particular "profession" (merchants), ethnic group (Jews), or clan. It is likely most correct to picture them as akin to a sort of "order" of merchants that accepted people of various backgrounds, who nonetheless possessed the necessary skills and the ability to step into a social network founded on trust and often reinforced by family ties. It is known that these merchants spoke many languages and kept up a caravan trade network along the whole length of the Silk Road and along the rivers of eastern Europe. One can assume their presence in Atil: after the destabilization of the region by the Irano-Byzantine wars of the sixth century and the Byzantines' imposition of unreasonable tolls on passing caravans, the trajectory of the Silk Road was altered. The caravans began to round the Caspian Sea not from the south, but from the north, passing through Atil. Given the tense and ceaseless confrontation between the Muslims and Christians with the beginning of the Arab Caliphate's expansion, the primarily Jewish Radhanites were the only group able to exercise neutrality and to be present in both Islamic and Christian territories. In one way or another, even without manifesting itself as an organized political force in the region, Judaism gave the Khazars strategic benefits and, moreover, confirmed their status as defenders of the caravan trade. [12]

The Khazar Hybrid Model of Nomad Statehood

The transitional character of the Khazar Khaganate revealed itself in the emergence of new forms that did not obliterate the old ones, but rather came to coexist with them. Thus, having transferred the capital to Atil, the Khazars did not neglect Semender, but merely altered its status. The proliferation of trade and agriculture did not lead to the total rejection of nomadic pastoralism. Bulan's adoption of Judaism did not entail radical religious reform: multiple faiths coexisted in Khazaria. Crimea was populated by animists and Christians (Christianity spread to Dagestan as well), the khaganate's professional soldiers were Muslims officially permitted not to make war on their brethren, while the khagan himself remained the embodiment of the divine power of Tengri. However, the true rulers of Khazaria at the turn of the ninth century became precisely those descendants of Bulan who had converted to Judaism. They held the position of *bek* (provincial governor) and passed the office down from father to son, rather than according to the traditional ladder arrangement. The khagan remained more of a sacred figure and a purely nominal ruler in this system of double rule. Corule was characteristic of nomadic political entities, but in Khazaria, it seems that it was not merely a question of "senior" and "junior" rulers who were responsible for different districts, but of fundamental differentiation between the essence of each ruler's power and even between orders of succession. The effective end of raids to the south and the lessening importance of such raids to the Khazars' economy also played a significant role in contributing to the diminishment of the khagan's political weight.

Thus, throughout the eighth century, a typical nomadic confederacy, Khazaria went through a profound structural transformation. Previously, nomadic alliances fell apart as soon as access to the riches of sedentary neighbors ceased. The chief lost power when he could no longer demonstrate his right to it through successful raids. The Khazars transcended this cycle by taking a step in the direction of developing the state as a mechanism for maintaining social order by redistributing internal resources (not those captured in raids). Nomadic alliances—at times even called "empires"—are not states in the strict sense of the word: the nomads do not pay taxes, they do not have a distinct class of civil servants and judges, and have no specialized penal system that monopolizes the right to employ force. Clan aristocracy replaces what would be government officials, the entire adult male population is simultaneously an army; and force, though regulated by traditions and rituals, is not the exclusive privilege of a certain category of officials. Not entirely breaking with its nomadic past, toward the ninth century, Khazaria managed to create a hybrid political and socioeconomic system that permitted it to survive under new conditions.

The khaganate was divided into several districts that differed in population composition, methods of governance, and economic activities. The region between the Volga and the Don Rivers was the center of the khaganate, where the Khazars maintained a traditional nomadic way of life. Every year, between April and September, the bek toured the central district, to which likewise the heads of aristocratic clans migrated. Adherence to old nomadic traditions not only supported the bek's authority but also helped withstand the pressures of other nomads moving in from Asia. For a while, the Khazars were able to absorb these newcomers into their social organization. For instance, at the beginning of the ninth century, tribes of Magyars (Hungarians) crossed the Volga and, for several decades, settled in the area north of the Black Sea. They chose to join the Khazars as a nomadic confederacy of various tribes instead of destroying and plundering their towns and crops—as would have happened had Khazaria been an ordinary sedentary polity.

The capital, Atil, constituted an antithesis to the traditional steppe. Justice was meted out by seven special judges: two for each monotheistic religion, and one for the animists. The population of the capital district was obliged to carry out regular duties (which was unthinkable in a nomadic environment), whereas craftsmen and merchants paid a tax. Instead of the general mobilization of nomads, the military force consisted of professional "foreign" Muslim soldiers, who depended on regular salary and thus retained their motivation and combat readiness even in times of peace.

Khazar garrisons protected key trading centers, and special crown officials collected tolls from the caravans that came by land or down the Volga. In a few accounts, in Crimea, where Khazar interests intersected with Byzantine ones, the delegates of the bek were active at some point. At the same time, the extensive territories populated by tribes subject to the khaganate were not directly governed from Atil and thus retained their internal organization, as was common in nomadic confederacies. The Hungarians and Alans in the south and the Slavs and Bulgars in the north paid tributes and were expected to contribute troops in wartime—this was the extent of their "khazarianism."

Volga Bulgaria and the Appearance of Early Statehood

The Khazar Khaganate was not the most powerful or extensive unified political entity in Northern Eurasia for its time. It is enough to note that the khaganate's transformation after the adoption of Judaism by a section of the clan aristocracy, as well as the consolidation of the bek's authority, occurred contemporaneously with the rise of the Frankish Empire under Charles the Great (Charlemagne) in the final decades of the eighth century. The case of the Khazars is notable in the sense that they created new forms of statehood, without the possibility of using the experience of predecessors, whether these were conquered peoples or those who had willingly adopted the new rule. The Byzantine Empire, the Arab Caliphate, and the ancient polities of the South Caucasus all played the role of external factors in Khazaria's becoming an entirely original Northern Eurasian political entity. The Khazars created

Political Ecology   19

a new social space that overcame the natural borders of biomes and connected to other developed sociocultural spaces, thus creating the possibility of conceptualizing a portion of the earth's surface as a "region." Functioning as a type of bridge, Khazaria connected the different cultures of the north and the south and exerted a particular influence over the northern periphery of the khaganate.

The unevenness of Khazaria's contribution to the renewal of Northern Eurasia's political culture manifested itself clearly in a crisis situation. Around 899, the Hungarian tribes that were part of the khaganate migrated to Pannonia, beyond the Carpathians, and with them three tribes of Khazar origin left. This situation is fairly typical for steppe confederacies and testifies to the fact that the khaganate, in its capacity as the steppe polity, had created nothing fundamentally new. Whether the reason for the departure of the friendly and even kindred tribes was the pressure of the new nomadic hordes moving west from Asia (the Pechenegs), dissatisfaction with the rule of the Judaic beks, or simply the nomadic desire for a change of scene—the solution to the problem was simple enough. They gathered up their tents and set off.

The Bulgars Adopt Islam: A Secession without a Confrontation

A totally different approach to secession was demonstrated sometime later on the opposite northern border of the khaganate. Gradually migrating north along the Volga from the steppes of the Caspian Sea, by the beginning of the tenth century, the Bulgars who had remained in Khazaria ultimately settled in the Middle Volga near the confluence of the Kama River on the border of the forest steppe and taiga. The leader of the Bulgars was part of the clan aristocracy of the Khazar Khaganate, bearing the title of *elteber*, or ruler of a vassal people. As with all subordinate tribes, the Bulgars were obligated to bear certain duties to the khaganate: to provide warriors and to pay a tribute, which was, incidentally, quite moderate, almost symbolic—one fur skin per household. Even so, a moment came when the Bulgars attempted to secede from Khazaria. Traditional political strategies of the steppe society envisioned two possibilities in this situation: a departure for new lands (as the Hungarians had done) or a destruction of the previous sovereigns with the objective of taking their place (as the Khazars had done in their time when they replaced Great Bulgaria). The Bulgars wanted neither to leave nor to wage war against the khaganate and demonstrated a radically novel understanding of the social and spatial boundaries when, instead, they decided to adopt Islam as their official religion. The very concept of a free choice of faith and the strategic considerations behind this choice reflect the influence of the new Khazarian political culture. Volga Bulgaria was not contiguous with any Muslim country, so adopting Islam allowed the drawing of a symbolic border between the Bulgars and the Judaic and Tengrian rulers of Khazaria. Furthermore, this move neutralized a threat from the Khazarian standing army, which would not engage with fellow Muslims. Thus, learning a lesson from the Khazars, who used religion as a political instrument, the Bulgars went one step farther. Their leaders declared the new religion—Islam—as mandatory for the entire land, thereby achieving in the area a heretofore nonexistent degree of cohesion within society and control over the population. [13]

We do not know when and how Islam began spreading among the Bulgars. Probably, to symbolically mark the adoption of the new religion, in about 921, Elteber Almysh invited a mission from Baghdad, the recently founded capital of the Arab Caliphate, located over 2,000 miles to the south. A direct trip would have taken longer than three months to complete. In reality, the mission's journey took eleven months: flanking the Khazar lands in the east, crossing Khwarezm in Central Asia, the caravan of official delegates, merchants, and spiritual leaders, carrying books and contributions for the construction of a mosque, arrived in the Bulgar city only in May 922. The converted Elteber Almysh began to be called Emir Jafar ibn Abdullah: both the title and the name made the chief of a tribe subordinated to the Khazar Khagan an "Islamic prince" who now joined an entirely different social hierarchy. The caliph officially had authority over the emir of Volga Bulgaria, but Baghdad was so far away that the caliph could not practically exert any influence over Bulgar affairs.

In this manner, deep within the continent and beyond direct and systematic contact with ancient centers of written culture and developed political entities, the nomadic tribe self-organized into a more complex political formation. This process involved reconceptualizing their own society using ideas and categories borrowed from a new universal culture that had emerged far beyond the boundaries of the Bulgar tribe and even the steppe nomadic world—Islam. The Bulgars, sitting at the border of the taiga biome far in the north, found themselves included in a common imagined cultural space along with ancient Khwarezm, Baghdad, and even Medina far away in Arabia, making their distant land a part of this space. By the same token, the Bulgars' local knowledge about their region and neighbors was also included in this broadening universal vision of the inhabited world. The process of the expansion of knowledge regarding the inhabited universe can easily be seen in Ahmad Ibn-Fadlan's *A Travel Account*. Ibn-Fadlan, member of the mission in 922, left invaluable observations about the Bulgars and the peoples surrounding them. Having become part of one universal vision of the world (in this case a Muslim Arabo-Persian vision), the Bulgars' local knowledge could now be "translated" into other universal "languages," such as Christian Byzantine culture. This is how exploration and appropriation by broad written cultures of previously inhabited but "invisible" northern Eurasia took place. Until then, separate local collectives of people simply had not possessed a common cultural language, the need to conceptualize this territory as a whole or to transmit their knowledge about its different corners.

The Bulgar Model of Statehood

In many ways, Volga Bulgaria continued the revolutionary transformation of nomadic society from within that Khazaria had begun. Having proclaimed himself emir, the former elteber Almysh established a primogeniture (linear) order of succession, transmitting power along the male line from father to son as did the Khazar beks. This broke with the steppe's traditional ladder system of inheritance. Even more important, the adoption of Islam made it possible to bring the diverse tribes closer. They constituted the Volga Bulgars' alliance under Almysh's rule—those who had come along with the Bulgars from the Lower Volga, and those who had inhabited this place before the

Bulgars' arrival. Having declared Islam a mandatory religion for everyone in the land, Almysh elicited resistance from a part of the Bulgar clan aristocracy. (It appears that Bulan in Khazaria had managed to avoid protests after converting to Judaism because this remained a personal and voluntary choice.) There is evidence that some Bulgar aristocrats, headed by Prince Askal, rebelled in protest against the adoption of Islam, but were subdued by force. The reliability of this testimony is uncertain, as with many accounts about this era and these regions. Still, it was logical to expect just such a reaction, given that the conversion of the entire population to Islam—a calculated rational decision of the rulers—could not have been "natural" or unanimous.

The restructuring of the economy in Volga Bulgaria was also more radical than that in Khazaria. Cattle breeding continued to play an important role, likely remaining nomadic in Bulgaria's southern regions. We know that 300 years later, at the time of the Mongolian invasion in 1236–7, the Mongolian army spent a year on Bulgar lands, having turned its capital, Bulgar, into the khan's headquarters. This meant that the pastures of Volga Bulgaria were capable of sustaining enormous numbers of horses and cattle. But it was farming that became the main activity of the Bulgars: they planted wheat, barley, millet, lentils, and beans. Chronicles from pre-Mongolian times mention not just a grain trade in Volga Bulgaria, but how it turned into the last resort for the inhabitants of neighboring principalities stricken by poor harvests, who survived famine only by bringing in cereals from Bulgaria. Farming in the forest-steppe biome permitted an increase in population density, and this gradual increase led to another important consequence: the formation of state institutions.

It is hard to systematically control and exploit nomadic herdsmen wandering the steppes, even if their migration routes are restricted by the ancestral territories of summer and winter pastures. Establishing control over a rare resource, such as a wellspring, gives much more power somewhere in a desert but not along the banks of one of the continent's major rivers such as the Volga. In other words, it is difficult to create a system of rule that does not solely depend on a chief's charisma and the nomads' interest in participating in campaigns seeking bounty. A sedentary agrarian population is quite another matter. It is not as easily prepared as are pastoral nomads to flee oppression, cannot as quickly gather troops to resist a chieftain's retinue, and, to the contrary, is interested in being defended by professional warriors. Land suitable for agriculture, especially around settlements, is a limited resource. In time, the growing population of a village or region begins to need new arable land, but control over communal ancestral lands as potential new crop fields often belongs to the chief. All these conditions lead to the strengthening of the power of the leader "in general" ("the government"), regardless of one's personality and the customs regulating the rights of ordinary members of society and elders.

A society that, until quite recently, had been a nomadic federation of clans and tribes, reaches a crucial turning point when a ruler begins to collect taxes from his own people and not only from conquered or subordinate tribes, as before. There is evidence that this had occurred in Volga Bulgaria, where the gradual diffusion of Islam across the population, which should have taken many decades, created a common social space. Real differences between tribes, such as languages and structures of kinship, still retaining their relevance, were leveled in one important aspect. With the proclamation of Islam as the universal religion, it became possible to perceive some supratribal entity that encompassed as equal members the "native-born" Bulgars, the kindred tribe of Suvars, and even the indigenous Finno-Ugric people conquered by arrivals from Khazaria.

Of no less importance was the emergence of a distinctive public social space as "official" and differentiated from the private. Islam was the "official" religion, which coexisted with the privately practiced paganism, just as the official authority of the emir was paralleled by the enduring hierarchies of local tribal chiefs and elders, and the official "crown" court was paralleled by the active traditions of common law. It is precisely the gradual division of the public and private social spheres that lays the basis for the creation of a state in the form of institutions. This means that social networks and connections complexify to the extent that a portion of them takes on an abstract form, disassociating itself from its concrete carriers and becoming specialized. The power of the head of a clan becomes distinct from the power of a military commander, a high-ranked priest, or a ruler (prince, elteber, emir). A warrior is no longer just any member of the tribe in the hour of armed conflict, but an individual who has specially dedicated himself to the military profession and makes his living only by means of this occupation. The traditional ritual exchange of gifts between the members of a clan or tribal alliance (the symbolic confirmation of social unity), and the payment of tribute as a substitution for a military raid (an acknowledgment of submission), gradually transform into a system of duties and taxes. The majority of such levies goes not into the prince's personal household, but into public necessities such as the building of fortifications or temples. Although it is the prince himself who has control of these resources, the distinction between his private affairs and the public interest testifies to the appearance of state elements.

The state is not a material and visible edifice, but a system of relations and a particular way of social thinking; it is therefore never simple to measure its degree of development, especially in the early stages. Given the extant (but quite limited) accounts of Volga Bulgaria, it can be regarded as an example of the autochthonous development of certain elements of statehood—in other words, a development that does not rely on previously existing forms and is not predetermined by the threat of external aggression. The importance of Khazaria's role in the formation of a new political mindset among typical steppe nomads such as the Bulgars, who gradually migrated across the entire territory of the Khazar Khaganate from the Northern Caucasus to central Volga, cannot be overemphasized. And yet, in many respects, Volga Bulgaria turned out to be a fundamentally new political entity, with more evident indicators of statehood. To examine in closer detail the process of how state institutions crystallized out of traditional familial and tribal relationships, in Chapter 2, we turn to the history of a political entity that has enjoyed incomparably more scholarly attention over the course of the past century than have Khazaria and Bulgaria combined: the polity that Russian historians of the nineteenth century had named "Kievan Rus."

The Cultural Self-orientation of the Region

There would have been nothing new or unusual about it if the Khazars had adopted Islam in 737 after the defeat of the khaganate by the forces of the Arab Caliphate—as they had indeed promised. Many peoples who found themselves under Arab rule or influence had converted to Islam. What is surprising is that, after 740, a part of the Khazar aristocracy adopted a monotheistic religion on its own initiative, and especially that it was a religion that did not practice active proselytizing. Less than two centuries later, history was to repeat itself on the northern periphery of the Khazar Khaganate: in 922 Volga Bulgaria looked to distant Baghdad to adopt Islam as its official religion. It is known that Khazaria had a considerable Muslim population and that Muslims may well have existed within the limits of Bulgar territory, but it is important to note that the initiative to adopt Islam belonged to the Bulgar rulers themselves. A few decades later, in 988, on the northwestern border of the region over which the khaganate had once exerted influence (now declined), and over a month's journey away from the capital of Volga Bulgaria to the southwest, in Kyiv on the Dnieper, Christianity was declared the official religion by Prince Vladimir Sviatoslavich.

Structurally, the situation here was identical to the adoption of monotheistic religions in Khazaria and Bulgaria. Strategic considerations explained the choice of religion—not that of the closest neighbor (in this case, Bulgar Muslims and Judaic Khazars), but that of an ally too removed to potentially interfere—Christian Byzantium. Chronicles repeat the same archetypal story about this selection of a faith. According to a later record, the Kyivan prince Vladimir, before adopting Christianity from Byzantium, listened to the arguments of representatives of Islam (Bulgars), Judaism (Khazars), and "Germans" who represented "Western" Christianity (which had in fact not yet separated itself from "Eastern" Byzantine Christianity at the time). Likewise, a debate among representatives of the three monotheistic religions had preceded the adoption of Judaism by the Khazars: Muslims argued the superiority of Islam over Christianity, the Christians argued the opposite, but both acknowledged Judaism as the "most truthful" religion after their own. The adoption of Christianity at the end of the tenth century by the sedentary multitribal population of the forest steppe and forest biomes, from the Upper Dnieper lands to the Baltic Sea, turned out to be an important step in the process that had begun back in the eighth century in the Caspian Sea steppes. The enormous territory stretching in the meridional direction from the Caspian to the Baltic Sea, and from the Danube River and the Carpathian Mountains in the west (the borders of Byzantium and those Hungarian tribes that had migrated to the Danube), up to the Ural Mountains in the east became included in several intertwined and often intersecting universalist cultural spaces: those of Christianity and Islam.

Inclusion in the mental maps upheld by Christian and Islamic universal cultures radically altered the status of the geographical space in this part of Northern Eurasia: previous vast areas were conceived of as distinct "lands"—bounded territories with characteristic populations—situated in a particular way and possessing certain relationships to one another. The physical category of "space" thus gained a cultural dimension, borders (often disputed), and chronological perspective (history and predictions of the future). Henceforth, any political entities began to be conceived of within the coordinates of an imagined geography, whereas geographical space itself was politicized. Cultural proximity and economic competition found an "objective" basis in spatial configuration, and the geographical abstraction of Northern Eurasia,

24   *New Imperial History of Northern Eurasia*

at least its stretch from the Baltic Sea to the western foothills of the Urals, acquired internal substantiation.

Reverse Perspective: The Year 862 in the South and West

The earliest known historical chronicle created in Northern Eurasia and offering relatively reliable dating of events is "The Tale of Bygone Years" (also known as the Primary Chronicle). It was composed in Kyiv on the Dnieper River at the beginning of the twelfth century. This Primary Chronicle is likely based on some earlier records, possibly from the first half of the eleventh century, and registers 862 CE as the time of the earliest event relating to the region. Unfortunately, neither Khazar nor Bulgar chronicles have survived—if indeed any had ever been produced. That is why the few surviving written accounts left by these cultures, whether a letter of a Khazar bek from the mid-tenth century or Bulgar tomb epitaphs from the thirteenth, present an extremely fragmented sequence of the events and participants. Historians try to make sense of these bits and pieces in conjunction with the fragmented correspondence of foreign travelers, and by comparing these with the relatively straight (although selective) chronology presented in the Primary Chronicle. But before turning to the events registered in the chronicle, it is necessary to put its narrative in a broader historical and geographical context. The Primary Chronicle is perhaps the first, or at least the most influential manifesto of independence and self-sufficiency of the emerging common space of cultural interaction between the Carpathian and Ural Mountains, and between the Baltic and the Black Seas. It is impossible to comprehend the logic and uniqueness of processes of political and cultural self-organization in the lands of Northern Eurasia without a survey, however brief, of the contemporaneous histories of the neighboring literate, agrarian societies.

The Abbasid Caliphate and the Perseveration of Historical Lands: Political Disintegration and Cultural Consolidation

In 862, the Arab caliph al-Musta'in, who had just ascended to the throne in Baghdad, acknowledged Prince Ashot of the Bagratuni clan as the "prince of princes" of Armenia, a dependent territory of the caliphate in the South Caucasus. Armenia (Arminiya) was the name of one of the most ancient lands on the periphery of the Mediterranean–Middle Eastern world, known as early as 521 BCE as a satrapy (province) of the First Persian (Achaemenid) Empire. On this territory with its multicultural population, political entities formed and fell apart, occasionally subjugating distant neighboring lands or becoming subjects of conquest themselves. The fact that this land was perceived as a distinct entity for more than a thousand years—whether as an Achaemenid satrapy, a viceroyalty of the Seleucid rulers, or the Kingdom of Greater Armenia since the second century BCE—was the result, first and foremost, of its natural geographical location. In various periods, the name referred to a territory roughly corresponding to the borders of the Armenian highlands: the east of today's Turkey, the western parts of Azerbaijan and Iran, the south of Georgia, and Armenia itself. But this geographical factor was gradually perceived as a historical and cultural one. [14]

Regardless of the altering of names of kingdoms and the changing of dominant languages and religions, the inhabitants of the region grew accustomed to thinking of Armenia as a distinct land—a specific territory with a particular population. Its distinctiveness was now no longer perceived by virtue of its landscape and the economic specialization adapted to it, but by virtue of the fact that Armenia had "always" existed and had already transformed into a crucial marker on the cultural map of the inhabitants of the Mediterranean and the Middle East. New provinces and kingdoms came to be inscribed within these culturally conditioned "natural" borders of the political imagination, even when, as a result of military confrontation, the territory of the Armenian highlands became divided between powerful neighbors as happened in the seventh and eighth centuries as a consequence of the rivalry between Byzantium and the Arab Caliphate. It is thus unsurprising that the part of the Armenian highlands belonging to the Arab Caliphate had been designated a separate province by the new overlords, or that the representative of the local ancient Bagratuni family, whose members staffed the same office during the preceding Byzantine reign, had been named the head of the province. Yet the appointment in 862 of Ashot Bagratuni as the prince of princes of Armenia provoked a string of unintended consequences when rational political logic was distorted by the powerful inertia of spatial imagination.

Perceiving Armenia as a separate province, Caliph al-Musta'in expected Ashot to serve the caliphate. However, from the perspective of the region itself it looked as if a representative of a local aristocratic family was recognized as the region's legitimate ruler by the caliph himself. Because of the expansionism of the ambitious Ashot, as soon as 863, a punitive expedition was sent out against him, but the caliph's troops (more precisely, the troops of the emirates that neighbored Ashot's lands and served the caliph) were defeated. In 875, the districts surrounding the city of Ani in the South Caucasus submitted to the rule of Ashot Bagratuni, and in ten years' time the Baghdad caliph as well as the Byzantine emperor had acknowledged Ashot as king of the independent Ani Kingdom, occupying a buffer zone between the two competing empires. [15]

The appearance of an independent Christian kingdom in caliphate territory of the South Caucasus was part of a general process of growing decentralization of the Abbasid Caliphate. Toward the beginning of the ninth century, local dynastic regimes appeared in all the provinces, even in direct proximity to Baghdad. In 875, the Samanid dynasty of Persian rulers of Central Asia became practically independent. The Samanid Emirate included the regions of Khorasan and Mawarannahr with their ancient cultural centers: Merv, Bukhara, Samarkand, Khwarezm, and Fergana. [16]

The name of the caliphate's northernmost province in Central Asia, Mawarannahr (Arabic for "beyond the river"), highlights the importance of geographic factors in determining the borders of historical regions, but it also transmits the particular perspective of an observer in the cultural space of the local mental geography. From the times of Alexander the Great's conquests, which had Hellenized the culture of Central Asia, the territory north of the Amu Darya was called Transoxiana, which means the same thing: the land on the other side of the river from a southerner's point of view.

26   *New Imperial History of Northern Eurasia*

Indeed, for many centuries there was no alternative perspective of the "northerner" as the representative of another, stable and relatively universalist culture: beginning north of the fertile Fergana Valley and the Syr Darya River were deserts and steppes inhabited by nomadic tribes. The nomads had their own vision of the surrounding world, including of Transoxiana/Mawarannahr with its tempting riches, but there was no desire or opportunity to make this knowledge accessible outside the boundaries of local society. Therefore, Samanid lands in the ninth century belonged to the old "southern" cultural world and not to that of "Northern Eurasia," which did not yet exist as a social space. [17]

Paradoxically, the disintegration of the caliphate as a unified political whole was brought about, in significant measure, precisely by the development of state institutions. Factors that gradually made the existence of a single ruling center redundant included the proliferation of a single system for the collection of taxes, for legal proceedings, and for the staffing of local garrisons over the vast territories conquered by the caliphate, and the growing sophistication of local administrations. With the new system in place, it was quicker, cheaper, and more effective to govern states that were smaller in size. The preservation of local regional traditions also contributed to fragmentation, especially when these traditions were strengthened, as in the case of the Armenian lands of Ashot Bagratuni, by the preservation of another religion.

At the same time, political fragmentation along the borders of historical "lands" contributed to the strengthening of a common Islamic self-identification, despite growing polarization between the Sunnites and Shiites. (The religious break itself within Islam may be viewed as a consequence of the intensification of religious sentiment and complexification of the belief system.) It is the reign of the Abbasid dynasty (749–1258) over the fragmented caliphate that witnessed the heyday of "Arab culture," which it would be more correct to call Arab-speaking culture, given that Arabic had become the universal language of high culture for the most diverse peoples, inhabiting territories from the Fergana Valley to Northern Africa. Political fragmentation brought about more specificities to the mental map of the inhabited world: new states, dynasties, and even peoples appeared on it, but the map itself remained more or less shared across the entire space of Arab culture and the periphery acquainted with it.

The Byzantine Empire: Political Effectiveness and Social Dynamism

The rapid appearance, victorious expansion, and beginning of the fragmentation of the Arab Caliphate took less than two centuries, occurring between 632 CE and the beginning of the ninth century. Compared to this historical dynamism, the western neighbor and chief rival of the caliphate, usually referred to as Byzantium, seemed to be a bastion of tradition and stability.

The actual name of this polity was the Eastern Roman Empire, which proclaimed its independence of the Western Roman Empire in 395 CE. Until 330, its capital New Rome was called Byzantium; afterward, it was better known by its unofficial name of Constantinople. Changes in dynasties and internal crises, the loss and regaining of territory, and clashes over different interpretations of the Christian religion were unable to undermine the fundamental stability of the Byzantine Empire. About 500 years after its inception, in the mid-ninth century, it entered yet another phase of ascent, connected with the rise to power of the so-called Macedonian dynasty in 867. A period of internal strife came to an end, foreign policy was successful, and the state apparatus achieved a degree of specialization and scope unthinkable at the time anywhere in the world—except perhaps in China. [18]

Interestingly, the formalization of the institutions of government and methods of administration did not lead Byzantium to decentralization and fragmentation, as occurred in the caliphate's case.

First, the church, which was under the control of the emperor, played a very important role in maintaining the unity of the country. Unlike Islam, the Christian church is structured as a rigid vertical hierarchy. If the caliph remained the symbolic leader of all Muslims (which did not necessarily presuppose direct political rule), then the Constantinople patriarch as well as the emperor who was closely connected to him relied on the organized clergy. The Christian clergy was a branching social structure that penetrated all strata of society in all provinces and was unequivocally subordinated to Constantinople.

Second, Byzantium's state institutions were developed by the imperial powers not ad hoc but consciously, relying on the legal tradition of the Roman Empire and Byzantium's own experience. Special treatises were written on the art of public administration and preparation of professional civil servants, and the administrative system was optimized through rational reforms. One of the most important reforms in the eighth century changed the traditional administrative delimitation of the country as provinces to a system of military districts, called *themes*. The borders of the *thema* did not correspond to historical lands, and the leading position in them did not belong to a member of the local aristocracy, but to a general (strategos) holding joint military and civil authority, specially appointed by the emperor. For an empire that was located on territories with ancient traditions of self-rule (or, at the very least, with their own clan aristocracies), this was not only a military reform. As the story of the Bagratunis or the Samanids illustrates, it was no accident that the Arab Caliphate broke apart along the borders of provinces that aligned with historical regions or conquered kingdoms. [19]

Third, the population of the Byzantine Empire was genuinely interested in the preservation of its unity. The Christian majority feared the expansion of Arab Muslims, who were barely being held back by imperial troops. (That said, many followers of dissenting Christian sects, declared heretics by the authorities, fled Byzantium and hid from pursuit within caliphate territory.) The inhabitants of the borderlands—the majority of the population, given the specificity of Byzantium's geography—suffered from the raids of nomadic and seminomadic tribes arriving from the East European Plain. Moreover, Constantinople was not just a capital city, but the greatest trading center of its time. This was the most important market for goods of every kind that were produced in the empire, and the main source of any goods that were imported into the empire. In this era, trade was the chief source of wealth and the incentive for keeping up contacts between different lands and peoples. In that respect, trade was only equal to successful warfare. It was profitable to be subjects of Constantinople.

Finally, despite the cult of traditionalism and the unprecedented level of formalization in state institutions in the early Middle Ages, Byzantine society retained a very high degree of social mobility. At this point in history, society was divided not along closed social estates belonging to one of which was hereditary, but along syndicates—warriors, guild masters, monks, civil servants, and so on—with open membership. A person born into the lower classes had a real opportunity to rise to the higher spheres (for instance, on the bureaucratic ladder) and even to become emperor. Byzantine political doctrine sacralized supreme authority as an institution, and not the actual person who wielded it. Unlike in the caliphate or in China, one did not have to be a descendant of the Prophet or a member of the ruling dynasty to become emperor. Any ordinary person could make his way to the position, even if through a bloody coup. The ascent to power itself was evidence of holy approval of the new emperor, and the ritual anointing of the monarch "washed away" any unspeakable past that had preceded the ascension.

In this respect, the story of the founder of the Macedonian dynasty, Basil I, was quite typical. Basil, the son of a peasant, came from a family of Armenians who had moved to Macedonia. His native tongue was Armenian and he spoke Greek with a strong accent his entire life. Having arrived in Constantinople, Basil began his ascent in the service from the imperial stables, was appointed chief minister (*parakoimomenos*) to the emperor, married the emperor's mistress, took part in a few conspiracies. Strictly speaking, the result of the conspiracies was that Basil the Macedonian founded a new dynasty—one of twelve that ruled Byzantium in the first eight centuries of its existence—and not that he ascended to the imperial throne. That a peasant from the empire's outskirts could become emperor was wholly possible under Byzantine law. The title of emperor was not automatically passed down as an inheritance; it was conferred via a special ceremony, as a rule, with the sanction of the previous emperor, the highest officials, and the army. The emperor had one and often, several official corulers, theoretically elected by the populace, but in the ninth century, actually directly appointed by the emperor. These could be the children or other relatives of the emperor in a dynastic succession, but they could also be entirely unassociated people such as Basil the Macedonian. Precisely these "junior" emperors were the main legitimate candidates for the position of the "senior" emperor who had appointed them, and a coup might help secure this position more quickly or displace a more legitimate successor-competitor.

This is how, over the course of many centuries, the Byzantine Empire was able to combine a certain degree of flexibility and permeability of social boundaries with a developed system of state governance. Suffice it to mention that the fiscal apparatus was capable of collecting taxes from the populace two times a year and regularly monitoring changes in the cadastral value of individual plots of land. In the absence of democracy, the primitive mechanisms for feedback and the selection of the most capable candidate for a leadership position relied on idiosyncratic measures, such as actions taken by the office of the emperor's coruler or even a palace coup.

The "Viking Era" of Violent Encounters

On the opposite northwestern outskirts of Europe, the year 862 was marked, first of all, by the raids of Normans, both from the outside and from "within." Those who were called Normans (from Old French, *northman*, a person from the north) were Germanic tribes inhabiting Scandinavia—Norway, Sweden, Denmark, Jutland. Their raids were sowing horror among the population of the Atlantic and Mediterranean coasts. These representatives of various Scandinavian tribes called themselves Vikings—*vikinger*. The three centuries from the ninth to the eleventh are called the "Viking Era" in the history of northern and western Europe. The beginning of their destructive raids in the 790s strangely coincides with the reign of Charles the Great, who declared himself emperor of the West in the year 800. A short time before this, the Franks entered into conflict with the Danes, and some historians argue that it was precisely this Frankish expansion and aggressive spreading of Christianity that triggered the counterraids of the Vikings, which were marked by especially brutal attacks on monasteries and churches and reprisals against the clergy. Of course, there should have been more fundamental reasons that the Viking expansion lasted several centuries. Of equal importance could be climate change as warming led to a population explosion in Scandinavia; a political crisis within old tribal communes that forced the chiefs of small and midsized tribes to set off in search of new space for themselves; or cultural factors. No less important were the internal fragmentation of western European lands and the weakness of their leaders, both of which made the continuation of raids an especially attractive occupation for the Vikings/Normans. [20]

In January 862 a troop of Normans, settled on the territory of what is now the Parisian suburb of Saint-Maur-des-Fossés—almost an island formed by the river Marne as it bends before flowing into the Seine—undertook a raid on the episcopal residency in Maux about twenty-five miles north along the Marne. In April the Vikings, commanded by Bjorn Ironsides, returned to the mouth of the Rhône after a raid on the cities of the Eastern Mediterranean, Northern Africa, and Spain. The cities farther north along the Rhône likewise fell victim to their raids: Arles, Nimes, and even Valances (well over 100 miles from the sea). The Normans used waterways to effectuate their raids, navigating them in narrow, flat-hulled vessels. Rivers were their roads. Franks and the Normans had a fundamentally different perception of space: the former perceived it as the totality of forests, plains, and crop fields, and the latter—as a structured network of waterways. Although these spaces coincide on a map, each space was actually mastered by different groups of people who were governed by different political forces.

In June 862 Charles the Bald, the king of West Francia, which encompassed a large portion of today's France, gathered a diet at Pistres (modern spelling Pîtres) to discuss how to rein in the Normans. It was decided that fortifications should be built on the Seine to prevent the movement of the Normans from the sea along this river and deeper into the mainland. It was not so simple, however, to halt the encroachment of the Normans into the geographical as well as the political Frankish space. Half a century later, Charles III (Charles the Simple) was forced to come to an agreement with the Norman leader Rollo (Hrólfr), in which Rollo permanently received the entire territory in the north of the Frankish kingdom henceforth known as Normandy. Granted the title of count, christened, and married to the daughter of Charles, Rollo (Christian name Robert) acknowledged the rule of the Frankish king. Normandy became an important obstacle in the path of new Viking bands seeking to invade the kingdom. It served as both barrier and "magnet," because it retained newly arrived Normans. The Vikings quickly integrated with the local population and when, in 150 years' time, they went off to take over England under William the Conqueror, they considered themselves to be vassals of the king of the Franks and spoke the Norman French.

Thus, political demarcations of space (the dividing of territory and power over it between the Franks and the Vikings) helped to breach the isolation of ecological niches—river valleys and the lands far away from them. Both political and cultural, this transformation contributed to weakening the role of climatic and demographical factors in the Norman expansion. Toward the end of the eleventh century, the Scandinavian homeland of the Vikings becomes Christian, and the Danish, Norwegian, and Swedish kingdoms replace the former petty warring princedoms, of which there were dozens. These changes definitively altered the character of the Norman expansion: the uncontrollable raids of bands of pagan chieftains were replaced by a foreign policy of Christian kingdoms as medieval states.

The Problems of Political Consolidation on "Unhistorical" Lands: The Carolingians

The events of 862 revealed the weakness or the absence of "the state" in the kingdom of Charles the Bald. Unchecked, small gangs of Vikings penetrated tens and even hundreds of miles into the country, established their settlements and staged their raids from there or set off on naval expeditions to other countries. This means that no single and solid territory was constantly controlled by the state as one network of officials and organizations representing central power, such as the police or the army. The authority of the king was composed of many direct bilateral relationships with those individuals and societies (communes, cities, tribes) that were subject to him. The conditions of this subordination could have been of various natures: some were completely subordinate thanks to the use of force, some acknowledged themselves as vassals of the king and swore an oath of loyalty in return for patronage and protection, and some were connected to the king through family ties. A personal conflict and, even more so, the death of the king could completely alter the configuration of power and the parameters of "the state."

Before Charles the Great proclaimed himself emperor in 800, Frankish kings were kings of "the people," the Franks, rather than of a particular territory. Their title reflected the relatively recent formation of these kingdoms during the Great Migration between the fourth and seventh centuries CE. Frankish kings had virtually no "historical lands" with clear borders to rule over, or any indigenous aristocratic dynasties to reckon with. The kingdom lacked even a permanent capital as a primary embodiment of the state's territoriality. Charles himself was constantly on the road, but he deliberately selected a former Roman settlement, Aachen, as the capital of his future empire. The capital represented the emperor's power architecturally in a majestic Byzantine-style cathedral (it was still 250 years before the schism between the Catholic and Orthodox Christians) and a palatial complex. [21]

Taxes in Frankish kingdoms were not collected on a regular basis, and of course never twice a year, as in Byzantium. The natural economy provided the owners of farmsteads with food and basic necessities, but there were not enough resources to make other payments on top of that. Besides, the idea that some Franks ("Franks" meaning literally "free people") should pay duty to other Franks was unpopular. The main sources of kings' income were war and raids on neighbors, and therefore one can see the grandiose expansion conducted by Charles the Great not only as an empire-building and Christianization campaign but also as a profitable economic enterprise. The chronicler highlights how wars against the belligerent tribes of Saxons and Avars in the east permitted the Franks to capture fantastic booty, which the defeated parties had accumulated over the decades of their own raids against neighbors. After the victory over the Avars in Pannonia in 796, the treasure was carted away on fifteen enormous wagons, and this bounty permitted Charles to finance subsequent wars and ambitious construction projects, including that of Aachen.

Unlike the Byzantine Empire or the Arab Caliphate, the Frankish Empire formed by subjugating individual population groups ("tribes"), rather than through conquering historical regions with existing administrative systems. Therefore, it was necessary to find ways not only of subjugating the conquered collectives but also of maintaining them as a unified whole.

Elementary Statehood

One important element of statehood as a systematic mechanism of governance introduced by Charles the Great was the convocation of spring and autumn diets (counsel meetings), a modification of the traditional Frankish annual assemblies—vestiges of the earlier democratic social order. Only the top ranks of the aristocracy and the clergy were invited to the autumn diet to discuss important matters with the king; decisions on these matters were drawn up in capitularies (ordinances). The spring diet, just as traditional assemblies, could be attended by all free Franks to report local needs and situations. Now they also affirmed the contents of the capitularies that were composed in the fall. In this case, the use of the old institution of tribal democracy is evident in a new role as an element of governance that also helped maintain a feedback system in an extensive empire.

No less important an element of statehood, though evidently rudimentary, was Charles's establishment of the institution *missus dominicus* (pl. *missi dominci*): "the envoys of the sovereign." Charles appointed the representatives of the crown in pairs: one was a secular aristocrat and the other, a high-ranked member of the clergy. The representatives embarked on a permanent mission to provinces that were far removed from their own native homes. They were tasked with obtaining oaths of loyalty and with ensuring that the interests of the emperor were being obeyed and his orders executed. The representatives explained to the local officials—military leaders and the counts of territories—their functions, and distributed copies of capitularies. The mission to each district was dispatched four times a year. Each time the emperor's representatives remained in the district for a month and they were accommodated by local residents.

By 862, little remained of the new practices Charles the Great had brought into state-building. Seeking to tighten control over the extensive empire, Charles himself ordered that the direction of different regions be divided among his sons as early as 806. Following extensive conflicts, the empire was divided in 843 among three of Charles's grandsons by the Treaty of Verdun. These were Middle Francia (by 855 fractured into three kingdoms), the kingdom of Western Francia (the basis of future France), and the kingdom of Eastern Francia (within the approximate boundaries of future Germany). The institution *missus dominicus* was retained only by the Western Franks, but it had lost its original meaning entirely: the representatives of the sovereign were now appointed by a diet that increasingly resembled a council of aristocrats. The representatives were selected from the very locality they were supposed to monitor, and the regions under their control now began to coincide with the boundaries of an earldom or province, although this practice had been carefully avoided previously. As a result, instead of representing the interests of the sovereign or even "the crown" (i.e., the impersonal higher authority) in the provinces, the *missi dominici* transformed into conduits for the interests of local noble families at court. By the end of the ninth century, the *missi dominici* had completely disappeared from records.

It is likely that the most fundamental consequence of Charles the Great's actions turned out to be the overcoming of the tribal character of western kingdoms. His empire was a unified whole more in name than in reality; it contained the previously independent Franks, Langobards, Saxons, and West Goths. Yet when Charles's single holding fell apart into kingdoms, they were already largely organized by territorial principle and contained mixed populations.

Territorialization of State Power through Interpersonal Contracts

The Viking raids created a unique threat to the Franks: an external enemy, they attacked from within the kingdom, penetrating deep into the country along the rivers flowing into the sea. It was therefore impossible to raise an army and embark on a punitive expedition against them, as had been done against the Avars or the Arabs. To an external observer, the Frankish state was embodied by its formidable military force, but "within" the kingdom the state was practically nonexistent by 862. Evidently, it was precisely the Norman threat that became the reason for the definitive transformation of Frankish kingdoms in the ninth and tenth centuries, from "kingdoms of peoples" into "territorial kingdoms." The newly forming kingdoms were not, however, states in the strict sense of the word. After the failure of Charles the Great's attempts to introduce even rudimentary formal, independent of personalities, institutions of government, Frankish kings began to build the foundations of territorial authority from scratch, as bilateral personal relationships.

As was already mentioned, after the two Viking raids of 862 (along the Seine and the Rhône), the king, Charles the Bald, issued an edict following the Diet of Pistres. The edict forbade, on pain of death, the sale of arms and horses to the Vikings; prescribed the building of fortified bridges over rivers blocking the Vikings' access; and demanded that every freeman in possession of enough means to obtain a horse and armor serve as a mounted warrior or chevalier, the predecessor of the future nobleman. This was

Political Ecology

a truly comprehensive program, but its actual execution wholly depended on local notables and counts, whose functions were becoming more and more hereditary. It was no coincidence that the very same edict of Charles the Bald attempted to simultaneously curb local independence: it forbade the construction of new castles without the king's permission and limited coinage to "only" ten mints—previously, every large market city minted coins. Yet the attempt to strengthen the kingdom by making local lords plenipotential transformed the king into little more than a symbol of power, while the real control over territories transferred into the hands of large landowners or counts, who used to be merely representatives of the crown. Castles continued to be built, despite the bans, even by landowners of humble origin. The class of nonaristocratic professional warriors-knights (chevaliers) formally recognized by Charles's edict needed economic support, which it received from the landed aristocrats by swearing an oath of fealty in return for the right to use a tract of land—a fief (Latin: *feudum*). Gradually, both the knight's fief and the count's office began to be inherited, and in 877, the very same Charles the Bald affirmed in his capitulary the hereditariness of the title of count. This, by extension, meant the hereditariness of the entire chain of conditional grants for service, up to the lowborn knight.

Thus, during the reign of Charles the Bald, efforts to counter the Viking expansion in many ways had contributed to the formation of the social order that would later be called feudalism. Generally speaking, this order was characterized by the relaying of key public ("state") functions through a chain of private relationships and responsibilities. A person acknowledging the authority of a suzerain (lord) as a vassal pledged fealty and promised to provide services in return for protection and patronage. These relationships permeated all of society, from peasant to king. Free peasants acknowledged their dependence on a local landowner capable of protecting them against raiders. Simple knights offered their swords and loyalty to the lord, in return for which they received land or monetary compensation. The local lord swore an oath to the count, and the count swore to a duke or directly to the king. Execution of the king's will was conditioned by how well it coincided with the interests of those carrying it out, and likewise with the presence of material and symbolic rewards, by which the king could attract the more disinterested of his vassals to his cause.

Transferring power relations and the mechanism of government into the sphere of interpersonal connections, feudalism laid the foundation for a new type of territorial authority. Governing the territory was thus conditioned not by a shared tribal connection to a historical "land" with blurred boundaries, or by the subjugation of a neighboring tribe or even princedom (with equally vague borders). It was a legally formalized right to rule, which presupposed the meticulous delineation of land and mutual obligations between the parties involved. The right to property was becoming inextricable from the relationships of submission and rule, and landownership determined what duties and taxes the vassal owed the suzerain. Simultaneously, the chain of feudal relationships that stretched from peasant to king created vertical links that thoroughly permeated all strata of the complex society and replaced the previous horizontal mechanical connections between distinct lands/tribes/provinces. Family and clan ties continued to play an important role in feudalism (the concept of aristocracy itself founded on blood lines), but the "vertical" link of lord and vassal proved stronger than the "horizontal" familial relations.

The baron or knight in control of a castle (castellan, chatelain) ruled the surrounding area to the degree that local inhabitants accepted his protection, either willingly or through coercion. In exchange for his protection they acknowledged his judicial jurisdiction, worked the fields belonging to the castle, and performed various natural duties. The peasants used the land, given that their obligatory duties were connected to it, while their lord wielded power over them only to the extent that he fulfilled the functions of the state in terms of protection, economic development (organizing the construction of windmills, bridges, roads), and governance (including judicial process). The lord himself had the right to exercise state functions to the extent that this right was acknowledged by his own suzerain, such as a count—the title, formerly given to a province's governor appointed by the king. The owner of the castle was obligated to serve the count, above all in times of war, and the latter guaranteed the rights of the vassals and served as an arbiter in cases of conflict among them. The count was a vassal of a duke or a prince, or, in the central parts of the country, of the king directly. This hierarchy was virtually unaffected by the distinctions between Franks, West Goths, Langobards, or Saxons, and thus became a universal mechanism of social cohesion, while state power—in personified form—reached every peasant commune and controlled every square inch of land.

This system may seem archaic, but only until one pictures the multitude of individual vertical strings of feudal loyalty as comprising a common imagined community of "nation" and envisions that the hitherto dispersed state functions are consolidated into special institutions of governance. Then it will appear that the situation of the vassal is not so different from the status of today's citizen. Recognizing the supreme authority of a suzerain-nation (now exercised through the apparatus of the state), the citizen has economic and natural duties (taxes, military service) and acknowledges the supremacy of this suzerain's law over religious or tribal traditions. Today the state is territorial because power over territory is inextricably linked with conceptions of the territory's property, whether personal or collective, while the right to property, in turn, is guaranteed only on the condition of acknowledging the authority of the state. The understanding of the relationships of authority and property as two distinct universal categories became possible only when feudalism used these relationships to tie together concrete individuals, having differentiated the previous syncretic familial and tribal links (at once, of dependence–partnership–ownership–responsibilities).

In the mid-ninth century, however, the western part of Europe was at the very beginning of the development of statehood. It lagged not only behind Byzantium with its highly organized, centralized state institutions, but also behind the Arab Caliphate, which relied on a more archaic system of governance that had been formed earlier on conquered lands, during the time of Roman, Hellenistic, or Persian rule. These old administrative structures and traditions were supplemented by Islam, a complex system of ideas and legal norms regulating almost every sphere of life. The Byzantine Empire, as was already mentioned, relied on an elaborate codex of laws, developed state institutions, and also on the parallel hierarchy of the Christian church that permeated society from the local congregation to the Constantinople patriarch.

Against this background, the Frankish kings, who had relatively recently settled upon the lush forest-covered lands of what were once the outskirts of Roman provinces, after a lengthy period of large-scale political cataclysms and population migrations, could boast only of the codification of Franks' customary law (the so-called Salic Law) and the preservation of elements of the Roman heritage. Even this heritage was predominantly passed down through the texts, however, and not through any functioning institutions.

Frankish tradition and the Roman heritage contributed an important element of private-law relationships into the establishing of connections between vassal and suzerain. Vassal connections—subordination and the performance of duties in return for patronage and protection—were also discovered by peoples of different corners of Northern Eurasia, independently and at different times. Everywhere, this was the first stage in the formation of political structures. Unlike the Franks, however, the self-organizing societies of Northern Eurasia could not even indirectly rely on the old traditions of formal statehood, whether Roman, Byzantine, Persian, or Chinese. On these lands, no one had ever before collected taxes with the goal of financing public works, attempted to govern a strictly demarcated territory, or described society in any terms other than those of kinship or tribal solidarity. Chapter 2 will discuss how political organization could come about under these circumstances, and which locally available social forms and practices were used in the process.

Further reading

Bassin, Mark. "Russia between Europe and Asia: The Ideological Construction of Geographical Space." *Slavic Review* 50, no. 1 (1991): 1–17.

Christian, David. *A History of Russia, Central Asia, and Mongolia*. Vol. 1. *Inner Asia from Prehistory to the Mongol Empire*. Malden: Wiley-Blackwell, 1998.

Forte, Angelo, Richard D. Oram, and Frederik Pedersen. *Viking Empires*. Cambridge: Cambridge University Press, 2005.

Golden, Peter B. *Central Asia in World History*. Oxford: Oxford University Press, 2011.

Golden, Peter B. *Turks and Khazars: Origins, Institutions, and Interactions in pre-Mongol Eurasia*. Farnham: Ashgate Valiorum, 2010.

2

Mechanisms of Political and Cultural Self-Organization of Northern Eurasia's First Polities

The Formation of the Rous' Lands

Rurik

The Primary Chronicle, the oldest known annals in Northern Eurasia, was composed in Kyiv on the Dnieper River at the beginning of the twelfth century. It begins the tale of local events from the year 6370 (862 CE) since the creation of the world. Two seemingly contradictory events happened that year in the forest area between the Ladoga and White Lakes in the northeast of Europe, extending from the sixtieth parallel southward for 125–200 miles, to Lake Ilmen and the Upper Volga.

The Invitation of Varangians

Lake Ladoga is connected to the Baltic Sea (its easternmost arm, the Gulf of Finland) by the forty-five-mile-long Neva River [1]. It is thus not surprising that Vikings from Scandinavia (called Varangians in this part of Europe) penetrated the territory. In contrast to England and France, the taiga area to the south and east of Ladoga had no large ancient cities or abbeys with rich sacristies, and thus rapid raids would yield no significant bounty. Therefore, according to the chronicle, "the Varangians coming from beyond the sea collected tribute from the Chuds, the Slavs, the Merians, the Ves', and the Krivichians," the tribes populating this area.[1] Under 862, the chronicle mentions the rebellion of these tribes against the Varangians: "And they drove the Varangians [back] beyond the sea, and did not give them tribute, and set out to govern themselves [literally, 'and began to own themselves']."

However, in the same year these tribes made the directly opposite decision:

There was no law among them, and the clan rose against the clan, and there was a quarrel among them, and they began to fight each other. So, they said to themselves, "Let us seek a prince who would rule over us and judge us according to the agreement and the law." They went overseas to the Varangians, to the Rus'. Those Varangians were called Rus', just as others are called Swedes, and yet others Normans and Angles, or Gotlanders, and so were these. The Chuds, the Slovenes, the Krivichians, and the Ves' told the Rus': "Our land is large and plentiful, but there is no order in it. Come to rule and reign over us." And three brothers were elected with their clans, who took with them all the Rus' and arrived: the elder, Rurik, in Novgorod, the other, Sineus, at Beloozero, and the third, Truvor, in Izborsk. And from those Varangians came the name "the Rus land." Novgorodians are descendants of the Varangian kin, and before that they were Slovenes. Two years later, Sineus and his brother Truvor died. Rurik acquired all the power, and began appointing his men to cities: one to Polotsk, another to Rostov, yet another to Beloozero. The Varangians in these cities are newcomers, and the indigenous population in Novgorod are Slovenes, in Polotsk—Krivichians, in Rostov— Merians, in Beloozero—Ves', in Murom—Muroms, and Rurik reigned over all of them.

Over the past three centuries, this story has provoked fierce debates among historians and politicians: Does it mean that statehood was brought to the "Rus' land" (and hence, as many believe, to Russia), which was unable to govern itself, by the overseas Varangians-Vikings? Why were Varangians called "Rus," who was Rurik—and was he a real figure at all? And, of course, the question remained: Why expel the Varangians, only to immediately invite them back to rule?

At the same time, few historians have noted that the alleged arrival of a Viking chieftain with his retinue to rule a territory outside Scandinavia was not the strangest part of this story: for example, just fifteen years earlier, in 847, the Norman Jarl Oscar was invited to rule the city of Bordeaux. Much more surprising was the composition of the "host party." The Chuds were Baltic Finns (possibly proto-Estonians or Karelians), who inhabited the seashore areas. Slovenes were the East Slavic tribe living south of Ladoga, around Ilmen Lake, which was connected to Ladoga by the 140-mile-long Volkhov River. Judging by the annals and archaeological data, Slovenes had migrated to this region in the mid-first millennium from the southwestern coast of the Baltic (present-day Poland). By the early eighth century, they reached Ladoga and invaded the territory of the Finnish-speaking tribes. The Finns themselves moved to these lands from the Urals in the east, but by the time of the Slavic colonization, they had already lived here for several centuries. Merians were another Finnish-speaking tribe residing southeast of the Chuds and Slovenes, in the Upper Volga. Krivichians were Slavs who arrived in the vicinity of Lake Peipus (125 miles to the west of Lake Ilmen) in the sixth century, either from the Carpathians or from today's northern Poland. Gradually, they settled farther south at the upper reaches of the Dnieper River. Living intermittently in the forests surrounding rivers and lakes, these various Slavic and Finnish tribes were equally vulnerable to Viking expeditions, although it is not quite clear how the Vikings could extract tribute from a small population scattered across a forest area of many thousand square miles. At least theoretically, one can imagine that the goal of expelling a common enemy could unite tribes that spoke different languages (and there could be significant differences even among assorted Slavic and Finnish dialects). It seems completely improbable, however, that they would demonstrate this same unanimity and determination by inviting a common ruler for themselves. Such a grassroots initiative would have required at least a prehistory of a fairly centralized single administration of these peoples—but there is no evidence of this in historical documents, folklore, or archaeological data. Therefore, the truly puzzling aspects of this story are the most mundane and practical: In what language and for what purpose did the local multicultural population negotiate the invitation of a common prince, and why from outside? [2]

The Volga–Baltic Trade Route: Cooperation, Interdependence, Protection

There is one explanation for the Vikings' interest in the region adjoining the Eastern Baltic. Historical documents and archaeological excavations confirm that the Volga–Baltic trade route from Scandinavia to the Arab Caliphate began here. It was the earliest of the three routes linking northern Europe to the Middle East, older than the routes along the Dnieper and Dvina Rivers. Beginning in the 780s, after the spread of Judaism in Khazaria and the migration of Bulgars to the Middle Volga, this became a busy logistical line. Hundreds of thousands of Arab silver dirhams were shipped north to Scandinavia (along the way, leaving a "trail" in the form of hoards later discovered at transfer points) as well as silk and spices. In exchange, goods of northern forests and the sea were carried to the Middle East, including amber, honey, wax, slaves, and, of course, fine furs. According to modern estimates, from the ninth to the eleventh centuries, at least ten million marks of silver were transported from the caliphate along the Volga–Baltic route, mainly through Novgorod on the Volkhov River. Of this amount, six to seven million marks (up to 1,400 tons, more than three million pounds) remained in circulation on the territory between the Volga and the Baltic. Given the low density of the not numerous local population, this is an extraordinary volume of bullion. [3]

This strategically important route began in the shallow Gulf of Finland, which Vikings—mostly Swedes, but also Norwegians and Danes—could cross even using smaller river vessels and not necessarily on large seagoing ships used for raids on the Franks and England. They entered the mouth of the Neva River and advanced along it to Lake Ladoga through the lands of the Baltic and Finnish tribes, primarily Chuds. On reaching Ladoga, they had to travel about sixty miles to the point where the Volkhov River flowed into the lake. The settlement of Old Ladoga (Staraya Ladoga) was situated in this strategic place, and the lands of the Slovenes began. The Volkhov led them south to Lake Ilmen—Novgorod is located near this critical juncture. From Ilmen, along one of the smaller rivers, such as the Msta and the Tsna, they traveled eastward to the network of tiny rivers of the Valdai Hills, eventually reaching the upper Volga. Along the way were portages, which necessitated carrying or dragging the vessels and cargo between adjacent waterways (e.g., the portage between the river Tsna leading to Ilmen and the river Tvertsa flowing into the Volga was 1.5 miles long). This was the area already occupied by Merians, with Krivichians gradually penetrating their territory and mixing with them. Merians' southern neighbors were the Bulgars, whose capital, Bulgar, was an important transition point on the Volga. And the Lower Volga was controlled by the Khazars. The Great Silk Road passed through their lands north of the Caspian Sea, leading southwest to Baghdad or southeast to Mawarannahr (Transoxiana). [4]

Thus, the initial leg of the route from the Baltic Sea to the Volga was the most challenging in terms of navigating through the maze of lakes and rivers. It passed through the lands of the Chuds, Slovenes, Krivichians, and Merians. Even as they traveled along waterways, the Viking traders depended on the local population. At night, they moored their boats and set large tents either directly on the ship or on the shore. In addition, twice a day, they stopped and went ashore to cook because they did not allow open fire onboard. Several dozen crew members of a ship or a larger convoy, even if heavily armed, stood no chance of fighting their way for weeks past riverbanks inhabited by hostile tribes, particularly in smaller rivers no more than thirty feet wide. It was of equal concern to obtain a guide among the locals who would be capable of navigating the labyrinth of waterways and finding the entrance to a rivulet behind reed thickets. Viking shallow draft boats were relatively light and could be carried over portages, just as cargo, but local hands were indispensable in speeding up this process: helping with the load, clearing the way, and manufacturing sledges or rollers to facilitate dragging the ships. [5]

Archaeological remains of settlements along the Volga–Baltic route reveal the simultaneous presence of Varangian, Slavic, and Finnish cultural elements. This, combined with hoards of Arabic coins, indicates a high degree of cooperation among different population groups and their involvement in the trans-Eurasian trade, which would not be possible without such cooperation. This also means that Slovenes were engaged not only in slash-and-burn agriculture, and Merians—not only in hunting. The tribute could be collected from them not just in grain and furs but also in silver coins. In this case, it was sufficient to enforce the tribute on the easily accessible inhabitants of the settlements along waterways, who were accumulating revenues from "logistics services."

The chronicler dates the beginning of the Varangians' taxation of local tribes to 859 CE, three years before their expulsion. The early dates and events of the chronicle are not fully credible, but noteworthy is the chronological proximity and direct logical connection of the tributaries' rebellion with their attempt to renew tributary relations. By the mid-ninth century, the Volga–Baltic trade route had been in operation for many decades, so the episodes mentioned in the chronicle in any case occurred much later than the first contacts of local tribes with the Vikings. One can only speculate whether the imposition of tribute that sparked the rebellion was the result of a onetime raid by a squad that followed the route of regular trade convoys, or an attempt to put the income from the transit trade under systematic control. What is important is that this attempt failed at the very beginning, which means that the common interest in preserving the trade route prevailed over the temptation of one of the parties involved to seize control of it. This structural situation explains the conflict of local tribes that followed after the "expulsion of the Varangians": the chronicler points out that "there was no law among them," that is, no legal basis for joint action. In boundless forests, the migration of sparse population did not have to provoke a confrontation among tribes. Neighbors gradually assimilated each other or could relocate to unoccupied lands to avoid unwanted contacts. The sole reason for open conflicts would be control over strategic settlements at the mouths of rivers or near portages. It is the common interest in sustaining transit trade that can explain the joint invitation of a prince, given the initial absence of a common "principality." This also indirectly testifies to the multilingualism of the region's diverse population, which made complex economic and political cooperation possible. The invitation of a Varangian chieftain from "overseas" to protect against raids and resolve conflicts in adjacent sectors of the trade route was a logical compromise, considering the varied composition of the "caretakers" of the trade route and their jealous attitude toward each other.

Varangians: Rulers by Contract

Varangians themselves were not a single people, and even less were they representatives of a single political organization, so it is not surprising that one group of "Varangians" was expelled, and another invited almost immediately. Frankish emperors and kings did the same on a regular basis, trying to use some Viking squads to defend against new raids. However, there was a significant difference: Charles the Simple yielded part of his own kingdom—the territory of future Normandy—to the leader of the Vikings, Rollo, as a fief, that is, a territory at his full disposal pending the formal recognition of the Frankish king's supreme authority. In this way, Rollo became Duke Robert, the sole source of power in Normandy, who had the right to transfer his title and possession of the duchy to his heir. Unlike Rollo, Rurik was invited by his future subjects themselves to administer local affairs "according to the contract" ("by agreement" and "by law," as the chronicle says). The tradition of inviting a prince with his retinue from outside to perform clearly defined duties—first of all, military protection—had persisted in the Lake Ilmen region for many centuries. The Novgorod popular assembly, the veche, invited the prince in accordance with an "agreement" (*riad*) and could expel him in case of dissatisfactory service. Therefore, the consolidation of princely power in the upper reaches of the Volga–Baltic trade route markedly differed from the history of the dukes of Normandy. The invited prince could not merge the tribes that recognized his authority into a homogeneous mass of subjects with the same legal status, residing on a common territory—at least not before the tribes themselves, with their popular assemblies and clan elders, had lost their differences in the process of assimilation. Nor could the prince claim the office, consecrated by tradition and law, of the local supreme ruler, because various Slavic, Baltic, and Finnish tribes of the region never had such a common ruler. In medieval western European tradition, a prince is usually perceived more as a supreme proprietor of lands and power itself than a top manager—an administrator and military commander. But being a prince like Rurik implied the latter responsibilities, and a prince's status and responsibilities were stipulated by a formal contract.

Not being the "leader of all" Slavs or Finns (like the "king of all Franks") or the representative of the supreme ruler in a certain distinct territory (like a duke on the outskirts of the Frankish kingdom), the commissioned prince found himself at the center of a complex process of social self-organization. Paradoxically, the foundations of his power in this remote forest region were much closer to pure political relationships and elements of "statehood" than was the power of the Frankish kings over territories, some of which had a thousand-year-old tradition of statehood since Roman times. The power of Frankish kings relied on several preexisting social regimes of authority: those of tribal elders, landowners subletting their possessions, or victorious military leaders. Rurik's power had no ready form or even object for its implementation: a single people or a separate historical territory to rule or preexisting property relations intertwined with political domination. In other words, there were no structural preconditions for the role of supreme authority that anyone could claim on whatever grounds. There was not even a situation of conquest, whereby the conquerors could impose their norms and values on the local population. This is why the question of Rurik's real identity is all but irrelevant, since the decisive factor was not the figure of the contender for the authority but the emergence of this authority from scratch, in the process of intercommunal self-organization.

The Whole of the Rous' Land

In technical terms, Rurik's power was implemented similarly to the power of west European rulers of the time: the prince relied on a squad of warriors that was sustained by the resources of a territory specifically designated for their "feeding." In Europe, such a land grant for the duration of service was called a "fief" and was provided by an overlord. In Rurik's case, apparently, the burden of sustaining the retinue of the invited prince was distributed among the federated tribes. According to the chronicle, Rurik settled in Novgorod; some historians believe that his residence was in Ladoga, but in any case, he controlled the initial key segment of the Volga–Baltic trade route along the Volkhov, between lakes Ladoga and Ilmen. His two lieutenants (the chronicle mentions them as his brothers) received "fiefs" in Izborsk and Beloozero. Both places were located at about the same distance to the west and east of the Volkhov River (200–250 miles) and not closer to any other point of the Volga–Baltic trade route. This means that Rurik's retinue was expected to live off Slovenes' fields in the west and the hunting grounds of Finnish tribes in the east, but not to exploit the trade route itself, which they were invited to protect and control. Their power was dissociated from economic ownership even territorially, in contrast to the syncretic nature of European feudalism.

This surprising functionality and "extraterritoriality" of power was reflected in language. The lands in the northeast of England, conquered by the Vikings-Danes at about the same time, became known as the Danelaw. The region in the north of France that was yielded to the Normans fifty years later was called Normandy. However, no "Varangianland" formed on the territory administered by the Varangians at the invitation of the local Finns and Slavs. The new polity began to be called "the whole of the Rous' land" (*Rous'kaia*, written in the annals with the digraph Uk—"oy"). This notion referred to a new political union rather than the tribal territory of the Slavs, Finns, Balts, or Scandinavians-Vikings, or a province in a kingdom. An abstract (political) phenomenon was given an equally abstract name that was dissociated from the reality of any particular people or tribe. The locals identified the invited prince's retinue as *Rus'*, although neither the Scandinavians themselves nor the Finns or the Slavs called their own warriors by this name.

We observe here a situation of mutual creative misunderstanding, when, as a result of misperceptions by all the interacting parties, a new—common, if somewhat distorted—social reality is being forged. Most likely, the original name *Rous'*, the Rous' Land (later transformed into Rus') derived from the Old Scandinavian root roþs- (in modern English transcribed as roths-)—to row, a rower. This is how the newcomer Vikings must have identified themselves. It is known that the size of Scandinavian ships was classified by the number of rowers: in the Old Norse language, they were counted by the number of rowing benches, in Old Swedish—by the actual number of rowers (therefore the "twenty-rower" ship in the former corresponded to the "forty-rower" in the latter). There is even a version stating that Norsemen were known in western Europe as Vikings, since the Old Norse feminine noun *víking* implied an expedition across the sea that required the rowers to take shifts (*fara í víking*). In the same logic, the entire group received its name in the Eastern Baltic region due to the central role of the oarsmen during shorter trips along the Gulf of Finland and farther along the rivers, which required smaller boats. To this day, Finns call the Swedes *Ruotsi*, Estonians— *Rootsi*, and the old Slavic spelling with the digraph Uk (oy) fits this pattern well: *Rous'* (роусь). [6]

Rous' versus Rus'

This or any alternative explanation of the origins of *Rous'* remains a more or less plausible hypothesis. Whatever the actual origins of the term, one thing is unambiguous: the local written sources from the period call the polity established in the ninth century along the waterways from Lake Ladoga to the Upper Volga, the Rous' Land. Therefore, this is how we will keep calling it in this text, using the digraph Uk. Besides the reasons of historical accuracy, it is politically imperative to distinguish this phenomenon from various versions of Rus' of a later time. Otherwise, inconspicuously, just by using the language carelessly, one can get used to the unsubstantiated idea that Rous' and Rus' (Russia) are one and the same in terms of territory, population, or political legacy— just because their modernized spelling is identical. Moreover, for the sake of a more adequate translation, we will use the term in plural—the "Rous' Lands," to convey the fluidity of this polity's boundaries and its composite character.

Even if referring originally to newcomer Scandinavians, the term *Rous'* soon came to denote the prince's retinue: a social group that was apparently unknown to local tribes, in which the entire male population took up arms in a time of war and a cast of professional warriors did not exist. The chronicles begin to mention Rous' separately from the Vikings when registering events that took place a hundred years later (after the mid-tenth century), in a context that implies a social group rather than an ethnicity. In a similar vein, the very first article of the oldest collection of local legal norms compiled in the early eleventh century, the Rous' Law (Pravda Rous'kaia), equalized the value of the life of a "Rousin" and a "Sloven" in Novgorod, at a time when the prince's retinue had long been recruited from locals and the Vikings had been assimilated.

"The prince and the entire Rous," according to a stable formula of the chronicles, became the main instrument for creating a new polity, which from the very beginning was supratribal and "multicultural," if this modern term is applicable to a society 1,000 years ago. Their military potential was not the main source of the new authority: a detachment of professional warriors could maintain control over local tribes only with the population's general consent, otherwise they would be expelled or destroyed. By sheer force alone, only a huge occupation army can subjugate a territory exceeding many thousand square miles. Moreover, the functions and privileges of the retinue were detailed from the very beginning by the treaty (*riad*) with inviting tribes. Thus, the initiator and main subject of this early state-building was a conglomerate of multilingual and multicultural local populations united by a pragmatic task: maintaining a profitable trade route. Should one of the tribes selfishly attempt to exploit its strategic location (whether it was the passage from Ladoga to the Volkhov or the portages in the upper reaches of the Volga), the entire common source of income would have been jeopardized. This mutual dependence required the main "shareholders" of the route to seek an arbiter and a general manager of the enterprise "from the outside."

The center of the new political union was Novgorod (literally, a "new city") on the Volkhov River, not far from Lake Ilmen. The choice of this location can be explained by the source of the main threat—Viking raids along the Neva and Lake Ladoga. The small number of professional warriors under Rurik's command could be used effectively only to guard a single strategic bottleneck that could not be easily bypassed via alternative waterways. According to the testimony of Ibn-Fadlan (a member of the embassy in Bulgar in 922) and the calculations of modern historians, a Rous' princely retinue in the tenth century numbered between 200 and 400 men, and initially it could be even smaller. Volkhov was the main waterway to Lake Ilmen, from which there were already alternative routes toward the Volga along small rivers (such as the Msta or Polya), so it was important to establish control over Volkhov.

Whatever the strategic considerations for choosing Novgorod as the prince's residence, the result was the rising role of the Ilmen Slovenes, on whose territory a "new city" was built. In any case, the Slavic population prevailed in the area of residence and gradual assimilation of the invited Scandinavians. Subsequent events further shifted the balance in the original Slavic-Finnish confederation in favor of various Slavic tribes.

The Dnieper Route

Two years after his arrival in Novgorod (864 CE, according to the chronicle's dating), Rurik sent an exploratory expedition to the south to find a direct route to Constantinople that would bypass the Khazar Khaganate. Only a few decades earlier, the route along the Dnieper to the Black Sea and farther to Constantinople was unknown or inaccessible to the Scandinavian merchants. The existing Volga–Baltic trade route via Bulgaria primarily served commerce with the caliphate. The route to

Self-Organization of Northern Eurasia's First Polities   45

Constantinople along the Volga or Don Rivers was very long and, in both cases, passed through the Khazar lands. The route to Byzantium through western Europe was even more difficult: it required passing through the territory of the Viking's sworn enemies, the Franks, or circumnavigating the Iberian Peninsula through the precarious Atlantic Ocean. Yet the Vikings knew about Constantinople and its enormous wealth, calling it Miklagard—"the great city." The first documentary mention of the "Rhos" who reached Constantinople dates to 838 CE. According to the Annals of Saint Bertin (the chronicle kept in the Abbey of Saint Bertin in the north of the Kingdom of the West Franks), in June of the following year 839, the son of Charlemagne, Emperor Louis the Pious, received Byzantine ambassadors at the imperial palace in Ingelheim on the Rhine. The Byzantine emperor instructed his diplomats to obtain confirmation of allied relations and peace between the empires.

> He also sent with the envoys some men who said they—meaning their whole people—were called Russians [in the original: Rhos], and had been sent to him by their king whose name was the Khagan [Chacanus] for the sake of friendship, so they claimed. Theophilus requested in his letter that the Emperor in his goodness might grant them safe conducts to travel through his empire and any help or practical assistance they needed to return home, for the route by which they had reached Constantinople had taken them through primitive tribes that were very fierce and savage and Theophilus did not wish them to return that way in case some disaster befell them. When the Emperor investigated more closely the reason for their coming here, he discovered that they belonged to the people of the Swedes [*gente esse Sueonom*]. He suspected that they had really been sent as spies to this kingdom of ours rather than as seekers of our friendship, so he decided to keep them with him until he could find out for certain whether or not they had come in good faith.[2]

If the "Rhos Swedes" came to Constantinople along the Volga–Baltic route, then one can understand why they chose a different route to return home to their "king" (the Scandinavian name Hákon that can be spelled Chacan was common among the Viking chieftains). They had to cover about 4,500 miles to get from the southern tip of the Scandinavian Peninsula to Constantinople through Ladoga, Bulgar, Atil on the Volga (or via the lower reaches of the Don). The direct way back to the north through the Frankish kingdoms was shorter by almost half, about 2,500 miles. Besides, this road was controlled not by a dozen different tribes, but by one ruler of the Frankish Empire. The only problem was that the Franks considered the Vikings mortal enemies and were well-acquainted with them. So, when the Swedish Vikings introduced themselves as "Rhoses," they were immediately identified and detained as Normans. If they had an opportunity to return from Constantinople along the Dnieper, they could have altogether avoided the risk of meeting with the Franks—the Dnieper route was only 200 miles longer than the dangerous "Frankish" one. Apparently, in 839, this road was not yet known, as evidenced by the absence of Scandinavian traces in the archaeological excavations on the Dnieper and in the Byzantine documents of the first half of the ninth century.

Expedition to Constantinople

That is why it seems logical that Rurik sent part of his retinue to search for a direct route to Constantinople soon after his arrival in Novgorod. As the gateway to the trade of northern Europe with the "Global South" of that time, Novgorod could add the lucrative Byzantine route to the well-established caliphate one. According to the chronicle,

> There were two men with him [i.e., Rurik], not relatives of his but boyars. They asked permission to leave for Tsar'grad [i.e., Constantinople] with their kin. They thus set off down the Dnieper, and along the way they saw a small town on a mountain. And they asked: "Whose is this town?" [The locals] responded: "There were three brothers, Kyi, Schek and Horeb, who built this town and then were gone, and here we are, their descendants, paying tribute to the Khazars." Askold and Dir stayed in this town, gathered a lot of Varangians around them and began to dominate the Polianian land. Rurik was ruling at Novgorod [at the time].

Thus, for the first time, the Vikings found themselves in Kyiv, the center of the Slavic Polianian tribe on the remote northern periphery of the Khazar Khaganate. Khazar political authority over the territory was expressed, among other things, in the practice of regular payment of tribute. Four years later (866 in the chronicle's timeline), Askold and Dir undertook a military expedition to Constantinople. According to the chronicle, only divine intervention helped the Byzantines to withstand the attack of 200 ships.

This legendary story is generally confirmed by Byzantine and European sources, but dated to 860 CE. In early June 860, Emperor Constantine led the army for yet another campaign against the Abbasid Caliphate. He left Constantinople and even took part of the city's garrison with him. Suddenly, at dusk on June 18, a squadron of 200 (in other sources—360) ships of Normans ("Normannorum gentes") approached the city from the Black Sea, at the less fortified section of the walls along the Golden Horne. The invaders plundered the suburbs, captured rich bounty, and withdrew. Byzantine authors mention a single leader of the Normans. Likewise, the great Arab historian of the tenth century, Al-Mas'udi mentions a "Slavonic king" "al-Dir" without a coruler. The use of the singular grammatical form in the Primary Chronicle suggests that Rurik sent one emissary to the south, but several centuries later the name was misinterpreted by copyists of the chronicle as two names, belonging to two different people. [7]

While dates and personal details of the earliest episodes mentioned by the chronicle are of questionable accuracy, the overall dynamics conveyed by the chronicler are important. Almost immediately on assuming the office, the contracted Scandinavian prince known as Rurik sent an exploratory expedition south. The expedition found a suitable base to prepare for the attack on Constantinople and spent several years building and equipping an "invasion fleet" of up to 360 boats. The military expedition did not contradict the plans for strategic trade cooperation; to the contrary, it was a prerequisite for concluding a trade agreement on terms favorable to a previously unknown or minor partner. Indeed, as early as 867, Byzantine sources mentioned the embassy of Rhoses, who signed a treaty in Constantinople and even expressed their

Self-Organization of Northern Eurasia's First Polities 47

readiness to be baptized. Historians still debate the circumstances and the very reality of the "first baptism of Rus'" but, in principle, baptism was necessary for negotiating more favorable conditions of the treaty: Christian Byzantium could not recognize pagans as equal partners. This does not mean that the Vikings had to faithfully keep their promise.

Kyiv the "Mother of the Rousian Towns," and Control over the New Trade Route

According to the chronicle's timeline, in 879, Rurik, the first prince commissioned by the confederation of Slavic and Finnish tribes, died. Three years later, in 882 his successor, Prince Oleg, together with Rurik's young son Igor, headed the joint forces of the confederates as they went south along the Dnieper.

> Oleg set forth, taking many warriors with him: Varangians, Chuds, Slovenes, Merians, Vesians, and Krivichians, and came to Smolensk of the Krivichians, and assumed the authority over the city, and appointed his sheriff [literally: man] there. From there he went down and took Lyubech, and also appointed his man there. They came thus to the Kyiv Mountains, and Oleg found out that Askold and Dir were ruling here. He hid some warriors in the boats, left others behind, and moved forward, carrying the baby Igor. After hiding his warriors, he approached the Hungarian Mountain and sent to Askold and Dir, telling them that "we are merchants, traveling to the Greeks [i.e., Byzantines] on behalf of Oleg and the little prince Igor. Come to us, your kinsmen." When Askold and Dir arrived, all the others jumped out of the boats, and Oleg said to Askold and Dir: "You are not princes and not of a princely lineage, but I am." He presented Igor: "And this is Rurik's son." And so, they killed Askold and Dir. . . . And Oleg began ruling in Kyiv and announced: "Let this be the mother of Rousian cities." He had [relied on] Varangians and Slovenes, and others, who were called Rous'. That Oleg began to build cities and imposed tribute on the Slovenes, and Krivichians, and Merians, and set the Varangians to pay tribute from Novgorod of 300 grivnas annually for the sake of preserving peace.

Twenty years after the Askold–Dir expedition departed southward from Novgorod, the task was no longer to explore a new trade route to Constantinople but to take it under direct control—and this was not solely a Viking enterprise. The mission was accomplished by the coalition of all the Finnish and Slavic tribes that participated in the "calling of the Varangians." They had to cover almost seven hundred miles to reach Kyiv. The first half of the expedition followed the relatively recent migration route of the Krivichians to the south. Perhaps this is why in Smolensk, the center of Southern Krivichians, Oleg "assumed authority" rather than "seized" it or "conquered" the land. The Slavic Krivichians were recent settlers among the Baltic tribes, of whom they assimilated part and drove other parts to new places. Today Latvians call Russians Krivichians (*krievi*, or *krīvi* in Latgalian), and Russia is known as Krievija. Farther south lay the lands of the Radimichis—judging by the archaeological data, these were Baltic tribes that had experienced some influence of Slavic settlers from the west. The designation *Radimichis* is close to the modern Lithuanian words *radimas* (location) and *radimviete* (place of origin), and thus, it means "locals." A typical group self-identification in eastern Europe through the twentieth century, it preceded and transcended ethnoconfessional and political categorization (cf. "Tuteyshyya / Tutejszy" and "Krajowcy," which have the same meaning). [8]

Moving farther down the Dnieper, Oleg "took" Lyubech, an inland port of the Severians that played a central role in the grain trade along this river. Severians made up an alliance of the tribes that inhabited a vast forest steppe and even open steppe territory to the east of the Dnieper. Historians formerly interpreted their name as a reference to the north (cf. Russian *sever*), but Severians were by no means the northernmost Eastern Slavic alliance. Therefore, some historians suggested not a Slavic but a Scythian-Sarmatian (Iranian) origin of "Severians" and most hydronyms (names of bodies of water) in the area—the basins of the rivers Seymitsa and Desna. The name of the river Seym derives from ancient Iranian and means "dark river" (cf. Avestan *syāma-* and Sanskrit *syāma-* "dark"). The river Sev, which could give the name to Severians, means "black river" (cf. Avestan *syava*, "black"; Sanskrit *syava*, "black-brown, bay, dark"). The name of the Severians' main city, Chernigov, is a Slavic translation of this term ("blackish"). The Scythian-Sarmatian background of the cultural landscape of the forest steppe and the steppe inhabited by Severians did not exclude their Slavic origin. Moreover, they could indeed interpret their name as a reference to the north, except that their "northernness" was apparently determined not in the Slavic system of coordinates. In the region of ever-migrating population, farmers-Severians did not come to an empty place when they settled in the area dominated by Iranian- and Turkic-speaking nomads. The nomads of Northern Eurasia indicated the four cardinal directions using colors and following the path of the sun: red (east), yellow (south), white (west), and black (north). Thus, Severians really lived in the north—in the north of the steppe belt, inhabited by Scythian-Sarmatian Iranian-speaking, and later Turkic and Mongolian nomadic tribes. Both versions of the origin of the name "Severians" and the names of their settlements and rivers imply Iranian linguistic and nomadic geographical influences. The important thing is not the etymology itself but the fact that these categories seemed to be fully understood by the local Slavic-speaking population and translated into their own language. This means that the degree of cultural interaction and mutual influence was high, and multilingualism was the norm in the south just as it was in the north, around Ladoga.

Finally, the expedition approached Kyiv on the territory of the East Slavic tribe of Polianians. Whether they lured Askold–Dir out of the city by cunning, as the chronicler writes, or he went out by himself to collect a toll from a passing caravan (which must have been the main source of income for Kyiv's master, concealed from the Novgorod prince), he was killed. This episode demonstrated the role of the invited prince and his retinue as not just a military detachment that was collecting duties from local tribes, but as the institution of an elementary state already based on the law. The governor of Kyiv was blamed not for the fact that he (or they) collected tribute from a local tribe for two decades and, probably, tolls from passing caravans, but that this was done unlawfully by a Viking of humble origin.

Self-Organization of Northern Eurasia's First Polities 49

According to the chronicler writing in the eleventh century, Oleg declared Kyiv "the mother of Rousian cities," that is, "metropolis" (in Greek): the residence of the prince was transferred here. Novgorod remained in the orbit of the new political center, as evidenced by the establishment of a tribute of 300 grivnas. The "old" Novgorod grivna weighed about 1.8 ounces (51 grams), so the annual tribute was less than 34 pounds (15.3 kilograms) of silver, which was rather a symbolic act of recognition of the Kyiv prince's sovereignty. As we have seen, every year caravans transported many tons of silver along the Volga–Baltic route via Novgorod, which became a powerful stimulus for political self-organization on the lands along this route.

At the same time, the transfer of the capital of the confederation to Kyiv, 700 miles south of Novgorod, a key center of the Volga–Baltic transit, attested that princely authority had developed a logic and motivation of its own besides the protection of the caravan route. A supratribal institution from its inception, princely power surprisingly quickly acquired the traits of territorial statehood. The boundaries of its territory were determined by strategic trade routes as well as by inhabited lands that had not yet been claimed by other polities. Thus, Rous' Lands emerged as a common social and subsequently cultural space of territories and communities that had never before constituted a single whole, either imaginary or organizational. The political unification of the stretch of North Eurasia from the Baltic Sea to the Black Sea steppes for the first time created the prerequisites for envisioning this new territorial and political unity as a world of its own, using the metaphors of a historical and geographical (and later, cultural) whole.

Consolidating Lands along the Route "from the Varangians to the Greeks"

Moving the headquarters to Kyiv was clearly aimed at establishing control over the new trade route "from the Varangians to the Greeks," which depended only partially on Novgorod. There was a route from the Baltic to the Black Sea that completely bypassed the Ladoga waterways system. It started at the confluence of the Daugava (Western Dvina) River and the Gulf of Finland in present-day Riga, proceeded eastward through the lands of the Baltic and Finnish tribes (Livs, Latgalians, and Selonians), then turned south along the tributaries of the Dvina, lakes, and rivers—to the Drut River (on the territory of the Dregovichians), which flows into the Dnieper about halfway between Smolensk and Kyiv. [9]

Yet another alternative route to the Black Sea bypassing Novgorod, along the Pripyat River, could only be controlled in Kyiv. In addition to receiving income from the transit of caravans from the Baltic, relocation to Kyiv opened up an important prospect for organizing direct bilateral trade with Byzantium without the involvement of intermediaries. Taking a tithe from transit trade was a common practice of large polities. Byzantium did so as well with regard to the Great Silk Road and Khazaria, which taxed merchants on the Volga. It is possible that in Novgorod, they collected a comparable fee for passage through the Ladoga system. Even if less organized tribes along the trade route were content with a lower toll on merchants sailing through their lands, the transit trade along the Volga–Baltic route entailed huge overhead costs. It is no coincidence that archaeologists and numismatists believe that only 30–40 percent of the transit Arabian silver ended up in northern Europe, and the rest remained with various intermediaries along the way. Staging direct trade with Byzantium along the Dnieper promised the Rous' Lands immense benefits.

One major caveat was associated with this plan: the forest-steppe zone along the Dnieper was already controlled by the Khazar Khaganate. As the beginning of the Primary Chronicle states, "And the Khazars collected [tribute] from the Polianians, and from the Severians, and from the Vyatichians—a silver coin and a squirrel from every hearth." In that era, the payment of tribute was the main form of acknowledging one's political subjecthood. It was precisely the inclusion of this territory in the relatively stable political space of the khaganate that made it possible to develop agriculture in the fertile forest-steppe zone, as farmers were no longer afraid of the nomads' raids. Archaeologists trace the intensive development of Slavic settlements in the Dnieper region from the start of the eighth century (the time of the khaganate's transformation as discussed in Chapter 1). Located across the Dnieper, Kyiv was the farthest outpost of Khazar influence, as the local toponymy reflected: one of Kyiv's hills, Khorevitsa, was most likely named after the biblical Mount Horeb (also known as Sinai), on which Moses received the Ten Commandments. The existence of this Kyiv toponym long before the appearance of Christians points to the only other group upholding biblical cultural associations: the Khazars. The mid-tenth-century treatise of the Byzantine emperor Constantine the Porphyrogenitus, *On the Administration of the Empire*, refers to the "Kyoav fortress, also called Sambatas"—most likely named so in honor of Sambation, the legendary "Sabbath River" of Talmudic legends, which, outside the limits of the inhabited world, was flowing with rocks. This is how the Khazars could identify the Dnieper River on the outskirts of their possessions, with its famous unpassable rapids: according to legend, Sambation rages six days a week and calms down only on the Sabbath. Most likely the Khazar outpost on the right bank of the Dnieper was located in close proximity to Oleg-occupied Kyiv, which only increased the ambiguity of the Rous' position on the land of the Polianians— official tributaries of the Khazar Khaganate.

It is in this situation of at least nominal Khazar hegemony in the region that the prince from Novgorod began to systematically subjugate the surrounding territories:

In the year 6391 (883). Oleg began to fight against the Drevlians and, having subdued them, took tribute from them of [the skin of] a black marten [the household].

In the year 6392 (884). Oleg attacked the Severians, and defeated the Severians, and imposed a light tribute on them, and did not allow them to pay tribute to the Khazars, saying: "I am their enemy and you have no reason [to pay them]."

In the year 6393 (885). [Oleg] reached out to the Radimichis, asking: "To whom do you give tribute?" They answered: "To the Khazars." And Oleg said to them: "Do not give anything [to] the Khazars but pay me." And so they gave Oleg a shilling [from the household], as they used to give the Khazars. And Oleg ruled over the Polianians, and the Drevlians, and the Severians, and Radimichis, and fought with the Ulichians and the Tivertsians.

Self-Organization of Northern Eurasia's First Polities 51

We see that without becoming involved in a direct conflict with the Khazars, Oleg first of all busied himself with imposing control over the Drevlians, whose territory the alternative route from the Baltic to the Black Sea passed through, along the Pripyat River. Characteristically, Drevlians alone were obliged to pay tribute in furs rather than in silver coins—unlike the Severians, Radimichis, and (several decades later) Vyatichians. It was hardly a matter of different levels of economic development: the chronicler had an extremely low opinion of the tribes who could pay in precious metals:

> Radimichis, Vyatichians, and Severians had common customs: they lived in the forest, like all the animals, ate everything unclean, and blasphemed in the presence of their fathers and daughters-in-law. They did not know marriage, but instead organized carnivals among the villages. They gathered for these carnivals, for dances and various devilish songs, and here they abducted wives for themselves, in collusion with them [i.e., the women]; each had two or three wives.

The only thing that set the Drevlians apart from these tribes was their location beyond the Khazar sphere of influence or proximity to transcontinental trade routes (the alternative path from the Baltic to the Dnieper through Pripyat was more a possibility than an actively used itinerary). Therefore, Drevlians did not have access to Arabic silver. Contributing one animal pelt per family in the forestland is not a burdensome tax, more a "token of recognition" than extortion.

The chronicle presents the political subordination of the Severians by Oleg as a onetime action, which is doubtful. The Severians directly bordered the grazing lands of the Khazars, whose power Severians could experience in the most immediate way. Open to the predatory raids of nomads and punitive expeditions of the Khazars, Severian farmers were hardly interested in a conflict with the khaganate. Coercion alone could not force them to break off established relations with the Khazars. The chronicler specifically mentions that they had been assigned a "light tribute"— apparently, even less than the usual "marten skin" from a hunter's household and a silver coin from the rest, and certainly less burdensome than the tribute paid to the Khazars. It was impossible to completely relieve Severians of paying tribute: it symbolized the establishment of regular relations between groups, albeit unequal (that is, political). In this political function, tribute was analogous to the exchange of gifts at the level of interpersonal or tribal relations.

Finally, Oleg turned to the Radimichis, whose lands were located higher along the Dnieper, north of the Severians who had already acknowledged his authority. According to the chronicle, Oleg did not even have to demonstrate his military strength to subdue the Radimichis, who found themselves surrounded by the tribes that had agreed to join the Rous' Lands. For the same reason, unlike their strategically located neighbors, they did not receive a discount and simply began to pay the same tribute—one silver coin per household—to the prince of the Rous' instead of the distant Khazars.

Thus, Oleg claimed the right to collect tribute from neighboring tribes rather than the Khazars, which in legal terms meant the annexation of part of the fiscal territory of the khaganate. These actions should inevitably have led to conflict with

52 *New Imperial History of Northern Eurasia*

the Khazars—or were a response to some hostile actions of the Khazars. The efforts to subjugate neighboring lands appeared to pursue a political rather than an economic goal. We see that the prince of the Rous' was ready to draw former subjects of the Khazar Khaganate to his side at any cost, especially in the case of borderline Severians.

Circumstances behind the Crisis of the Volga–Baltic Trade

It is difficult to say what the real motives of the Novgorod prince were and why the expedition to Kyiv was supported by the joint forces of the tribes who had invited Rurik. This invitation had a specific goal: to ensure the protection and functioning of the Volga–Baltic trade route from Ladoga to the territory of Volga Bulgaria. A 700-mile journey through the forest to the south diverted enormous material and human resources from the original task.

Several important events occurred almost simultaneously with the expansion of the Rous' into the Dnieper region, but their sequence is unclear. First, archaeologists and numismatists have noted an interruption in the flow of Arabic silver to Europe in the last quarter of the ninth century, which was not restored until the 910s CE. Coinage did not stop but, obviously, the key intermediary in the transit chain from the caliphate to the north—the Khazar Khaganate—blocked the flow of silver coins. The transit of silver was restored almost simultaneously with the separation of Volga Bulgaria from Khazaria and the adoption of Islam by the Bulgars. Whereas before the crisis in supply, the coins transported to the north were mainly Abbasid dirhams from Baghdad, now they were mostly Samanid dirhams. They were transported from Central Asia through Bulgar, bypassing Khazaria. Some historians suggested that the Khazars blocked the trade along the Volga River in order to punish the Rous' for invading the khaganate's zone of interests along the Dnieper. The available data from the period are so scattered that the reverse interpretation is equally plausible: for some reason, the Khazars began to keep all the silver for themselves—for example, to finance ongoing large-scale social transformation, which included expensive public works (the building of fortresses and government edifices), and to finance professional administrators and mercenaries. Either way, the blockade significantly affected not only the Novgorod prince and his retinue but also the entire confederation of tribes living along the Volga–Baltic trade route. Perhaps that is why they dispatched a common military expedition to search for an alternative passage to the south, which demonstrated restrained but evident hostility toward Khazar interests.

Given the transcontinental importance of the Volga–Baltic trade route, it is highly unlikely that the Khazar Kaganate disrupted it solely out of the desire to annoy the newcomers from the Baltic. If the Khazars already had a fortress in close proximity to Kyiv, they were able to send troops there to punish the Rous' more directly, simply, and inexpensively than by sabotaging trade along the Volga, hundreds of miles away from the Dnieper—the location of the assumed foe. Indeed, the Khazar documents mention military victories over the Rous' but referring to the events of the early tenth century. In its turn, the Primary Chronicle does not write about any military clashes with the Khazars in the Dnieper region in the late ninth century, so the hypothesis of a conflict between the Khazars and the Rous' as a cause of the Volga trade disruption remains pure speculation. The disruption itself is a fact, however, and the first significant factor accompanying the arrival of the Rous' in Kyiv.

The second important historical event from this period was the resettlement to the west of the Hungarian tribes from the steppes north of the Black Sea. As previously mentioned, at the beginning of the eighth century, the Hungarians (Magyars) moved from the foothills of the Urals to the territory of the Khazar Khaganate. They recognized the sovereignty of the Khazars and occupied the territory between the rivers Volga, Don, and Seversky Donets—more than 250 miles east of the Dnieper. Around 830 CE, the Hungarian tribes and some Khazars left the khaganate and settled in the area of the Southern Bug River, between the lower reaches of the Dnieper and the Carpathian Mountains. Almost immediately, they began staging reconnaissance raids farther west: in 836, Hungarians appeared on the Danube on the border with Byzantium; in 862, they invaded the Kingdom of the East Franks for the first time; and in 881, they reached Vienna. In the early 890s, Hungarians resumed their westward migration along the explored routes: bypassing the Carpathian Mountains from the south, through the lands of present-day Moldova and Romania, in 896 they occupied Transylvania, from which they captured Pannonia (today, western Hungary and eastern Austria). The space occupied by the Hungarians in the Khazar Khaganate before their departure in the 830s suggests that it was they who exercised the khaganate's control over the adjacent territories of Severians and Polianians. Therefore, when Hungarians migrated to the Southern Bug, a temporary vacuum of power emerged in the steppe zone along the Dnieper in the second half of the ninth century. Newcomers from Novgorod were able to take advantage of this situation, spreading their authority over the lands that Khazaria could no longer effectively control. [10]

A third factor probably connected the two circumstances mentioned above (the interruption of the flow of silver along the Volga through Khazaria and the departure of the Hungarian tribes from the Don and Black Sea steppes). One reason for the resettlement of Hungarians farther west was the mounting pressure on them of new migrants from the east: the Pechenegs, Turkic nomads. They clashed with the Hungarians for the first time no later than 854 CE. By 882 the Pechenegs had reached Crimea. Pechenegs called themselves "baja-naq" or "bajinaq"—"brother-in-law" (specifically, "husband of an older sister"). This ethnonym betrays the archaic social organization of a group that defined itself solely in terms of interclan relationships. Unlike the Hungarians, who recognized the supreme authority of the Khazars for two centuries, the Pechenegs immediately demonstrated hostility to the khaganate, seizing pastures and destroying cities on their way, along the Don River and on the Taman Peninsula. Sometime between these years (854 and 882), the Pechenegs crossed the Volga. They pastured their herds along the Volga and they very likely completely blocked the transit of trade through Khazaria.

The Ambiguity of the Tribal Division of the Rous' Lands

Thus, whatever happened first—the arrival of the Rous' in the Dnieper area in the wake of the Hungarians' departure, the trade blockade by the Khazars, or the temporary

54 *New Imperial History of Northern Eurasia*

disruption of this trade by the Pechenegs—it created a radically new situation. The crisis of the Volga–Baltic trade route forced a reconfiguration of the Rous' Lands, and this process had little to do with unification along any ethnocultural lines. The chronicler says nothing about the Viking prince's interest in uniting exclusively Slavic tribes. On the contrary, even writing several centuries later, he emphasized that the Slavs were only one component of the Rous':

> By the White Lake [Beloozero] the Vesians are settled, and by the Rostov Lake— the Merians, and by the Kleshchina Lake [the original, Merian name of Lake Pleshcheyevo]—also Merians. And along the Oka River, where it flows into the Volga, there [live] the Muroma, a people of their own, and the Cheremisians, a people of their own, and the Mordvins, a people of their own. These are the only Slavic peoples in the Rous' [Lands]: the Polianians, the Drevlians, the Novgorodians, the Polochans, the Dregovichians, the Severians, [and] the Buzhans, who were called so because they lived along the Bug River.

The Slavs themselves were not perceived as a single community. As the chronicler specified while telling the history of Slavic tribes, "all these tribes had their own customs, and the laws of their fathers, and traditions, each had customs of their own." Different Slavic tribes could be in conflict with each other (compare, "The Drevlians and other neighbors began to oppress the Polianians"). Therefore, it would be misleading to interpret the consolidation of territories under the rule of the Kyiv prince as a unification of Slavic tribes.

By itself, the language of "tribal" organization used by the chronicler and adopted by later historians of Northern Eurasia, can be misleading. Kinship ties, from immediate family relationships to broadly extended and almost abstract ones, could be the most suitable foundation of initial social organization. Suffice to recall the Pechenegs, who found no better way to distinguish themselves from other Turkic-speaking Oguz nomads than by referring to their place in the common hierarchy of kinship. However, when a nominal "tribe" occupies a territory of many thousands of square miles and has tens of thousands of members, references to common kinship become purely symbolic. The unity of such an extensive human collective and its ability to act unanimously, in peace and war, are ephemeral if based solely on the idea of tribal solidarity. This is especially true in regard to sedentary farmers of the forest zone. They are physically deprived of the mobility required for a tribe to come together to contemplate important decisions—unlike the nomads, who can gather very quickly around the headquarters of the clan's elder.

In speaking of the "tribe," modern historians usually have in mind a more analytical concept of a primitive polity, in which structures of authority are inseparable from family ties and extended clan relationships. It is believed that at this stage of "primitive democracy," the main source of power was the general assembly of clan members. The assembly made the important decisions, elected the elder (or the council of elders) and the military chiefs. The power of these elected figures, however, was not separate from their high ranks in the clan hierarchy and was not consolidated as distinctive permanent offices. That is, the holder of power was not distinguished from other clansmen of

Self-Organization of Northern Eurasia's First Polities 55

similar seniority in terms of everyday activities. The society was regulated by the norms of customary law, which did not differentiate between religious beliefs, legal norms per se, and the rules of everyday conduct. This structural description of the initial social organization, rooted in the works of the first anthropologists and sociologists of the late nineteenth century, captures the general logic of decision making and taking collective actions but cannot explain the existence and functioning of large "tribes."

The material accumulated by modern political anthropology suggests that in some cases a distinctive "tribe" is merely an appellation assigned to its neighbors by a better-organized society. In other cases, a tribe appears as a nascent form of indigenous statehood. A third meaning of the term implies a degree of linguistic and cultural affinity. This latter factor would have been particularly important in the segment of Northern Eurasia stretching from the Black Sea to the Baltic Sea during the turbulent last centuries of the first millennium CE, which were characterized by permanent population migrations. Local communities did not have to be subordinated to a common hierarchy of authority in order to consider themselves members of one or another "tribe" in the sense of a single social space of people who understand each other and therefore enter more intensively into all sorts of relationships, including armed clashes. Those belonging to a different tribe were not necessarily more hostile; it was just easier to communicate with members of the same "tribe." Accordingly, the opposition "us versus them" did not necessarily mean "friend or foe": one of "us" could be much more dangerous precisely because of access to vital insider information.

The chronicle's systematic mention of various tribes highlights the composite character of the Rous' Lands without necessarily implying the homogeneous nature of individual tribes as its "building blocks." It seems more accurate to speak of the Rous' Lands as an agglomeration of territories rather than "tribes." Thus, according to the chronicler, Oleg began collecting tribute from the Radimichis in 885, but the complete subordination of the Radimichis is registered only a century later, after a major battle in 984. This means that parts of "tribes" were autonomous enough to establish special relations with neighbors, including something as serious as paying tribute to a new sovereign, while the tribe "as a whole" did not deem it necessary or possible to demonstrate solidarity— for example, by attempting to bar the imposition of tribute on their fellow tribesmen.

So, how did the broad coalition of territories and "tribes" that made up the Rous' Lands function at the beginning of the tenth century?

Confederation of Lands along the Waterway "from the Varangians to the Greeks"

The Byzantine emperor Constantine the Porphyrogenitus left a detailed description of the organization of the Rous' Lands along the Dnieper in the first half of the tenth century:

> [Let it be known that] some of the *monoxyla* [dugouts made from a single tree trunk] coming from outer Rhosia to Constantinople are from Nemogard, where

Sfendoslav, the son of Ingor, archon of Rhosia, had his seat, and others from the city of Milinisk and from Teliutza and Tzernigoga and from Vusegrad. And so, they come down the Danapreos River, and are collected together at the city of Kyova, also called Sambatas. Sclaves (Σκλάβοι) and their *paktiotai* [i.e., allies],—namely, Krivitiens, Lendzanens and other Scalvinians,—cut the *monoxyla* on their mountains during winter, and, having equipped them, with the onset of spring, when the ice melts, they bring them on to the neighboring lakes. And since these [lakes] lead to the river Danapreos, they too enter thence on to this same river, and come down to Kyova, and draw the ships along to be finished and sell them to the Rhos (Ῥῶς). The Rhosians buy these bottoms only, furnishing them with oars and rowlocks and other tackle from their old *monoxyla*, which they dismantle; and so they fit them out. And in the month of June they move off down the river Dnieper and come to Vititzeve, which is a *paktiotikon* fort of the Rhos, and there they gather during two or three days; and when all the *monoxyla* are collected together, then they set out, and come down the said Danapreos river.

The author goes on to describe this long and dangerous trip in great detail, but the circumstances of preparations for the expedition are also very interesting. Without much disagreement, historians have deciphered most of the proper names mentioned—in any case, the general geography is understandable. Ingor is Igor (Scandinavian *Ingvarr*), who was brought to Kyiv (Kyova) on the Dnieper (Danapreos) River by Oleg as a "minor"; he is the prince of "Rhosia" (documents of the era routinely translate "prince" as "archon"—Greek "chief, ruler, head"). His son Sviatoslav (Sfendoslav) is the governor in the Novgorod region, most likely in Old Ladoga: it is possible that a scribe erred and "Nemogard" should be read "Nevogard," which is the Varangian name of "the city on Lake Nevo" (i.e., Ladoga). It is difficult to say whether the reference to "outer Rhosia" is a reflection of Byzantine geographical concepts or there was an actual division of the Rous' Lands into "inner" and "outer:" for example, the territories along the Dnieper versus the territories along the old Volga–Baltic route.

Historians believe that Milinisk is most likely Smolensk of the Krivichians and speculate that Teliutza must be Lyubech of the Radimichis. There are few doubts that Tzernigoga is Chernigov of the Severians, Vusegrad—Vyshgorod, about ten miles from Kyiv up the Dnieper River. Vititzeve (Vitichev of later sources) down the Dnieper is a guard post at the Dnieper ford (Scandinavian *viti, vete*—"signal light, bonfire").

A System Based on a Formal Political Contract

In general, the narrative of Constantine the Porphyrogenitus completely corroborates the map of the Rous' Lands of the period as known from the chronicles. It is thus all the more significant that in speaking of the "tributaries" of the Kyiv prince, he uses the term "pactiots" (*paktiotai*), which means allies under the treaty ("pact"). They are not just rafting dozens or hundreds of boats downstream to Kyiv but selling them to the Rhos, apparently for money. The treaty (*riad*) with the tribes that invited Rurik in the north and the treaty (*pact*) with the Dnieper tribes indicate the complex nature of political power in the Rous' Lands.

First of all, this means that the local population was politically organized enough so that its representatives could conclude an agreement, on certain conditions recognizing the subordination of the whole society ("tribe") to the prince and his retinue. Second, this subordination was political in nature: that is, in exchange for paying tribute, it implied military and logistical support of the "tribe" by the prince and his retinue as an extraterritorial institution of a rudimentary state, rather than as a victorious foreign entity. Under the treaty, everyone had to pay tribute to the prince—even Novgorod, which, compared to the recently subordinated Dnieper lands, could be perceived as the prince's "own" territory ("domain" in terms of the feudal Frankish world). Outside the negotiated sphere of exploitation and subordination, other interactions could be based on the equality of both parties (including the sale of boats).

The Economic and Political Role of the *Poliud'e*

The trip to Constantinople took several weeks: first along the Dnieper through the rapids, whose names Constantine the Porphyrogenitus listed separately "in Rhosian" and "in Slavic." Then through the Black Sea along the Bulgarian coast, to the border with Byzantium in the town of Mesembria (today, Nessebar). Here, the crewmen stayed and rested while goods were loaded onto Byzantine ships and, accompanied by merchants and envoys, sailed to Constantinople. There, outside the city walls in the vicinity of the Saint Mammes monastery were the headquarters of the Rous' merchants, who had the right to reside there up to six months a year.

At the beginning of autumn, the caravan returned to Kyiv and the second stage of the organizational and economic activities of the Rous' Lands began, this time directed not outside but inside the commonwealth:

> When the month of November begins, their archons together with all the Rhoses leave Kyiv and go off on the *poliudia* (πολύδια), which means "rounds," that is, to the Sklavinías of the Vervians [i.e., Drevlians] and Drougouvitos [Dregovichians, to the north of the Drevlians] and Krivichians, and Severians and the rest of the Slavs who are *pactiots* of the Rhosians. There they are fed throughout the winter, but then again, starting from the month of April, when the ice of the Dnieper river melts, they come back to Kyiv. They then pick up their *monoxyla*, as has been said above, and fit them out, and come down to Romania [i.e., to the Eastern Roman Empire, Byzantium].

The cruising of the subject territory by the Kyiv prince was reminiscent of the practice by the emir of Volga Bulgaria or the visits of tribal pasturelands by the Khazarian khagan and bek during the summer months: it was a way of visually representing supreme power on the local level in the absence of regular institutions of central government. In addition to the representative function, the *poliud'e* ("going out to the people") fulfilled an important economic task, as the prince and his retinue were fed by their subjects during this period. However, even this "economic" aspect of the ritual was inextricably linked to its political function. Offering meal and joint feasts were parts of the ancient rituals of exchange and gifting as the foundations of sustained social ties. In these rituals that have been preserved in private relations to this day, an element of reciprocity is extremely important: one is obliged to reciprocate for a gift-in-kind, and the value of the response must be equivalent. Otherwise, the hierarchical relationship between the patron and the dependent (the generous and the stingy, senior and junior, rich and poor) is immediately established. The fact that the exchange was disproportionate—the hosting tribe fed the prince and his retinue—symbolically put the "guests" in a dependent position, emphasizing the contractual and conditional nature of their power. "You only get when you give," and accepting food and shelter from subordinated "tribes" not only confirmed friendly relationships and the impossibility of committing violence against the hosts but also obliged the prince and his retinue to render them future services. The priority of political symbolism over economic pragmatism in this practice is underscored by the fact that *poliud'e* lasted only six months of the year—in contrast to the practice of "feeding" (*kormlenie*) of later centuries, when crown officials were completely financed by the local population. If the retinue could survive for half a year at the expense of other sources, it was theoretically possible to obtain food without leaving the residence of the prince. True, this would either become an additional burden on the Polianians, whose territories surrounded Kyiv, if food were to be delivered free of charge, or put them in a privileged position, if they were to be paid for the food. The "cruising" of tribal territories in the *poliud'e* evenly distributed the load of rudimentary statehood among all the Rous' Lands without discriminating against individual union members—"pactiots."

Conspicuously, there is no mention of Novgorod and "outer Rhosia" in general in the description of the circular *poliud'e* route, which headed northwest from Kyiv before turning northeast, southeast, and farther, completing a clockwise movement. One can only guess whether this was due to the fragmentary information available to Constantine the Porphyrogenitus or because he meant the Ladoga region when he wrote about "the rest of the Slavs." Or perhaps the territory of the original Rous' Lands was traveled in the same manner by the retinue of the junior ruling prince residing in Ladoga or Novgorod. The question also remains open as to whether the goods that were sent along the Dnieper to Constantinople in June were connected in any way to the preceding stage of "circling" the lands. If the *pactiot* tribes paid tribute in silver, what was their role in transcontinental trade, the only source of coinage? If slaves and forest products (honey, wax, furs) delivered to Constantinople were taken from the tribes for sale, then on what conditions? Was it part of the tribute collected by the prince and the retinue, or were the goods entrusted to the organizers of the caravan trade by the tribes themselves?

Either way, during the first decades of expanding the Rous' Lands to the Dnieper region, the relations of the prince-led retinue and local tribes were built on approximately the same foundation as in the north during the time of Rurik. The main incentive for collaboration in a more complex social organization was a common interest in maintaining transit caravan trade and participating in it. Moreover, if the Volga–Baltic route depended equally on at least four "shareholders" controlling different sections of the route—the Varangians in the Baltic, the local tribes from Ladoga to the Volga River, Volga Bulgaria, and the Khazar Khaganate—the Dnieper route "from the Varangians to the Greeks" was completely monopolized by the rulers of the Rous' Lands. The Kyiv

The War as Diplomacy

The last statement may sound paradoxical, but, from the point of view of the authorities of the Eastern Roman Empire, this was the only way for "barbarians" and "pagans" to achieve the status of equal partners with the empire, including in trade. Byzantine treaties were usually concluded for a period of thirty years, and this rhythm is visible in the known military campaigns of the Rous' against Constantinople. As registered for 907 CE, the Primary Chronicle reports a massive assault of the Byzantine capital from Kyiv:

> Leaving Igor in Kyiv, Oleg marched against the Greeks taking with him numerous Varangians, Slovenes, Chuds, Krivichians, Merians, Polianians, Severians, Drevlians, Radimichis, Croats, Dulebs, and Tivercians, who were renowned interpreters: these were called the "Great Scythia" [by the Greeks]. With all of them Oleg sallied forth by horse and by ship, and the number of his vessels was two thousand. He arrived before Constantinople, but the Greeks blocked the strait and locked up the city. Oleg disembarked upon the shore and ordered his warriors to beach the ships. They ravaged the city suburbs, slaughtered many Greeks, destroyed many palaces, and burned the churches. Of the prisoners they captured, some were slashed, some were tortured, others were shot, and still others thrown into the sea. Also, much other harm the Rous' inflicted upon the Greeks as enemies usually do. Oleg commanded his warriors to make wheels and put ships on wheels. When the fair wind rose, they raised the sails amid the field and began moving to the city. The Greeks, seeing this, were frightened and said in a message sent to Oleg: "Do not destroy the city, we will agree to [pay] any tribute you want." Oleg stopped his troops, and [the Greeks] brought out to him food and wine, but he would not accept it, for it was poisoned. . . . So Oleg demanded that they pay to his warriors, for two thousand ships at the rate of twelve grivnas per oarlock, and then pay tribute to the Rous' cities: first of all, for Kyiv, then for Chernigov, Pereyaslavl, Polotsk, Rostov, Lyubech, and for other cities, for there resided grand princes subject to Oleg.

One cannot help but notice a very detailed list of the participants in the expedition, which included all the tribes of the Rous' Lands, the Varangian retinue, and some who did not belong to the confederation—inhabitants of the lower Dnieper and the Bug Rivers (a region the Byzantines traditionally called "Great Scythia")—who were translators. The legendary mounting of ships on wheels that shocked the Byzantines does not seem incredible to modern historians, particularly given that this maneuver was later repeated by the Turkish troops of Mehmed II during the siege of the city in 1453. Then the Turks were able to transport about seventy vessels by land in carts to

60   *New Imperial History of Northern Eurasia*

bypass the chain stretched across the mouth of the Golden Horn harbor by the city's defenders. Once in the harbor, the ships directly approached the low and less fortified city wall. In 860, the Askold–Dir attack was so unexpected that the defenders of the city had not pulled the chain across the Golden Horn. They believed that only divine intervention prevented the enemies from breaking into the city through a weak section of the walls. When part of Oleg's flotilla bypassed the chain, the Byzantines hastened to conclude peace. [11]

Oleg did not accept food and drink from the Byzantines—as he had accepted the offerings of the "pactiots" during the "circling." The reason might not be potential poisoning, but the political significance of the ritual itself. Oleg treated the Byzantines "as enemies usually do," demanding tribute rather than establishing mutually binding relations. The size of the tribute seems enormous: even if calculated in the "old" grivnas, each boat was entitled to one and a half times more silver than the annual tribute from the entire Novgorod territory. This would amount to a total of forty-nine tons of silver, but Oleg also demanded tribute for each of the tribal centers that delegated its warriors to the campaign. It seems strange that the share of the prince's permanent retinue was not negotiated separately, nor was that of the horsemen. So it is possible that only the Rous' rowing squads received "twelve grivnas per oarlock" (fifty-four pounds of silver per boat), while the rest had to be content with their personal loot, plus the tribute paid to their "cities."

It is even stranger that such a large-scale military disaster was not reflected in Byzantine sources. Some historians explain this by suggesting that the chronicle was actually describing the Askold–Dir expedition of 860, although from a military point of view the two campaigns were fundamentally different. Others believe that the events took place in the year 904, when, indeed, the Byzantines mention the attack of the "Rhos." In any case, the main outcome of the campaign was a treaty concluded several years later, as in the case of the campaign of 860. The authenticity of this treaty, dated 911 CE, can be considered proven. The document specified in detail the terms of the Rous' trade with Byzantium. Apparently cited by the chronicle in a reverse translation from the Greek original, the treaty begins with the list of the Rous' Lands' political leadership: "We are of the Rous' kin: Karla, Inegeld, Farlaf, Veremud, Rulav, Hudy, Ruald, Karn, Frelav, Ruar, Actev, Truan, Lidul, Fost, and Stemid are sent by Oleg, Grand Prince of Rous', and by all the serene princes and boyars under his sway." Even after the triple transliteration (by ear to Greek, then to Cyrillic, then to Latin script), most of these names clearly betray their Scandinavian origin (Karl, Ingjald, Farulf, Vermund, Hrollaf, etc.). Only the Kyiv prince and his Varangian retinue (the Rous') could force Byzantium to conclude a favorable trade agreement with the confederation of distant tribes, and in doing so, they acted in the common interests of all members of the confederation.

Thirty years later, in 941, the prince of Kyiv, Igor, embarked on a new expedition against Constantinople. This time the chronicler does not mention the coalition force manned by all the allied tribes, but cites a breathtaking number of ships headed to Constantinople—10,000. From other sources, it is known that Igor relied on the Pechenegs as his allies. His troops plundered the coastline but they were defeated. "Upon his return, Igor began to collect many warriors and sent [messengers] overseas to the Varangians, inviting them to [join the campaign against] the Greeks, for he again planned to attack them." The new campaign of 944 was already organized on the model of successful joint expeditions in the past, as opposed to the retinue's raid on boats in 941:

> Igor gathered many warriors: the Varangians, the Rous', the Polianians, the Slovenes, the Krivichians, the Tivercians, and hired the Pechenegs taking hostages from them, and advanced upon the Greeks by ship and by horse, wanting to avenge himself. . . . When the Emperor heard this news, he sent to Igor his best boyars with a plea: "Do not come [here] but take the tribute which Oleg had received, and I will add some more." He likewise sent silk and much gold to the Pechenegs. When Igor came to the Danube, he called together his retinue to consult with them, telling them about the Emperor's offer. Igor's retinue then replied, "If the Emperor says so, then what else do we need—without fighting, take gold, silver, and silks? Who knows who will be victorious, we or them? Who has the sea for his ally? For we are not walking by land, but [sailing] over the depths of the sea. Death lies in wait for us all." Igor heeded them, ordered the Pechenegs to assault the Bulgarian Land, while he himself, after receiving from the Greeks gold and palls for all [his] warriors, returned back to Kyiv.

This time the campaign took a ritualized form, which indicates a certain stabilization and even routinization of relations with Byzantium: the joint army of the Rous' Lands, led by the retinue, had only approached the Byzantine border on the Danube before the emperor hastened to confirm readiness to conclude a new treaty. The chronicle dates the treaty to 945 CE; like previous treaties, it was concluded during a purely diplomatic mission after some time had passed since the military campaign. The new treaty repeated the treaty of 911 but also significantly expanded it. The rules stipulating the conduct of the Rous' on the Byzantine territory or within its sphere of interests were particularly detailed, which testified to a more systematic engagement of the Rous' Lands with the Byzantines. As in 911, the treaty assumed that merchants arrived not only from Kyiv: a monthly allowance in Constantinople was granted "first [to] those who were from the city of Kyiv, then from Chernigov and from Pereyaslavl and from other cities."

Cooperation of Primitive Communities as Self-organization into a Complex Polity

Thus, by the mid-tenth century, when Constantine the Porphyrogenitus had documented the established routine in the Rous' Lands, the rudimentary state apparatus as embodied by the prince and his retinue seemed to have fully proved its effectiveness. It allowed the members of the confederated local tribal unions to trade with the richest country in Europe, enjoy military protection, and have an external arbiter in case of intertribal disputes. At the same time, princely power did not intervene in internal tribal affairs, but remained an external force focused more on a commonality of interests than on coercion. Characteristically, the tribe that systematically showed dissatisfaction with the princely power was the Drevlians, who were the least integrated into the Dnieper trade. They alone were allowed by Oleg to pay the tribute not in silver, obtained only through the trade, but in animal pelts. In 913, the Drevlians broke off relations with the prince of Kyiv, so Igor had to subjugate them by force, and their tribute was increased. The exception only confirms the general rule: princely power was more stable where it brought benefits to the local population, at least equivalent to the burden of duties.

The early model of princely power in Russia was built on the principle of an exoskeleton: elements of state institutions personalized by the prince and the retinue existed and were territorial (supratribal) in nature, but there was no formal structure that streamlined the relations of the subjects with these "professional managers." The prince and the retinue regulated the sphere outside tribal unions, such as war and trade, but internal activity was governed by traditional political institutions: the clan elders and popular assemblies.

The retinue of the prince was itself merely a fragment of another, equally prestate society, albeit organized in a slightly different way. In the ninth century, the Varangians (Vikings, Normans) had nothing like the vast and "multitribal" confederation of the Rous' Lands in Scandinavia, especially on the territory of future Sweden, from which the Varangians mainly came to eastern Europe. The majority of the Scandinavian population consisted of free peasants, who also made up the troops of numerous principalities that were constantly fighting among themselves. These endless clashes with neighbors and the beginning of pirate raids against western Europe strengthened the role of the retinues grouped around a prince or a charismatic leader. The function of these detachments of professional warriors was nothing but war, so their existence depended entirely on the availability of bounty. Accordingly, the authority of the leader was based on his reputation as a warrior and the ability to lead his retinue to the source of rich bounty and distribute it fairly. The consolidation of the political space on the Scandinavian Peninsula was driving various "jarls" (nobles) outside, into predatory and aggressive raids, since they had fewer and fewer opportunities at home.

The arrival of the Scandinavian warriors along with invited rulers of the confederation of Slavic-Finnish tribes resulted in the overlapping of two political and economic systems, which had an unexpected consequence. In Scandinavia, the warriors did not rob members of their own principality, therefore, the Rous' did not raid the territories of the allied tribes. They still received the bounty they were accustomed to from raids beyond the borders of the Rous' Lands, as well as in the form of tribute paid under the agreement of the confederation of tribes. Essentially, the prince's retinue preserved a traditional way of life: they obeyed the prince as a military leader who found potential sources of bounty and redistributed the spoils among his minions. Local tribes also preserved their traditional way of life: their domestic affairs were controlled by clan elders and popular assemblies. But together, the two almost isolated systems, based on different logics of economic activity and the legitimacy of power, constituted a structure of primitive statehood. This structure was characterized by the territorial principle of power, the specialization of different categories of the population in economic, military, and administrative activities, as well as the systematic alienation of resources for sustaining nonproductive activities for the benefit of the entire community. These abstract and impersonal state functions existed in their pure form, separately and independently from the hierarchies of kinship (in contrast to nomadic societies) and from private property relations and legal subordination (unlike in the early feudal Frankish kingdoms). It is all the more surprising that such a complex state organization was based on quite primitive elements: a redistributive community of warriors and a union of communities of hunters and farmers.

This composite model of early statehood probably was typical of Northern Eurasia's societies, which were formed in the process of political self-organization on the basis of numerous multicultural groups. If there was no foreign conqueror who could impose a fundamentally different political culture due to overwhelming military superiority, the preservation of local traditions and power structures in the process of political evolution seemed inevitable.

Political Institutionalization as a Destabilizing Factor

However, the success of self-organization based solely on the coincidence of various actors' strategic interests can become the main source of its crisis. What will keep former allies together on the same terms after all or some of them achieve their goal? The treaty of 945 with Byzantium confirmed the provisions of the 911 trade agreement, in which the "Rhos" somewhat vaguely promised "to the best of our ability, to maintain with you Greeks, in future years and forever, an unbroken and unchanging friendship." The new treaty stipulated such minuscule details of the broad variety of possible conflict situations and their resolution that it left no doubt: this was the foundation of a permanent strategic partnership. Even the fact that the new agreement introduced some restrictions on the rights of merchants from "Rhosia" (e.g., from now on merchants could take no more than a certain amount of silk cloth outside the city walls and only after a Byzantine official examined and sealed the purchase) testified to the normalization and routinization of contacts: only those transactions that become typical require formal regulation. The presence of merchants "from the city of Kyiv, then from Chernigov and from Pereyaslavl and from other cities" in the suburbs of Constantinople was normalized by the privileges granted to them and the restrictions imposed.

But what did the prince and the retinue gain from the new treaty? As a state institution, they received full recognition from the most highly developed state of that time. The agreement assumed that the signatories (the prince and the retinue) were the highest source and guarantor of law in the Rous' Lands, they controlled all the armed forces in their jurisdiction, conducted a coherent foreign policy, and systematically collected taxes. From this vantage point, the 945 treaty was a triumph—and perhaps it was important for the prince himself to have this "statist" aspect of his role formally recognized. But for the retinue as a community of warriors with their own economic interests, the 945 treaty was a severe blow. On the one hand, the treaty imposed highly detailed restrictions of the Rous' raids on territories subject to Byzantium, which apparently were carried out in the past along with trade missions. The document explicitly presumed the unilateral responsibility of the Rous' retinue for possible breaches of the treaty. Besides prohibiting raids and generally limiting the presence of the Rous' warriors in "neutral waters," the treaty also directly dictated foreign policy in the south: "If the Black Bulgarians come and start to fight in the Korsun country, then we order the Rhosian prince not to let them in, otherwise they will damage his country too."

On the other hand, besides limiting the arbitrariness of the retinue's actions "as a state," the treaty also substantially narrowed their field of activity as a private detachment of professional warriors. In 911, the Rous' were guaranteed virtually unlimited employment in the Byzantine service:

> Whenever there will be a need to go to war and these [Rous'] want to honor your Emperor, whatever number of them come at a time wishing to remain in his service voluntarily, then so be it. . . . With respect to the Rous' serving the Christian Emperor in Greece, if any one of them dies without setting his property in order and has no kinsfolk there, his estate shall be returned to his closest younger relatives in Rous'. But if he makes a will, the person whom he has designated in writing as his heir shall receive the property of which he thus disposed.

The 945 treaty no longer viewed the Rous' warriors as private individuals entering the Byzantine state service. They could enter the country only as part of an allied expeditionary force at the invitation of Constantinople and within the established quota. The personal property affairs of individual warriors were beyond the scope of the treaty: "If we . . . shall want to have your warriors against our enemies, let us write about that grand prince of yours, and he will send us as many of them as we wish; and from here they learn in other countries what amity the Greeks and the Rous' have toward each other." In fact, the very perspective of discussing the problem of joining the Byzantine service had changed: in 911, the agreement registered Kyiv's point of view, and in 945, the text was written on behalf of the emperor.

Thus, the formal recognition of the Rous' Lands as a polity and partner, albeit the junior one, of the Eastern Roman Empire inadvertently provoked a serious problem for the political system, which functioned "as a state" without having a proper state structure. The Rous' warriors were the first to suffer: for them, the new treaty ruined the traditional economy of raiding neighbors, the richest and closest of whom were clients of Byzantium. Sporadic attempts to preserve the traditional economic model of the retinue would continue over the next several decades but the status quo was never restored. Events began to unfold rapidly, according to the chronicles—in a matter of months after concluding the treaty: "Thus Igor began to rule in Kyiv [after signing the treaty], in peace with all countries. And autumn came, and he began to plot to go to the Derevlians, wanting to take a large tribute from them."

The Disruption of Political Symbiosis: The Case of the Drevlians

The need to maintain peace with neighbors in the summer, the season of traditional raids, forced the retinue to seek compensation for the missed bounty inside the Rous' Lands, which meant increasing the amount of tribute. The first stop on the "circling" route were the Drevlians, who probably participated less than others in trade with Byzantium (their capital is not mentioned in the treaties), which means they paid

Self-Organization of Northern Eurasia's First Polities   65

less to the prince for sustaining and protecting trade. The Byzantines only accepted merchants from special lists compiled by the prince, who probably did not do this for free. The desire to take a larger tribute from the Drevlians was not a whim of the prince, but a demand of his retinue—the community of warriors on which he depended as much as they depended on him:

> Igor's retinue said to him, "The lads of Sveneld adorned themselves with weapons and fine raiment, but we are naked. Go forth with us, oh Prince, after tribute, that both you and we may profit thereby." Igor heeded their words, and went to the Drevlians for a tribute, and added a new tribute to the old one, and his men committed violence against [the Drevlians]. After collecting the tribute, he headed to his city. On his way back, he said to his retinue, after some reflection: "Go home with the tribute, and I will come back and walk around more." He dismissed his retainers on their journey homeward, but being desirous of still greater booty he retraced his tracks with a small part of his retinue. The Drevlians, hearing that he was coming again, consulted with their prince Mal, saying, "If a wolf gets in the habit of coming after the sheep, he will take away the whole flock one by one, unless he be killed. So is this one: if we do not kill him, he will destroy us all." They then sent forward to Igor, saying: "Why are you coming again? You have already collected all the tribute." But Igor did not heed them, and the Drevlians came forth from the city of Iskorosten and slew Igor and his retainers, for there were few of them.

Sveneld (Sveinaldr) was a Varangian warrior, whose name is found in several sources from the mid-tenth century but is not mentioned among the two dozen signatories of the 945 treaty from the Kyiv side—senior associates of Prince Igor. Perhaps he was the leader of a minor detachment that made a successful raid beyond the Byzantine zone of influence during the summer season, while Igor was demonstrating his peacefulness. Inspired by Sveneld's example and following tradition, the retinue expected Igor to lead them to a source of rich bounty, and they disregarded the changed circumstances.

The reaction of the Drevlians was also predetermined by traditional expectations and conventions: a onetime collection of annual tribute was deemed a legal instrument for sustaining political relations with the prince. However, additional requisitions were perceived not as an unwarranted increase of the same tribute, but as an unconnected criminal act of robbery. Both the Slavs and the Varangians called a criminal "wolf": in Old Norse, *vargr* meant both the enemy and the wolf; in Old Swedish, *warag* stood for the villain and the wolf, compared to the Russian *vrag* (the enemy). In the eyes of Drevlians, Igor and his retinue made outlaws of themselves by violating the contract regulating the relations of the tribe and the prince. Thus, the collusion of the two traditional political and economic regimes undermined the spontaneous symbiosis that had produced the effect of a state. As it turned out, in reality there was no universally upheld "state" perspective that would perceive the prince as a legitimate ruler even if he committed an injustice in relation to his subjects. Two different "truths" clashed, which in the tenth century meant two legal regimes: the right of warriors to

Princess Olga: The Formalization of Elementary Statehood

In response to the murder of Igor, his widow, Olga, took brutal revenge on the Drevlians, burning their tribal center of Iskorosten, killing residents or selling them into slavery. However, of much greater consequence was the reform of relationships between the princely power and the *pactiot* tribes carried out by Princess Olga:

> She imposed upon them a heavy tribute, two parts of which went to Kyiv, and the third to Olga in Vyshgorod, for Vyshgorod was Olga's city. She then went through the land of Drevlians, accompanied by her son and her retinue, establishing legal provisions and tribute. The sites of her camps and hunting grounds are there still. Then she returned with her son to Kyiv, her city, and remained there for one year. In 6455 (947) Olga went to Novgorod and established coaching inns (*pogosty*) and dues along the Msta [River] and the Luga [River]. Her hunting grounds still exist across the lands, as well as boundary markers, sites, and coaching inns. . . . Her sleighs stand in Pskov to this day. Her fowling preserves still remain on the Dnieper and the Desna, and her village of Ol'zhichi is in existence even now. And so, having established everything, she returned to her son in Kyiv and stayed with him in amity there.

Using the demonstratively brutal suppression of the Drevlians as a measure of intimidation to prevent possible resistance from other tribes, Olga for the first time formalized the relations of statehood that had previously emerged spontaneously in the process of interaction of primitive communities that differed in "specialization" and way of life. First of all, she clearly separated the tribute collected for common needs in the "state treasury" in Kyiv—the main city of the Rous' Lands—and the personal income of the prince (and the retinue?), which was sent to Olga's residence in Vyshgorod.

Second, in place of the archaic "circling" by the prince and the retinue as "guests of honor" through the lands of the "pactiots," when the collection of the tribute intertwined with ritual feasts, a system of direct tax collection was introduced. For this purpose, next to but separate from the old community centers, the prince's permanent missions, called coaching inns (*pogosty*) were founded. Clearly identifiable in archaeological excavations, they served as fiscal district centers to which the local population brought their taxes in the established amount. Introduced as coaching inns for the prince on the lands belonging to *pactiot* tribes, these permanent missions functioned as an exterritorial symbol of princely power. The introduction of permanent missions, possibly with special staffs, physically separated the hitherto synchronous acts of the bringing of tribute by locals and its acquisition by the retinue. A technical office representing the crown as the abstract ("state") power substituted for the intimate interaction of the prince with the local population. As a result, the symbolic meaning of paying tribute was reversed: the important moment of offering the duty in person

Self-Organization of Northern Eurasia's First Polities 67

as a gift was gone, and the appropriation of someone's property in an impersonal form came to the fore. Reciprocal relationships gave way to unilateral obligations.

Another mechanism allowing the intervention of princely power into the hitherto autonomous sphere of tribal jurisdiction was the allocation of special hunting grounds for the prince "across the lands," and fowling preserves along the rivers. It is unlikely that the prince and the retinue had nowhere to hunt until then. Allocation of a part of the territory of each tribe specifically for princely use symbolized the loss of the tribe's monopoly on "their own" land. Landownership was based not on legal property rights but on the very fact that the collective used it. This collective—"tribe" whatever this term means—could be forced to pay tribute, but the land remained the exclusive possession of the tribe as long as that tribe lived on it, that is, was not driven away by the conqueror. Olga did not resettle the tribes or conquer them but, receiving part of their land for specific "use," she became co-owner of the territory. This symbolic significance of separating the hunting lands of the sovereign from public lands was fraught with further important legal consequences. It is especially important that Olga carried out her reform throughout the entire Rous' Lands, from Kyiv in the south to Novgorod in the north, from the Baltic (where the Luga flows) to the Volga portages (the upper Msta), in the lands of various Slavic and Finnish tribes.

The Dilemma of the Sovereign and the State

What did state-building mean in the mid-tenth century in eastern Europe? The surviving written sources and archaeological evidence allow an extremely fragmented reconstruction of the events and circumstances of this era. Historians argue even about the existence of the rulers of Kyiv featured in the documents, not to mention the details of their biographies—age, family relations, and accomplishments. Nevertheless, the most general and least controversial information available to us today makes it possible to understand, if not how the state was organized, then at least how it was doable in principle. Specifically, one may ask, how was it possible to manage the vast Rous' Lands from a single center on a regular basis as a whole, using which institutions of power, and for what purposes? The princely reformers themselves lacked ready answers to these questions, as can be concluded from the inconsistent and even contradictory policies of the second half of the tenth century. The contradictions in the chronicle's narrative reflected this lack of a coherent political narrative.

Olga and Sviatoslav: Two Scenarios of Power

According to the chronicle, the widow of Igor, Princess Olga, was the supreme ruler of the Rous' Lands for nearly a quarter of a century, until her death in 969. This raises a question about the status of their son Sviatoslav, who according to the chronicle was born around 942. Thus, by local demographic standards, he would have reached maturity by 956 and, consequently, have taken over power from his mother. (The chronicle explicitly states that Olga retained her parental authority over Sviatoslav— that is, "she raised him to manhood and adult age.") Viking women enjoyed significant legal rights, but rule by a woman when there was a direct male heir to the throne, adult and fully capable, appears quite extraordinary. Instead of a formal transfer of power to her son, according to the annals, in 955 Olga traveled to Constantinople, where she was baptized. Politically, this step meant not only the strengthening of relations with Byzantium in the spirit of the treaty of 945 but also the enhancing of the position of monotheistic religion in the Rous' Lands, since the prince was also the high priest in eastern Europe. The adoption of Christianity would have contributed to the formalization of state institutions in the Rous' Lands, carried out by Princess Olga, and creating a new basis for the supratribal unity of the population. This was all the more important because both the external borders of the Rous' Lands and their internal integrity required new substantiation if the country was becoming something more than a confederation of autonomous tribes interested in the fair and skillful administration of the trade route passing through their lands. However, Olga's attempts to persuade Sviatoslav to be baptized met his staunch refusal. Both Olga's persistence and Sviatoslav's perseverance testify that it was not just a matter of their moral choice or that Sviatoslav's political role was far more significant than is suggested by the chronicle: "But he did not heed her exhortation, answering, 'How shall I alone accept another faith? My retinue will mock that.' But his mother replied, 'If you are baptized, then everyone will do the same.' He did not heed his mother, and continued to live according to pagan customs."

The chronicler begins to mention Sviatoslav as an independent figure only after 964, when he must have been at least twenty-two years old:

> When Prince Sviatoslav had grown up and matured, he began to gather many brave warriors [around him]. After all, he himself was brave, walked light as a cheetah, and fought a lot. He did not carry carts or cauldrons with him, and boiled no meat, but cut off small strips of horseflesh, game, or beef, and ate it after roasting it on the coals. Nor did he have a tent, but he spread out a horse-blanket under him, and set his saddle under his head; and all his retinue did likewise. He sent [messengers] to the other lands saying, "I want to attack you."

By the demographic and legal standards of that time, Sviatoslav "had grown up and matured" much earlier: by the age of twenty-two his son Vladimir would already have several children. He must have begun to gather a retinue of professional warriors at least around the time of his mother's baptism, which was reflected in the debates with Olga regarding the adoption of Christianity. Sviatoslav is always mentioned in documents together with the retinue, most often in the context of military campaigns. Olga rightly believed that the retinue would have followed Sviatoslav's example if he had been baptized—but, apparently, Sviatoslav himself had a fundamentally different understanding of princely power and the mission of the retinue, so the initiative to preserve the old ways was coming from him, not from his entourage. There is not a single mention of his retinue participating in routine "government" activities within the framework established by Olga's reform: visiting local permanent missions (*pogosts*), enforcing "legal provisions," and so on. Instead, Sviatoslav revives the mores and lifestyle of the Varangian bands of the past that already appeared archaic and therefore exotic—note the chronicle's tone in describing his camp life. The chronicle mentions only his campaigns during the past five years of the life and reign of Princess Olga, whom he survived by only three years. This does not exclude the possibility of his raiding neighboring lands from the very beginning. Even before his first raid as mentioned by the chronicle under 964, Sviatoslav "sent [messengers] to the other lands saying, 'I want to attack you.'"

Thus, Sviatoslav's activities were separate from those of Olga not so much chronologically (as her heir), as politically. The chronicle's constant refrain about Olga and Sviatoslav's ruling together in amity should not mask the fundamental antagonism of the two political strategies that they chose and embodied for many years: the logic of state-building and the logic of embodying the ideal of the "sovereign" according to the canons of a "barbaric" cultural tradition (the Viking, Slavic, or steppe one). The difference between these two strategies seems obvious today: the first involves large-scale organizational activities, the creation of a unified cultural and legal space, and the second requires a systematic personal heroic behavior based on direct action and intimate contact with followers. However, the "scientifically substantiated" advantage of the former strategy to create an effective state was far from obvious in the tenth century, whereas the tested tradition supported the choice made by Sviatoslav.

Sviatoslav's Neotraditionalist Body Politics

At the same time, the reformer Olga and the "neotraditionalist" Sviatoslav equally broke out of the political culture of the past decades, consciously searching for new political solutions. It seems obvious in the case of Olga, but the demonstrative brutality of the appearance and primitiveness of Sviatoslav's life was equally politically innovative. It was the result of his conscious and even deliberate choice as an element of the symbolic "body politics" and performance of the ideal leader. Both local people and Byzantines, who had a good idea of how the "archons of the Rhoses" typically looked, were shocked by his appearance. According to the classical depiction of Sviatoslav by the Byzantine chronicler Leo Deacon,

> His appearance was the following: he was of moderate height, neither taller than average, nor particularly short; his eyebrows were thick; he had gray eyes and a snub nose; his beard was clean-shaven, but he let the hair grow abundantly on his upper lip where it was bushy and long; and he shaved his head completely, except for a lock of hair that hung down on one side, as a mark of the nobility of his ancestry; he was solid in the neck, broad in the chest and very well articulated in the rest of his body; he had a rather angry and savage appearance; on one ear was fastened a gold earring, adorned with two pearls with a red gemstone between them; his clothing was white and differed from his confidants only in cleanliness.[3]

The heroic leader, the first among equal warriors (distinguished from them only by the cleanliness of his clothes), Sviatoslav demonstrated behavior that is most consistent with Scandinavian religious beliefs: the cult of war and weapons, contempt for luxury despite the constant pursuit of fortune as proof of one's chosenness and luck.

According to this worldview, warriors who die heroically get into Valhalla, and those who tremble cover themselves in shame forever. Sviatoslav made a famous appeal to his warriors who were frightened by the appearance of superior enemy forces: "We have nowhere to go already, whether we will or no, we must fight. So let us not disgrace the Rous' Lands, but rather die on the spot, because shame is not known to the dead. If we flee, shame will be upon us." This can be read as an expanded quotation from the epic poem *Beowulf*, created in England at the beginning of the eighth century by recent Anglo-Saxon migrants from Scandinavia, in which the hero Wiglaf speaks to the soldiers who fled from the battlefield (in Seamus Heaney's translation):

> Then a stern rebuke was bound to come
> From the young warrior to the ones who had been cowards . . . :
> ". . . A warrior will sooner
> Die than live a life of shame."

It looks as if Sviatoslav began raids on neighboring lands without any special plan, just for the sake of doing it: "And so he went to the Oka River and the Volga, and came across the Vyatichians, and asked the Vyatichians: 'To whom are you paying tribute?'" Subsequently, he devastated Volga Bulgaria, the rich inner territories of the Khazar Khaganate, which never recovered from this blow, and imposed tribute on the Slavic tribal union of the Vyatichians in the Oka basin (historians disagree about the actual sequence of these enterprises of Sviatoslav). After that, he went to fight in the Danube Bulgaria and even declared the trade city of Preslavets (Little Preslav) on the lower Danube to be his capital. [12]

Since the nineteenth century, historians have habitually referred to Sviatoslav's campaigns as manifestations of active "foreign policy" of the "Kyiv state." This formula is itself misleading because the separation into "foreign" and "domestic" policy is a relatively recent phenomenon. It implies not only a systematic demarcation of the country's territorial borders but also a clear division of the population into "native" and "foreign," as well as the differentiation of foreign and domestic policy in terms of their methods and goals. Unlike Olga, who was preoccupied with the management of lands belonging to the initial confederation of tribes along the Volga–Baltic and Dnieper trade routes, Sviatoslav demonstrated not a territorial but a "situational" understanding of his possessions. "His" territory was where the prince and his retinue were currently present, procuring bounty by force of arms. It is the differences in understanding princely power that became the topic of the last argument between Olga and Sviatoslav not long before she died. According to the chronicler, Sviatoslav declared to his mother: "I do not like to remain in Kyiv, I want to live in Preslavets on the Danube, since that is the center of my realm, where all riches flow to: gold, silks, wine, and various fruits from Greece, silver and horses from Czechia and Hungary, and from Rus'—furs, wax, honey, and slaves."

Olga perceived the Rous' Lands as a distinctive contiguous territory spanning from Kyiv to Novgorod, which she was trying to consolidate through a network of administrative centers and symbolic spaces like hunting grounds representing princely power. Sviatoslav's actions revealed a different understanding of the Rous' Lands as a zone dominated by the retinue (the Rous'). This already archaic political vision was extraterritorial in the sense that it aspired to exercise control not over people ("tribes") or historical regions, but over the flows of material resources. In the same manner, Rurik could say about Ladoga, and Askold–Dir—about Kyiv: "That is the center of my realm, where all riches flow to." At the same time, Sviatoslav did not consider himself the ruler of the Bulgarians, on whose lands he tried to establish himself with his retinue, nor did he have any control over the vast territory between the lower Danube and Kyiv. His power was "singular" in space and "discrete" in time, that is, existing only there and at that moment in which he and his retinue were present, and only as long as they were victorious.

From the vantage point of the old economic logic and anthropology of power of the Viking warrior community, Sviatoslav's actions were rational, and he embodied the ideal leader. He constantly led the retinue to new places promising rich booty, instead of procuring systematic revenues from the already conquered population. But from the vantage point of the Rous' Lands as a territorial whole, Sviatoslav's "foreign policy" was meaningless and directly destructive.

Thus, in 968, when Sviatoslav was away raiding Bulgaria, the Pechenegs besieged and nearly captured Kyiv. Only a detachment of "people" (*liudei*), who hastened to the rescue from the opposite (Severians') bank of the Dnieper under the command of the tribal militia leader (*voevoda*) Pretich, forced the Pechenegs to lift the siege and move down the Dnieper. Afterward, a letter was sent from Kyiv to the Danube with an eloquent rebuke of Sviatoslav:

> You, prince, are seeking a foreign land and take care of it, and you will lose yours, because the Pechenegs have all but taken us captive, along with your mother and your children as well. If you do not come and protect us, then they will finally capture us. Do you really have no pity on your native land, your old mother, and your children?

As it appears from this letter, the Kyivans themselves believed that Sviatoslav was not acting in the interests of Kyiv, and that his country was relevant for him only as a "native land"—he did not care about it as a ruler. It is of even more interest that, apparently, Sviatoslav took with him to the Danube the entire retinue, that is, all the professional warriors, and therefore, Kyiv was nearly captured by enemies and the siege had to be lifted by "people" under the command of a man with a Slavic name Pretich (Pretić). But this means that the vast territory of the Rous' Lands was administered by Olga without the participation of the retinue in the sense of a special military organization, an autonomous warrior community, relying solely on the network of local missions (*pogosts*) and the help of local tribal military commanders, such as Pretich. True, Sviatoslav's adventures on the Danube made Kyiv vulnerable to enemy attacks, but in peacetime they apparently did not feel the need for Sviatoslav's retinue in Kyiv, less so in his Danube conquests.

Even more harmful and meaningless from the "foreign policy" point of view were Sviatoslav's attacks on Volga Bulgaria and the Khazar Khaganate. None of his predecessors could even conceive of setting off to plunder the main trading partner on the Volga–Baltic route, the gateway for the flow of silver from Baghdad and Khwarezm. Even though Bulgar was located much closer to the Rous' Lands and was a much weaker opponent than Constantinople—the target of several military campaigns organized from Kyiv—the chronicles do not mention similar attacks on Bulgar before Sviatoslav. The Khazar Khaganate once collected tribute from "tribes" east of the Dnieper River—that is, exercising political dominance over them. However, from the end of the ninth century, the khaganate no longer posed a direct military threat to the new rulers of Kyiv. The departure of the Hungarian tribes westward and the arrival of the Pechenegs in their place resulted in the physical, territorial isolation of the Rous' Lands from Khazaria. Having dealt a fatal blow to the already-weakened khaganate, Sviatoslav destroyed not only the key intermediate center of caravan trade along the Volga and the northern route of the Great Silk Road but also the barrier that for centuries contained the migration of nomadic tribes from beyond the Urals. After the fall of Khazaria, the Pechenegs became unrestrained masters of the steppe from the Volga to the Danube, destroying the agriculturist settlements of the forest-steppe zone including Slavic ones that flourished under the protection of the Khazar Khaganate. For many centuries, the steppe inhabitants were the main existential threat to the lands ruled from Kyiv.

Despite these irrational attacks and brazen raids in the zone of Byzantine influence, fighting both in alliance with Byzantium and against it, together with former enemies, in July 971 Sviatoslav signed another treaty with Byzantium—thirty years after the first unsuccessful campaign against Constantinople by Prince Igor. As always, the chronicle presents the treaty as an extraordinary concession forced out of the Byzantines, but its text appears completely standard compared to the previous documents signed every thirty years:

> I, Sviatoslav, Prince of Rous', even as I previously swore, now confirm by oath upon this covenant: I, along with all the Rous' under my command, boyars and others, want to have peace and perfect amity with all the great Emperors . . . until the end of the world. I will contemplate no attack upon your country, or any territory under Greek rule, or Korsun' (Chersonesus) and its cities, or against Bulgaria. And if someone else plans to attack your realm, I will oppose him and wage war upon him.

The short text of the treaty cited in the chronicle differs from the treaty of 945 only in terms of the more extended obligations of allies to Byzantium, as well as the presentation of the Rous' side. In 945 the treaty was signed by twenty-three envoys and twenty-nine merchants on behalf of "Igor, the Grand Prince of Rous', and from each prince and all the people of the Rous' Land." Besides Igor, special envoys represented his wife, Olga, their son, Sviatoslav, nephew, Igor, and three other dignitaries. Sviatoslav signed the treaty alone—which is natural, given the circumstances of a long campaign away from home. But he did not deem it necessary to indicate that he was acting on behalf of anyone other than his retinue. In his opinion, perhaps this was how a true sovereign should act: not burdened by social obligations that condition and hence limit his absolute power.

His death soon thereafter symbolized the marginality of an ideal sovereign without a state: Sviatoslav was killed in a battle with the Pechenegs at the Dnieper rapids, on "no-man's-land," either hesitating to return to Kyiv after the failure of his Danube expedition or awaiting the arrival of reinforcements from Kyiv to continue his raids in the south. According to a legend, the Pechenegs made a drinking cup from the skull of Sviatoslav for their Khan Kurya, as was customary in "Great Scythia." According to Herodotus and Strabo, the Scythians did the same with their enemies, and as late as 811 CE, the Bulgarian Khan Krum ordered that a goblet be made from the skull of the Byzantine Emperor Nicephorus I, who had been slain in battle.

The Sovereign as a State Institution

Five years after the death of Sviatoslav, a dispute for power began between his sons Yaropolk, Oleg, and Vladimir: they were fighting each other at the head of their retinues, besieging and capturing towns, and killing each other. This plot seems overly ubiquitous for medieval Europe (and, of course, not only Europe). Therefore, it comes as a surprise that such a typical conflict was registered by the Primary Chronicle for the first time only under the year 977 CE—almost 120 years after the Rous' princes established their rule in the region. Even according to the chronicle's own semilegendary list of rulers, the conflict between Sviatoslav's heirs broke out only in the fourth generation of Rurikids. Given the demographic standards of the era—age of marriage and childbearing age, life expectancy—it would be more realistic to talk about the fifth or even sixth generation. The situation would have been exacerbated by the fact that Varangian chieftains fathered numerous children with different wives and concubines, and even children born of a slave had a legal right to part of the paternal inheritance. Nevertheless, the chronicle suggests that Rurik had no other son, except Igor, who was "minor" at the time of Rurik's death after seventeen years of reign; and that Princess Olga gave birth in 942 to the first and only son, Sviatoslav, thirty-nine years after her marriage to Igor.

The Secret of Initial Political Stability in the Rous' Lands

We have no way to verify this information today, but it is clear that until the last quarter of the tenth century, the probable rivalry among the heirs to the Rous' Land's ruler never reached the level of an open confrontation. This can only be explained by the semi-isolated coexistence of the "pactiot" tribes' confederation and the community of retinue warriors as holders of the supreme power over these lands. To become the prince of the Rous' Lands, one had to be the retinue's chieftain, and it was meaningless to wage a fratricidal struggle, recruiting supporters and bribing opponents, in order to be recognized as the retinue's leader. As a community upheld by the rules of military democracy, the retinue members were choosing a leader for themselves or sustaining more complex and shaky political arrangements (for example, if the nominal office was held by a descendant of the previous charismatic chieftain as a purely symbolic figure, while the real power belonged to the new leader recognized for his prowess). One way or another, the figure of the new prince reflected a consensus already achieved within the retinue.

Despite numerous speculations by professional and amateur historians, it is unclear whether the rest of the Rous' Lands had princes of their own. The chronicle only mentions at that time Prince Rogvolod in Polotsk of the Krivichians and Prince Tur in Turov of the Dregovichians: "This Rogvolod had come from overseas and held power in Polotsk, and Tur held power in Turov, so Turovians were named after him." "Rogvolod" can fairly confidently be identified as Ragnvald Olafsson, the illegitimate son of King Olaf Haraldsson of Norway's Vingulmark, who was born in Oslo in 925. The identity of "Tur" has not been established and some historians do not regard him as a historical figure, although it seems likely that he was another Varangian *konungr* with the popular name Thor (after the God Thor; as a personal name of historical actors, it is still transcribed in Russian as "Tur"). The fact that we know about only these two local princes might be an exception that proves the rule: the status of invited princes with their retinue, which at the time necessarily meant Varangians, was higher than that of local tribal chiefs and elders. The chronicle's failure to mention native Slavic and Finnish princes may therefore be interpreted either as their absence, or as the result of their lower prestige compared to the Varangian leaders.

Either way, we witness here a result of a well-calculated and rational political strategy rather than the evidence of local underdevelopment and an inferiority complex toward the overseas chieftains. Since the days of Rurik, the invited princes helped local populations to achieve a more complex and efficient political organization while preserving the fundamental separation of power and possession of communal resources. The Varangian princes and their retinues did not lay claim to the land of the tribal union they ruled, being content with the tribute paid to them. At this relatively low cost, the political sphere remained separate from other areas of public life. This was the important difference between the Rous' Lands and the Frankish kingdoms, where the kings of "all Franks" and dukes combined supreme power with a claim to supreme ownership of the tribal territory. Local Finnish, Baltic, and Slavic tribes could elevate their elders and wartime leaders to the role of permanent plenipotentiary princes, but this development was fraught with the same coalescence of power and possession as in the Frankish lands, which threatened the sovereignty of communities and their unions. At the same time, the invited Varangian prince "owned" only his community-retinue, so even after several generations of princely rule the dualism of the prince's power and the sovereignty of the tribe persisted. It manifested itself most vividly in the continuous identification of territories with tribes rather than rulers or dynasties. The "private" power of the prince, who came "out of nowhere" as the bearer of a certain amount of authority (backed up by personal qualities and the size of his retinue), was separate from the tribe's "private" ownership of territory by the right of colonization (formalized in beliefs and customs).

The Crisis of 977 as a Disruption of the Demographically Territorial Distribution of Power

This delicately balanced system functioned for over a century, until a radical turnover violated the separation of power and possession of the Rous' Lands. The conflict of

Self-Organization of Northern Eurasia's First Polities   75

977 became possible because of an unprecedented decision made during the life of Sviatoslav: "Sviatoslav installed Yaropolk in Kyiv and Oleg with the Drevlians. At this time, the Novgorodians came asking a prince for themselves: 'If you will not come to us, we will find a prince ourselves.'... The Novgorodians accepted Vladimir, and Vladimir went with Dobrynia, his uncle, to Novgorod, and Sviatoslav [departed] to Pereyaslavets."

Because the chronicle tells this story when listing the events of the year 970, immediately after reporting the death of Olga, it is usually perceived as a description of Sviatoslav's last arrangement before leaving Kyiv for the Danube. However, the time line of the Primary Chronicle, particularly when referring to early periods, is not exactly one of physical time, with accurately measured continuities and registered moments of transition. It is possible that this was not an instantaneous decision, but a phased process of appointing the sons of the Kyivan prince to the community centers of subject tribes as governors. The need for the introduction of direct rule by the Kyiv-appointed viceroy might have emerged back in 945, when Olga had exterminated the entire elite of the Drevlians during a multistage, large-scale retaliation for the murder of Igor. Therefore, Sviatoslav's decision to send his son Oleg to the Drevlians might not be the first appointment of a Kyivan representative to their land or could have taken place much earlier. Sviatoslav's own early rule in Novgorod around 950 CE, which was mentioned by Constantine the Porphyrogenitus, at the time when Olga occupied the princely seat in Kyiv, could also be a precedent of these later appointments.

Whatever the exact prehistory of the decision to appoint sons of the Kyivan prince as administrators of confederate lands, it was the sole measure that equally corresponded to the otherwise incongruent political strategies of Olga and Sviatoslav. On the one hand, this measure enhanced the presence of the supreme authority on the ground, in line with Olga's political reform. Besides, a young prince in the role of a viceroy was less likely than an ordinary appointee to provoke resistance from local community leaders who had already recognized the supreme power of the Rous' prince. Perhaps this was the rationale behind installing these regional princes when they were very young: Sviatoslav was not even ten years old when his rule in Novgorod was registered by Constantine the Porphyrogenitus, his sons were sent to preside over the Drevlians and Novgorodians at about the same age. Actual decision making probably belonged to an older relative or some other representative of the Kyivan prince (Vladimir went to Novgorod with his uncle), while the figure of the young prince made the governor's power more legitimate in the eyes of the local population. In the alternative political logic, those who embraced the political ideal of the prince as a heroic warrior-leader chosen by the gods saw his children as inheriting some of this divine grace and luck. The prince's children could share this unique resource with local populations, whereas their father Sviatoslav was determined to keep his divine gift all to himself and his retinue, raiding in faraway lands.

To sum up, Yaropolk Sviatoslavich (members of the dynasty were addressed by their given name and patronymic), who was probably the eldest of Sviatoslav's sons, occupied the metropolitan princely seat in Kyiv. This could be either a temporary appointment for the duration of Sviatoslav's campaign on the Danube, just as Igor stayed in Kyiv while Oleg was besieging Constantinople, or a permanent arrangement, similar to the division of responsibilities between Olga and the mature Sviatoslav. Oleg

Sviatoslavich became the prince of the Drevlian land, which was a less prestigious but also a less ambiguous position: his status would not have changed in the event of Sviatoslav's return. If there had been a tradition of appointing a representative of the Kyivan prince to Novgorod in "outer Rhosia" from among the younger kin, the frustration of Novgorodians as conveyed by the chronicle is quite understandable. The appointment of Oleg raised the status of the Drevlian land and left the Novgorodians with the prospect of receiving a prince's servant or, at best, a senior retinue member as governor, which meant lowering the prestige of Novgorod relative to other lands. In Scandinavia and eastern Europe, the popular assembly (a *thing* in Scandinavian and Germanic societies or Slavic *veche*) had the right to invite a military leader—*konungr*, or prince. The assembly chose among several candidates and upon selecting one concluded an agreement (*riad*) with him. The prince promised to comply with local laws and protect the region. So, the Novgorod elders had every right to seek a prince on the side, if the Kyiv prince failed to offer them a candidate of high status.

Neither Yaropolk nor Oleg showed interest in trading his position for the office of Novgorodian prince, so the retinue member Dobrynia saved the day when he proposed Sviatoslav's youngest son, Vladimir, as the third candidate. Vladimir's mother was a servant of Princess Olga and, by a happy coincidence, Dobrynia's sister. Neither the Novgorodians nor Sviatoslav seemed disheartened by Vladimir's birth out of wedlock and his mother's low social standing, but it is clear that initially Sviatoslav did not consider Vladimir as a regional prince. This arrangement—which envisioned junior princes supervising some of the Rous' Lands on behalf of the Kyivan prince and even temporarily substituting him in the metropolitan seat—might not have been new. What changed in the 970s was the sudden collapse of kin hierarchy based on demographic seniority: two years after Sviatoslav's departure from Kyiv, he died. The Rous' Lands remained under the supreme command of his son in Kyiv, Yaropolk, whose siblings Oleg and Vladimir presided, respectively, over the neighboring land of the Drevlians and the distant but strategically important Novgorod. On the one hand, the simultaneous reign of members of the same family in three different tribal centers erased the discreteness of tribal territories, each of which was previously directly subordinate to the prince of the Rous' Lands on individual terms. Moreover, since Yaropolk, Oleg, and Vladimir were not strangers from overseas but the heirs of the Rous' Lands' prince, their power rested not only on the retinues but also on the embryonic state institutions established by Princess Olga. This transformed the bilateral relations of the prince and the tribe that invited him by the veche's decision. The junior prince representing his father's authority in a given land acted in the interests not only of the local tribe and his own retinue but also of the nascent state as a collective and public subject of power, not limited to a tribe's territory. Power lost the former character of private relations between two parties and became universally abiding and collective. By the same token, subordination changed its former individual and circumstantial character, so that subordinated tribesmen lost their discreteness as a particular group.

On the other hand, several princes representing a single state power were faced with the problem of its distribution. Unlike earlier times, as brothers and almost coevals, Yaropolk and Oleg found themselves in the position of two independent princes rather

Self-Organization of Northern Eurasia's First Polities 77

than traditional corulers belonging to different generations, like Oleg and Igor, Olga and Sviatoslav. Moreover, as the heads of separate territories, still clearly delineated by their tribal affiliation, they did not differentiate their responsibilities functionally, unlike the khagan and the bek in Khazaria. They equally represented the universal state power, which enhanced their authority as local princes but also made their position insecure: after all, any other "Sviatoslavich" could take their place as representative of the state.

Forest Law as the Reason for Fratricide

The structural conflict of the universality of state power and the private role of the invited "tribal" prince inevitably led to a political conflict, particularly when several princes embodied both these aspects. The scarce details provided by the chronicle confirm the political, not the personal reasons for the brothers' mutual enmity. In 977, Yaropolk of Kyiv went to war against his brother Oleg in the land of the Drevlians. The only explanation for this campaign in the chronicle was an insult inflicted on Yaropolk back in 975: while hunting, Oleg deliberately killed the son of Yaropolk's senior commander (*voevoda*), Sveneld:

> Once, Sveneldich [i.e., the son of Sveneld], named Liut, left Kyiv to hunt and was chasing a wild beast in the forest. Oleg saw him and asked his own people: "Who is this?" And they answered him: "Sveneldich." Oleg attacked and killed him, for he himself was hunting there. From this the enmity between Yaropolk and Oleg began, [since] Sveneld constantly urged Yaropolk, seeking to avenge his son: "Attack your brother and seize his domain."

The chronicle's suggestion that Yaropolk spent two years preparing to avenge his brother for the murder of a junior warrior, Liut, seems implausible, so some scholars have proposed explanations of a conspiratorial and psychological nature. More than 1,000 years later, reconstructing the interpersonal relations of historical actors is neither possible nor necessary, particularly given the information provided by the chronicle: in response to the murder of Liut, Yaropolk was going to seize the territory under his brother's purview. The land itself belonged to the tribe of Drevlians, not Prince Oleg, which meant that the conflict somehow concerned delineating the princes' spheres of sovereignty.

As was mentioned earlier, one of Princess Olga's political reforms was the allocation of special hunting grounds for the exclusive use of the prince on the land of each of the former *pactiot* tribes. Claiming part of the sovereignty over tribal territory, this measure symbolized the authority of the Kyivan prince as present across the entire Rous' Lands. Over a century later, during the Norman conquest of England after 1066, when royal power became as "extraterritorial" with respect to the local population as in the early Rous' Lands, William the Conqueror used the forest laws to undermine the preexisting common law. The legal regime of the royal forest became one of the few new institutions extended to the whole kingdom, thereby extending the power of the king countrywide. Royal hunting grounds were "afforested" throughout the country, the forest law was personally regulated by the king, and its violation incurred cruel punishments similar to penalties for an assault on the monarch's power. Thus, according to the law of William the Conqueror, killing a red deer warranted blinding, while his son, William II, introduced the death penalty in forest laws. In the course of a hundred years, the area of royal hunting grounds had reached one-third of the country's entire territory, with its legal regime spreading to some adjacent villages and even small towns. Actually, the woods began to be known as "forests" after these territories were taken outside the sphere of common law (Latin *foris*—outside, out of doors), subordinate to the regime of the royal forest laws.

The land of the Drevlians bordered on the Polianian territory near Kyiv, so it is not surprising that a young Kyivan hunter, carried away by the pursuit of game, could find himself on territory subject to the neighboring prince. What seems strange is the sequence of and motivation for Oleg's actions: first, he clarified who was in front of him, and only then, after some calculations, "killed him, for he himself was hunting there." Obviously, the reason was not that the woodland was too small for the two hunters, but that the forest was the hunting ground established by Princess Olga for the exclusive use of the Kyivan prince and the retinue as the symbol of supreme authority. The rights of Yaropolk, Oleg, and Vladimir to the hunting grounds belonging to the prince of the Rous' Lands mirrored the distribution of the supreme power among them. If Yaropolk was not just the ruler of Kyiv and the surrounding Polianian territory but the full prince of the Rous' Lands like Princess Olga, did he not have the sole right to hunting grounds in all subject lands? But if, by right of birth, his brothers had the same powers as Yaropolk, at least within their regional jurisdictions, did they alone not enjoy the privilege of using the hunting grounds on their territory? In other words, the dispute over the right to hunt, possibly along with a similar conflict over the use of *pogosts*, manifested the general problem: was the division of powers among Sviatoslav's sons a matter of territorial delimitation or different rights?

Liut "Sveneldich" believed the Kyivan prince possessed the supreme power, and therefore members of his retinue could hunt everywhere. Oleg, after clarifying that the young man did not belong to his retinue, killed Liut as a violator of the Drevlian prince's sovereignty. Whatever the personal relationship between these people, the legal framework for their conflict was disagreement about supreme authority over a given territory.

Political and Cultural Consolidation of the Rous' Lands

The Resolution of a Systemic Crisis through a Fratricide

Two years after the hunting incident, the Kyivan prince Yaropolk led the troops against his brother Oleg in order to "seize his domain," according to the chronicle. There was a battle, which Oleg lost. In the rush to retreat behind the protection of the walls of his capital Ovruch, Oleg fell from the bridge spanning the moat and died, having been crushed by horses falling from above. Yaropolk mourned the death of his brother, blaming Sveneld for it, according to the chronicle. When Vladimir learned about these

Self-Organization of Northern Eurasia's First Polities 79

events, he panicked and fled from Novgorod "beyond the sea" to the king of Norway Haakon Sigurdarson "The Mighty." Obviously, everyone understood the political subtext of Yaropolk's campaign as the only way to resolve their ambiguous situation: an attempt to force the prince-brothers to recognize the exclusive authority of Yaropolk as the supreme prince of the Rous' Lands.

In 978, Vladimir returned to Novgorod with the Varangian retinue (the chronicle, possibly erroneously, dated his return to 980) and expelled Yaropolk's administrators from the city. Coming back with the military force made certain a confrontation with Yaropolk, so Vladimir wasted no time heading south. On the way to Kyiv lay Polotsk, ruled by the already mentioned Rogvolod/Ragnvald. An alliance with him could increase Vladimir's chances of victory, so Vladimir proposed to Rogneda (Ragnheið or Ragnhild in another transcription), the daughter of Rogvolod/Ragnvald. Rogneda rejected Vladimir in a most insulting way: she preferred to marry Yaropolk rather than Vladimir, the "son of a slave." Infuriated, Vladimir captured Polotsk, murdered Rogneda's father and brothers, and forcibly took her as his wife. After that, he besieged Kyiv, tricked Yaropolk into leaving the city under the pretext of negotiations, whereupon Vladimir's warriors murdered Yaropolk. Vladimir became the sole ruler of the Rous' Lands, eliminating not only his brothers but also at least one local dynasty of invited Varangian princes in an important tribal center.

It might seem that in his rise to power, Vladimir followed in the footsteps of his father Sviatoslav: he relied on the Varangian retinue, claiming lands that he had no right to claim as his domain. Later, he led military campaigns against the same targets as Sviatoslav, including the Bulgars and Khazars. He challenged the Byzantine Empire, demonstrated a commitment to paganism, and even arranged the persecution of Christians in Kyiv, and eventually appointed his sons to reign over different Rous' Lands. However, this was rather a mirror image of Sviatoslav's policies. Unlike his father, who constantly strove for distance from Kyiv, Vladimir made the city the center of all his undertakings; and in contrast to Sviatoslav's spartan ideal of the chieftain always on the warpath, Vladimir famously indulged his carnal urges: according to the chronicle, Vladimir kept several hundred concubines in harems at three of his residences. Still more significant was the difference in political culture. Whether acting consciously and purposefully or demonstrating spontaneous political intuition, over his thirty-seven-year reign Vladimir had consistently implemented a certain political scenario, clearly rooted in the reforms of Princess Olga. This consistency can be traced simultaneously in three interconnected spheres, fundamental for the Rous' Lands: in the institution of the princely retinue, in the religious-cum-cultural sphere, and in the organization of princely power. The apparent contrast between Vladimir's personal preferences and many of his political decisions highlights the nonaccidental and purposeful character of his actions.

The Retinue

Vladimir owed his success entirely to the Varangian force that he brought to Novgorod from the Norwegian ruler Haakon the Mighty. This action does not seem to be unequivocally necessitated by security considerations alone. It is unclear whether

Yaropolk actually planned to strike against Novgorod after defeating Oleg or whether there was any immediate threat to Vladimir residing over 600 miles from Drevlian's town of Ovruch, where Oleg accidentally died. The chronicle only mentions that Vladimir fled "beyond the sea" as soon as he heard about Oleg's death. Novgorodians, who were so enthusiastic about having Vladimir as their prince, would likely have defended him in the event of Yaropolk's attack. But if Vladimir was planning a campaign against the legitimate ruler of Kyiv in order to cut the political Gordian knot in his own favor, the support of the Novgorodian popular militia and their enthusiasm could not be taken for granted. In this case, a unit of Norman mercenaries was indispensable.

The Varangians earnestly completed the task, made Vladimir master of Kyiv, and expected fair remuneration: "After all this, the Varangians said to Vladimir: 'This city belongs to us, we captured it [and] want to take a ransom from the townspeople— two grivnas per person.'" The leader of a traditional Varangian retinue would have eagerly satisfied this request, as it was his primary duty to provide a community of warriors with spoils of war. However, Vladimir's response was completely unusual. He played for time for a whole month under various pretexts, and then sent his Varangian warriors off to join the service in Byzantium without paying them himself. Moreover, Vladimir sent a special messenger to the Byzantine emperor with a letter that completely compromised his former allies: "Here Varangians are coming to you, do not try to keep them in the capital, or else they will do the same evil to you in the city as they have done here. Scatter them around and let not even one come there [i.e., to the capital]." And yet, throughout his long reign, Vladimir enjoyed the reputation of a benevolent retinue patron. The chronicle constantly mentions him along with his retinue, and he is credited with organizing weekly feasts for retinue members for whom he even purchased silver spoons, saying: "'With silver and gold, I won't find a retinue for myself, whereas with a retinue I will procure silver and gold, just as my grandfather and father had obtained gold and silver.' For Vladimir loved the retinue and consulted with them regarding administering the country, matters of war, and legislation."

These words stand in stark contrast to Vladimir's treatment of his Varangian associates, which suggests a single explanation: Vladimir considered himself the head of the country, who relied on the retinue, rather than the leader of the community of professional warriors, whose authority was applicable only on the territory currently occupied by his warriors. The prince's retinue itself had changed under Vladimir. From an extraterritorial commune of Scandinavian warriors, it had evolved into a social institution of the Rous' Lands, even structurally reproducing the specifics of this supratribal political formation. Describing Prince Vladimir's retinue feasts among the events of the year 996 (i.e., sixteen or eighteen years after Vladimir captured Kyiv), the chronicle provides a detailed nomenclature for different categories of participating warriors: boyars, bodyguards (*gridi*), constables (*sotskie*), tithingmen (*desiatskie*), and notables ("best men," *luchshie muzhi*).

The term "boyare" denoting senior retinue members had been borrowed from the Turkic language of the Bulgars before part of them relocated to the Danube from the Caspian steppes (*baj*—master, *är*—man, originally from Old Iranian). The Danube Bulgarians already pronounced the word as "bolyare." *Gridi* were junior status retinue members. This Scandinavian term originally referred to a prince's bodyguard and was

Self-Organization of Northern Eurasia's First Polities   81

used only in "outer Rhosia," in Novgorod. *Sotskii* and *desiatskii* are Slavic terms and direct equivalents of historic English terms "constable" (who supervised a "hundred") and "tithingman" (leader of a tithing) as administrators of, respectively, 100 or 10 units: hides, families, or warriors. The decimal principle for organizing the population was widespread in Nordic as well as nomadic societies, where both the Khazars and the Hungarians (Magyars) used this system, including for the organization of detachments of their Slavic subjects. Thus, the "collective portrait" of the retinue during the heyday of Vladimir's rule demonstrates its hybrid "intertribal" character, which was a far cry from the original Varangian model. Archaeological finds from the end of the tenth century further confirm the cultural synthesis of Slavic, Varangian, and steppe elements, when Viking sword hilts remained the principal Scandinavian detail in the burials of warriors.

The strongest blow to the original Varangian retinue culture must have been delivered by Prince Sviatoslav, who tried to embody the ideal of a Norman king devoutly worshipping the northern God Odin. Constantly fighting far from Kyiv and even farther from the Baltic, Sviatoslav was exposed to the influence of the steppe zone's martial culture, from the Volga to the Danube. He also had to replenish inevitably high casualties at the expense of local warriors: Volga Bulgars, Khazars, and Pechenegs. According to historical documents, while fighting on the Danube, Sviatoslav recruited Bulgarian soldiers into his army. His portrait as described by Leo Deacon cited earlier in this chapter depicts more a steppe warrior than a Viking.

Having ceased to be a Scandinavian community of warriors, the prince's retinue did not become Slavic, because it lost its homogeneous communal character altogether. The retinue transformed into a key political and social institution, the basis of a princely administration operating throughout the entire Rous' Lands and therefore open to all groups of indigenous population. So, in 988 when Prince Vladimir became concerned about protecting Kyiv from the Pecheneg raids, he turned to the tribal elites ("best men") of different lands and was not in the least concerned about their "otherness." "And Vladimir said: 'It is bad that there are few cities around Kyiv.' He began to build cities on the Desna, Oster, Trubezh, Sula, and Stugna [rivers] and, recruiting the best men from the Slovenes, Krivichians, Chudians, and Vyatichians, to populate [these] cities, for there was a war with the Pechenegs."

Vladimir combined this indiscriminate attitude to diverse populations of the Rous' Lands with an acute awareness that tribal (linguistic, cultural, religious) differences were a political problem.

Religion and Culture

What language did Prince Vladimir speak? The answer obviously depends on a clarifying question: With whom? With Polianian elders in Kyiv, Slovenes in Novgorod, or with the Norwegian king who sheltered him? There is no doubt that at least with these people Vladimir conversed without an interpreter. Furthermore, for the inhabitants of the Novgorod land that Vladimir ruled for almost ten years, a knowledge of the Finnish Chudian language was highly relevant, whereas the Severians and Polianians regularly interacted with their southern steppe neighbors: the Khazars, Hungarians (Magyars), and later the Pechenegs. Thus, describing the first siege of Kyiv by the Pechenegs in 968, the chronicle tells the story of a teenager (*otrok*), who managed to sneak through the Pecheneg camp to bring help from the other side of the Dnieper:

> Then one lad said: "I will be able to get through [the enemy lines]." The townspeople were delighted and said to the lad: "If you know how to get through, go." So he went out of the city, holding a bridle, and walked through the camp of the Pechenegs, asking them: "Did anyone see a horse?" For he knew the Pecheneg language, and they took him for one of their own.

Besides, local people had to communicate with Varangians on a regular basis, and hundreds of Rous' merchants spent many months in Constantinople every year, so a knowledge of the Old Norse (Scandinavian) and Greek languages was also quite common. Vladimir's grandmother, Princess Olga, who was baptized in Constantinople, probably spoke and read Greek. Vladimir's grandson, Vsevolod Yaroslavich (1030–1093), according to his son, "knew five languages while sitting at home" (that is, without ever leaving his country). Historians believe that, in addition to Slavic, these languages were the Scandinavian language of his mother, the Greek language of his wife, the Turkic Cuman language of the steppe neighbors, the Polovtsians, and, possibly, the English language of his daughter-in-law. Although it seems more likely that the fifth language spoken by Vsevolod after almost two decades spent as Prince of Rostov was the Finnish language of the local Merian population. The very phenomenon of the Rous' Lands became possible because back in the mid-ninth century, members of the confederation of Slavic and Finnish tribes along the Volga–Baltic trade route understood each other well enough to agree on the invitation of a common administrator—Rurik. Until the rise of modern nation-states at the beginning of the twentieth century, multilingualism and the cultural ambiguity of tribal borders were the norm in Northern Eurasia. This openness to cultural hybridity greatly facilitated spontaneous social mobility but hampered efforts to establish a centralized government.

Obviously, Vladimir was well aware of this problem: according to the chronicle, his first action after capturing Kyiv was to establish a pantheon of pagan deities representing the beliefs of different tribes of the Rous' Lands: "Vladimir began to reign in Kyiv alone and placed idols on a hill behind the palace's courtyard: wooden Perun with a silver head and a golden mustache, and Khors, and Dazhd'bog, and Stribog, and Simargl, and Mokosh. [The people] made sacrifices to them, calling them gods."

The very idea of the pantheon as a lineup of various gods in one place was unusual for local peoples, and its composition was extremely selective. The figure of Perun—the god of thunder and patron of warriors—was rooted in the oldest (Indo-European) stratum of Slavic mythology of the first millennium BCE. Common ancient roots explain why the god of thunder of the Balts had an almost identical name: *Perkūnas* in Lithuanian, *Pērkons* in Latvian. Another Slavic deity in Vladimir's pantheon was the goddess Mokosh, the patroness of women; Dazhd'bog—the all-Slavic god of the sun and fertility; and Stribog—the wind god or, according to some interpretations, Father Sky. At the same time, some of the most important Slavic deities were left out. For example, Veles (Volos), the god of earth, cattle, and the underworld, was particularly revered by the Ilmen Slovenes. When Rous' dignitaries signed treaties with Byzantium, they swore by the name of Veles, along with Perun. Of no less importance was Yarilo (Jarylo), the son of Perun, who represented the cyclical flow of time: the lunar phases, the sequence of seasons, and in general the cycle of death and rebirth.

Whereas the Slavic gods Veles and Yarilo seemed to be excluded in the officially sanctioned pantheon of gods, deities of the Khazar steppe's Iranian-speaking population were included in this pantheon. Scholars trace the significant influence of Iranian-speaking nomads (Scythians, Sarmatians, later Alans) on Slavs' beliefs back to the mid-first millennium CE. Even the Slavic word for "god" (*bog*) was borrowed from them, replacing the common Indo-European designation of deity *divъ. Therefore, both Dazhd'bog and Stribog bear Iranian influence in their names. But Khors and Simargl were purely Iranian deities. Khors is the "shining sun" (Persian *xuršēt*), Simargl is probably Simurg, the prophetic bird who nests in the mountains, also present in the mythology of the Turkic peoples of the Middle Volga. Traces of the Iranian-speaking Alans—subjects of the Khazar Khaganate—have been discovered by archaeologists on the territory of ancient Kyiv, and it is known that one of the city's quarters was called "Kozare" (Khazars). The inclusion of "Iranian" deities in Vladimir's pantheon confirms the significant presence of the steppe factor on the cultural map of the Rous' Lands.

It is also known that a Jewish community with ties to Khazaria existed in Kyiv. A letter written in Hebrew in the early tenth century and signed by eleven members of the Kyivan community has been preserved. The names of two, Gostiata bar Kiabar Kohen and Judah, "who is called SWRTH" (Severyata), present riddles that are open to daring interpretations. Thus, a person with the typical Slavic name Gostiata (literally, "merchant") must have been born to the Khazar tribe Kabar (Kiabar)—one of the three that seceded and migrated with the Hungarians to Pannonia. And yet, he called himself Kohen, that is, he belonged to the Levitical priest clan of *kohanim*, who had to obey strict marriage taboos and by no means could marry a non-Jew. The second man had an ancient Jewish name, Judah, but the nickname Severyata indicates his origins in the land of Severians, which until the end of the ninth century remained in Khazaria's sphere of influence. Judging by the letter, the Kyiv Jewish community was neither numerous nor rich, which should not be surprising given that Judaism was not widespread in the Khazar Khaganate outside its ruling elite. What is puzzling is how entangled cultural and tribal ties in the Rous' Lands were at the time.

From the 945 treaty with the Byzantines, it is known that the first Christian church of St. Elijah was built in the "Khazarian" Kozare quarter of Kyiv, which suggests its somewhat marginal status. On the other hand, it was characterized as "the cathedral church," as if distinguishing it from other Christian places of worship existing in the city. As the chronicle explains, "there were many Christians among the Varangians." This assessment is confirmed by the fact that the two victims of violent anti-Christian persecutions that followed the establishment of the pantheon of pagan deities by Vladimir were the Varangians Fyodor and his son Ioann. Princess Olga's baptism in 955 must have further enhanced the prestige and influence of Christianity in the Rous' Lands.

A hypothesis backed by archaeological evidence proposes that the spread of Christianity during this period had a distinct "feminist" character: the new religion was embraced, first of all, by Varangian women or local women who married Varangians and were dissatisfied with the pagan regulation of marriage. In many ways, the social and legal status enjoyed by Scandinavian women during the early Middle Ages was outstanding and by far superseded the standards of that time. They had the right to divorce and fully retain any property brought to the family after marriage. They were also given custody of all younger children, while older children were to be divided between former spouses. Children of concubines, including slave girls, suffered no legal discrimination and participated equally in the distribution of paternal inheritance (Prince Vladimir was a vivid example of this). Women could take part in campaigns and even battles along with men; cases are known of women commanding teams of Vikings. This unprecedented equality of Scandinavian women had one major downside: the custom required the ritual murder of a widow and joint burial with her deceased husband (as described by witnesses and fully confirmed by archaeological data). High-ranking families could make a slave girl perform the role of the ritual wife, but, obviously, not everyone had this opportunity and even fewer were willing to die this way. For wives of Varangians, this perspective, along with the legitimacy of male polygamy and recognition of the illegitimate children's right to claim a share in family property were important incentives to convert to Christianity. The patriarchal regime of Christianity as a monotheistic religion appealed the most to pagans who were ready to abandon the collective equality of women as a social group in order to protect their individual rights.

As was discussed earlier, Sviatoslav did not follow Olga's example when she was baptized. He entirely relied on the support of pagan, most likely Scandinavian gods. By some reports, he even ordered the execution of Bulgarian Christians in his army on the Danube when he decided he had run out of luck precisely because of them. Vladimir also did not resemble a person capable of honoring even one of the Ten Commandments. Nevertheless, in 988, according to the nominal chronology of the Primary Chronicle, Vladimir received baptism in the Byzantine Chersonesus in Southern Crimea (Korsun of Russian chronicles). Upon returning to Kyiv, he ordered the destruction of his pantheon of pagan deities, and forcefully baptized all the city inhabitants.

In the story of Vladimir's turn to Christianity as told by the Primary Chronicle, facts are tightly and often seamlessly intertwined with literary tropes. The most famous of these tropes is "the choice of faith": representatives of different religions advertised their creeds, and the party making a choice among them critically assessed each. The Primary Chronicle was created in the early twelfth century, after the East–West Schism in 1054 had divided Christianity into the Catholic and Eastern Orthodox churches. Therefore, speaking of the much earlier events of the 980s, the chronicle anachronistically insinuates that Vladimir was choosing not just among three monotheistic religions (Judaism, Islam, and Christianity), but also separately between Byzantine Orthodoxy and the "Latin" faith. This detail compromises the historicity of the account, which itself appears to repeat stories of the choice of faith by the Khazars and the Volga Bulgars. Still, the story of Vladimir's selection of religion should not be dismissed completely as a literary iteration of the archetypal plot. The structural situation of choosing a monotheistic religion—particularly in the radically new status for the Rous' Lands of "official" confession—was real. It is also important that the chronicle separates by chronology and plotline the testing of different religions from Vladimir's actual decision to baptize, thus complicating the familiar scenario. It is further altered by not attributing to the prince the original initiative to compare the merits of different religions or even to consider monotheism in the first place.

According to the chronicle, in 986, an embassy from Volga Bulgaria arrived in Kyiv and invited Vladimir to convert to Islam. This initiative followed the successful military campaign of the Rous' army against the Bulgars in 985. Unlike the looting raid conducted by Prince Sviatoslav in the past, this campaign by his son aimed at establishing a partnership with the Bulgars and led to the conclusion of the "perpetual peace." From the point of view of the Bulgars, who had made Islam their official religion back in 922, the treaty would be much more secure if the Kyiv prince were a Muslim, and not a pagan. Their proposal that he convert to Islam interested Vladimir so much that he organized the legendary test of alternative monotheistic religions. But only two years later, in 988 (according to other sources, already in 987), Vladimir went on a campaign to the Crimean possessions of Byzantium. He besieged and captured the important port city of Chersonesus (Korsun)—either planning in advance to be baptized there or vowing to become Christian in the event of a successful siege. Allegedly, he demanded that the Byzantine Emperors Basil II and Constantine VIII allow him to marry their sister Anna as a condition of the Rous' troops' withdrawal from the city. They agreed, but requested that Vladimir first adopt Christianity.

Byzantine and Middle Eastern sources place these events in a broader historical perspective: there was yet another military mutiny in Byzantium, Emperor Basil II asked the Rous' prince for military assistance in subduing it, promising in exchange to marry Anna off to Vladimir. Vladimir agreed and sent an expeditionary force (an Armenian chronicler cites the figure of 6,000 soldiers). Still unclear is the sequence of all these events, and whether Vladimir captured Chersonesus–Korsun by force or was allowed there as an ally. However, the general structure of relationships seems obvious: Vladimir made the strategic choice in favor of Byzantium as a priority partner of the Rous' Lands, offered his military assistance as an ally, but demonstratively maintained an aggressive stance to sustain the symbolic distance from the politically and culturally kindred hegemonic power. As a result, the acceptance of Christianity from Byzantium by the Rous' is presented by the Primary Chronicle as the most precious prize of war captured by the victorious Kyiv prince from the defeated emperor.

The relinquishing of paganism by Prince Vladimir and his retinue essentially undermined the traditional religion centered on the tribal elders and the prince as the chief priests and embodiments of benevolent divine power. However, the demise of paganism across various Rous' Lands was not synchronous and directly depended on the degree of the Kyiv prince's authority in a given locality. Apparently, in Kyiv the compulsory mass baptism of residents took place in 988 without provoking active protests, but in the second major Rous' city, Novgorod, it took place only two years later, in 990. In the recently subordinated lands of the Merians, near Rostov and Murom, formal Christianization took more than a hundred years. Even in the cities of this region, pagan idols survived until the 1070s. As to spiritual religiosity, the process of the dissemination and rooting of a Christian worldview across the Rous' Lands continued for many centuries, blending with old cultural forms that included survivals of pagan beliefs.

Other consequences of Christianization revealed themselves much sooner, almost immediately. The unity of the Rous' Lands had previously been constituted as parallel submissions of individual tribes to the prince and his retinue, so the act of political submission to the same authority was the main thing the multicultural populations had in common. Now, the Rous' Lands were redefined, at least nominally, as the common territory of Christians. The East–West Schism of 1054 completed the convergence of political and cultural borders of the Kyiv prince's country, now surrounded by the lands of pagans, Muslims, or Catholics.

The adoption of monotheism as a spiritual system based on book knowledge led to the dissemination and even institutionalization of literacy in the bookish Church Slavonic language, across all the Rous' Lands. As per the chronicler,

> He [Vladimir] began to build churches in other cities [besides Kyiv] and to appoint priests to them, and to bring people for baptism in all the cities and villages. He ordered taking children from the best people and subjecting them to book learning. The mothers of these children cried for them as if they were dead, for they were not yet strong in faith.

By mastering the new, universal cultural canon, the children of the "best people" of local tribes were losing connection to specific local traditions and thus "dying" as members of old cultural groups. Instead of reproducing the ancestral cultural canon, they participated in the formation of a new pan-Rousian Christian culture and a new, common tradition.

The formation of a unified Christian high culture did not mean that the previous diversity of lands and tribes was obliterated. Such an impression can form only when one perceives the few preserved literary texts of that era, created within a narrow layer of the cultural elite, as representative of the spiritual world of the entire population. The idea that this whole population spoke the common Old Russian language is similar to the assumption that everyone in medieval Europe spoke the same Latin language because it was the language of high culture and hence of the majority of primary sources at our disposal. The nontextual cultural traditions and vernacular languages of various Slavic, Finnish, Baltic, Iranian, and other tribes persisted and continued to develop after 988, but simultaneously the common transtribal cultural space of Eastern Christianity was broadening and evolving. Without abolishing the need to command at least the basics of several languages spoken by neighbors, this new common cultural space created an entirely novel context for the development of political forms.

Organization of Princely Power

As soon as he established himself in Kyiv, Vladimir undertook a series of military campaigns, largely following in the footsteps of his father Sviatoslav. But even the scanty information provided by the chronicle conveys the important difference between the

Self-Organization of Northern Eurasia's First Polities

two rulers: Sviatoslav was seeking booty for his retinue, and Vladimir was trying to consolidate control over adjacent territories. Thus, in 981, "Vladimir defeated the Vyatichians and imposed tribute upon them [levied] from each plow, just as his father did." Indeed, fifteen years earlier, "Sviatoslav defeated the Vyatichians and imposed a tribute upon them," but for some reason Vladimir had to conquer them again. Moreover, the following year (982), "the Vyatichians took up arms, and Vladimir went against them and defeated them a second time." This is the Primary Chronicle's first mention of a subordinate people's rebellion, at least since reporting the Drevlianians' attempt to cancel membership in the Rous' Lands after the death of Prince Oleg in 913. Apparently, Sviatoslav raised levy from the Vyatichians as a onetime measure: he never returned to their land again and did not create a mechanism securing their subordinate status in his absence. Vladimir tried to achieve exactly this, much to the surprise of Vyatichians who seemed not to understand the nature of their new subordinated position judging by their attempt to restore the status quo right after their initial defeat.

The same logic is revealed in Vladimir's actions toward Volga Bulgaria and Khazaria. The description of his campaign against the Bulgars in 985 explicitly defies its predatory motives. Sviatoslav would have been shocked to learn that his son refused to levy a tribute on a people who looked too rich to him!

> Vladimir advanced on the Bulgars with his uncle Dobrynia by boats [via Novgorod and the Volga–Baltic route from the north?] bringing the Torks on horseback along the shore [from the south?], and thus defeated the Bulgars. Dobrynia said to Vladimir: "I have checked the captured prisoners: they are all in jackboots. They will not pay us tribute—let's go and look for [other] people, who wear bast shoes." So Vladimir made peace with the Bulgars, and they pledged an oath to each other, and the Bulgars said: "There will be peace between us until the stone begins to float and the hops to sink." And Vladimir returned to Kyiv.

Obviously, once defeated, people "in jackboots" were a much more preferable object of pillaging than a poor tribe in bast shoes, but their political subordination to the distant and less sophisticated Rous' society was highly problematic. Instead of ruining Bulgaria, Vladimir concluded a treaty with the emir and seriously considered conversion to Islam. The subsequent 1006 treaty with Volga Bulgaria allowed merchants of both countries to freely trade along the Volga. In 1024, the starving population of the upper Volga Rous' Lands turned to the Bulgars for help: "There was great disorder and famine throughout that country; everybody went along the Volga to the Bulgars, and transported bread [from them], and thus recuperated (*ozhili*)."

The same pragmatism manifested itself in relations with waning Khazaria: according to the chronicle, in 985, Vladimir went to war on the khaganate and defeated it. Instead of pillaging it, Vladimir imposed a regular tribute on Khazaria, which signified a recognition of political dependence, and put his son Mstislav in place as ruler of the former Khazar port city of Tamantarkhan on the Taman Peninsula (Tmutarakan of Russian sources). In this way, Vladimir symbolically claimed the political legacy of the Khazar Khaganate, its lands now under varying degrees of subordination to the Rous'

Lands—of course, with the significant exception of the steppe belt, now completely controlled by the Pechenegs.

To maintain the cohesion of the old and newly annexed territories, Vladimir integrated local clan and tribal elders in the ranks of town constables (*sotskie*) and chiliarchs (*tysiatskie*) into the nascent administrative apparatus. Thus, they were becoming part of the unified "civil" hierarchy, parallel to the military hierarchy of the retinue. He also resorted to a method tried by his father with dire consequences: appointing his sons as governors of individual lands. The libidinous and prolific Vladimir fathered at least thirteen sons, twelve of whom were given control over different regions. What was novel in this decision is that their principalities did not coincide with the old tribal territories but were formed around significant cities. According to the chronicle, this was Vladimir's first undertaking after the adoption of Christianity. He inaugurated a triple system of integration of the Rous' Lands— through a single cultural and confessional space, governed by members of one princely family, and structured by administrative rather than tribal units.

To avoid the paralysis of central power, similar to the crisis of 977, Vladimir established an official political and genealogical hierarchy: the eldest of the male siblings was to become the grand prince of all the Rous' Lands and rule in Kyiv, and all the local princes were subordinate to him. The next oldest brother was the immediate successor to the office, followed in line of succession by the third brother, and so forth. Then the elder brother's eldest son would begin to rule, and the succession sequence was repeated. This "ladder" order of succession was completely unfamiliar to the Scandinavian princes and alien to the Slavs, but characteristic of the Eurasian nomads. Obviously, it was deliberately adopted by Vladimir, and precisely as a rational political principle, since it did not rely on the corresponding kinship structures in Slavic, Finnish, or Scandinavian clans.

Equally consciously, Vladimir adopted another element of the nomadic society's political culture. The author of the *Sermon on Law and Grace* compiled around 1040, Kyivan Metropolitan Hilarion, calls him "khagan," using the same title to address Grand Prince Yaroslav, who ruled during the writing of the *Sermon*. In the diplomatic relations of Khazaria and Byzantium, it was assumed that the "khagan" was equivalent to the "emperor" as the ruler of ordinary princes and kingdoms. Arab and European authors had called the Rous' princes "khagans" back in the ninth century, but it is difficult to say how adequately some original meaning was conveyed by this term, after several stages of cultural and literal linguistic translation, and whether those princes used this title themselves. However, in the case of Hilarion, we have a junior contemporary of Vladimir, who shared his language and culture yet addressed him as "khagan" despite the double Christian and Slavic alienation from the religiously Judaic and Turkic- and Iranian-speaking political elite of the Khazar Khaganate. Apparently, both the Orthodox Metropolitan Hilarion and the prince of the Slavic-Finnish-Scandinavian Rous' Lands realized that the single cultural and political space created by Vladimir, uniting different tribes and local political unions, was not comparable with an ordinary principality, even a very large one; its ruler deserved the highest title known in Northern Eurasia: khagan.

The Emerging Rous' Lands as a Form of Groupness

And so, the story went full circle, closing a certain stage of the complex historical process, which began in the eighth century CE at the southern border of Northern Eurasia—at that time, a space that was not structured or marked in any universal cultural categories. The emergence of the Khazar Khaganate in the steppes of the northern Black Sea and the Caspian Sea regions was the result of the revolutionary transformation of yet another steppe confederation of Turkic and Iranian-speaking nomadic tribes. As a result of spontaneous processes of self-organization and response to the challenges of their sedentary southern neighbors, these tribes consolidated on new principles, partially integrating into the wide cultural space of ancient agricultural civilizations on their own terms. The Khazars gave an impetus to the further cultural exploration of Northern Eurasia in the universal language of monotheistic religions: Judaism, Islam, and Christianity. Scattered territories of friendly or hostile tribes who worshiped their own deities, spoke their own languages, and led diverse ways of life began increasingly coming into contact in the process of population migrations and raids. More than anything else, it was mutual interest in trade that made sporadic interactions systematic; to make them meaningful, cultural models needed a way to envision society beyond the local solidarity of a clan or a tribe. The Bulgars who resettled up the Volga River distanced themselves from the Khazars by means of universal cultural (primarily religious) mechanisms. The Bulgars became an intermediate link in the emerging chain of local ties that soon developed into a transcontinental channel of economic and cultural interaction, crossing Northern Eurasia from Scandinavia to Central Asia along the Volga–Baltic trade route.

Part of eastern Europe from the Karelian Isthmus to the lower reaches of the Dnieper presents a vivid example of the processes of social and political self-organization at work, similar to the ones that had led to the emergence of the Khazar Khaganate. Of course, the historical circumstances of the Lake Ilmen region in the mid-ninth century differed from the conditions of the northern Black Sea region at the beginning of the eighth century, but the basic principle of historical transformation was similar. One can see how quite random circumstances coincided with the conscious efforts of people who belonged to different cultures but were trying to find a common language to achieve a common goal. They often misunderstood the intentions and behavioral logic of the "other," but these erroneous mutual projections and misunderstandings produced not only conflicts but also a new—common—social and cultural reality.

The impossibility of single-handedly monopolizing control over the strategic Volga–Baltic trade route forced various sociocultural communities ("tribes") to seek compromise and coordinate their efforts. The wandering communities of the Scandinavian warriors entered into a rather unexpected symbiosis with the local communities of farmers and hunters. The cooperation of two fairly primitive social systems produced very complex relations of territorial control and the redistribution of resources in common interests—elements of nascent statehood. Relying not on any, then nonexistent, theoretical schemes, but on precedents of contemporary political formations—the Scandinavian chiefdoms, Volga Bulgaria, Khazaria, and Byzantium— the rulers of the territory that became known as the Rous' Lands tried to find their way.

It was an irony of history, both accidental and logically prearranged, that the ruler of the most extensive autonomous cultural space of Northern Eurasia at the end of the first millennium CE called himself a khagan, just like the ruler of Khazaria, which gave the initial impetus to the internal crystallization of social and political unity in this part of the continent.

From the very beginning, the Rous' Lands emerged as a supratribal and supracultural community. Initially connected only by a common interest in maintaining trade routes and the supreme political power of the Varangian retinue, by 1000 CE, the Rous' Lands became so culturally and politically integrated that the name of the country, derived from the designation of its ruling institution (the retinue–Rous'), began to be perceived as an ethnonym (name of the people). Indeed, after the 980s, the chronicle ceases to mention the former tribal names of territories. Instead of historical lands, from then on, it began referring to new political formations—cities and the principalities surrounding them. This does not mean that numerous cultural, linguistic, and even religious "tribal" differences had disappeared. However, along with them and gradually marginalizing them, appeared new ways of thinking of the Rous' Lands, which envisioned the territory under the control of the Kyiv grand prince as a single cultural and political space inhabited by a population cognizant of this unity. In reality, the stratum of people for whom this unity was the lived experience, communicated and remembered via the medium of a common literary language and texts, was very small. But many people at least had the possibility of thinking of themselves as part of a vast cultural entity under certain circumstances—for example, during a political crisis. Christianity provided that common language and common cultural environment capable of shaping the idea of a broad cultural and political unity.

According to modern social scientists, an imaginary collective of people who have never met in person, but who think of each other as members of a single community, is called a nation. Theoretically, nation is opposed to ethnos (or ethnicity) as a community based on shared ideology and culture—to a commonality of origin, customs, and everything that is associated with "corporeality" and biologically determined behavior. Sometimes this opposition is interpreted as a contrast between an "invented" community and an "objectively existing" kinship. These interpretations and this very opposition between the two forms of groupness are rather archaic, popular in the mid-twentieth century, but rooted in reasoning dating back to the nineteenth century. As studies by anthropologists or historians of nomadic cultures show, "ethnicity" and "tribe" are no more "objective" collectives than modern nations that are formed under the influence of standardized schooling, common literature, and the political process. On the example of Northern Eurasia—be it the Great Steppe or the forests of the north—we see how a constant mixing of the population perpetuates in the course of migrations, wars, and reconfigurations of nomadic confederations, even if the previous tribal names are preserved. In practice, it is impossible to clearly distinguish between the Iranian-, Turkic- and Mongol-speaking groups of nomads, even when we know the names of the tribes. Likewise, it is impossible to determine the proportion in which different Slavic, Baltic, and Finnish tribes "intermixed" in different territories. Disputes continue today about the origin

Self-Organization of Northern Eurasia's First Polities 91

of the "Slavic" pagan gods and their differentiation from the Baltic or Iranian ones. The concept of "ethnogenesis" as a biological process going on for centuries emerged at the beginning of the twentieth century from a combination of limited historical knowledge and nationalist (ranging from romantic to fascist) ideological fantasies of intellectuals and politicians of that time. The popular fascination with ideas of "the purity of the race" and the unity of "blood and soil" in the twentieth century forced historians to seek the "original" inhabitants of the territories in Europe, where, a millennium later, attempts were made to carve out mononational and monocultural states.

It would likely be a wild exaggeration to call the people of the Rous' Lands around 1000 CE a "nation," but any speculations about the formation of one or another common "ethnicity" are even more arbitrary. At least, the term "nation" does not describe some physical reality, but only the way we depict—from the outside, as students—a particular logic in which a society functions, as demonstrated by its members. "Ethnicity," on the other hand, is a fantasy about the reality of blood kinship and common historical fate based on this circumstance, which is doubtful by itself. True, the historical sources suggest that the inhabitants of the Rous' Lands gradually began to identify themselves as Rus', Ruthenians (_rus'kie_), and eventually as Russians, and later they invented myths of common origin for themselves. However, historians should not forget that this emerging unity was rooted in a political community of elementary statehood and a universal cultural code forged by Christianity and the literary Church Slavonic language. These foundational elements by themselves did not make everyone "Slavs" or "Russians." Like a modern nation, the emerging community of the Rous' Lands was held together by common ideas, economic interests, and political institutions. At the same time, it was susceptible to radical reconfigurations in the event of fundamental changes in circumstances.

What is truly surprising is that on a territory exceeding the area occupied by the empire of Charlemagne during the heyday of its brief existence, from an extremely culturally diverse population, lacking any preexisting unifying tradition, a fairly integrated and stable cultural and political entity was formed, called the Rous' Lands. Still, history never stops: this relatively integrated space, which many have already begun to take for granted, has become the arena of a new stage in the history of Northern Eurasia as a space that is being simultaneously mastered and interpreted by its inhabitants.

Notes

1 This and the following quotes from the Chronicle are translated from the Russian edition prepared by Oleg Tvorogov on the basis of the Hypatian codex as, arguably, more authentically representing the phrasing of the initial version of the text. The available English translation of the Primary Chronicle is _The Russian Primary Chronicle: Laurentian Text_, translated and edited by Samuel Hazzard Cross and Olgerd P. Sherbowitz-Wetzor (Cambridge, MA: Medieval Academy of America, 1953).

2 English translation: *The Annals of Saint Bertin*, translated by Janet Nelson (Manchester, 1991), 44. The original spelling of key terms is added in square brackets.
3 *The History of Leo the Deacon: Byzantine Military Expansion in the Tenth Century*, Introduction, translation, and annotation by Denis F. Sullivan and Alice-Mary Talbot (Washington, DC: Dumbarton Oaks, 2005), 199.

Further reading

Franklin, Simon and Jonathan Shephard. *The Emergence of Rus, 750–1200*. London: Longman, 1996.

Montgomery, James. "Ibn Faḍlān and the Rūsiyyah." *Journal of Arabic and Islamic Studies* 3 (2000): 1–25.

Obolensky, Dimitri. *The Byzantine Commonwealth, 500–1453*. Ann Arbor: Praeger Publishers, 1971.

Pritsak, Omeljan. *The Origins of Rus'*. Cambridge, MA: Harvard Ukrainian Research Institute, 1981.

Raffensperger, Christian. *Reimagining Europe: Kievan Rus' in the Medieval World*. Cambridge, MA: Harvard University Press, 2012.

3

Consolidation of New Political Systems

State-Building in Northern Eurasia
(Eleventh–Thirteenth Centuries)

In 1000 CE, Northern Eurasia was already very different from the loose conglomerate of semi-isolated cultural worlds that it had been only two centuries earlier. Its frontiers were drawn into the sphere of influence of one or another southern universalist culture (e.g., the Bulgarian Kingdom on the Danube—into the sphere of Byzantium). Taking place in western Europe was a complex synthesis of Roman statehood's reconsidered heritage and the customs of various "barbarian" tribes. By contrast, Volga Bulgaria and the Rous' Lands presented an example of the autochthonous development of complex political forms still based on the cultural code of one of the world religions. As a result, the habitable space unknown to the surrounding world—unintegrated or not expressing itself in universal categories—was shrinking.

In the summer of 1000, Iceland, an island that the Vikings began to colonize in the days of Rurik, voluntarily converted to Christianity. Much more dramatic was the conversion to Christianity of the Viking homeland—Norway. Starting from the mid-tenth century, its kings made attempts to convert its subjects to the new faith but encountered unified resistance. Around 1000 CE, King Olaf I (Olav Tryggvason) made the Christianization of Norway a systematic policy, erecting the first church in 995. Implementing this policy, he was not shy about resorting to torture and death threats and lost his own life in 1000 largely as a result of his aggressive proselytism. His ambition to become the Christian ruler of all Scandinavia brought him into armed conflict with a coalition of opposing kings and he died in a sea battle. However, his death did not stop the Christianization of Norway during the next decades, under Olaf's successors.

On Christmas Day 1000, or January 1, 1001, the leader of the Hungarian tribes, Vajk, was crowned by the papal legate (authorized representative) as King Stephen (István) I of Hungary. Pope Sylvester II conferred on him the previously unheard-of title of His Apostolic Majesty, in recognition of his efforts to spread Christianity. Indeed, by the end of his reign, Stephen I had established up to ten new dioceses. Just as it had happened in the Rous' Lands, the Christianization of the Hungarians contributed to the process of political consolidation, when the old tribal division was replaced by new administrative and diocesan boundaries. In this way, the western outskirts of the

Great Steppe on the Middle Danube, once controlled by the militant Avar Khaganate and occupied since the late ninth century by nomadic Hungarians (Magyars) from the Khazar Khaganate, became part of the Christian world. The parallel Christianization of Norway and neighboring Scandinavian kingdoms transformed northern Europe—the homeland of the Vikings—from a forbidden land, the abode of infernal evil in the eyes of the Franks, into a part of the common cultural space. Integration into a common cultural space did not offer protection from wars and predatory raids, but it brought the conflict into a more productive plane of interaction between parties capable of understanding each other and negotiating.

Populated areas of Northern Eurasia were integrating into the "big world" in the east as much as in the west. In the tenth century, Islam began to spread among the Turkic-speaking nomads of Central Asia, whereas they began to interact more and more closely with the agricultural oases of Mawarannahr (Transoxiana). In 1001 CE, the Samanid dynasty fell: the territory to the north of the Amu Darya was now controlled by the Turkic-speaking Kara-Khanid Khanate, and to the south—by the Oghuz Turks ruled by the Ghaznavid dynasty. The policy of these Turkic rulers was largely shaped by old tribal alliances and conflicts but now staged in the new, universal context of the vast Islamic world. Between 1001 and 1026, the Ghaznavids invaded the Indian subcontinent seventeen times, each campaign accompanied by colossal destruction and plunder. However, unlike the usual devastating raids of the nomadic Turks, the Ghaznavids' expansionism had much more fundamental consequences: the northwest of the Indian subcontinent was included in the sphere of the Islamic world. The Turkic rulers (in both the north and the south) adopted the Arab-Persian culture and administrative system and found themselves assimilated into the Islamic cultural canon. Obviously, it was only a matter of time before the steppe neighbors of the Turks farther to the east—various Mongol tribes and confederations—would follow their example and enter into direct and systematic interaction with the "big world." [1]

Against the backdrop of the gradual integration of Northern Eurasia's periphery into the orbit of neighboring universalist cultural and political formations, the inner territories of the region, which did not share borders with influential neighbors, present particular interest. They were also "opening up" to the world and contemplating their inner space in one of the universal cultural codes, but at the same time they did not rely on any ready-made borrowed sociopolitical scenarios. The Volga Bulgaria and the Rous' Lands were early examples of such societies that developed in dialogue with global cultural centers (the caliphate and Byzantium), without recourse to any preexisting local traditions of statehood and universal culture.

Political Processes in the Rous' Lands in the Eleventh–Thirteenth Centuries

The multifaceted reforms of the Kyiv prince Vladimir Sviatoslavich (Sviatoslav's son) completed the formation of the Rous' Lands as a common cultural and political supratribal space. Calling this space a state is possible only with numerous reservations,

Consolidation of New Political Systems

since the power of the Kyiv prince reached many territories in such a mediated and delegated form through a chain of representatives or surrogates that it lost the very character of "central power." The empire of Charlemagne (800–14) offers some historical parallels to the Rous' Lands of the post-Vladimir period (he died in 1015), although the differences between them are very significant. For one, despite the fact that the Carolingian Empire at its peak covered just half the area of the Rous' Lands, it began to disintegrate almost immediately after the death of the first emperor. The Treaty of Verdun, signed thirty years later in 843, fixed the boundaries of the divided empire between Charles's three grandchildren. The political transformation of the Rous' Lands took more than one century, and the divisions of the common cultural and political space were revised and reconfigured many times. The modern concept of "commonwealth" implying a voluntary recognition of the central government's legitimacy and the commonality of political space seems to characterize the Rous' Lands more accurately than "empire." This legitimacy and commonality were little more than a very general framework that implied common norms of behavior, administrative techniques, and legal norms. Individual princes could rely on this framework in their policies or ignore it, since the commonwealth, unlike the empire, suggested a more loose organization.

The Veche as a Cornerstone of the Political System

The complex political system of the Rous' Lands included as only one of its elements the imperial, nesting-doll-like hierarchy of power, in which the "kings" of individual countries obeyed the "emperor," and the "dukes" and "counts" of provinces and regions obeyed the "kings." True, Vladimir Sviatoslavich tried on the imperial title of "khagan," perceiving himself as the "prince of princes," and some of his successors followed suit. But the grand prince of Kyiv was not the only or even the main source of local rulers' authority. Even after the original confederation of tribes was converted to a more integrated political entity by the reforms of Vladimir Sviatoslavich, the old community centers retained their role as independent political factors. Now they were institutionalized as urban communes and expressed their collective will at popular assemblies—the veche. The versions of old chronicles that have survived explicitly demonstrate a strong anti-veche bias, directly related to their apologetic attitude toward princely power. Nevertheless, historians have been able to find evidence in the chronicles of the veche's existence in most of the Rous' Lands and to reconstruct the main functions of this institution. The majority of researchers agree that the city veche was an independent element of a complex political structure, supplementing princely power and putting certain constraints on it. City communes usually emerged on the basis of the former tribal centers, and even when the communal will was not expressed through formal veche convocation, there were other ways of communicating the interests of the local population, especially its most influential and patrician part.

Theoretically, the veche of the eleventh century might have been a continuation of the tribal popular assemblies of the previous centuries, like those that probably concluded a contract–agreement (*riad*) with the first invited Varangian retinues. Unfortunately, no reliable information has been preserved about them, unlike the veche of the eleventh century. It is known that the veche was an urban phenomenon—apparently, the veche was not convened in villages and suburbs. It was anything but a spontaneous rally: the meeting followed a clear ritual with its own rules, and it is possible that the proceedings were recorded. The participants of the veche were sitting, not standing, and the designated veche squares were probably furnished with benches. This "technical" detail—capacity of the squares—allows us to estimate the number of veche participants confidently, even in famous veche centers such as Novgorod or Kyiv as no more than 300–400 people. This means that the veche was not the popular assembly imagined by historians as a convocation of all free adults or just free men. Apparently, only members of a certain privileged stratum of townspeople and possibly some in the adjacent countryside could participate in the veche. So far, we can only guess about the social composition of these urban "notables": what role, if any, was played by the former tribal aristocracy, merchants (especially in Novgorod), the new civil administration—constables (*sotskie*) and chiliarchs (*tysiatskie*).

The political model formed in the Rous' Lands by the beginning of the eleventh century was based on the balance and functional differentiation of the authority of the veche and the prince. The veche expressed the consolidated position of the "land" as a forum of local elites: the clan aristocracy, the wealthy, elected or appointed magistrates. In this capacity, the veche entered into a relationship with the prince, who remained an alien political force to the commune: the princes moved from one city to another, dreaming of eventually occupying the Kyiv throne. At the same time, the veche was not a body of executive power: it did not manage the city and adjacent region on a day-to-day basis and could not even control the implementation of its own decision if it required time to execute. The veche's main task was to maintain relations with the prince as head of the local government. Without the consent of the veche, even if a forced one, the prince could not take office. The veche was in a position to invite another candidate for the job in the event that the previous prince violated the accepted norms, died, or fled the city. Therefore, the occasional expression of the communal will by the veche did not make it purely a formality: the veche sanctioned the very legitimacy of the princely power.

Scenarios of the Transfer of Princely Power

Although Vladimir Sviatoslavich attempted to formalize the system of princely rule to avoid the risk of fratricidal conflicts, even in the most ideal case, the transfer of princely power could proceed according to one of three legitimate scenarios, which modern historians characterize as *invitation, consent,* and *conquest.*

According to the chronicle, Rurik was invited to reign by a confederation of Slavic and Finnish tribes, and Vladimir Sviatoslavich himself was invited by the Novgorodians, who simply demanded that his father provide them with a legitimate ruler—a representative of the princely family. The *invitations* of princes by the veche are registered in later periods as well, in different parts of the Rous' Lands, including Kyiv in the eleventh and twelfth centuries. This may even seem surprising, since the invitation scenario implies that demand exceeds supply, such that there are many vacant offices and a city commune had to make an extra effort to find the most suitable

Consolidation of New Political Systems

candidate. However, by the beginning of the eleventh century, every city of the Rous' Land already had princes who tried to preserve their power and even transfer it to their heirs, so there were more contenders than there were princedoms for them. The fact that the institution of the prince's invitation did not disappear during this period confirms the potency of the veche. It continued to convey the political will of the city commune, and the princes had to reckon with it.

The transfer of power to the prince's heir was by no means guaranteed—hereditary monarchy did not exist in the Rous' Lands. In those cases when power was transferred to a close relative without conflict, there is always a mention of *consent* to this transfer of the retinue and the city commune, with the latter having the final say. Notable precedents included the transfer of the principality to an uncle, brother, son, or nephew. Often the heir was the prince's former coruler, de facto or officially (as, apparently, was the case with Princess Olga and her son Sviatoslav). In any event, the main candidate for the next "invitation" was already present, familiar to the retinue and the commune, so unless they had special objections, he was "glorified." This was a special term for the inauguration of a "domestic" candidate for the office. In cases when the prince was invited from outside, he was "accepted." Although the transfer of princely power to an heir was possible, only the Polotsk princes managed to keep the city under the rule of one family for several generations (from 987 to 1129), forming a separate dynasty. In other cities, even if the retinue and the veche agreed on the successor chosen by the prince, intervention by contenders-outsiders was almost inevitable, thus making the arranged transfer of power highly problematic.

Indeed, the number of qualified candidates for the office of local prince exceeded the available vacancies, and the more prestigious the place, the greater the number of contenders seeking it. Leading their communes of warriors–retinues, princes conducted something similar to primaries among themselves according to their own rules, before seeking recognition of their claims to power by the veche. Actually, military prowess and resolve were the main qualifying criteria for the successful candidate, so when city communes accepted the victorious prince, they were not only submitting to force but recognizing his princely worthiness. The story of the confrontation between the sons of the Kyiv prince Sviatoslav, discussed in the previous chapter, is a classic illustration of the *conquest* strategy as the combination of a routine political process and an extraordinary form of military confrontation. Key to this combination was the use of violence within clearly outlined boundaries: it was not to affect the city, its inhabitants, and their property, so opponents engaged each other on an open field. In the event of a prolonged siege of the city, the besieged prince was obliged to come out for battle or negotiate—this is how Vladimir's half-brother Yaropolk, who reigned in Kyiv, was killed. Having occupied Kyiv, Vladimir did not allow his troops to plunder the city, in contrast to many conquerors in later periods, but he even refused to collect the ransom from the townspeople, which he had promised to the retinue. By the twelfth century, killing the opponent was no longer perceived as a necessary prerequisite for victory, and a military defeat alone disqualified a pretender to the princely seat.

Simultaneously with such legitimate wars as elements of a ritualized process of political competition, there were also devastating raids on neighboring principalities characterized by merciless plunder and the taking of numerous captives. Instances of such raids became increasingly frequent in the second half of the eleventh century, when even monasteries and churches were pillaged. These predatory raids also had political meaning, undermining the authority of the prince, who had failed to protect his subjects from invaders, and hence weakening the rival principality. However, if such a raider conquered the city, the legitimacy of his claims to power in the devastated principality remained questionable in the eyes of both other princes and locals: the prince was an alien political force, but this force could not be openly hostile to the city commune, acting as an "occupant."

The prince's complex relations with the city commune were reflected in the ritual of assumption of power. The successful contender for the office was solemnly met outside the city walls by the entire population—as if emphasizing his status as a stranger, not a local. When the prince approached, everybody bowed in a sign of general recognition of his rights to power. Then the prince entered the city and proceeded to the main cathedral, where he was greeted by the higher clergy. The ceremony of enthronement took place in the cathedral or in the prince's official residence. After that, leaving the cathedral or the palace, the prince was greeted by a jubilant crowd, "glorifying" the new ruler: a personal manifestation of joy was an expression of individual loyalty. The prince publicly concluded an "agreement" (oral contract) with the city, secured by a mutual oath ("kissing the cross"). The ceremony ended with a common feast at the prince's court, which was a relic of an ancient ritual of unequal exchange: the prince treated the townspeople, symbolically putting them in a dependent position. Now they had to repay him with a good attitude and loyalty.

Prince Vladimir's Model of the Harmonious Rurikid Princedom and Its Failure

Prince Vladimir's attempt to turn the Rous' Lands into a single cultural and political entity under the rule of one princely dynasty had only partial success. Vladimir and his sons succeeded in spreading the power network centered in Kyiv to a vast territory, bringing under its sway the former subjects of the Khazar Khaganate in the forest-steppe zone along the Dnieper and those lands along the Volga–Baltic and Baltic–Dnieper trade routes, in which independent Varangian retinues remained. However, instead of consolidating all power under the coordinated control of one family, what happened was a radical reconfiguration of both the princely power and the nature of family relations in the princely clan. This is the fundamental quality of complex and heterogeneous societies: an attempt to rationalize and regulate their diversity only results in enhancing their complexity.

After three and a half decades of Prince Vladimir's reign, it became universally accepted that only a direct descendant of Rurik, the founder of the clan, could be considered a legitimate contender for any princely seat. However, instead of an orderly distribution of principalities by seniority as envisioned by Vladimir's original scheme of succession, the Rurikids entered into open political competition with each other. The ruling family, united by ties of kinship, transformed into a particular legal estate of certified princes. Only belonging to this estate gave the right to reign but in no way guaranteed the occupation of a certain princely office. Once again, we witness the

Consolidation of New Political Systems

transformation of private (family) relations into a public (political) institution. The very idea that the prince occupies the throne temporarily, until, in order of seniority, he moves to a more significant one, as well as the conditionality of this transition in practice by the consent of the city commune, greatly accelerated the transformation of personal ties into political relations. To become a ruling prince, it was not enough to be the eldest in the family—it was also necessary to demonstrate one's princely fitness, which usually required a battle with another family member. Under these circumstances, political considerations necessarily undermined familial sentiments.

Prince Vladimir himself damaged the ideal system he had created when, at the end of his life, he elevated the status of one of his younger sons, Boris, by appointing him commander of his retinue. In fact, this meant the announcement of Boris as coruler, which gave him a great chance to become Vladimir's successor as the grand prince of Kyiv following the scenario of the city commune's consent. The eldest of Vladimir's sons, Sviatopolk, rebelled against the blatant violation of the rules: contrary to the official principle of seniority, Vladimir did not allow him to leave Turov (the former tribal center of the Dregovichians on the territory of modern Belarus) for almost thirty years. The Novgorod prince Yaroslav also rebelled, although, unlike Sviatopolk, he was making an exemplary princely career: in about 1011 he moved on from his initial position in Rostov to more prestigious Novgorod and had every reason to expect Kyiv to become the next station. On the side of Sviatopolk was formal seniority, while Yaroslav occupied the key Novgorod princely office. In addition, Yaroslav was Vladimir's own son, whereas Sviatopolk was the adopted child of Vladimir's slain elder brother Yaropolk.

These circumstances might be of secondary importance from the standpoint of intrafamily relations, but their political significance was great. Apparently, Sviatopolk arrived in Kyiv to confront his father in a peaceful way, because he ended up being arrested along with his wife and her confessor, and put up no resistance. Yaroslav acted from a distance and more aggressively—he refused to send his father the usual share of the locally collected annual tribute, and instead invited Varangian mercenaries to Novgorod to beef up his forces. Judging by these few details, Sviatopolk, who arrived in Kyiv with his wife, intended to negotiate; Yaroslav was contemplating an armed coup. In the summer of 1015, Prince Vladimir died. When the news came, his young son Boris was far from Kyiv with his retinue, repelling the raid of the nomads the Pechenegs. The retinue and the Kyiv militia offered that Boris take power as the Kyiv prince "by consent," but Boris categorically refused to violate the order of succession established by his father and recognized his eldest brother Sviatopolk as Vladimir's legitimate successor. Kyivans released Sviatopolk from captivity and proclaimed him their prince—but only after Boris publicly denounced any intent to claim the Kyiv throne and after Sviatopolk won over the sympathies of the veche "electorate" by generous distribution of gifts. Yaroslav did not recognize Sviatopolk's legitimacy and went to war against Kyiv. [2]

A series of battles outside the city walls followed. First, Yaroslav defeated Sviatopolk and took over Kyiv. Then Sviatopolk returned, bringing as allies the nomadic Pechenegs and also the army of his father-in-law, the Duke of Poland and future first Polish king, Bolesław I the Brave. Yaroslav was defeated and fled to Novgorod. He even tried to escape overseas to the Varangians, but the Novgorodians damaged the ships that were ready to sail and forced their prince to continue the fight. They raised funds to hire new Varangian mercenaries and mobilized the militia for the new military campaign. Thus, both sides acted within the logic of the accepted scenarios of contentious politics, with the city commune playing an important role as the final arbiter and even a key ally (as in the case of Yaroslav). At the same time, adherence to certain rules of the political process did not prevent participants from violating ethical norms and demonstrating extreme cruelty toward opponents–siblings.

During the first period of confrontation, three sons of Prince Vladimir, who were not even active contenders for the Kyiv throne, were killed. The murder of all three was later attributed to Sviatopolk, whom the chronicles nicknamed "The Accursed" and condemned for fratricide. However, two of the victims—Prince Vladimir's favorite son Boris and the Murom prince Gleb—were the only brothers who immediately and unconditionally recognized the legitimacy of Sviatopolk as the next grand prince of Kyiv. Both of them were killed on their way to Kyiv, where they set out for upon Sviatopolk's invitation, and their murder could only be politically beneficial to Yaroslav. The third victim of the conflict, the Drevlianian prince Sviatoslav, was killed in the Carpathian Mountains while trying to escape to his Czech or Hungarian allies. It is assumed that he was also slain by Sviatopolk, but the information about Sviatoslav is too scarce to either confirm or question this version. It is not even known exactly when Sviatoslav was born. According to one version, Sviatoslav was older than Yaroslav, which meant that he was one step closer to the Kyiv throne and thus, legally, a rival of Yaroslav. Finally, in 1019, Yaroslav's army defeated Sviatopolk's army in a battle on the Alta River (in about the same place where Boris was killed). Wounded, Sviatopolk fled to the Pechenegs and allegedly vanished in the steppes. Besides the chronicle that was closely censored by ruling princes, another main historical source about these events is the saga *Eymundar þáttr hrings* from a fourteenth-century Icelandic compendium, which tells about the participation of Varangian warriors in the conflict between Yaroslav and Sviatopolk. According to the saga, the main enemy of the "king Jarizleif" led the army of Turkic nomads to Kyiv and was killed by the Varangians with the tacit approval of Jarizleif, who said, "I will do none of this: I will not encourage anyone to clash with king Burizleif, nor will I blame anyone if he is killed."

The name of the King Burizleif and the circumstances of his murder (sleeping in his tent, at night) coincide with the history of Prince Boris, whereas the general description of his confrontation with Jarizleif (Yaroslav) as the main enemy, a contender for the Kyiv throne, relying on the Pechenegs' support instead identifies Burizleif with Sviatopolk. Either way, Yaroslav sanctioned the murder of his brother by the Varangians, although he did not want to take personal responsibility for his brother's death. He was engaged in political struggle, not personal confrontation, so the murder was a "technical" episode in this struggle. It was left to the discretion of the military to decide how to eliminate the threat from Sviatopolk, who repeatedly returned with new reinforcements. Characteristically, during the fratricidal conflict a generation earlier, in which Prince Vladimir emerged victorious, the death of rival siblings was perceived as collateral damage. The murder of one's brother was mourned

Yaroslav the Wise: Consolidation of a Common Space of Persisting Diversity

In 1019, the political crisis was overcome, Yaroslav became the unchallenged grand prince of Kyiv and ruled until his death in 1054—as if repeating the thirty-five-year reign of his father, also in the wake of the fratricidal war. Whatever Yaroslav's actual role in the deaths of his siblings–rivals, which was extremely reprehensible by the standards of the recently established Christian morality, he made sure that all the responsibility was put on Sviatopolk "The Accursed." By contrast, Yaroslav became known as "The Wise." This flattering epithet was substantiated not least by Yaroslav's role in codifying the customary law into the codex of laws known as *The Rous' Justice* (Pravda Rous'kaia). Just as Prince Vladimir took on the role of baptizer of the Rous' Lands, laying the foundations for their cultural unity, Prince Yaroslav became a legislator spreading uniform legal norms throughout the Rous' Lands. *The Rous' Justice* is usually compared with similar "barbaric law codes" of medieval Frankish kingdoms, composed centuries earlier, but there is also a significant difference: unlike *leges Visigothorum*, *lex Burgundionum*, and other monocultural codes, *The Rous' Justice* incorporated the customary law of the multitribal Rous' Lands. Therefore, the unification of the diverse local "tribal" norms became an important element in the development of state institutions, transforming traditions rather than exploiting them.

During the long reigns of Yaroslav and his father Vladimir, the complex political system of the Rous' Lands was consolidated and, from the outside, resembled a single, even centralized state. The grand prince personified the highest authority if not the central power itself: local princes sent two-thirds of the annual duties collected in their lands to Kyiv. Besides semicentralized taxation and putting together the code of law, this period witnessed the first minting of coins in the region. The latter measure had a purely political significance as a declaration of sovereignty. The coins produced numbered in the hundreds, which made their economic value insignificant as a means of payment in the vast Rous' Lands, although they actually circulated. Almost all known coins were minted in a short period at the turn of the eleventh century, during the formation of Vladimir's political legacy and the ensuing fight over inheriting it. The first was the gold coin minted on the initiative of Prince Vladimir, which imitated the gold solidus of the Byzantine Empire. Numismatists believe that very few of them were minted over a short period of one or two years.[3] Besides the gold coin, at the end of Vladimir's reign, a small number of silver coins was produced.[4] Around 1015, soon after Vladimir's death, the new grand prince Sviatopolk minted his own silver coins in Kyiv, while simultaneously in Novgorod Yaroslav (the Wise) produced his silver coins, which are remarkable in their perfection in comparison with the crude coins produced by his father and brother. [5] This resembled competing claims to supreme power. After that, the minting of coins in the Rous' Lands ceased for centuries. Notable exceptions were the silver coins minted in 1070 by the "outcast prince" Oleg of Tmutarakan, which circulated exclusively on the Taman Peninsula. His desperate attempts to secure a principality for himself (substantiated by this limited coinage) will be discussed later in this section.

However, the consolidation of power in the hands of the senior prince and even the minting of coins do not necessarily equal the institutionalization of statehood. Thus, simultaneously with the production of their own coins, at the beginning of the eleventh century the Rous' Lands witnessed the final division of the hitherto single monetary and weight system into two—the northern and the southern systems. The main measure of weight and currency, the grivna, became heavier in Novgorod than in Kyiv, and the greater weight of silver made its nominal purchasing power higher. This is another example demonstrating that the common space (in this case, economic) does not necessarily imply its unification. In the same way, even during the reign of Yaroslav, the internal structural pluralism of the political system persisted. The clan–class of the Rurikids continued to compete for the princely offices, and the power dualism of the prince and the city commune with its veche did not disappear. Having eliminated his brothers as rivals, the victorious grand prince appointed his sons to the regional principalities, thus laying the foundations for a new outbreak of competition among the junior princes after his death.

An Attempt to Ease Political Competition through Corulership

In the shadow of Yaroslav the Wise, ruling in Kyiv as the unchallenged grand prince, his sons migrated from one principality to another in the established order of seniority and prestige without any major conflicts. Every city needed a prince, and disputes between the competing brothers, if they occurred, were peacefully resolved by the supreme arbiter—their father, the grand prince. After Yaroslav's death, his sons managed to avoid bloodshed and come to an agreement. Following the order of succession, the eldest of the brothers, who held the position in Novgorod, Iziaslav became the next grand prince of Kyiv. However, his brothers, the Chernigov prince Sviatoslav and the Pereyaslavl prince Vsevolod, became his corulers. Together they reformed the legislation, editing *The Rous' Justice* and adopting its extended version— *The Yaroslaviches' Justice* (Pravda Yaroslavichei). Together they participated in military campaigns against the nomads and made decisions regarding the appointment of new princes to vacant offices. To equalize access to the growing political and cultural resource of the church, they established, in addition to Kyiv, two new archbishoprics, in Chernigov and Pereyaslavl. This triumvirate of the Yaroslaviches was an attempt to improve the complex political system of the Rous' Lands by alleviating its main destabilizing factor—political competition.

Corulership proved but a palliative solution to the problem. By refusing to eliminate the rival brothers, each of whom fathered numerous children, the sons of Yaroslav had greatly expanded the circle of potential contenders for power in the next generation. Now, not only brothers but also uncles and nephews entered the competition. All of them had legitimate rights to the princely office under the "ladder" order of succession inaugurated by Vladimir, but it was no longer feasible to reach a compromise that would accommodate most of the contenders as corulers. Besides, the competition among the princes without the office was only part of the problem involved in maintaining

Consolidation of New Political Systems 103

political stability. Another key player was the city commune, whose role increased as the competition among the princes intensified. The Yaroslaviches triumvirate held out for thirteen years and fell apart not so much because of contradictions between the corulers, but because one of them, Grand Prince Iziaslav, discredited himself as a legitimate prince in the eyes of the Kyiv city commune.

In 1068, the united army of three corulers, the Yaroslaviches, was defeated in a battle with the Polovtsians—a new powerful alliance of Turkic nomadic tribes who replaced the Pechenegs as masters of the steppe. After the defeat, Iziaslav fled to Kyiv. Although military defeats happen, it was still possible to lose one battle but win the war. Just a few months later, Iziaslav's brother Sviatoslav with only 3,000 troops managed to compensate for the earlier setback and defeat the fourfold superior forces of the Polovtsians, which afterward stopped their attacks for a quarter of a century. The problem was that Iziaslav, unlike his brother, refused to continue fighting and, even worse, neglected his direct obligation to the city: to protect it from enemies at any cost. The Polovtsians were ravaging the suburbs of Kyiv, so the townspeople convoked the veche, which demanded that the prince arm the militia and drive out the invaders, but Iziaslav ignored this resolution. From that moment, in the eyes of the townspeople, Iziaslav lost the right to rule and they expelled him. As his replacement, they invited the only prince who happened to be nearby—Prince Vseslav of Polotsk, who was held in Kyiv imprisoned in a dungeon. This representative of the Polotsk dynasty of princes constantly warred with the triumvirate and raided Novgorod and their other lands, for which he ended up in captivity in Kyiv. To the city commune, according to the generally accepted political scenario of that time, a foreign prince imprisoned by his rival had more rights to the local throne than their old prince, who had breached the agreement-contract for his reign.

Later, Iziaslav temporarily regained the Kyiv throne, but the triumvirate could not be restored, not least because Iziaslav discredited himself as a politician and the brothers no longer viewed him as an equal, much less senior coruler. Subsequently, on several occasions the most influential princes of the Rous' Lands would successfully arrange a peaceful redistribution of power and even corulership, albeit on a much smaller scale. For example, in 1093, after the death of the grand prince of Kyiv, Vsevolod, his son Vladimir Monomakh voluntarily renounced his claims to become the next grand prince in favor of his cousin. After weighing the odds and referring to the "ladder" order of succession (in reality, rarely observed), he thus explained his decision: "His father was older than mine and reigned in Kyiv before my [father]." Vladimir Monomakh became the grand prince of Kyiv only twenty years later, at the invitation of the Kyiv veche and the retinue. This time, nobody seemed concerned about the strict observance of the ladder principle of succession. However, the old ideal of political subordination of the entire Rous' Lands to the grand prince of Kyiv due to the filial devotion of regional princes (as in the time of Yaroslav the Wise), was already unattainable.

The "Overproduction" of Princes and an Attempt to Localize Their Competition

By the end of the eleventh century, the Rurikid princes formed a distinctive estate of the realm that was so sizable that its members had to severely compete even for offices in minor cities. The "overproduction of princes" allowed city communes to become more discriminating in the choice of a ruler and often act as the supreme arbiter in disputes between claimants. The rising independence of communes was especially visible in the north, in the Novgorod land. Since 1095, the Novgorodians had stopped considering arguments based on the formal order of succession when deciding on the candidacy of a new prince, and they began inviting princes of their choice. Legitimate but unwanted contenders were not allowed into Novgorod and could even be arrested until the arrival of the invited prince, as happened to Vsevolod Mstislavich in 1136. In the south, the city veche did not act so demonstratively, but the influence of city communes was comparable to that of Novgorod.

Many princes were frustrated by the growing competition and infuriated by the need not only to defeat their rivals but also to secure support and an invitation from the city commune. Since the last quarter of the eleventh century, battles between competing princes had more and more often violated the rules of duel-like "political" fights between two retinues on an open field. Their confrontation became more reminiscent of the ruinous invasions of foreigners trampling fields, burning down suburbs, and plundering churches and monasteries. In the old political logic, such an attitude to the city that the prince-contender wanted to rule was counterproductive. It was quite understandable if the goal was to terrorize the townspeople and break their political will. Submission was prioritized over economic prosperity.

A typical example of this new political culture was Oleg Sviatoslavich—the one who minted silver coins in Tmutarakan. His father was a member of the Yaroslaviches triumvirate, the famous victor over the Polovtsians. The fourth son of this Chernigov prince, Oleg Sviatoslavich, belonged to a growing group of "outcast princes." To these younger grandchildren of Yaroslav the Wise, not only the office of the grand prince in Kyiv but even their fathers' principalities remained out of reach. Having no means to sustain a retinue of his own, Oleg Sviatoslavich was one of the first to use the Polovtsians as allies in the struggle with other princes for the office once occupied by his father. In 1078, he captured Chernigov with the support of the Polovtsians but he was soon forced to flee to Tmutarakan. The next time he succeeded in taking hold of Chernigov in 1094, again thanks to the Polovtsians. They ravaged and plundered the outskirts of Chernigov, but even having captured the city, Oleg Sviatoslavich did not try to stop them. On the one hand, he probably had no other way to pay off his allies. But on the other hand, it was a deliberate policy of terror pursued by the ruler, who was aware of the insufficient substantiation of his claims to power (legitimacy) and therefore relied only on brute force.

His predecessor was Vladimir Monomakh, a legitimate heir to the grand prince of Kyiv, who ruled Chernigov as the son of the last local prince, apparently with the consent of the city. Vladimir acted as a legitimate prince whose duty was to protect the interests of the city by all means. After eight days of siege and visible ruin of the neighborhood by Oleg's Polovtsians, unable to repel them, Vladimir fled from Chernigov when it became clear that continued resistance would only worsen the damage to the city. Oleg Sviatoslavich, who began the siege by burning monasteries around Chernigov to intimidate the townspeople, could hardly count on their loyalty. His low prestige in the eyes of the population was demonstrated the next year, in

1095, when the inhabitants of Murom, which was part of the Chernigov principality, refused to obey Oleg Sviatoslavich and agreed to recognize as their prince Vladimir Monomakh's son. In 1096, when the joint troops of the Kyiv prince and Vladimir Monomakh marched against Oleg Sviatoslavich, he decided that he could not rely on Chernigovians and escaped to the Starodub fortress in the north of the principality.

Such aggressiveness and adventurism were typical of the "outcast princes," who tried to compensate for their lack of legitimacy with utter resolve. Further escalating competition within the political system of the Rous' Lands, they brought this system to the brink of destruction by the end of the eleventh century. To resolve the crisis, in 1097, on the initiative of Vladimir Monomakh, a conference of the six most influential princes was convened in the city of Lyubech on the Dnieper. It turned out to be unrealistic to reconcile the interests of all parties and come to an agreement on the scale of the entire Rous' Lands. As a compromise, it was then decided that claims to the office should be restricted by the fathers' domains: the children of the Chernigov prince could claim the princely offices only in the Chernigov land, and so forth. This should have lowered the intensity or at least the scope of political rivalry and made politics a family matter once again, so that all the junior rulers would be subordinate to the authority of the eldest prince as his children. In addition, this decision severely restricted the autonomy of city communes, which were forced to choose their rulers from a smaller number of contenders, all of them close relatives.

This measure had only a temporary effect. One generation later, brothers competing for patrimony in local principalities were joined by their uncles and nephews, so the generic problem of the Rous' Lands reproduced itself with the same urgency on the local scale. Moreover, the Lyubech Conference did not regulate the rules pertaining to the office of the Kyiv grand prince. The old principle of transferring from one principality to another in order of seniority, until reaching the Novgorod office as the last step before Kyiv, was undermined by the conference decisions, but theoretically, the Kyiv office was still open to any Rurikid. In the absence of any formal mechanism for selecting legitimate candidates for the office of the Kyiv grand prince, military force became the main argument. Throughout the twelfth century, Kyiv had been repeatedly captured by princes seeking this title. Acting now as representatives of their home principalities, they did not perceive Kyiv as the sole source of their prosperity that should be protected by all means. On the contrary, candidates for the office did not hesitate to punish the city and its stubborn citizens for putting up resistance, burning down entire districts, and robbing churches—as happened in 1139, 1169, and 1203. Kyiv became a symbol of supreme power rather than its actual, therefore cherished, source.

The Formalization of the Rous' Lands as a Confederation

This new attitude to the "mother of Rous' cities" explicitly revealed the essence of the Rous' Lands' political system, which was previously masked by the nominal commonality of the territories participating in the political process. As it turned out, the office of the grand prince of Kyiv embodied the pinnacle of the individual prince's career after he moved from less prestigious principalities to more prestigious ones, rather than the supreme power for all other princes. In the past, all the princes participating in "circling" from one city to another recognized the importance of Kyiv as the main prize in the political game they were playing. Therefore, they agreed to the special status of the grand prince of Kyiv and the need to send him the lion's share of taxes collected in their principalities—everyone hoped to become the new Kyiv prince one day, and everyone had a chance to achieve this status. With the delimitation of the Rous' Lands among individual dynasties, most of the princes lost their legitimate right to claim the Kyiv principality, even theoretically. To the rest, Kyiv turned into a sports trophy of sorts, an object of vanity and extraction of resources.

Unable to alleviate the "overproduction" of princes in the long run, the Lyubech Conference's spatial division of the Rous' Lands into "patrimonies" with clear boundaries and under the control of local dynasties was highly consequential in other respects.

The eldest of the princes gathered in Lyubech, Sviatopolk Iziaslavich, kept the title of grand prince of Kyiv and in addition received control over the northwestern Turov and Pinsk principalities in the former land of the Dregovichians (in modern Belarus). Vladimir Monomakh retained the Pereyaslavl principality on the left bank of the Dnieper, at the edge of the steppe, as well as the Smolensk principality in the center of the Rous' Lands and its northeastern neighbors: the Suzdal and Rostov Land and Beloozero. The main culprits of the crisis, two of the "outcast princes" Oleg Sviatoslavich and David Sviatoslavich were allowed to receive their father's Chernigov with the Seversk Land, as well as Ryazan and Murom lying to the east. Other dynastic formations recognized by the Lyubech Conference were Volhynia to the west of Kyiv and Red (Chervona) Rus' farther to the southwest, on the border with the Kingdom of Poland, later known as Galicia. [6]

The imposition of new political boundaries at first simply reproduced the logic of "big" politics at the local level. The senior ruler functionally began to play the role of the grand prince, and numerous representatives of the local princely dynasty competed for his throne. The younger princes moved from one secondary city to another in the hope of eventually occupying the main "paternal" office. Therefore, it comes as no surprise that, by the mid-twelfth century, in addition to the main and the only one grand prince of Kyiv, several new offices acquired the grand prince title. The grand prince of Vladimir ruled in the new capital of the Suzdal land, which was originally part of Vladimir Monomakh's domain. The patrimony awarded to the outcast princes Oleg and David was divided, to the effect of creating two grand principalities: in Chernigov and Ryazan. The grand prince of Galicia reigned over Volhynia and Red Rus'.

The allocation of individual territories of the Rous' Lands as heritable domains of several princely dynasties, while maintaining the old principle of accession to power, did not change the political situation overnight. Depending on the political talents of princes, the number of pretenders to the highest office, the outcome of wars with neighbors, or relationships with city communes, the local political system could consolidate (as did the western lands united in the Galician-Volhynian principality), or could continue dividing under the pressure of internal conflicts (as in the case of Chernigov and Ryazan). By itself, the Lyubech Conference made the political system of the Rous' Lands neither more fragmented than it was nor more stable in its individual regions. As before, the entire growing clan-legal estate of the Rurikids retained the exclusive right to hold princely offices, but one's ability to exercise this right depended on a complex of factors including the complicated order of succession, ability to defeat competitors, and the support of the city commune. What really changed after the formal delimitation of the Rous' Lands into regions under the control of individual dynasties of the Rurikids was the creation of conditions for political differentiation and "specialization" of these regions. Each of them embraced one of the many possible scenarios for the further evolution of the traditional political system, so simultaneously several of them were explored and consistently implemented. Previously, the effect of individual innovations was leveled by the constant rotation of princes across the Rous' Lands. Now, "political specialization" was creating prerequisites for dividing the common political space into separate political systems.

New Regional Political Systems

Thus, in the Novgorod land, by the mid-twelfth century, the dualism of the princely power and the authority of the city commune was decided in favor of the commune. The veche was transformed from an extraordinary gathering of townspeople into a regular government body that elected magistrates: the mayor and chiliarchs, whereas the invited prince mainly concentrated on military affairs and the civil court. Historians call the regime established in the Novgorod land a "boyar republic," since real power belonged to elective bodies, with the key role played by representatives of the local aristocratic and wealthy families (*boyars*). The formation of the Novgorod Republic after 1136 (when the townspeople expelled the grandson of Vladimir Monomakh—Vsevolod, who had lost the trust and respect of the Novgorodians) is directly related to the political weakening of Kyiv. Traditionally, the prince of Novgorod was the most probable candidate for the office of grand prince of Kyiv, so after the Lyubech Conference, Novgorod was left under the purview of the Kyiv prince. But his grand title now meant little more than "first among equals," and the ensuing demise of Kyiv's military power made it extremely difficult to control Novgorod, located almost 700 miles away. Previously, all the princes of the Rous' Lands were interested in sustaining the office of the Novgorod prince. Now, the Kyiv prince was alone and could rely only on his own authority—which, as it turned out, was insufficient.

The northeastern lands presented the opposite dynamics. The princely power there was able to suppress the resistance of city communes and acquire the most authoritarian forms. It is likely that all the princes dreamed of this degree of control, but in the old cities that emerged on the site of tribal communal centers—Chernigov or Smolensk, not to mention Novgorod or Kyiv—the authority of the city commune was very high. The northeast was a sparsely populated forest region, mostly a tribal territory of the Finnish-speaking Merians, which was colonized by the Slavic settlers. The oldest city there was Rostov, home to one of the oldest dioceses in the Rous' Lands, founded back in 991. However, the remaining local cities were founded relatively late: Suzdal is first mentioned in the chronicle under the year 1024, Vladimir was founded by Vladimir Monomakh in 1108 on the site of a fortified garrison, the border town of Moscow on the lands of the Vyatichians was first mentioned under the year 1147. It is thus all the more remarkable that the ruler of the region, Prince Yuri Dolgoruky (son of Vladimir Monomakh) in 1125 moved his capital from ancient Rostov to Suzdal, which was barely a hundred years old. In 1157, his son Andrei Bogoliubsky again transferred the capital—to Vladimir, which was not even half a century old then. All the inconveniences of relocating the seat of power, the risks of moving it farther south, closer to the steppe, and the investments needed to bring smaller towns to new capital status were compensated by one advantage: the city community in each new capital was younger and weaker than in the previous one. The city of Vladimir was founded by the prince virtually from scratch, and therefore could not match the princely power in the same way as the older cities that emerged on the basis of former tribal centers. Moscow, from its very foundation, developed under the political system of a princely monopoly on power. When it became the capital of an appanage principality in the thirteenth century, and later the capital of the entire former Vladimir principality, the city commune of Moscow did not play any independent political role. Authoritarianism should not be mistaken for consolidation of statehood: unlike the republican Novgorod land, which was only expanding its territory, the northeastern lands were characterized by powerful centrifugal tendencies and internal fragmentation.

The Smolensk principality demonstrated a third political scenario. Although Smolensk was an old urban community in which the merchants played an active role similar to Novgorod, or perhaps precisely for this reason, the principality came close to the ideal of continued princely power as envisioned at the Lyubech Conference. Throughout much of the twelfth and thirteenth centuries, Smolensk was characterized by greater political stability than many of its neighbors but it also was not split into appanages as a way to ease competition for the main princely office. Power was passed directly from father to son for many generations. At the same time, the Smolensk princes pursued an active foreign policy in the interests of the security and commercial needs of the principality. Apparently, in Smolensk, they intuitively found a mutually beneficial balance of power between the prince and local commune, similar to the more radical Novgorod scenario (princes do not interfere too much in communal self-government) and maintained this balance for many decades.

Marriage Diplomacy as an Indicator of Political Boundaries

One unexpected effect of the territorial division of the Rous' Lands among several dynasties of the Rurikids was a higher cohesion of this clan-legal estate of princes, as demonstrated by a change in the marriage policy. Representatives of different dynasties began to systematically intermarry, whereas previously the spouses were chosen outside the Rous' Lands. Thus, the mother of Yaroslav the Wise (one of the wives of Prince Vladimir) was a Polotsk princess Ragnhild, a representative of a different Varangian clan. Yaroslav himself in 1019, after winning the struggle for Kyiv, married Ingegerd, the daughter of the king Olof Skötkonung of Sweden. His eldest sons—members of the triumvirate—married the sister of the Polish King Kazimierz I (Iziaslav), a German aristocrat (Sviatoslav), and daughter of the Byzantine emperor Constantine IX Monomachos (Vsevolod). Yaroslav's daughters married the Norwegian King Harald Sigurdsson (Elizabeth), the Hungarian King András I (Anastasia), and the French King

Henry I (Anna). The children of the "triumvirs" followed suit: Vladimir Monomakh was married to a daughter of the last Anglo-Saxon king of England Harold II, and after, probably to a Byzantine woman. His rival Oleg Sviatoslavich first married a Byzantine aristocrat and then a Polovtsian khan's daughter. A son of the third triumvir, Sviatopolk Iziaslavich, was also married twice: the first time, probably, to the daughter of a Czech prince, and the second time to a daughter of a Polovtsian khan.

The established trend abruptly changed in the next generation: at the beginning of the twelfth century, the first marriages were concluded between Rurikids—representatives of different princely dynasties of the Rous' Lands. A particularly striking example is the son of Vladimir Monomakh and his successors as the grand prince of Kyiv, Mstislav. Three years before the Lyubech Conference, a Swedish princess became his wife, and after her death, he married in 1022 the daughter of a Novgorod mayor: not only not a "foreigner," but a representative of the local nobility rather than the princely estate. Since the mid-twelfth century, marriages to representatives of dynasties outside the Rous' Lands (with the important exception of the Polovtsian khans) had become very rare.

Viewing marriage as a unique resource for building strategic alliances, members of the princely families were choosing spouses outside their political space. The fact that after the Lyubech Conference they began marrying representatives of other Rurikid clans suggests that they actually started to perceive the patrimonies of other dynasties as foreign countries. This is an important circumstance, testifying that the formation of autonomous political centers in the common space of the Rous' Lands was under way. This common space had never been homogeneous or monolithic before, but now its fragmentation was confined to relatively stable boundaries. The reality of this emerging boundary was confirmed more from the outside (through recognition by other dynasties) than from inside, as a result of internal political consolidation. The change in marriage patterns also means that networks of close family relations between princes began to take shape only in the twelfth century: earlier, most members of princely families were connected only through one common, often distant ancestor.

A Common Space Characterized by Political and Cultural Diversity

Thus, by the beginning of the thirteenth century, the Rous' Lands as a single cultural and political supratribal space had undergone significant evolution. Its original political system was formed in the second half of the ninth century and persisted, with some improvements, for almost 250 years. It was based on the coexistence of two semiautonomous power structures: local city communes (former tribal centers) and the corporation of Rurikid princes. The Rurik clan claimed a monopoly on princely power throughout the entire territory of the Rous' Lands, but the right to a particular princely office was determined by victory in the competition with the most legitimate contenders. Winning over support from the city commune (often by military means) was instrumental in becoming a ruler. From the capital it was impossible to govern a vast country with a highly diverse population organized around local centers of power, and it was unrealistic to ensure the loyalty of local princes to the central government. The only technique for securing the loyalty of regional administrators at the disposal of the Rurikids was the family relationship between father and sons. But even family ties did not guarantee against conflicts, and keeping power in the hands of one family was unrealistic. Therefore, in 1097, it was decided to abandon attempts to build a unified system of power for the entire Rous' Lands as a common sphere defined by Eastern Orthodox Christianity and the Rurikids monopoly on power. Over the twelfth and early thirteenth centuries, the initial political dualism of the prince and the city commune was revised along different scenarios in different principalities: from the republic in Novgorod, where the city commune prevailed, to the Vladimir-Suzdal principality in the northeast, where the princes undermined the commune.

The Rous' Lands, once named after the only institution connecting different territories—the Varangian (later princely) retinue, never existed as a unitary state, and after 1097, this space was formally divided into separate "countries." At the same time, several centuries of common political history, religion, and written culture contributed to the fact that the Rous' Lands increasingly became viewed as a category of cultural identification. It is still unclear how "multilayered" the sense of cultural belonging in different parts of the medieval Rous' Lands was. We know that Christianity got along with the remnants of pagan beliefs and rituals, but it is not clear how complete the assimilation of representatives of the Slavic, Baltic, Finnish, and Turkic tribes into a common cultural entity was; or how much local spoken dialects differed from each other. The surviving written sources of the period are mainly written in the Old Russian literary language, which gives the impression of cultural unification. This impression is probably no more correct than it is to assume the cultural unity of the kingdoms of western Europe merely because most European sources were written in the same medieval Latin language.

In a sense, the Rous' Lands can indeed be compared to "Europe"—an even more ambiguous and indefinite construct of mental geography of a much later period. Unlike "Europe," the Rous' Lands for several centuries actually functioned as a single political space in which princes migrated from one city to another, carving out principalities almost without regard to the boundaries of historical lands and tribes. Like the imaginary space of "Europe," the inner unity of the Rous' Lands was a unity of a familiar and understandable—but not necessarily a friendly—social world, a common space of interaction and conflict. This familiarity did not make the clashes between the principalities less bloody than the wars with the infidels, and it did not prevent some Rousians from using Varangians, Polovtsians, or Poles as allies against other Rousians. The commonality of experiences could serve as the basis for a new political integration at some point in the future, but it also stimulated a demarcation from neighbors, whose cultural proximity required emerging countries to take additional measures to secure their political autonomy and separateness.

Political Integration of the Steppe

The Rous' Lands were able to form and evolve over the course of several centuries as a common political and cultural space, firmly present in the mental mapping of neighboring societies, from Scandinavia to Byzantium, not least because there were no serious external threats. With the exception of the southern forest-steppe zone, the Rous' Lands were a forest territory connected by a network of rivers as the main means of transportation. This forest region, moreover, for the most part was surrounded by relatively sparse, less organized populations. Only in the southwest, on the border with the Kingdoms of Poland and Hungary, was there a zone of competition and cooperation with politically developed societies. Connected by family ties with the Polish and Hungarian rulers, the princes of the Volhynian and Galician lands fought with them for border towns or came to their aid as allies. However, on the scale of the entire Rous' Lands, there was no serious threat coming from the western neighbors until the thirteenth century.

The real sources of concern were the steppe nomads in the south: the Pechenegs, the Torks, and later the Polovtsians. However, even they did not present an existential threat. The people of the steppe besieged Kyiv several times, they regularly raided the southern lands—Pereyaslavl and Chernigov, but even more often they participated in numerous interprincely conflicts as invited allies of one or both of the parties. Rous' princes periodically organized expeditions to the steppe to oppose the nomads and built defense lines—for example, the "serpent ramparts" constructed by Prince Vladimir Sviatoslavich (earthen ramparts stretching for many hundreds of miles, with a palisade on top connecting a chain of outposts). At the same time, relations with the nomads were by no means limited to war, and the integration of the Polovtsians into the political and cultural space of the Rous' Lands was so deep that some historians consider it possible to recognize them as equal participants in this space. Some of the Polovtsian khans and their subjects adopted Christianity, and, after the mid-twelfth century, the majority of the Rous' princes married a Polovtsian woman at least once.

Compared with the situation of many of its neighbors, including Byzantium, the Rous' Lands enjoyed unprecedented security for three centuries. The initial consolidation of this space, its subsequent enhanced complexity, and eventual tendency toward differentiation were results of mostly domestic factors rather than a response to external pressure. However, in the thirteenth century, the Rous' Lands lost their exclusive position as the most politically and culturally integrated (both internally and with the outside world) part of Northern Eurasia and relative immunity from foreign invasions. In the northwest, the colonization of the Baltic southern coast by the knights of the German (Teutonic) Order and the Swedish knights resulted in a direct clash with Novgorod over the territories inhabited by Finnish pagans, which both sides perceived as their colonies. In the west, out of former "buffer" forest territories in the twelfth century emerged an important independent political force of consolidated Baltic tribes, whom neighbors called "Lituans" ("Litva" in Russian sources). Still, the greatest threat to Rous' Lands was the Mongol invasion from the steppes to the southeast. It should be noted that in the thirteenth century, the politics in Northern Eurasia finally transcended the boundaries of ecological niches, so the "forest" ceased to serve as an insurmountable obstacle for the "steppe." New political formations arose from the manipulation of differences and solidarity among various population groups, and not from the uniformity of natural conditions.

Nomadic Peoples of Northern Eurasia

Yeke Mongɣol Ulus, better known as the Empire of Chinggis Khan, emerged at the beginning of the thirteenth century in southeastern Siberia. In some aspects this political and cultural phenomenon was similar to the Rous' Lands, formed in the tenth century in the east of Europe. Both political formations played an important role in the transformation of Northern Eurasia from a geographical abstraction into an internally structured cultural and political space, integrated into the surrounding world. Like the Rous' Lands, the Yeke Mongɣol Ulus was an original, largely unprecedented experiment in consolidating an extremely culturally diverse population into a single whole. The clash of the two political formations was a conflict of different cultures, economic systems, and political scenarios. Even the self-designation of these western and eastern versions of self-organization of the "nonhistorical" part of Northern Eurasia differed in a characteristic way: "Rous' Lands" implied the political formatting of a certain territory, and "Yeke Mongɣol Ulus," or "Great Mongol Ulus," emphasized the unity of the population (*ulus*—Mong., meaning people, tribe, nationality, detachment, army, and only in a figurative sense, the state). However, the result of their long struggle was a certain synthesis of different traditions of statehood and the gradual integration of the region's western and eastern borderlands.

The nomads of the eastern part of the continent more than once took an active part in the historical processes in its western part. Migrating from across the Urals, individual tribal associations crossed the Volga, traversed the steppes of the northern Caspian and Black Sea regions, and moved farther west across the Carpathian Mountains to the Danube valley, or southwest to Asia Minor, or to the Northern Balkans. In the period described in Chapter 2, this trip was made by the Magyars (Hungarians)—the Ugric tribes related to the taiga hunters, the Khanty and Mansi, who left the forests and engaged in steppe cattle breeding. By the thirteenth century, they were already Catholic Christians, sedentary inhabitants of the Hungarian Kingdom, which occupied the territory once dominated by the nomadic Avar Khaganate, and before that—by the western wing of the nomadic Turkic Khaganate.

The Hungarians were followed by the Pechenegs, a conglomerate of Turkic, Iranian-speaking, and Ugric tribes. For nearly a century they terrorized the population of the forest-steppe zone subject to the Kyiv princes, but from the mid-eleventh century begin to settle along the southern borders of the Rous' Lands as allies of local princes. They are known from chronicles as "Black Hoods" (*chernye klobuki*) and are probable ancestors of the Zaporozhian Cossacks of later times. Some Pechenegs, who continued to nomadize in the steppes along the Don River, were displaced by a wave of newcomers and migrated farther west—to the Czech and Hungarian lands. In the Hungarian Kingdom, the Pecheneg khans held senior government positions and even governed the city of Pest and its vicinity.

The newcomers who drove out the Pechenegs were Torks, representatives of the western group of Oghuz Turks. The Oghuz tribes participated in the process of Turkization of the ancient cultural centers of Central Asia, laying the foundation for the Kara-Khanid and Ghaznavid khanates mentioned at the beginning of this chapter. Later, they would spread the Turkic language and culture to a significant part of the Middle

Consolidation of New Political Systems   113

East and the South Caucasus. However, the Torks, who came to the eastern European steppes, themselves shared the fate of the Pechenegs: less than a century later, they had to leave their pasturelands and flee to Byzantium, becoming its subjects, or settle in the Rous' Lands and joining the semisettled borderland tribes of the Black Hoods.

The Torks retreated under the pressure of the Polovtsians—the Turkic-speaking Kipchaks. The name in Russian chronicles, *polovtsy*, most likely, comes from the Old Slavic word for yellow color (*polovyi*). This must be a translation of their self-given name, "Yellow Kipchaks" (*Sara Kipchak*), either because of their hair color or because of the southern ("yellow") location of the ancestral clan territory. In the eleventh century, dozens of scattered tribal unions of the Kipchaks dominated the vast steppe belt from the Altai Mountains to the Danube River. This prompted the Persian author Nasir Khusraw to call this entire vast territory Desht-i Qipchaq—"the [foreign] land of the Kipchaks." The Kipchaks did not represent political or economic unity: some of them led a sedentary lifestyle and inhabited large trading cities, and others were nomadic pastoralists; sharp conflicts broke out between the tribes. However, it is noteworthy that the very idea of the unity and distinctiveness of the Great Steppe is associated with the Kipchaks. For the first time, instead of the image of separate predatory hordes appearing "out of nowhere" from a hostile and unknown external world, the steppe was plotted on a universal cultural map as an ordered space with a population living according to its own laws and customs. [7]

Following the Pechenegs and Torks, the Polovtsians went through a stage of territorial expansion and military confrontation with the southern principalities of the Rous' Lands, which gave way to the establishment of closer contacts and even alliances between individual Rousian princes and Pecheneg khans. Just like the Torks and Pechenegs, the Kipchaks were swept away by a new nomadic force that came from the east—the Mongols. However, the Mongols were fundamentally different from all their predecessors, and the consequences of their invasion for the polities in their path were completely different.

The Nomads' Strategic Symbiosis with China

By the beginning of the thirteenth century, nothing indicated that in a matter of a few decades the Mongols would create the largest empire in human history. Initially, the Mongol-speaking tribes lived in the valleys squeezed between the mountain ranges of South Transbaikalia, between the Argun and Onon Rivers. In the eighth century, most of the Mongol tribes migrated to the south, settling near the Turkic and Tungus tribes, and over the next three centuries demonstrated a tendency toward internal strife and fragmentation.

Inhabitants of the steppes east of the Altai Mountain range, in which the Mongols settled, had by this time been in a complex symbiosis with the sedentary Chinese culture for over a thousand years. Essentially, it was the development of powerful Chinese polities in the south that helped this steppe region turn into a kind of "incubator" of nomadic tribes. As has been mentioned several times in this book, highly specialized nomadic herding is unsustainable without the constant influx of strategic products of the agricultural economy by means of raids, trade, or the collection of tribute.

114   *New Imperial History of Northern Eurasia*

The rich economy of Chinese societies was a strong magnet that attracted northern nomads. During the periods of prosperity, the nomad's numbers swelled at the expense of sedentary and semisedentary tribes from the forests of Siberia in the north and Manchuria in the northeast. An economic or ecological crisis would compel the "surplus" nomadic population to escape westward along the Eurasian steppe belt in search of resources to survive. Such migrations took the form of nomadic hordes crushing all along their way, reaching the western outskirts of the continent and in the end peacefully settling and assimilating there. China's economic success meant more opportunities for nomadic peoples who were getting more and more resources. Accordingly, the political unification of Chinese societies forced the nomads to unite, and the crisis and devastation in China led to the collapse of powerful nomadic confederations. The very spatial-political imagination of the nomads was structured by the exceptional role of China: the traditional dual organization of nomadic confederations assumed a division into left and right wings, and the left (senior) wing was always on the east flank, and the right wing was on the west. Thus, nomadic federations "faced" the south, where China was situated, whereas in the rear were the not always friendly Turkic and Tungus tribes of Siberia.

The first centralized Chinese state was created in 221 BCE, and was followed by the first "nomadic empire" of the Xiongnu in 209, twelve years later. The powerful First Turkic Khaganate was formed in the steppe by 552 CE, which, in turn, gave impetus to the unification of China from several polities under the Sui dynasty in 581. The Tang dynasty that replaced it had to deal with the new nomad opponent in the north—the Uyghur Khaganate. In these periods, when the united China was opposed by multitribal nomadic confederations, there was no room in the steppe for nonaligned tribes, and the border with China clearly differentiated between "the nomads" and "the settled" (i.e., "barbarians" and "civilization"). During the times of political fragmentation in China, hybrid states were formed in the north: borderland tribes (mainly the Tungus-speaking Jurchens) established political control over both the nomadic population of the steppe and the sedentary Chinese population. They managed to maintain control of these states by dividing the system of government into Chinese and nomadic. The Chinese population obeyed Chinese officials and Chinese traditions, but the upper stratum of administration was occupied by Jurchen tribal aristocracy. The Jurchen rulers zealously protected their monopoly on extracting resources in China from the steppe competitors by sustaining anarchy and tribal fragmentation among the nomads. Unlike the inner Chinese dynasties, which tended to ignore the nomadic world until it began to pose an open threat, the Turkic and Jurchen rulers of China actively intervened in the steppe politics they were well familiar with. Their tactical goal was to prevent the strengthening of any tribal alliance and destroy the most promising candidates for the formation of a new steppe confederation, which they did using their own army or the hands of rival nomadic groups.

It was during this period of externally supported fragmentation in the steppe and decentralization of China that the Mongols became involved in big steppe politics. In 840 CE, the Uyghur Khaganate, the last significant confederation of nomads, collapsed, and in 907 CE, the once mighty Chinese Tang Empire fell. It was replaced in China, according to official historiography's eloquent definition, by "the Five Dynasties and Ten Kingdoms period." By the beginning of the thirteenth century, three large states existed on the territory of the former Tang Empire: the Great Jin created by the Jurchens—Tungus tribes who annexed vast territories of Northern China to their possessions in Manchuria and the Amur region; Xi Xia (Western Xia)—the state formation of the Tanguts, the people of the Tibeto-Burman language group, west of Jin; and the Song Empire of the Han Chinese in the south. [8] Of these three states, the most powerful was the Great Jin, which pursued an aggressive policy both in the south, against the Song, and in the steppe. In the first half of the twelfth century, Khabul Khan—the great-grandfather of Chinggis Khan—for the first time united most of the Mongol clans in the "Hamag Mongol Ulus." His troops defeated the punitive expedition dispatched by the Great Jin emperor and began raiding the Jin territory.

The rise of the new autonomous force in the steppe seriously worried the Jurchen rulers of the Great Jin. Although the Mongolian confederation collapsed after the death of Khabul Khan, starting in the mid-twelfth century, the Jurchens began to pursue a policy of "reduction of the adults" in the steppe. Every three years, the Great Jin army invaded the steppes of Eastern Mongolia, exterminating or enslaving the male population of nomads. To support punitive expeditions against the dangerously strengthened nomadic tribes, the Jurchens usually recruited some weaker tribes by rewarding their leaders with imperial titles. These recently titled allies could become the targets of the next punitive expedition, and the former defeated enemies could become vengeful assistants of the Jurchen imperial forces. For example, in 1196, the Great Jin troops attacked the tribes of the Central Asian (probably Mongolian-speaking) Tatars and invited the leader of a small Mongol ulus, Temuchin (the future Chinggis Khan), to take part in the expedition. Temuchin accepted this offer, all the more so because he considered the Tatars to be responsible for the death of his father. As a result of a successful campaign, Temuchin strengthened his authority among the Mongols, but by 1198, a new expedition of the Jurchens to the steppe had already followed—this time against the Mongol tribe, closely related to Temuchin's clan.

Temuchin and the Rise of the Mongols

This was the situation in the steppe in the 1180s, when Temuchin began to gather loyal followers around him. Information regarding his biography is limited and often contradictory, starting with his date of birth: according to some sources it was 1155, others cite 1162. As a teenager, Temuchin lost his father, and after that his ancestral lands and herds. The family was in poverty, Temuchin barely escaped the murderers who were pursuing him, and only the support of his father's sworn brother—the leader of a kin tribe—saved Temuchin and his family. The story of his twenty-year-long ascent to the heights of power over the steppe is the story of an endless series of coalitions with friendly tribes against hostile ones. The goal of the clashes was not the destruction or ruin of rivals, but their inclusion in the assembled confederation of tribes, so the lives of the defeated enemies were usually spared, contrary to the customs of the steppe at that time. In 1206, in the upper reaches of the Onon River at the heart of the Mongols' ancestral lands, representatives of the nobility of all tribes convened for a congress (*kurultai*). They proclaimed Temuchin the ruler of all the nomads with

116   *New Imperial History of Northern Eurasia*

a new title—Chinggis Khan. It is still not entirely clear what this title means, except that Temuchin wanted to emphasize his difference from all previous steppe rulers. [9]

In 1211, Chinggis Khan launched a full-scale offensive against the Great Jin. In 1219, he suddenly redirected his forces to Central Asia against the Shah of Khwarezm—the Turkic ruler of the enormous polity that by 1200 had absorbed most of the possessions of the Kara-Khanid and Ghaznavid khanates, stretching from modern-day western Iran and Azerbaijan to eastern India. The victorious war continued until 1224, but the Shah of Khwarezm Ala ad-Din Muhammad II had already fled from the Mongols to foreign lands in 1220. Chinggis Khan found it necessary to allocate 30,000 troops for the mission to search and apprehend the Shah. This expeditionary corps under the command of Generals Jebe and Subutai covered a great distance in 1220–4. Having reached the southern coast of the Caspian Sea, the pursuers learned about the death of Ala ad-Din Muhammad.

Chinggis Khan ordered that the mission continue—now obviously for reconnaissance purposes. The troops of Jebe and Subutai invaded the South Caucasus, defeating the forces of the Armenian princes and the army of the Georgian King Lasha Giorgi (George IV), and fought their way to the North Caucasus. In the steppes of the Northern Caspian region, the Mongols defeated the sedentary Alans and nomadic Polovtsians. In the battle of the Kalka River in the Azov Sea region, the Mongols crushed the joint army of the Rous' princes, who came to the aid of the Polovtsians. Pursuing the remnants of the defeated enemy fleeing to Kyiv, Jebe and Subutai stopped halfway to the city and turned their depleted forces back to the east. Having crossed the Volga, the Mongols suffered a devastating defeat by the Volga Bulgars. As a result, according to some sources, only 4,000 soldiers returned from the campaign, which lasted three and a half years. In 1224, Chinggis Khan returned to the east with the main army to continue the war in China. This time he led his army against the western neighbor of the Great Jin, the Tangut kingdom of Xi Xia, fearing that these two old rivals could make an alliance, which would complicate his main task—complete victory over the Jurchens. Chinggis Khan died in the late summer of 1227 during a campaign in western China. [10]

A Balance of Idealism and Pragmatism

What were the goals of Temuchin-Chinggis Khan? Biographical information about him recorded by his younger contemporaries, along with the idea of his "chosenness" by God, emphasize his personal uncompromising hatred of traitors and betrayal, regardless of whom they benefited. He had experienced betrayal at an early age: the Tatars poisoned his father when he was their guest, while the head of a kindred Mongol clan impoverished his family and almost killed him. Afterward, he methodically punished betrayers—whether by persecuting the Tatars or by invading the Central Asian Khwarezmian Empire of Ala ad-Din Muhammad II after he ordered the execution of the peaceful Mongolian envoys, which was the worst form of treachery in Chinggis Khan's view.

The latter may seem an especially irrational response, since a spontaneous decision to invade the huge Khwarezmian Empire required the halting of a long war against the Jin Empire, for which Chinggis Khan had been preparing for many years, and the transfer of almost all his forces thousands of miles to the west. And after Ala ad-Din Muhammad fled, Chinggis Khan dispatched a significant part of his army to capture him, weakening the forces that suppressed the resistance of the Khwarezmian army. Apparently, the drive to establish justice and law in the steppe made Chinggis Khan especially intolerant of treacherous violations of rules and agreements. The disproportionate response to these violations can be seen as an impetus for the large-scale military expansion when the pursuit of one perfidious politician (Ala ad-Din Muhammad) eventually led the Mongolian troops across the continent westward, to the Caucasus and eastern Europe.

On the other hand, analyzing the political situation in the steppe during Chinggis Khan's rise to power, one has to admit that he acted in the most pragmatic way as he tried to neutralize the main threats to himself and his clan. Considering the Jurchens as the main danger, he began to unite the nomads. Instead of the traditional policy of consolidation of kindred Mongol tribes, which would inevitably have provoked concern and opposition from the Turkic and Tungus peoples, Chinggis Khan announced the revival of the Turkic Khaganate that existed half a thousand years earlier. The memory about that khaganate was preserved only in the Chinese chronicles and legends of the steppe people, but the idea of uniting "people of the felt walls" (that is, in the nomads' yurts) turned out to be popular. Preparing for a clash with the Jin Empire, which was considered invincible, Chinggis Khan managed to subjugate, for the most part peacefully, not only the numerous inhabitants of the steppes but also the tribes of southern Siberia, including the forest dwellers (Buryat Mongols, Turkic-speaking Yenisei Kyrgyz).

Chinggis Khan's Supratribal Political System

To prevent this complex confederation of tribes from crumbling, in 1203–6, Chinggis Khan introduced a unified system of administration that divided the population into tens, hundreds, and thousands. The decimal division itself was the traditional principle for organizing the army of the nomads in Northern Eurasia, but Chinggis Khan applied it to families. From then on, "one hundred" designated a number of the population that was capable of providing and equipping a hundred warriors. This created a unified social structure that did not coincide with the boundaries of the traditional tribal hierarchies. Chinggis Khan's appointees to the highest posts were primarily his most trusted and proven companions rather than representatives of the clan aristocracy. The priority of the new organizational principles over the old tribal system was most clearly manifested in the army: commanders were chosen not from the senior clansmen but from the warriors, who earned promotion in battle; representatives of different tribes had to serve in the same detachments, and it was forbidden to transfer to a different unit; severe military discipline regulated all spheres of life, even regulating the process of pillaging the captured cities.

Whatever Chinggis Khan's personal motives were—an irrational desire for power and the imposition of his understanding of justice, or a pragmatic calculation—he played a key role in creating a fundamentally new type of nomadic society with a highly developed statehood. Unlike the traditional steppe confederations, the central power revealed itself not only "outside," in the sphere of interaction with the outside world, but also "from within," duplicating or even replacing the traditional hierarchies of kinship. For the first time, the political organization created by the nomads proved to be so strong as to be able to absorb vast territories of highly developed sedentary societies. The fact that this political organization was used for military conquests that were unprecedented in scale and destructiveness resulted from a combination of circumstances, but also from the essential qualities of the state created by Chinggis Khan. The "Mongols"—from now on this tribal name denoted a multilingual polity—practiced warfare that was fundamentally different from the previous nomadic raids.

The Art and Economy of Warfare

Beginning in the first centuries CE, after the collapse of the first "nomadic empire" of the Xiongnu, waves of nomads from the eastern steppes migrated all the way to the Danube valley or broke up at the borders of Byzantium. The collapse of another steppe confederation raised a new wave of migrants striving to escape the civil strife and "overproduction" of nomads in the Mongolian steppes—the result of increased "surplus products" obtained from China during the previous period of prosperity. The nomads lacked the skills to besiege fortresses and they fared poorly against regular armies, so they moved westward past the fortified oasis cities of Central Asia until they reached the fertile steppes between the Volga and the Ural Mountains. The arrival of the next wave from the east pushed them farther, across the Volga, Don, and Dnieper, until they collided with state power far to the west that was as organized as China—Byzantium. The Rous' Lands were away from the path of migrating nomads. Besides, despite the lack of centralized administration and coordination, the Rous' Lands proved to be a strong enough polity, which the nomads could not systematically exploit.

The city fortifications of the sedentary states did not stop the Mongolian army. After the first conquests in China and Central Asia, the Mongols adopted sophisticated siege weapons from the defeated opponents, and used these widely. But even before obtaining this equipment, Chinggis Khan's army successfully captured fortresses, at relatively low cost to itself. Ravaging the surrounding villages, Chinggis Khan's warriors drove the local residents from their places, sowing panic in the enemy's rear. Healthy men were used for slave labor and as human shields: unarmed, scores of them were driven to storm the city walls on pain of death. The garrison wasted arrows and stones to fend off the attacks of desperate slaves, whose dead bodies were filling the moat making it easier to cross. As a result, the Mongols themselves assaulted the already exhausted and demoralized garrison.

The cavalry formed the base of the Mongol army, and its deployment also differed from traditional nomad tactics. The army of nomads included all capable men who went to battle under the command of the clan elders, and the battle itself disintegrated into many individual skirmishes without a unified plan and leadership. The Mongol cavalry was rigidly organized along a formal military hierarchy, not as clan groups. It was no longer a mass of kinsmen temporarily switching from cattle breeding to warfare, but a regular army, superior to the regular armies of the settled states that fought mainly on foot. The actions of the Mongol warriors were much more coordinated and controlled at all stages of the battle than the actions of other nomads. The senior officer always remained behind the troops, observing the battlefield from an elevation and directing his forces.

Finally, the distribution of war booty was officially regulated in the army of Chinggis Khan, in contrast to the spontaneous looting of the enemy's property during typical raids of nomads, who might quit halfway through the fighting so as not to miss any valuables. In the Mongol army, marauding was forbidden until the end of the battle. After that, a fixed share of the loot was withheld in the interests of the great khan and the commander, and the remaining part (about four-fifths of the loot) was distributed among all the warriors. Moreover, those who had perished in battle were also counted, and their share was sent home to families. This scheme reversed the traditional "political economy" of raids, under which the khan received the lion's share of the spoils of war and redistributed it among the tribal aristocracy, who, in turn, redistributed their share along the chain of the clan hierarchy. This mechanism provided the material basis of power relations in the nomadic confederation but compromised military efficiency. Ordinary warriors were concerned with securing part of the loot for themselves before everything was taken by the khan, rather than focusing on the battle. Chinggis Khan created institutions of power, largely independent of the traditional redistribution economy. By leaving most of the loot to the army, he provided rank-and-file warriors with a powerful incentive to win battles and take an interest in new conquests.

The initial expansion of the Mongols led by Chinggis Khan into China and Central Asia was not always followed by occupation. Similar to the raids by nomadic confederations of earlier times, the initial Mongol campaigns had various explanations, including even accidental circumstances. However, the aforementioned innovations in the political system and military organization created a different logic and even a different economy of war. Purposeful military expansion turned out to be more profitable than pastoralism for most nomads, not just for the tribal aristocracy. Permanent occupation of the conquered territories allowed economic resources to be extracted and redistributed regularly and on a greater scale than previous occasional payoffs by the sedentary states to nomads in the past.

The Mongol Expansion on Four Fronts

In the spring of 1235, eight years after the death of Chinggis Khan, a great kurultai was convened on the banks of the Onon River (not far from modern Nerchinsk). It reviewed the results of the wars against the Great Jin Empire and the shah of Khwarezm and decided on further goals. The main threat to the nomads in the Mongolian steppes—the Jurchens—was eliminated; no powerful agricultural states remained in the region that were not already undermined by Yeke Mongγol Ulus, so no imperative need required the unification of nomads into a single confederation. However, the supratribal state created by Chinggis Khan, its central element being an offensive military machine, had already acquired its own logic of existence. If there were no prosperous agricultural societies around to conquer and exploit, the Mongol war machine needed to be delivered to those who were far away. At the kurultai, it was decided to continue the offensive on four fronts at once: to the east against the Kingdom of Goryeo on the Korean Peninsula; to the south against the Chinese Song Empire; to the southwest against the Abbasid Caliphate and farther to the Middle East; and to the west against Desht-i Qipchaq and its neighbors (including Volga Bulgaria and the Rous' Lands, which were specially mentioned among the targets of aggression). Unlike the previous waves of nomads that originated in the Mongol and Central Asian steppes, the Mongol invasion was not a massive migration of armed refugees, but a deliberate expansion of organized invaders. [11]

Contrary to popular stereotypes, the Mongol conquests were nothing like a "blitzkrieg" or an invasion by countless hordes. By the time of Chinggis Khan's death in 1227, the Mongol army was about 130,000 strong and probably only twice as many thirty years later, when half of Eurasia was ruled by Chinggis Khan's heirs. Occasionally, Mongols wiped whole cities off the face of the earth and devastated entire provinces, but in general their expansion was based on negotiating political subordination with local rulers. This was a time-consuming process. Thus, the Mongol troops made six campaigns to Korea, before the rulers of Goryeo surrendered in 1258 and, twelve years later, signed the treaty of 1270. Under its provisions, Goryeo was recognized as a tributary and vassal of the new Mongol Yuan dynasty in China. The Great Yuan State was founded in China by Chinggis Khan's grandson Kublai Khan after the defeat of the southern Chinese Song Empire in 1271. The conquest of the Song began immediately after the kurultai of 1235 and also took several decades.

Expansion in the Middle East had already begun during the war with the shah of Khwarezm, when the Mongols were conquering vassal states of the huge empire one after another. In the wake of the kurultai of 1235, Mongol forces captured Isfahan in central Iran. Then, Noyon (General) Chormaqan turned his expeditionary corps to the northwest, invading Anatolia and the South Caucasus. On this front, Mongolian expansion developed at a slow pace, largely due to the lack of human resources needed to conquer and control these vast, densely populated territories. The Mongol army did not grow much even after mobilizing the troops of the vassal and allied rulers, due to casualties and the need to keep garrisons in the conquered cities. In October 1253, when Chinggis Khan's grandson Hulagu launched a new large-scale campaign in Iran, his army numbered only 70,000. Later, it was beefed up by another Mongol expeditionary corps and allied forces, but still never exceeded 100,000 to 140,000 troops. Only by the end of 1257 had Hulagu's army put most of Iran under control, and at the beginning of 1258 had seized and brutally plundered Baghdad, whose caliph refused to recognize the great khan's power. Afterward, in alliance with the Christian states of Cilician Armenia and the crusaders' Principality of Antioch, Hulagu occupied Syria and invaded Palestine. He had to retreat in 1260, having learned about the death of Great Khan Möngke. Thus the Mongols did not succeed in gaining a foothold in Syria, although in 1300 Hulagu's grandson Gazan brought his troops all the way to Gaza. According to some sources, he occupied Jerusalem, which he even promised to hand over to the crusaders, but in the end the Mongols were thrown back beyond the Euphrates by the Egyptian Mamluk sultanate. [12]

Against this background of protracted advancement in Korea, South China, and the Middle East, the Mongol campaign in the west in 1236–42 is noteworthy for its dynamism. In six years, the conquerors marched 5,500 miles conducting incessant battles from the Altai Mountains to the Adriatic Sea. [13]

Chinggis Khan had personally formulated the task of conquering Desht-i Qipchaq and neighboring lands back in 1224, when he divided the territories under his control among his sons. Tolui, the youngest son of Chinggis Khan and his first wife, received ancestral territories as his ulus. The third son, Ögedei, was to succeed his father as the great khan. The second son, Chagatai, received the already conquered Central Asian possessions, from the Uyghur lands in the east to Mawarannahr in the west. The eldest, Jochi, received Central Asia and the territories to the north (Western Siberia), as well as all the lands to the west, "to be conquered in the future." Chinggis Khan transferred 9,000 yurts (about 54,000 people) under Jochi's rule and ordered his son to conquer the entire Desht-i Qipchaq beyond the Urals. Jochi evaded this mission: according to one contemporary Persian author, he was outraged by the "recklessness of his father in relation to lands and people." Tensions between Jochi and Chinggis Khan grew so high that an army was allegedly prepared to set off against Jochi, and only his death under unknown circumstances stopped the punitive expedition. In 1229, the new great khan Ögedei sent an expeditionary corps to the west, which reached Volga Bulgaria and probably subjugated the Urals region, but then turned back. A full-scale offensive beyond the Urals by the joint forces of all Mongol uluses began only after the kurultai of 1235, in the winter of 1236.

Initially, the army of Mongols probably numbered about 40,000 warriors, but in the fall of 1236, it received Mongol reinforcements from Iran as well as from the peoples who recognized the Mongols' power (the Bashkirs, some Kipchak tribes, and part of the Mordovians). According to some generous estimates, the maximum size of the joint army in the Western campaign might have reached 120,000–150,000 warriors. However, the figure of 70,000 seems more realistic, especially given that large-scale military operations were conducted simultaneously on three more fronts. The supreme command of the Western campaign was taken by Batu (*c.* 1209–55/6), Jochi's son and heir, who was joined by the sons of the rulers of all other uluses.

In 1236, using the already subjugated territories west of the Urals as the staging area, the Mongols conquered Volga Bulgaria. At first the rulers of the emirate voluntarily submitted to the conquerors and even received gifts for their collaboration, but in the autumn, the Bulgars rebelled. The uprising was brutally suppressed and the main Bulgar cities were burned down. The grand prince of Vladimir, Yuri Vsevolodovich, allowed scores of Bulgars who fled from the invasion to settle in Rous' cities along the Volga River.

The Invasion of the Rous' Lands and Desht-i Qipchaq

In 1237, Mongol troops established complete control east of the Volga River down to the Caspian Sea, thus displacing the Polovtsians beyond the Don. Divided into four corps, the Mongol army allocated three of them for the attack of the Rous' Lands, aiming at Suzdal, Ryazan, and Chernigov. With the end of the autumn mud season (*rasputitsa*) in December 1237, the Mongols invaded the Ryazan principality, defeated its army, and on December 21, seized and burned Ryazan. The future great khan Möngke personally participated in the battle. [14]

At the beginning of January 1238, Batu's troops moved from Ryazan in the direction of Kolomna to the southwest, intending to encircle the strong Vladimir-Suzdal principality. Chinggis Khan's son Kyul Khan died in the battle near Kolomna. This most likely means that at some point the Rous' forces were able to fight their way to the command post in the rear of the Mongol troops. Nevertheless, the army of Vladimir principality was defeated and Kolomna was captured. On January 20, after putting up a stubborn resistance, Moscow fell. After a weeklong siege, on February 7, the capital city of Vladimir was captured and burned down. Batu's army then passed through the entire principality from east to west, from Pereyaslavl-Zalessky to Tver. After a two-week siege, on March 5, Torzhok fell in the southeast of Novgorod land. At the same time (March 4), under the command of General Boroldai, a Mongol division that was raiding the northern regions of the Vladimir principality, defeated the remnants of Grand Prince Yuri's troops at the Sit River, northwest of Uglich.

In this wooded and swampy area, Prince Yuri set a meeting point for the militias from across the principality and for the troops sent to his aid by his brothers—the grand prince of Kyiv Yaroslav and the prince of Yuriev-Polsky, Sviatoslav. Not expecting the Mongols so early, the assembled troops camped in the villages scattered along the sixty-mile-long valley of the Sit River. Only from the west—in the direction of Tver and besieged Torzhok—were they guarded by some 3,000 soldiers. Boroldai attacked from the south, and his forces crushed Yuri's regiments before they could line up in battle formations. The defeat at the Sit River put an end to the organized resistance of Vladimir principality, its ruler, Grand Prince Yuri, was killed in that battle.

After the Sit River battle and the capture of Torzhok, Batu's troops marched toward Novgorod. However, just over 100 miles from the city, the Mongols turned sharply to the south. They were probably frightened by the perspective of meeting the spring season in the center of the swampy Valdai Hills, or perhaps the heavy losses and fatigue of people and horses made it risky to confront the fresh forces of the Novgorod principality. Or maybe they did not consider attacking Novgorod at all and just a small advance guard was pursuing refugees fleeing Torzhok.

Due to a fodder shortage in early spring, the retreat to the southern steppes was carried out on a wide front, by separate *tumens* (divisions, nominally 10,000-men-strong) moving along different routes through Smolensk, Ryazan, and Chernigov principalities. Dispersed and exhausted, and concerned about the beginning of the spring mud season, the Mongols avoided large cities on their way. When they attempted to capture the small appanage town of Kozelsk in Chernigov principality, the siege continued for almost two months. It was May by the time the Mongols took Kozelsk, at a huge cost of 4,000 besiegers killed, and only after the arrival of Batu's main forces at the scene.

After taking respite over the summer and having secured their rear and flanks by neutralizing any threat from Volga Bulgaria and Ryazan, in the fall of 1238 the Mongol army launched a full-scale assault on Desht-i Qipchaq: against the Circassians, Alans, and Polovtsians in the northern Black Sea and Azov Sea steppes. In winter, punitive expeditions of Mongols returned to the Middle Volga, completing the subjugation of the Mordovians and ruining the towns of the Vladimir-Suzdal land that were spared during the 1237 campaign. A new raid was also made against Ryazan principality.

Consolidation of New Political Systems 123

In March 1239, the Mongols captured Pereyaslavl on the left bank of the Dnieper, which could be considered Kyiv's shield from the southeast. However, throughout the spring and summer, their main efforts were concentrated against the highly mobile Polovtsians, who were putting up a stubborn resistance. In the fall, Batu's troops moved farther north through the Pereyaslavl land, into Chernigov principality, and on October 18, they captured the well-fortified Chernigov. Then the Mongols turned east, toward Putivl, destroying outposts on the border with the steppe. Thus, they repeated the maneuver already tried during the campaign against the Vladimir-Suzdal land and earlier, against Volga Bulgaria: similar to the blanket stitch used for finishing the raw edge of the fabric, the Mongols secured the edge of the steppe by periodic northward incursions into the Rous' Lands, then thrusting eastward (or westward) and returning to the steppe a hundred to several hundred miles from the point of incursion. The territory within this circular movement was cleared of enemy forces, providing a safe right flank for the next northward incursion.

At the end of December, the Mongols occupied most of the Crimea, where the Polovtsians had taken refuge from them. Another 40,000 Polovtsians led by Khan Köten were able to flee from the Mongols to Hungary. At the beginning of 1240, headed by Khan Möngke, the Mongols appeared near Kyiv, apparently for reconnaissance. Möngke did not storm the city, and only sent envoys to the prince offering peace. In the spring of 1240, the combined forces of Möngke and Güyük headed south to capture Derbent, seen as the gateway to the North Caucasus. They hoped to meet with the General Chormaqan's Mongolian expeditionary corps that were advancing from the South Caucasus northward. Their advancement was delayed for three months by the siege of the large Alanian trading city of Manas, which required exceptional efforts. After the entire Caucasus and the steppe north of the Black Sea fell under Mongol control in the summer of 1240, Great Khan Ögedei called back "the older boys"—the heirs of the Chagatai and Tolui uluses, as well as his son Güyük, together with their troops. Batu, the head of Jochi's Ulus and leader of the Western campaign, was left with his brothers and a few junior princes from other uluses. What began as a joint enterprise of all the Mongol uluses under the command of their leaders now turned into an internal affair of Jochi's Ulus with its modest military potential.

Batu's Transcarpathian Campaign

The Mongol casualties during the 1236–40 campaign are unknown, but they must have been very significant. The Mongol army had to storm dozens of well-fortified and strongly defended cities, fight with large and well-equipped armies, and make long, exhausting marches. Over the same period, the corps of Jebe and Subutai had avoided large fortresses but lost 87 percent of its men, and it is highly unlikely that the Western campaign took a lesser toll on the Mongols. However, by the fall of 1240 under the command of Batu, there were only about two times fewer troops than at the beginning of the campaign: from 40,000 to 70,000 by various estimates, not a maximum of 10,000–20,000 as could be expected (especially after the senior khans' departure for Mongolia). The only source of reinforcements for the Mongol army were the conquered peoples: it is known that the Mordovian contingent of the Batu army reached Germany; Bashkirs from the Southwest Urals fought on the side of the Mongols from the very beginning. Bulgars, Polovtsians, and probably Alans who did not escape the invasion, merged into the ranks of the Batu army when their leaders died or accepted the Mongol rule. Those Rous' principalities that recognized Mongol power also had to provide the Mongols, who traditionally demanded "a tenth of everything," with troops. If at the beginning of the Western campaign a significant part of the multiethnic Mongolian army consisted of the Turkic, Iranian, and Ugric tribes of conquered Central Asia, by the end of 1240, the majority of the troops should already have been staffed with multitribal natives of eastern Europe.

The return of other "princes" to Mongolia was a serious reason to stop further expansion to the west, but Batu decided to continue the campaign with his own forces. From the very beginning, his ultimate goal was to conquer the Kingdom of Hungary, and he even sent dozens of messages to King Béla IV demanding obedience. Apparently, taking the steppes of Pannonia under control was viewed by the Mongol elite as the culmination of Desht-i Qipchaq's conquest and the fulfillment of Chinggis Khan's historic promise to revive the Great Turkic Khaganate, uniting all nomads. Furthermore, the nomadic economy required a symbiosis with a prosperous sedentary society capable of accumulating significant resources for the payment of tribute. Besides King Béla, Batu also sent threatening messages to the emperor of the Holy Roman Empire, Frederick II, whose realm with a population of about six million was clearly more suited to the role of exploited sedentary partner-neighbor than were the warring rulers of a dozen Rous' principalities that, combined, had a much smaller population scattered over an immense territory.

The continuation of the campaign—beyond the Dnieper, Danube, and Carpathian Mountains—required safe flanks, so in November 1240, Batu's army assaulted Kyiv, the main potential threat on the steppe border between the Dnieper and Dniester. Like previous raids into the forest-steppe zone, this attack was carried out as a deep northward incursion from the steppe rather than a frontal expansion from the already subjugated adjacent territory in the east (in this case, from Pereyaslavl and Chernigov). Having crossed to the right bank of the Dnieper (probably at the rapids), destroying the border settlements of the Black Hoods—the Pechenegs and Torks who had settled along the Ros River and been baptized—Batu's troops besieged and captured Kyiv on December 6, 1240. Next came the turn of Galician-Volhynian principality, whose princes did not stage organized resistance and some even fled to Poland and Hungary. Several local towns were captured without a fight, a few, such as Galich and Volodymyr-Volynsky, fell after the siege, and the Mongols could not capture the fortress of Kremenets. The rulers of the neighboring Bolokhov land hastened to open negotiations with Batu and escaped the ruination of their principality by providing fodder for his army. After a respite, in early January 1241 Batu's army began the conquest of the Hungarian lands across the Carpathian Mountains.

Chinggis Khan's old general, Subutai, is credited as the main strategist of this campaign. The tactics he used in 1237–40, securing the northern flank of the army advancing along the steppe belt westward by a series of incursions into the sedentary territories, predetermined the plan of invasion of Pannonia. The Pannonian Steppe was protected from the rest of Desht-i Qipchaq to the east by the Carpathian Mountains and

Consolidation of New Political Systems

surrounded by strong potential allies in central Europe from the north and west. Batu personally led a small part of his army directly to Hungary through the snowcapped mountain passes, blocked off by abatises. Detachments under the command of Chinggis Khan's junior grandsons Kadan and Buchek bypassed the Carpathians from the south, through Transylvania and Wallachia (the traditional route of all nomadic migrants to Pannonia). Subutai stayed behind with the reserve force. The main part of the army, two or three tumens under the command of another junior grandson of Chinggis Khan, Baidar, bypassed the highest mountain ridge from the north, through Poland. By mid-March 1241, Batu's troops had fought their way to Pest, the rendezvous point of King Béla IV's army. At this time, the corps of Baidar was pushing through the Polish lands, forced to engage in repeated heavy battles with the detachments of Polish princes and dukes. On April 9, in the battle of Legnica, the Polish–German army was defeated, and High Duke of Poland Henry II the Pious, who commanded it, was killed. After a two-week respite, the remnants of Baidar's corps turned sharply south into Hungary. Almost simultaneously, on April 11, in the Battle of the Sajó River the united forces of Batu and Subutai, who came to his aid, defeated the Hungarian army. King Béla IV fled to Austria and then to Dalmatia to the shores of the Adriatic Sea. Kadan's detachment, which was moving around the Carpathians from the south, rushed after the runaway Hungarian king, and in March 1242 reached the westernmost point of the Mongol expansion on the Adriatic.

It is difficult to say how realistic Batu's plans were to establish himself in Hungary. On the one hand, in the summer of 1241, he began to establish the Mongol-Chinese system of government on the occupied territories, appointing *darugachi* (governors) and even minting the khan's coins. On the other hand, having taken Pest and small towns in the south, even one year later the Mongol army was unable to take under control about two dozen fortified cities—something that had never happened before. Apparently, the number of Mongol troops was insufficient for the task and they were "Mongol" only in a political sense, staffed mainly by contingents from the Rous' Lands, Volga Bulgaria, and the Polovtsian steppes. According to a chronicler writing in Latin, at the key moment of the Battle of Legnica, someone from the "Mongol" ranks in a "terrible voice" shouted "byegaycze, byegaycze!" The distorted transcription makes it difficult to precisely determine what the original said: either Polish "run!" or Russian "flee!" All the same, the Polish knights panicked in response. At some point, the losses of Mongolian commanders could become critical with regard to combat capability and the controllability of the motley crew of troops.

As to the size of these troops, the Mongol army is usually assessed by its number of tumens. Nominally numbering 10,000 soldiers, in reality, a tumen could be much smaller, particularly during a protracted war with many bloody battles. After the heavy losses sustained in Poland and Hungary, Batu's tumens might each have had only a few thousand combat-ready horsemen, which was a far cry from what was needed to hold the vast territory, much less completely subjugate it. The raid across Poland secured the northern flank of Mongol operations in Hungary, but this was only a temporary tactical achievement. By the fall of 1241, skirmishes with Czech-Austrian, Bavarian, and German forces along the western border of the Hungarian Kingdom had forced the "Mongols" to back away. In March 1242, one year after the beginning of the

126 New Imperial History of Northern Eurasia

invasion in Pannonia, none of its strategic goals had been fully achieved: many cities remained defiant, the legitimate ruler had not been killed or had at least been forced to sign a peace.

It is amid this uncertainty that Batu received news that Great Khan Ögedei had died on December 11, 1241. The most likely heir was Ögedei's eldest son Güyük, who became Batu's sworn enemy during the Western campaign and who had been consolidating his position in Mongolia after returning from the Polovtsian steppe in the summer of 1240. In the case of a military conflict with the new great khan, Batu could be trapped in sparsely populated and still insubordinate Hungary, isolated by the Carpathian Mountains from the resources of Desht-i Qipchaq. The Mongol army urgently left Hungary, retreating via the southernmost route, through the territory of the Bulgarian Kingdom that had hitherto been unaffected by the big war, and forcing its ruler to recognize himself as a vassal of the Yeke Mongγol Ulus.

The Peak and Collapse of the Mongol Empire

Batu had to abandon plans to settle in Pannonia near the borders of the Holy Roman Empire, as had the nomadic confederations of the past in the Mongol steppe near the borders of the Chinese kingdoms. As did other masters of Desht-i Qipchaq before him who were interested in controlling traditional trade routes and the steppe from the North Caucasus to the Urals, he decided to make the Lower Volga the center of his ulus. Following the tradition of nomadic confederations, Mongol uluses were divided into left (senior) and right wings, and Jochi's Ulus was no exception. The eastern, left wing, from the Urals to the Irtysh River, was ruled by Batu's elder brother Orda Ichen, who voluntarily recognized Batu as the head of Jochi's Ulus. Batu's right wing covered the entire east European steppe, from the Carpathian to the Ural Mountains. [15]

His fears about Güyük's coming to power were fully justified: after the interregnum, at the kurultai in 1246, Güyük was elected the next great khan and in 1248 moved an army against Batu. The first civil war in the Great Mongol Ulus ended as quickly as it began because Güyük suddenly died on the march. In 1251, a friend of Batu, Möngke was elected great khan. His bid was supported not only by Batu, who sent three tumens to make this support more convincing, but also by many leaders of other uluses— fellow veterans of the Western Campaign. Möngke's death in 1259 shattered the unity of the Mongol Empire. In 1260, two kurultais were convened one after the other: one in conquered China, the other in the capital of the empire, Karakorum. The two youngest sons of Chinggis Khan's youngest son, Tolui, were simultaneously proclaimed Möngke's successors: Kublai, who was leading the conquest of South China, and Ariq Böke, the guardian of the ancestral lands. The ensuing war between them escalated into a conflict among all four uluses, which supported one or another great khan. The Mongol Empire began to fall apart, and plunged into civil war. The open hostilities ended in 1304, only after the formal recognition by everyone of Temür, the ruler of the Yuan Empire in conquered China, as the sixth Great Khan of Yeke Mongγol Ulus. However, by this time, the Mongol Empire was a loose confederation of virtually independent uluses. In the fourteenth century, these uluses themselves began to fragment, and new ruling dynasties established in individual polities that emerged on their ruins were gradually losing even formal ties with the Mongol political tradition. In 1368, as a result of the Red Turban Rebellion, the Chinese Yuan dynasty was overthrown, and with it the formal title of the Mongol great khan ceased to exist.

The rise and expansion of the Mongol Empire transformed Northern Eurasia— from the Pacific Ocean to the Adriatic Sea—into a single space of political and cultural interaction, both in the lived experience of several generations of contemporaries and in the imagination of later historians and philosophers. The unprecedented magnitude of the multicultural population's relocations and the exchange of economic and administrative techniques radically transformed the map of the continent. At the same time, these radical changes brought about by Mongol conquests were largely structured by the contours of the old historical regions. On the one hand, this was because the spatial imagination of the Mongols was itself structured in the categories of ancient "lands." On the other hand, Mongol expansion was based on the subordination of the existing dynasties and governments that relied on established administrative and economic ties within certain political borders. Thus, initially, Jochi's Ulus included the lands of Khwarezm and the entire Caucasus, but the civil war of the 1260s introduced important corrections to its map. The borders between the uluses of Jochi and Chagatai and the so-called Ilkhanate became surprisingly close to the borders of the great Middle Eastern powers of past eras, which included both Mawarannahr in the northeast and the South (and sometimes North) Caucasus in the northwest. Now, however, the territory north of the ancient sedentary zones was no longer just a strip of steppes shared by multilingual nomadic tribes, but a politically highly organized society. This society was further united by a common cultural environment based on a single writing system and, as of the fourteenth century, a monotheistic religion.

The Long-Term Results of the Mongol Invasion

The integration of the continent's inner steppe and taiga regions into a common cultural space as a result of political self-organization and subsequent Mongol conquests produced colossal social upheavals from China to Europe. However, it is difficult to give an unambiguous and universally applicable answer to a popular question: To what extent did the Mongol invasion prove itself a destructive factor, and to what extent was its effect constructive? The very formulation of the question may be incorrect, since it implies a certain initial static state of things that the Mongols "worsened" or "improved" according to some objective yardstick of "historical progress." Known as the Golden Horde, the western wing of Jochi's Ulus is a case that demonstrates all the ambiguity of the question regarding the historical role of the Mongol conquests.

The available evidence, including archaeological data, can support mutually contradictory and equally speculative conclusions about the impact of the Mongol conquest on the polities north of the steppe zone—Volga Bulgaria and the Rous' Lands. What can be said for certain is that, in the mid-thirteenth century, Volga Bulgaria was included in the Golden Horde, whereas some of the Rous' Lands—first of all, the northeastern principalities—became vassals of the Golden Horde's khans (the so-called Tatar-Mongol yoke). At the same time, political formations of nomads (Polovtsians, Alans, and Circassians), who created complex societies with a diversified economy in the east European steppes, disappeared without a trace. Known only from Mongol sources is the existence of large cities in the steppe, vibrant centers of trade that Batu's troops captured with great difficulty after many weeks of siege. Judging by the chronology of individual operations during the campaign of 1236–40 and the number of references to various objectives of warfare in the texts created in the Mongol camp (including by European travelers), the Mongols spent most of their efforts and time on subduing the population of Desht-i Qipchaq that put up fierce and organized resistance to the invaders. The "usual" takeovers of one nomadic confederation by another, stronger one, in practice meant resubordination of the existing clan hierarchies to the new khan—mostly a political change. However, for the semisedentary population of the steppe that had elements of formal state institutions, the Mongol invasion meant the destruction of their entire way of life.

In contrast to this total catastrophe of the steppe society, the reaction of the Rous' Lands' rulers to the Mongol threat seems remarkable. Not only did this threat fail to mobilize the Rous' princes for unified action against the aggressor. There is also no evidence that the appearance of Batu's army in the steppe on the periphery of the Rous' Lands and even the raids he carried out were perceived as the main political problem of the moment. Judging by the Russian chronicles, the arrival of Mongols did not affect the regular political life of the Rous' Lands. For example, between 1235, when the great kurultai proclaimed the Western Campaign, and the Mongol sack of Kyiv in 1240, Kyiv changed rulers four times, in each instance in the form of an armed confrontation that harmed the fortifications and defenders of the city. Particularly destructive was the storming of the city in 1235 by Prince Iziaslav of Chernigov, although it was not so horrible as the assault on the city in 1203 by the prince of Smolensk, Rurik Rostislavovich: he plundered and burned Kyiv, including its churches and monasteries, and the city's inhabitants were driven into captivity by his Polovtsian allies. Moreover, the princes who replaced each other as masters of Kyiv, were not the least bit concerned about fortifying the city. Daniel (Danil) of Galicia, the nominal ruler of Kyiv at the time of its conquest by Mongols, was not even physically present in the city, which he administered through his chiliarch Dmitry. One of the princes of Kyiv during the Mongol invasion, Yaroslav Vsevolodovich, brother of the grand prince of Vladimir, Yuri Vsevolodovich, who was killed at the Sit River, took over Vladimir principality after Yuri's death. In the winter of 1239, just one year after the dramatic ruin of the principality by the Mongols, Yaroslav Vsevolodovich was able to gather a significant army and set off on an aggressive campaign against Smolensk, as if there were no Mongols around.

Thus, although the Mongol raids could be much more destructive than the usual interprincely wars as they inflicted a higher rate of casualties due to the large number of participating troops, they were not perceived by contemporaries as a fundamentally novel or different factor. The Mongols captured and burned cities (most of which had a population of no more than 1,000 people)—but this was also regularly done by neighboring Rous' princes. The appearance of Mongols nearby, even if they invaded, was not seen as a reason to form a defensive military alliance or to postpone another raid on the neighboring principality.

The permanent occupation of the forest and even the forest-steppe territory did not interest nomadic pastoralists. After delivering preventive strikes against the territories bordering on Jochi's Ulus (and the Bulgar lands, now incorporated in the ulus), the new masters of the steppe had no significant clashes with their northern sedentary neighbors for over a decade. The Mongols seemed to be included in the long-established political culture of universal competition and temporary alliances of the Rous' Lands, in which the factor of ethnocultural solidarity never played any role. In this situation, some of the princes made the important strategic choice of recognizing themselves as vassals of the Mongol Empire.

This meant that the great khan (and after 1266—the khan of the Golden Horde) became the supreme arbiter in any disputes between the princes (previously decided by military means). His representative in the Rous' Lands was granted the title of grand prince, and this title was confirmed by a patent (*yarlyk*—Mong. *Zarlig*, i.e., decree, diploma) issued by the khan. As it was during the formation of the Rous' Lands, political subordination was expressed through the payment of a fixed tribute and the provision of military contingents. In return, the Mongol ruler guaranteed a fair trial and military assistance. It would probably be an exaggeration to claim that the princes of the Vladimir-Suzdal land, who were the first to recognize the supreme power of the Mongols (Yaroslav Vsevolodovich and his son Alexander Nevsky), did it without any pressure from Batu. However, the ruler of Galician-Volhynian principality directly bordering on the steppe, Prince Daniel of Galicia, was able to avoid formal subordination to the khan and enjoyed a status as Batu's junior ally. Smolensk principality became the Golden Horde's vassal only after 1274 and had renounced this status by 1340. At the same time, a number of principalities had to recognize the supreme power of the Golden Horde, but their princes did not seek the privilege of acting as the khan's representatives in the Rous' Lands.

As it turned out, the Mongols' presence produced various results, largely depending on the priorities of the political players interacting with them. Representing a supratribal empire with a neutral confessional policy, the Golden Horde embodied a supreme political and military force that was neither less nor more alien than any other candidate for political domination in the region, be it a neighboring principality of the Rous' Lands, the Kingdom of Poland, Volga Bulgaria, or a confederation of Polovtsians. The initial patriarchal model for managing the Rous' Lands as a family matter, by the grand prince—father and local princes—sons subordinated to him, made political consolidation of the region practically impossible. Particularly after the demise of the father figure of the senior ruler in Kyiv, numerous principalities were governed by "brothers" having equal rights to the legacy of Rurik. As the kaleidoscope of successive masters of Kyiv shows, among the Rurikids, there was no one legitimate "royal" dynasty, whose representatives could insist on the subordination of other aristocratic families on the grounds of birthright or conquest—the main principles for legitimizing supreme power in medieval society. In this situation, recognition of the primacy of the Mongol Empire offered a universal solution by introducing a hierarchy of power into the horizontally organized political system. Many rulers in Central Asia, the Middle East, and the South Caucasus used this opportunity—and so did the grand princes of Vladimir in the Rous' Lands.

The rulers of Vladimir-Suzdal principality in the northeast of the Rous' Lands were able to use Mongol support to obtain an advantage over their neighbors–longtime rivals, but also to finally subjugate the city communes. The inclusion in the political hierarchy of the Mongol Empire, whose khans began to be called tsars (like the Byzantine emperors), raised the status of the grand princes approved by the Mongols. This created the preconditions for the emergence of a dynasty that stood above all other Rurikids. In the future, this dynasty would even lay claim to the political legacy of the Golden Horde as its most viable part.

Lithuania: The Birth of the Forest Monarchy

In the thirteenth century, simultaneously with the attempt to overcome the systemic crisis of supreme power in the Rous' Lands with the help of the external and "neutral" power of the Mongol Empire, a new political force appeared and claimed dominance in eastern Europe on different grounds—the Grand Duchy of Lithuania.

The heated debates between national historiographies (especially Lithuanian and Belarusian) about the "nationality" of lands and tribes that made up the Lithuanian principality only confirm the indispensability of multiculturalism and polyethnicity for any successful autochthonous political formation in the region. Like the Rous' Lands and the Great Mongol ulus, the Lithuanian principality emerged when it became no longer possible to employ clan ties as social institutions to solve the problems faced by society. Finding a way to establish the controlled collaboration of different "tribes" (i.e., groups that are not linked by common hierarchies of kinship) opens a path to building a polity of almost any size. As the relatively well-documented history of the Rous' Lands or the Mongol steppe shows, this political formation needs to be based on the common interests of local authorities (princes, the clan aristocracy), as well as the ability to use the immediate political and economic environment for the common good. From this perspective, the history of the rapid rise of the Lithuanian principality is of particular interest as an example of the political and cultural self-organization of lands that were originally on the periphery of the most intense historical processes of their time. Initially not even attracting particularly hostile attention from neighbors (certainly not comparable with the Jurchen threat to the Mongol nomads), the future Lithuanian principality in many ways created an acute political crisis in the region. The overcoming of the crisis was accompanied by the formation of a new polity, which in a short time managed to take a leading position in eastern Europe.

The East Baltic Region

The population of the southeastern coast of the Baltic Sea consisted primarily of Baltic tribes, or rather tribal unions, which the neighbors called Prussians and Curonians (Kurs). At the end of the first millennium CE, the Vikings (Danes and Swedes) regularly raided the coastline inhabited by the Prussians and Curonians. In the eleventh century, the Curonians and some of their neighbors themselves began raiding the Scandinavian coast and engaging in sea piracy in the Baltic. There is some information about the northern and southern peripheries of the area populated by the Baltic tribes. Strategic transcontinental trade routes that stimulated the coalescence of the Rous' Lands began

Consolidation of New Political Systems 131

farther to the northeast on the territories of the Finno-Ugric tribes of Livs and Aesti: the Volga–Baltic (through the Gulf of Finland and the Neva River) and the Dnieper–Baltic, its southernmost path running along the Daugava River (from the Gulf of Riga to Polotsk). The territories that are adjacent to this commercial route were mentioned in historical sources only inasmuch as they had drawn the attention of merchants and Varangian squads traveling along this way. At the opposite end of the Balts' area, in the south and southeast, the Prussian tribes bordered on the Polish principality (Civitas Schinesghe, and after 1025, the Kingdom of Poland) and the Rous' Lands. The central part of this wooded region, along the middle and upper reaches of the Neman River, remained isolated from the turbulent political developments of the turn of the millennium. The banks of the Neman River's upper reaches in Aukštaitija (from the Lithuanian *aukštas*—"upper"), the Upper Land, were inhabited by the Baltic tribes (Aukštaits) as well as Slavic colonists. Each group populated a significant part of the territory: the Aukštait tribes dominated in the western part, the Slavic tribes in the east. [16]

Considered predominantly Slavic, the territories along the upper Neman River entered the political system of the Rous' Lands relatively late. Chronicles begin to mention local princes only from the second quarter of the twelfth century, that is, after the Lyubech Conference. At this time, the main problem in the Rous' Lands was not the establishment of princely rule over free communes, but the regulation of relations among the growing clan-estate of princes. So, this westernmost part of the Rous' Lands, first of all, Grodno principality, was a latecomer lagging behind the general trends. Pine forests to the northwest of Grodno with larger or predominantly Baltic populations formed the periphery of this periphery inhabited by typical "forest folks" of Northern Eurasia.

Latecomers to the Rous' Lands

For the first time, the "border of Rous' and Litva" (confinio Rusciae et Lituae) is mentioned in a German chronicle under the year 1009: somewhere in the area of modern Western Belarus, the German missionary Bruno of Querfurt was killed by the Prussians. He participated in converting the Hungarians to Christianity, then proceeded through Kyiv to the Pechenegs and baptized several families, consecrating a special bishop for them. However, the sedentary Prussians, who became the next object of the daring missionary, turned out to be much more dangerous and aggressive than the nomads. Bruno's attempt to baptize the Yotvingians, a group that was part of the Prussian tribal confederation living in-between the Polish, Rous' and Lithuanian lands, proved fatal. The Yotvingians were mentioned in chronicles on several occasions as raiding neighbors or as victims of retaliatory campaigns. For example, as early as 983, having barely established himself in Kyiv, Prince Vladimir led his troops against the Yotvingians, and in 1038 Yaroslav the Wise followed in his footsteps.

In the 1040s, Yaroslav the Wise helped his brother-in-law, the Duke of Poland to subdue Mazovia in the north of the Polish lands. In this context, historical documents mention "Litva," either a separate territory known in English as Lithuania, or its population, which at the time was both Baltic (Lithuanians) and Slavic. While the modern term "Lithuania" can be used as a more or less accurate designation of that historical land, its population will be identified hereafter as Lituans: clearly related to modern Lithuanians but by no means identical with them. Yaroslav's troops marched to Mazovia through Lithuania, so he included this "no-prince's-land" under the authority of Polotsk principality, which, as usual, meant the establishment of tributary relationships. For the next century and a half, the vicissitudes of Polotsk history became the main external influence on the population of Lithuania. Over this period, apparently, the gradual integration of the Lithuanian lands and the western outskirts of the principality had been going on through trade, military affairs, and everyday contacts. [17]

After the death of Yaroslav the Wise in 1054, the principality of Polotsk entered a prolonged confrontation with the triumvirate of his successors. In 1067, they managed to capture the prince of Polotsk Vseslav, who waged endless attacks on his neighbors. However, he was released from captivity already in 1068, when the Kyivites, disappointed with their prince Iziaslav Yaroslavich, invited Vseslav to rule them. In 1071, Vseslav succeeded in returning to Polotsk, where he ruled until his death in 1101. Bad blood between the Polotsk and Kyiv princes persisted in the next generation, but this was in the post-Lyubech period, when the actual power of Kyiv reached a demise. The Polotsk land itself was divided among six or seven sons of Vseslav into appanage principalities, which continued to split up further. It is in this context, apparently, that new Rous' principalities such as Grodno appeared on the eastern border of Lithuanian Aukštaitija. In search of new territories and subjects, junior princes extended their authority to the Lithuanian lands.

The constant conflicts of the Polotsk princes with their neighbors involved the Lituans (as vassals participating in the campaigns of the overlords) in conducting raids on the neighboring Novgorod, Smolensk, and Volhynia lands, as well as in repelling retaliatory strikes. In 1127–30 the Kyiv prince Mstislav (son of Vladimir Monomakh) undertook several campaigns in an attempt to subjugate the Polotsk land. Divided into several appanage principalities, it was no longer controlled from a common center, so in order to finally neutralize the threat from the clan of Polotsk appanage princes, Mstislav took the nontrivial step of exiling all local princes to Byzantium. He made his son the ruler of the Polotsk land, but this change of dynasty was apparently not recognized by the Lithuanian lands: in 1132 Mstislav of Kyiv led a special campaign aimed at pacifying the Lituans. His troops ravaged Lithuania and took some prisoners, but on the way back the rearguard of the Kyiv army was beaten by the Lituans.

In the mid-twelfth century, the Lituans had already taken an active part in the struggle for power in the Polotsk principality between Vseslav of Polotsk's grandchildren, who had returned from Constantinople exile and immediately formed two rival parties. By supporting one or the other party, the Lituans acquired the role of important ally. Thus, in 1159, the leader of one local princely clan, Rogvolod, expelled a representative of the other clan, Prince Volodar, from Polotsk. The defeated Volodar fled to his allies in the Lithuanian lands, and they helped him to establish himself in Grodno, on the border with Aukštaitija. Three years later, Prince Rogvolod brought his army there in an attempt to achieve the final submission of the rival but was defeated by Volodar's allies from Lithuania.

Consolidation of New Political Systems   133

In this way, Aukštaitija, a part of the vaguely defined Lithuania, was gradually integrating into the political system of the Rous' Lands with its constant rivalry of contenders for princely offices and an economy of raids. The result was not long in coming. The inhabitants of Lithuania, who formerly lived from agriculture, fishing, and hunting, now acquired a stratum of professional warriors. Unlike usual tribal militia members, who returned to their customary occupations after the danger of a military confrontation was over, these warriors always looked for a new application for their combat skills. As late as 1180, detachments from Lithuania participated in a military campaign against Smolensk as allies of the Polotsk princes, but already in the winter of 1184, the Lituans set off on an independent raid against Polotsk and farther north, plundering the Pskov land. This raid cost the Novgorod prince Yaroslav Vladimirovich, whose duties included the defense of the vassal Pskov, to lose his office: the Novgorod city commune expelled him. Still more important was the symbolic significance of this raid: it marked Lithuania's joining the political system of the Rous' Lands as an equal part.

The Lituans played by the rules accepted in the Rous' Lands and within its territorial bounds. According to these rules, there was nothing extraordinary in Novgorodians' sacking of Prince Yaroslav Vladimirovich in 1184: after that, he returned twice to rule Novgorod and both times was expelled again for different reasons. Likewise, members of this political system were expected to raid neighboring principalities. In the vast Rous' Lands, the main threat to individual lands and urban communes came from escalating competition within the princely milieu, which was organized as a horizontal network and lacked a clear hierarchy of seniority or the priority of one princely dynasty over others. Within this network, a prince could increase his status by invading and pillaging the opponent's territory in a neighboring "cell." By contrast, enhancing the economic and political potential of one's own principality was not directly related to elevating the prince's status in the Rous' Lands.

The only obstacle to the official integration of Lithuania into the Rous' Lands was the absence of Rurikids among the local leaders, which made their power illegitimate. In principle, this obstacle could be avoided by a dynastic marriage, but it was not clear, who should claim the role of one indisputable leader—the main prince. The nascent stratum of professional warriors in Lithuania had not yet crystallized enough for this. When the political system of the Rous' Lands was only forming, individual lands received "ready-made" princes–leaders of the Varangian retinues. The local population accepted the legitimacy of their rule precisely because they were foreigners: the Varangians did not have to prove their right to exceptional status compared to other members of the community and they had the skills that the locals lacked. Lituans had to form princely power through a completely independent process.

Pushing Livonia into the Arms of Catholic Crusaders

In 1185 Lituans raided Livonia, the lands of the Livs, who were tributaries of Polotsk principality. This raid was as "domestic" as a raid on Pskov: the Lituans were operating in the political space of the Polotsk principality and the Rous' Lands in general, and not, for example, in the Prussian intertribal or Baltic territorial context. Clearly expressing

134   *New Imperial History of Northern Eurasia*

the claim to a share in the political legacy of the crumbling Polotsk principality, that raid led to some major unintended consequences.

Shortly before the Lithuanian invasion, the German missionary Meinhard von Segeberg arrived in Livonia. He settled in the trading post of German merchants at Ikšķile (German: Üxküll) on the Daugava River, some twenty miles from the sea, and began to preach Christianity, having secured the prior permission of the Polotsk prince. At first, Meinhard had very modest success with the locals, and he baptized only a few people in several years. But after the devastating raid from Lithuania, the Livs immediately agreed to build on their lands not just the first stone chapel, but two stone castles: in Ikšķile and in Salaspils down the Daugava, about halfway to the sea. Apparently, the nominal subjects of the Polotsk prince were not counting on his ability to protect them from the Lituans and welcomed the building of the fortresses. In 1186, Meinhard became bishop of Üxküll and obtained Pope Clement III's permission for any monk to join his mission in Livonia. In 1193, the new pope, Celestine III, called for any believers to join the Livonian mission, promising indulgence (official absolution) and the relaxation of strict monastic rules in return. Thus, in a matter of few years since the Lituan raid, the political situation in the southeastern Baltic had changed dramatically. On the site of trading posts established by private individuals—merchants—a diocese of the Catholic Church emerged under the special patronage of the papacy and with the goal of missionary expansionism.

In the 1190s, two parallel processes were unfolding: the Lituans were establishing themselves as a key force in the northwest of the Rous' Lands, and German missionaries were expanding their influence in Livonia. Lituans conducted systematic raids on Novgorod principality and its dependent territories in Karelia. Moreover, in 1198, they forced the Polotsk prince to join their attack on Velikie Luki in the south of Novgorod principality—just as two generations earlier they themselves were forced to participate in wars fought by Polotsk. Sometime at the turn of the century, Prince Vsevolod from the appanage principality of Jersika (Gerzika) in the northwest of the Polotsk land, in modern-day Latvia, married the daughter of the Lituan prince Daugirutis (Dovgerd). This first documented instance of intermarriage among Lituans and Polotsk Rurikids marked an important step toward the merger of Lithuania with the Rous' Lands.

At this time, the Livs attempted to expel the German missionaries who seemed to be establishing themselves permanently on the Livs' lands: after all, the church tithe was a much heavier burden than the tribute collected in the Rous' Lands. Many baptized Livs abandoned Christianity, and the rebel Livs seized the Salaspils castle. In response to the uprisings, in 1198, the new bishop of Livonia, Berthold Schulte, brought a caravan of ships from Lübeck containing armed monk–crusaders and the first German peasant-colonists. The peaceful preaching of Christianity gave way to the spread of religion and its political and economic institutions by the power of the sword, with varying success. In 1198, Berthold's army defeated the Livs, who tried to prevent his landing, but in 1199 the Livs were victorious, and Bishop Berthold Schulte himself was killed in the battle. The death of the bishop at the hands of the pagans triggered a more aggressive expansion of the German colonists. The third bishop of Livonia, Albert von Buxthoeven, sailed from Germany, accompanied by 1,500 "pilgrim"-crusaders. In 1201, at the mouth of the Daugava, they founded the city of Riga, where in 1202 a military order of "warrior monks" was established: the Livonian Brothers of the Sword. The Christianization of the Livs fully acquired the character of systematic military-economic colonization: moving inland from the coast, the crusaders built castles to control the conquered territory. Two-thirds of the colonized lands remained under the rule of the order, and one-third was transferred to the authority of the Bishop of Riga.

Thus, the consolidation of Lithuania as an independent regional power in the west of the Rous' Lands upset the existing balance of power in the region and, to a certain extent, brought about a new factor: military and economic colonization by the crusaders, mainly from the German lands. Initially separated from each other by the territories of the Baltic and Finnish tribes, the spheres of interests of the Crusaders and Lithuanians increasingly began to overlap, and at the end of 1201 in Riga, the Lithuanians concluded the first peace treaty with Bishop Albert: they had set out on a campaign against the Baltic Semigallian tribe on the left bank in the lower reaches of the Daugava and wanted to protect themselves from the threat of attack from the rear. From that moment, and for more than two centuries, the history of the Lithuanian lands became closely intertwined with the history of the crusaders in the Baltic.

A Recipe for Successful Political Self-organization

It can be added that simultaneously, as of the mid-1180s, at the opposite end of the Eurasian continent, Temuchin was consolidating his power over the nomadic tribes in the Mongolian steppe. Besides this chronological coincidence, common to the formation of the Mongol ulus and the Lithuanian principality was their reliance on the "pagan" religion of their ancestors. As was the case three centuries earlier with the Rous' Lands, the creation of large-scale political confederations on the basis of elementary "tribal unions" was probably facilitated by the absence of a universalist normative worldview. This gave the territorial expansion a strictly "political" character of "pure" power relations, almost dissociated from the dominance of a foreign and alien cultural code. It is at least known about the Mongols that although they were deeply devoted to their own shamanistic cult, they respected all religions. The boundaries of the Rous' Lands also took shape before the adoption of Christianity as an official religion, when local pagan cults got along with each other and did not interfere with political agglomeration. At some point, the grand prince of Kyiv and rulers of Mongol uluses discovered the need to adopt a monotheistic religion as the state religion, or rather the state-forming one. This happened when transcontinental trade and military expansion ceased to play the role of the main factors uniting the multicultural subordinate population. To keep the diverse populations together as subjects of a common polity, it became necessary to find an internal motivation for unity and a common language to express and disseminate ideas about the meaning of living together in a certain territory. Until that moment, external and foreign circumstances remained the main structuring factor: the borders of the conquered countries' provinces, some preexisting administrative and economic structures and networks, and so forth.

This explains the fact that the Lithuanian principality emerged in the sphere of the Rous' Lands, and not in the "natural" Baltic tribal context. Dealing with Rous' principalities must have been much more challenging than with the Prussian

136 *New Imperial History of Northern Eurasia*

confederation: they were more organized politically and economically, Christian and, presumably, Slavic-speaking even on its western outskirts. However, the Rous' Lands offered something that the neighboring Baltic tribes could not: a ready structure and scenario for Lithuanian political self-organization. In this situation, the hypothetical cultural and linguistic affinity was not an important stimulus for unification. The political solidarity of Baltic tribes began to form only in response to a new fundamental external factor—the expansionism of the crusaders. Before this, the Lituans were pushing their Baltic neighbors to side with the crusaders—in fact, the very arrival of armed crusaders instead of peaceful missionaries in the Daugava region was triggered by Lituan aggression against the Livs. Later, frightened by the Lituan raid of 1201–2, the Baltic tribe of Semigallians entered into an alliance with the bishop of Riga. They helped him suppress the resistance of the Livs, and in turn, in 1205, received military assistance from him against the Lituans. In 1207, Vyachko, the ruler of the Koknese principality in the northwest of the Polotsk land, so urgently needed protection from the Lituans that, in desperation, he promised half of his land and castle to the bishop of Riga in exchange for help (and the bishop did not miss this opportunity).

Polarization and Consolidation of the Baltic Peoples by the Crusaders

The beginning of the thirteenth century in this region was marked by a chaotic kaleidoscope of making allies and identifying enemies. As the scanty descriptions of conflicts in a few chronicles suggest, a radical reformatting of the political and cultural map was taking place on the territories of modern Lithuania, Latvia, and Estonia. Previously, various Finnish and Baltic tribal unions pursued different political trajectories and economic strategies: coastal tribes focused on overseas military and trade relations, hinterland tribes continued their socioeconomic practices, and those that entered the orbit of Polotsk and Novgorod principalities began adopting Orthodox Christianity. In response to the radically changed political situation in the region, two hostile centers were gradually formed by the 1220s. The crusaders and the Lituans led two opposing camps of voluntary and compulsory allies in the struggle for domination in the southeastern Baltics, or, as it was probably perceived by the local population, in the fighting either German Christianizing colonialists or Lituan expansionism. A "third force"—invaders from overseas or the remote forests—was uniting hitherto independent lands of equal status in the Baltic region by right of conquest. A similar process began in the Rous' Lands after the Mongol invasion only a few decades later.

After the final subjugation of the Livs, in 1207, the territory conquered by the crusaders along the Daugava River was proclaimed a principality within the Holy Roman Empire—Terra Mariana (Latin—Land of Mary, but also Land of the Sea in literal translation). After that, the crusaders directed their conquest northward, against the Aesti (related to modern Estonians). In alliance with friendly Latgalians, who were previously in the orbit of the Rous' Lands and even in some part converted to Orthodox Christianity, the crusaders attacked the individual lands (*maakonda*) of the Aesti one after another. In the decisive Battle of St. Matthew's Day in 1217, the Aesti were defeated by joint troops of the crusaders, the bishop of Riga, and the tribal

Consolidation of New Political Systems   137

militias of the Livs and Latgalians. The leader of the united resistance by the Aesti lands, Lembitu, was killed. As a result, the way was opened for the incorporation of the southern and central territory of present-day Estonia into Terra Mariana. (Shortly before that, in 1215, the status of the principality was raised: it came under the direct subordination of the papal Holy See.) The northern part of modern Estonia was under the rule of the Danish king, but in 1227, it too was conquered by the Livonian Brothers of the Sword. [18]

With some lag, the crusaders appeared on the opposite, southwestern end of the Baltic lands. Back in 1206, Pope Innocent III had announced a crusade against the pagan Prussians—a conglomerate of Baltic-speaking tribes who inhabited the territory along the Baltic Sea from the Vistula to the Pregolya River, which flows into the sea near present-day Kaliningrad. However, the actual crusade began much later, and the chain of events leading up to it had more to do with local conflicts than with some preexisting intervention plans by foreigners—just as it was with the formation of the Order of Livonian Brothers and the Riga Bishopric in the wake of Lituan assault on local tribes. In the south, the Prussian tribes bordered on the Polish Duchy of Mazovia (a few centuries later Warsaw would become the center of this territory). Ruled by a representative of the Piast princely dynasty, this was far from being the most prosperous and prestigious of the Polish lands. In an effort to enhance his status, Duke Konrad I of Mazovia attempted to seize some Prussian territories to the north under the pretext of converting the Prussians to Christianity, as stipulated by the papal decree. The Prussians responded with devastating raids and seizures of Mazovian territory. The north of Mazovia most likely had a significant Prussian population living alongside the Poles (like Balts and Slavs in the west of Polotsk principality). So, Konrad's confrontation with all Prussians as pagans could be met by Prussians' mobilization in the name of their territorial unification.

As in many other instances when historical lands or "tribes" acquired a single political organization and entered into a "state" conflict with neighbors, this confrontation was irresolvable in principle. It was no longer possible to reach a compromise through private agreements between the warring clans or other small collectives, as before, because now the whole principality was a party to the conflict as a collective political organization. There were also few chances to defeat enemies who were at about the same level of political and economic development. The Prussians could not conquer all of Mazovia (and hardly intended to), and Konrad did not have the resources to conquer the strong and numerous tribes of the Prussian confederation. In an attempt to break the deadlock after two decades of fruitless struggle, Konrad decided to seek help from a third force. This was a typical solution in that structural situation, which greatly complicated initial bilateral conflicts and intensified the process of unpredictable self-organization. Polish and Czech princes routinely appealed to the authority of the emperor of the Holy Roman Empire, while the Livs, fearful of the Lituans, accepted the help of German missionaries-colonists. Konrad chose the strategic partner halfway between these two options: in 1225, he invited the knights of the Teutonic Order (Order of Brothers of the German House of Saint Mary in Jerusalem) to protect the northern borders of the duchy from pagan raids. In exchange for this service, he ceded to them for twenty years the

Chełmno Land in the north of Mazovia—the bone of contention between him and the Prussians.

The Teutonic Order, founded after 1190 in Palestine, despite its name, was not perceived in the 1220s as a military and political instrument of the German emperor. In 1211, the king of Hungary András II granted the Teutonic knights the area in the southeast of Transylvania in exchange for their guarding the southern route from Desht-i Qipchaq to the Pannonian steppe, around the Carpathian Mountains, along which Polovtsian tribes migrated one after the other to Hungary. The knights were exempted from all taxes and duties, and they did not obey royal law or local church authorities. On the sparsely populated territory received by the order, they erected five fortresses and earthen ramparts. Colonists from the Hungarian and German lands resettled under the protection of these fortifications. Thus, in the 1220s the Teutonic Order was perceived as a frontier militarized self-governing entity performing the function of border guards, like Cossacks in the steppe or Grenzers on the border with the Ottoman Empire of later times. Therefore, it comes as no surprise that Konrad of Mazovia hastened to invite the Teutonic knights to his land as soon as he learned that András II had expelled them in 1225 for attempting to switch seigneurs, from the king of Hungary to the even more nominal and far-distant authority of the pope, which was also more prestigious. So, the knights came to the border with the Prussians from Transylvania—not from Germany.

In the deserted region of Transylvania on the border with the steppe, the Teutonic Order did not show any particular desire to conquer new territories. However, before arriving on the banks of the Vistula River in 1231, the order demanded a guarantee that any lands conquered in the future would be recognized as its possessions. This guarantee was provided by the Golden Bull of Emperor Frederick II in 1226. Pope Gregory IX, who bitterly struggled with Frederick II for supreme authority in the Catholic world, in 1234 decreed that all past and future land acquisitions of the Teutonic Order would have the status of the Holy See's vassal lands.

Formally a crusade aimed at forcible conversion of the pagan Prussians to Christianity, the territorial conquests by the Teutonic Order were only minimally accompanied by forceful acculturation: baptism and Germanization. Not only did the order have insufficient human resources for this work, but the very logic of the conquest of vast territory with a large bellicose population made the colonizers interested in using the already existing mechanism of social control, which only had to be reoriented to serve the new authorities. Therefore, like the Livonian Brothers of the Sword, the Teutonic knights tried to subjugate tribes one by one. As in Livonia, they built castles dominating the vicinity on the sites of former tribal centers, thereby taking over their former authority and administrative functions. The subordination of the tribal nobility meant the subordination of the entire tribe; the adoption of Christianity by the tribe's leader disorganized the local pagan cult and opened the way to the baptism of the majority in the future. Paradoxically, less intervention into tribal internal affairs meant higher control over the tribe. [19]

In the early 1230s, when the Livonian Order and the bishop of Riga established control over the entire northeast of the Baltic region, north of the Daugava River, the knights of the Teutonic Order began the region's conquest from the southwest.

Consolidation of New Political Systems 139

Crusaders from German, Polish, and Czech lands and Denmark joined this conquest. A giant arc of the emerging new common space stretched out from the Polish principalities and imperial lands along the Baltic Sea, to the periphery of Novgorod possessions, across the lands of the Prussians, Curonians, Livs, Latgalians, and Aesti. This common space was defined by unanimous opposition to the crusaders or equally wholesale alliance with them. Such a space of all-embracing solidarity had never existed here before—neither in the form of a political union nor as a cultural unity. It gradually expanded and encompassed new territories, already affecting the lands of Yotvingians and the Samogitians. As a result, Lithuanian Aukštaitija found itself transformed from a periphery of the Baltic world into a core territory not yet affected by the new political realignment.

The Lithuanian Aukštaitija as an Independent Political Actor in Search of Allies

Judging by the list of Lituan raids and campaigns, at first the Lituans saw their isolated position not as a potential threat but as an advantage that provided them with freedom of maneuver. Accordingly, after many of their military leaders perished in 1213 and 1214 during the raids on Livonia, now protected by the castles of the knights, the Lituans radically changed the direction of their attacks. Over the next decade, they undertook at least six major campaigns in the Rous' Lands: mainly against Pskov and Novgorod, but also in the distant Chernigov principality (1220) and Smolensk (1225). It is difficult to draw a formal line between predatory raids and regular political relations in the thirteenth century. The principalities of the Rous' Lands and their neighbors in the Polovtsian steppe or the Lithuanian forests did the same things during raids: they captured prisoners and looted valuables, including those belonging to churches and monasteries. At the same time, the parties of open conflicts sustained economic and political relations, and the former adversaries could become allies in the next conflict. That Lituan raids were an element of foreign policy (and not just plundering) is confirmed by the peace treaty concluded with the Galician-Volhynian principality in 1219 (in 1215 according to the chronicle's chronology), one of the first documents produced by the Lituans. [20]

First of all, the choice of ally was clearly strategic: Galician-Volhynian principality was the southern neighbor of the expanding Lithuanian land, which had apparently absorbed the buffer territories of the Polotsk land that initially separated the Lithuanian territory from Volhynia. The appanage Grodno principality was such a buffer territory, and the fact that chronicles stopped mentioning it after 1183 most likely means it had been absorbed by the Lituans along with other Polotsk peripheries. In the west, the Lituans neighbored Baltic tribes, in the east—Polotsk principality, which they had gradually been absorbing. Their raids were directed to the north and northeast against Livonia, Pskov, and Novgorod. So, only the southern border with a powerful Galician-Volhynian principality was a matter of special concern. Another important feature of the 1219 treaty was that it was signed not by one prince—the leader of a raid (as was the case in 1201 when the Lituans concluded a treaty with the bishop of Riga)—but by twenty-one princes, grouped by seniority and the territories they represented, just as in the early treaties between the Rous' princes and Byzantium. The first five signatories probably represented Aukštaitija, of whom the senior one was a certain Zhivinbud. They were followed by two princes from Samogitia (the "lower" Lithuanian lands down the Neman River, west of the "upper" Aukštaitija). Next mentioned were representatives of the Rushkovich clan (seven names), the Bulevich clan (three names), and four "princes from Diavolta" (Deltuva principality along the Šventoji River northwest of modern Vilnius). Several centuries later, the Bulevich clan (Billevich, Billewicz) was known as an ancient Belarusian szlachta (noble) family, the Rushkovich clan (Rushkevich) can also be identified with Belarusian names and toponyms known from later times.

Numerous attempts to prove the "primordially Lithuanian" or "typical Slavic" origin of the names mentioned in the treaty have not led to any unambiguous conclusions. The propinquity of Indo-European roots of the two language families that had been interacting for centuries makes it virtually impossible to tell with certainty the direction of influence and borrowing in each case. The princes who signed the treaty of 1219 most likely represent Lithuania as a wide confederation of lands and various Baltic and Slavic tribes that preserved their pagan beliefs. The cooperation of diverse cultural communities and multilingualism were typical of Northern Eurasia, making the question of the "nationality" of Lithuania as a political entity meaningless. Lithuania of this era was not a people, but a "land" inhabited by cooperating and warring multicultural groups, similar to the Rous' Lands. The absence of a single official religion and book culture did not hinder but instead helped Lithuania to expand at the expense of neighboring territories—just as the cultural sameness of the Rous' principalities at this time did not prevent them from fragmentation and fierce confrontation with each other.

By the 1230s, the Polotsk principality had come almost entirely under the control of the Lituans, who began ruling it formally from the beginning of the 1240s at the latest. Even if the Rurikids were retaining their status as the nominal rulers of Polotsk until that time, they had to take into account the factor of Lithuania's growing power. Thus, in addition to the pagan Slavic clans living in Aukštaitija and Samogitia, the predominantly Orthodox Christian and, apparently, Slavic-speaking population of future Belarus in the Polotsk land was joining the multicultural population of Lithuania. This population shift did not undermine the political supremacy of the Baltic princely families in Lithuania, but it made Lithuania a formal participant in the Rous' Lands. The 1219 treaty with Galicia-Volhynia, the absorption of Polotsk, and attempts to establish control over the Toropets principality between the Smolensk and Novgorod territories testified to this new status of Lithuania.

The rapidly changing situation in the west in the Baltic region did not allow Lithuania to commit itself completely to the eastern political sphere of the Rous' Lands. In the same year 1219, when the Lituan princes concluded an agreement with the Galician-Volhynian principality, the Semigallians broke their long-standing alliance with the Livonian Order and the bishop of Riga. This happened after the crusaders, having established control over the territories north of the Daugava, began their expansion to the Semigallian land to the south of the river. The Semigallians turned for help to their former enemies—the coastal Curonians and the inhabitants of Samogitia further inland. In 1228, Semigallians and Curonians attacked Riga: they could not capture the city but plundered the fortified Dunamünde Abbey at the mouth of the Daugava.

On February 9, 1236, Pope Gregory IX announced a crusade against Lithuania. The core of the crusader army consisted of the Livonian Order forces joined by about 2,000 German knights from elsewhere, but the main manpower was provided by the subordinated tribes of the region (Livs, Latgalians, and Aesti), as well as local Christian allies—Novgorod and Pskov. On September 26, 1236, the crusaders were ambushed by the combined forces of the Samogitians and Semigallians in the "Saule" area—either near Šiauliai on the territory of modern Lithuania, or Vecsaule in Latvia. In a fierce battle, the master and 48 knights of the Livonian Order died, as well as 180 of the 200 Pskov warriors. The defeat was so crushing that it called into question all of the order's previous conquests. Recently pacified by the order, the Curonians from the Baltic coast immediately revolted. The Semigallians and Selonians followed suite, which meant that the entire territory south of the Daugava seceded from Terra Mariana. Unable to cope with this damage on their own, on May 27, 1237, the Livonian Brothers of the Sword merged with the Teutonic Order, which inherited all the Livonians' property and political role in the region. Aukštaitija, Samogitia, and their Baltic neighbors, who were still evading occupation by the crusaders, found themselves bounded the Teutonic Order's expansionist state. [21]

The consolidating Lithuania faced several possible, not necessarily mutually exclusive prospects. It could continue its integration with the Rous' Lands. However, the Mongol invasion of 1237–40 delivered a decisive blow to this political system and altered the old rules of the game. Another possibility was the reconciliation with the crusaders. It implied the complete subordination to the Teutonic Order or the rapid voluntary Christianization of the Lituans as a necessary condition for negotiating a partner status with the order. Leading the anticrusader resistance in the Baltic was the third option. Multiple domestic circumstances and the logic of the unfolding political situation in the region determined the path taken by the Lithuanian confederation.

Further reading

Dimnik, Martin. *Power Politics in Kievan Rus': Vladimir Monomakh and His Dynasty, 1054–1246*. Toronto: Pontifical Institute of Medieval Studies, 2016.

May, Timothy. *The Mongol Empire*. Edinburgh: Edinburgh University Press, 2018.

Onon, Urgunge. *The Secret History of the Mongols: The Life and Times of Chinggis Khan*. New York: Routledge, 2001.

Rowell, S. C. *Lithuania Ascending: A Pagan Empire within East-Central Europe, 1295–1345*. Cambridge: Cambridge University Press, 2014.

Zelart, Anti. *Livonia, Rus', and the Baltic Crusades in the Thirteenth Century*. Translated by Fiona Rob. Boston: Brill, 2015.

4

From Local Polities to Hierarchical Statehood

Interaction and Entanglement of Competing Scenarios of Power (Thirteenth–Fourteenth Centuries)

By 1237, the vast territory to the east of the Holy Roman Empire between the Vistula River and the Ural Mountains—what we identify today as Eastern Europe—had become almost completely included in the horizontal network of principalities of approximately equal power. Even when a community developed political organization under the influence of more powerful neighbors, it was still a process of fairly spontaneous self-organization in which junior partners determined the outcome almost as much as senior ones did. More or less synchronous political self-organization of neighboring communities that were systematically exchanging information and practices explains why no principality was able to dominate the rest. The expansion of the crusaders in the Baltics and the Mongols in Desht-i Qipchaq created a fundamentally new political dynamic. It opened the possibility for previously independent polities to consolidate into more complex and powerful political formations through subordination to a single central power.

Reformatting the Rous' Lands

By 1237, for more than a century, the largest political system in the region—the Rous' Lands—had been in the same state of unstable equilibrium as the Baltic tribal unions or Desht-i Qipchaq. We find essentially the same predicament everywhere: neighboring appanage principalities or "tribes" could neither defeat one another nor completely abandon mutual pretensions since there were no clear state borders between them, and the concept of "foreign policy" in the modern sense was unknown (as separate from domestic policy, economics, or family relationships inside a dynasty). Endless clashes with neighbors resulted not so much from the excessive belligerence of people living in that era as from their social imagination, which differed from that of modern times. For them the concept of territorial border was extremely abstract, impossible to visualize and document before the development of precise cartography.

The division into friends and foes was situational and momentary, rather than strategic and permanent. New circumstances—often completely incongruent with abstract "objective interests," such as envy of the neighbor's war booty—could instantaneously realign the ranks of allies and enemies. At the same time, compared to earlier periods, it became much more difficult to resolve even mundane local conflicts, because the political self-organization of lands and tribes into principalities greatly expanded the scope of collective solidarity and responsibility. A conflict now concerned not only its direct participants and their close relatives, but all subjects of the local prince. This is the reason for the constant "war of all against all" that is routinely associated with the period of feudal fragmentation. The long-established historical lands—identifiable territories with a population sharing a sense of community—by the very fact of their existence, confirmed their distinction from neighbors. After receiving centralized political organization—basically a prince with a retinue nearby and deputies in community centers—those historical lands did not become stronger than their neighbors who had advanced to a similar level of political and economic development at about the same time. With enhanced combat capabilities, their tensions and conflicts became more systematic and widespread, but no one was able to take an unconditionally dominant position. Against this background, the almost synchronous appearance of three contenders for dominance in the region—the Teutonic Order, Jochi's Ulus, and the Grand Duchy of Lithuania—represented three alternative scenarios of political centralization and consolidation.

Northwestern Principalities and the Teutonic Order State

After extending its power to Livonia, the Teutonic Order emerged as a large polity with a centralized administrative structure, unlike any other power in the region. By 1241, five of the Prussians' seven main tribal unions recognized the authority of the order. The order neither sought to destroy the local clan aristocracy and tribal leaders nor recognized their authority as representatives of the central government or junior partners–vassals. To this religious-political organization, only Christians were deemed legitimate counterparts in any legal and political transactions. Naturally, the order preferred to deal with Roman Catholics, but the Orthodox subjects of neighboring Pskov and Novgorod further east were also viewed as full-fledged partners, which made an alliance with the order attractive in the eyes of some Rous' leaders, especially in Pskov. As a result, a new complex political and economic common space formed in the southeastern Baltics. Retaining their old political membership in the Rous' Lands, Pskov and Novgorod joined this new common space, as their economies largely depended on the Baltic trade with German market towns that would later form the Hanseatic League, via the mediation of Livonian merchants in Riga and Dorpat (Tartu). These ties with the Teutonic Order and German free cities of the Holy Roman Empire were particularly important for commercial and political elites in Pskov, who feared the rising influence of Novgorod and the Vladimir-Suzdal land. Novgorod, also interested in trade with Livonia, had more tense relationships with western neighbors vying with Teutonic and Scandinavian knights and missionaries for vast colonial territories in Karelia. Both Pskov and Novgorod eagerly invited Lituan princes as allies in their conflicts with each other and with the Teutonic Order. [1]

This medley of mutual interests and rivalries in the early 1240s occasionally led to open border conflicts between Catholic and Orthodox neighbors. In July 1240, at the mouth of the Neva River, the troops of the Novgorod prince Alexander Yaroslavich clashed with a Swedish punitive expedition that had come to subdue the rebellious Finnish tribes. This battle, for which prince Alexander was nicknamed Nevsky, was an episode of Novgorod's decade-long struggle for control over the Izhora land as a colony. Several months later, the former prince of Pskov, Yaroslav Vladimirovich, who was previously expelled from the city under the pressure of the Vladimir-Suzdal principality, returned to Pskov with the support of the Teutonic Order. Alexander Nevsky was the main overseer of Vladimir-Suzdal interests in the region, so he gathered forces and marched from Novgorod against the pro-German Pskov prince and the knights who supported him. On April 5, 1242, the Novgorodians fought with the troops of the Teutonic Order at Lake Peipus (Lake Chud). Despite its fierceness, this battle, in which twenty knights lost their lives and six were taken prisoner, was regarded by the order as a border skirmish caused by a political conflict of secondary importance. This assessment was confirmed by the relatively small scale of casualties, incomparable to those incurred in battles with the Lituans, particularly during the Saule battle in 1236.

The Teutonic Order's main concern remained their continued control over the conquered lands of the pagans. The long-lasting uprisings of the Prussians in the 1240s and 1260–1270s contributed to the consolidation of the order's regime of military occupation. The massive colonization of lands by immigrants from Christian northern Europe, the human losses and assimilation suffered by the Prussians, and their mass migration to Lithuania quickly shifted the population balance in favor of the colonists. It is believed that by the beginning of the fifteenth century, the Prussians made up only about a third of the population on the territories controlled by the Teutonic Order. Over the same period, the German colonists founded more than ninety cities there—an unprecedented rate of urbanization for Europe at that time. Crafts and trade flourished under the protection of the city walls, peasant settlers cultivated more and more fields. The order's political centralization and integration of the once independent tribes effectively created on their territories a completely new society defined by rigid cultural and legal norms of German-speaking medieval Christendom. This society largely ignored the existence of the indigenous peoples and their rights to land and property. The only entrée to this new society was baptism, which provided the right to legal protection and social integration.

The Principalities Forcefully Subjugated by the Mongols and Those that Kept Their Independence

A parallel process of unification of aboriginal societies took place in the southeast of the region. The Mongols' westward campaign led to the expansion of Jochi's Ulus to Hungary, and later to the establishment of the Golden Horde as an independent khanate claiming supreme power on the territory from Central Asia to the Carpathian

146 *New Imperial History of Northern Eurasia*

Mountains. The introduction of Chinggis Khan's administrative system throughout the conquered territory—the division of the population into thousands and tumens (ten thousands), regardless of clan and tribal boundaries—had the same effect of centralization and integration of previously independent tribes and lands. Unlike the Teutonic Order, the Mongol centralized statehood was inclusive and did not discriminate against anyone, but it did not allow anyone to escape its hold. Following Chinggis Khan's program of unifying all nomadic peoples ("people of the felt walls"), the diverse population of Desht-i Qipchaq was directly included in the single polity, which was only nominally "Mongol." The urbanized territories of Volga Bulgaria and the North Caucasus were also incorporated into this polity, probably because they still allowed nomadic cattle breeding while offering nomads the much-needed cultivation of cereals and production of manufactured goods, as well as established market towns. The status of the vast Rous' Lands remained uncertain after the Mongols subdued their main strategic centers on the border with the steppe in 1237–40.

On the one hand, the Mongols did not attempt to conquer the Rous' Lands and permanently occupy them in the same way that the Teutonic Order had occupied East Prussia and Livonia. Probably not only the northern forest part but also the southern forest-steppe zone of the Rous' Lands was of little practical interest to them. But on the other hand, immediately after the raids through the southern principalities, Mongol officials—darugachi (basqaqs of the Russian chronicles)—were appointed there. According to some sources, they were also appointed to those cities of the northeast, which voluntarily submitted to the Mongols during the raid of 1238 (e.g., in Uglich). Still, by itself, the presence of representatives of Jochi's Ulus in town alone did not yet determine the status of the principality.

It took two decades for the Rous' Lands to be practically drawn into the orbit of the Mongol political system. This process had unequal consequences for different territories and, despite the asymmetrical relations of power, it was bilateral. Beginning in 1243, the princes of the Rous' Lands began paying visits to Batu, who had retreated from Hungary. They were acting voluntarily or at an invitation that could not be turned down. Visitors pledged their loyalty to Jochi's Ulus, after which they were usually recognized as rulers in their principalities and returned home. This did not make Rous' princes formal vassals of Batu because there was no talk of paying regular tribute yet. The Mongol Empire would impose tribute on the conquered territories only after conducting the population census, so the first sign of the Mongols' formal political domination was not their victorious military raid, but the arrival of the khan's census takers. By 1246, censuses were completed in the Kyiv and Chernigov principalities and probably in other southern territories along the border with the steppe. This meant that these principalities became vassals of the Mongol Empire under the administration of local princes.

The prince of Galician-Volhynian principality, Daniel (Danil) Romanovich, evaded visiting Batu for a long time; he came to pay his respects and confirm his loyalty only under direct pressure: the Mongols threatened a punitive expedition against his capital, Galich (Halych). Already in the early 1250s, Daniel had expelled the Mongol officials from his land but he continued sending gifts to Batu every year and participated in joint military expeditions with the Mongols. Apparently the Mongols did not conduct

Local Polities to Hierarchical Statehood

a census in Galicia-Volhynia, and annual gifts to the khan were not regarded as tribute. The subtle difference in interpretation defined the political status of Prince Daniel as Batu's junior partner rather than a formal vassal.

By this time, Polotsk principality had been completely absorbed by Lithuania. The Mongols did not invade its territory or the lands of Novgorod and Pskov. Smolensk principality also remained largely unaffected by the new political reality in the south and was much more concerned with the expansionism of neighboring Lithuania. Smolensk entered the Golden Horde's sphere of influence only in the mid-1270s, when the Mongol army passed through its lands to aid the Galician-Volhynian prince Leo (Lev), who was at war with Lithuania. Afterward, in 1275, a population census was taken in Smolensk principality and was followed by the imposition of regular tribute— almost forty years after the Mongols' invasion of eastern Europe.

The Vladimir-Suzdal Principality and the New Model of Dealing with the Mongols

The vast Vladimir-Suzdal principality in the northeast found itself in-between the Rous' Lands that preserved their independence and those that became Mongol vassals. Like the southern principalities, it suffered the devastating Mongol invasion in 1238 and bordered on Jochi's Ulus (along the Volga). However, unlike the forest-steppe zone, its territory was not suitable for nomadic cattle breeding, and the Mongols did not appoint administrators to the principality's main cities or conduct a census there. Rather, the initiative to establish close ties with the Mongols belonged to the local princes themselves. In 1243, Grand Prince Yaroslav Vsevolodovich was the first of the Rous' rulers to visit Batu, who benevolently acknowledged his status as the senior prince of the Rous' Lands ("the elder of all the princes [speaking] the Russian language"). This meeting was most likely arranged by his son Alexander Yaroslavich (Nevsky), who, according to some sources, became acquainted with Batu in 1242. The timing suggests the possibility of alternative interpretations of this key event: the first meeting of a Rous' grand prince with Khan Batu, and the idea of using this meeting not only to confirm the prince's right to rule over his domain but also to endow him with the status of grand prince of the entire Rous' Lands. It could be that Batu began to summon the Rous' princes to determine their loyalty, starting with Yaroslav Vsevolodovich, or that Yaroslav himself proposed to Batu a new model for dealing with the princes.

Either way, the title of senior prince meant little in practice, other than the granting of control over ruined Kyiv: by that time, for almost two centuries since the death of Yaroslav the Wise, the Rous' Lands had not been subject to one supreme ruler. Nearly every principality had its own "grand prince." Moreover, obtaining this hollow title entailed additional troubles. To validate Prince Yaroslav Vsevolodovich's current status, Batu's approval would have been sufficient. But since Batu himself was only a coruler of one of the uluses of the Mongol Empire, only the great khan could officially confirm the elevation of the Vladimir prince's authority to supreme ruler of the entire Rous' Lands—a vassal of the Mongol Empire. Therefore, in August 1246 Yaroslav Vsevolodovich arrived in Karakorum, the capital of the Mongol Empire, where he witnessed the election of the next great khan, Güyük. His status as chief prince of

148 *New Imperial History of Northern Eurasia*

the Rous' Lands was confirmed, but on the way home Yaroslav Vsevolodovich died. According to the most popular hypothesis, he was poisoned on Güyük's order. This interpretation makes sense: it is known that Güyük hated Batu and thus could consider his protégé Prince Yaroslav an enemy. Not confirming the new status of Yaroslav, previously approved by Batu, meant discrediting the local Mongol ruler in the eyes of the vassals. Letting Yaroslav return home as the nominal master of the entire Rous' Lands meant strengthening Batu, against whom Güyük was preparing to go to war.

In 1247, two sons of Yaroslav Vsevolodovich traveled to Karakorum—the elder Alexander Nevsky and the third son Andrei. This time, Güyük was free to appoint the senior prince of the Rous' Lands himself, choosing from the two candidates: he selected not the elder Alexander, who was closely associated with Batu, but Andrei. Largely nominal, Andrei's grand-princely status was further deliberately compromised by provoking the resentment of the powerful Alexander Nevsky, who had been bypassed despite his seniority. After returning home, Andrei did not maintain close contacts with the Mongols. Great Khan Güyük, who appointed Andrei, died unexpectedly in 1248, just as he was about to depart for the war with Batu. In turn, Batu had strained relations with the grand prince, who had been selected by his enemy. Instead, Prince Andrei Yaroslavich became a close ally of Grand Prince Daniel of Galicia, and even married his daughter in 1250: in the Middle Ages, interdynastic marriages were much more "official" confirmation of a political union than written treaties. Many historians see their alliance as a preparation for anti-Mongol resistance by the two most powerful princes of the Rous' Lands. There is no evidence of their contemplating any such plans, but it is likely that Andrei followed the example of Daniel, who distanced himself from the Mongols as much as possible without directly alienating them. The situation radically changed in 1251, when the interregnum in Karakorum ended and Möngke was elected the next great khan with the support of his old friend Batu. Prince Andrei's elder brother Alexander Nevsky traveled to see Batu's son and coruler, Sartak. He denounced his brother Andrei as being disloyal to the Mongols and holding his title illegally, in violation of seniority. Alexander Nevsky returned to Vladimir-Suzdal principality with a large Mongol army.

Alexander Nevsky: A Rous' Prince Turned Mongol Viceroy

Thus, in 1252, for the first time since the Mongol Empire's Western campaign, a significant military force was sent against the Vladimir-Suzdal principality. According to the Russian chronicles, the army was led by a certain high-ranking Nevriui. Some historians believe this was Alexander Nevsky himself, interpreting "Nevriui" as a distorted Mongolian pronunciation of the Neva River as "Nevra." Others think it was Niuryn (Nurin), a military leader who came from Inner Mongolia and later made a rapid career under Möngke. Despite disagreements regarding the scale and goals of the Nevriui campaign, its immediate results are clear: the army of Andrei Yaroslavich was defeated near Pereyaslavl-Zalessky, the city was plundered, and he himself fled to Novgorod, and from there to Sweden. His grand prince's patent (*yarlyk*) was transferred by Khan Batu to Alexander Nevsky. According to the chronicle, Prince Andrei commented on his brother's actions: "How long will we quarrel among ourselves and set the Tatars upon [each other]; it is better to flee to a foreign land than to be friends with the Tatars and serve them!"

The same scenario was used by Alexander Nevsky to subjugate the mighty and unruly Novgorod land. Novgorodians had expelled him from the office of prince in 1240, and in 1255 and 1256 rebelled against his protégés. The Novgorod city commune was notoriously self-willed, and within the political system of the Rous' Lands, princes had to comply with its decisions. But in 1257 Alexander Nevsky brought a Mongol detachment to Novgorod and, acting on behalf of the Mongols, crushed the opposition to his authority, ordering that the noses of some local leaders be cut off and the eyes of others gouged out. In 1259, using the threat of bringing in the Mongols again, he forced the Novgorodians to partake in the census—thus, Novgorod recognized itself as a vassal of the Mongol Empire, obliged to regularly pay tribute. What was formerly a bilateral conflict between the city commune and the prince as two legal entities was now transformed into a political matter of subordination or disobedience to the general order established by the Mongols. Thus, a precedent was created for subduing city communes, which was later widely used by the Vladimir (and subsequently Moscow) grand princes. Previously, the princes of the Rous' Lands regularly resorted to the help of nomads (Pechenegs or Polovtsians) as military allies in order to gain power for themselves. Now, in the northeastern lands, the princely power itself was reconsidered as representing the supreme power of the Mongol Empire. From now on, it was based not on an agreement with the city commune, but on the right of the conquerors (Mongols) delegated to their vassals-princes, whose authority was officially confirmed by the khan's yarlyk as a patent to reign. Gradually, the status of the "grand prince" began to change. The empty formal title was acquiring practical weight as a ruler's rank in the centralized hierarchy of the Mongol Empire, and from 1266—the independent Golden Horde.

This transformation marked the final disintegration of the Rous' Lands in the second half of the thirteenth century into several political systems developing in different directions. The southwestern territories gravitating to the Galician-Volhynian principality retained their independence as a junior ally of the Golden Horde. Polotsk land in the west was absorbed by Lithuania. The northeastern Vladimir-Suzdal principality was actively integrating into the political system of the Golden Horde, simultaneously dragging into the Horde's political sphere the neighboring territories of Ryazan, Murom, and even Novgorod, which was located so far away from the steppe. This process was accompanied by linguistic differentiation, which affected the naming of diverging territories. The population of the northeast of the former Rous' Lands began to call themselves "Rusians" or "Russians" (*ruskie*), and the population of the southwest—"Ruthenians" (*rus'kie*).

The Formation of the Grand Duchy of Lithuania

As a polity ruled by the single prince, Mindaugas, Lithuania was first mentioned in historical records in 1238, when everything seemed to be working in its favor. Lithuania's main foe, the Livonian Brothers of the Sword, had suffered a crushing

150   *New Imperial History of Northern Eurasia*

defeat, and the rival Vladimir-Suzdal and Chernigov lands were devastated by the Mongols. In 1239, the Lituans captured Smolensk, a longtime rival for control over Polotsk principality, whose allies in the northeast and south had just been defeated by the Mongols. The political system of the Rous' Lands operated by the logic of a zero-sum game: the loss of one participant automatically meant the gain of the other.

The Demise of the Rous' Lands Political Scenario

However, just a year after the Mongol invasion, the new prince of Vladimir, Yaroslav Vsevolodovich, was able to assemble a strong army and expel the Lituans from Smolensk. No matter how destructive the blow inflicted by the Mongols was, it affected mainly a thin layer of the politically organized part of society concentrated in cities, most of which had populations of less than 1,000, and units of professional warriors (prince retinues), who never exceeded a couple of thousand or even several hundred men in the entire principality. This explains, why educated contemporaries invariably described enemy invasions in apocalyptic terms, even if the enemy troops were several hundred strong. This is also why a total military catastrophe always gave way to a rapid recovery: scattered over a vast territory, the bulk of a principality's population lived in small villages of a dozen households. A principality retained most of the human and economic potential it needed to rebuild the weak political infrastructure even after a most devastating enemy raid. Therefore, the demise of Lithuania's powerful neighbors could only be temporal.

Lithuania's success was jeopardized not so much by its vindictive neighbors as by the fact that it was achieved within a disintegrating political system. In the 1240s, after the final annexation of the entire vast Polotsk land, Lithuania became known as a grand principality (traditionally rendered in English the Grand Duchy of Lithuania), in accordance with the nomenclature adopted in the Rous' Lands. Thus, it was no longer a vaguely defined territory inhabited by a multicultural population but a political entity whose residents, regardless of their native tongue, were subjects of the Grand Duchy of Lithuania—Lithuanians. But the political principles that had constituted the system of the Rous' Lands and sustained the zero-sum game of grand principalities were rapidly changing under the influence of the crusaders and Mongols. The former "horizontal" network of political associations was undermined by more efficient "vertical," hierarchically organized political structures. One's victory over a neighboring principality no longer changed the overall balance of power if the defeated foe was a vassal of a powerful suzerain and bound by obligations of mutual support. Thus, the defeated Order of the Livonian Brothers of the Sword was reorganized as the Livonian branch of the Teutonic Order often referred to simply as the Livonian Order. As a result, the threat to Lithuania from the west and northwest only increased. Recognizing themselves as vassals of the Mongols, the defeated princes of Vladimir only strengthened, rather than weakened, their influence on the neighboring principalities. Since 1258, the rulers of Galician-Volhynian principality had received direct military assistance from the Mongols in campaigns against the Lithuanians. This structural political transformation made Lithuania's situation precarious despite the synchronous weakening of its rivals. The next campaign of the Grand Duchy of

Local Polities to Hierarchical Statehood 151

Lithuania against the Livonian Order in 1244 was a failure. The campaigns of 1245 to Torzhok and 1248 to the Vladimir-Suzdal principality also ended in defeat. The Rous' Lands provided a format for interaction of the principalities that emerged as a result of political self-organization. When this format disintegrated, instead of quick raids in different directions in the war of "all against all," the availability of powerful patrons, or at least partners, became the key to success.

A Strategic Partnership with Galicia-Volhynia and an Attempt to Integrate the Holy Roman Empire

In this situation, the Grand Duchy of Lithuania found a natural partner in Galician-Volhynian principality, its southern neighbor in the disintegrated Rous' Lands: not subordinate to a powerful suzerain and, unlike the Polish princes to the southwest, not shying away from close contacts with "pagans." In the mid-1240s, the two principalities entered into an alliance, sealed in 1248 by the marriage of Grand Prince Daniel of Galicia to the niece of Grand Duke Mindaugas of Lithuania. This rapprochement was followed by a break and several years of new confrontation, a new union in 1254, confirmed by the marriage of Daniel's son Shvarn to Mindaugas's daughter, and a new round of confrontation after 1255. By the standards of that time, such intense and systematic interaction was the closest possible analogue to the modern concept of "allies," while the recurring dynastic marriages laid the foundation for a possible future unification. Furthermore, it is a modern anachronism to perceive these conflicts as a confrontation between "Lithuania" and "Galicia-Volhynia." The authority of the first grand duke of Lithuania Mindaugas was constantly challenged by rival Lithuanian princes, particularly by his nephew, Prince Tautvilas of Polotsk and Prince Vykintas of Samogitia. Daniel of Galicia was married to Tautvilas's sister, and therefore, when Tautvilas quarreled with Mindaugas in 1249 and fled, fearing for his life, Daniel offered him shelter and support in the fight against his uncle. It was thus the deep involvement of the Galicians in Lithuanian politics that led to the conflict between Mindaugas and Daniel.

In 1250, Mindaugas found himself in a tight corner, simultaneously confronted by the crusaders, the Samogitians led by Vykintas, and the Galician troops supporting Tautvilas. In a seemingly desperate situation, Mindaugas made an extraordinary decision: he directly contacted the land master of the Teutonic Order in Livonia, informing him of his desire to be baptized. Mindaugas renounced claims to the lands of the Curonians, Semigallians, and Selonians, and in the spring of 1251 he was baptized according to the Catholic rite. Further concession of parts of the Samogitian and Yotvingian lands allowed Mindaugas to completely normalize relations with the order: on July 6, 1253, he was crowned Lithuanian king of the Holy Roman Empire. In his new capacity as a Christian king, Mindaugas introduced an in-kind tax on the harvest, similar to the church tithe: diaklo (*duoklė*), which was delivered to local fortified community centers and used to support the king's retinue of professional warriors.

Now Daniel of Galicia found himself in a difficult position. In 1252, his ally, Vladimir-Suzdal Grand Prince Andrei Yaroslavich, was overthrown by his brother Alexander Nevsky with the support of the Mongol troops. At the same time, the ruler of

152   *New Imperial History of Northern Eurasia*

the western region of Jochi's Ulus, Batu's nephew Kurumishi (Kuremsa of the Russian chronicles), invaded the southern possessions of Daniel. The union of Mindaugas with the order and the Polish princes left the Galician prince in complete isolation. In this situation, Daniel agreed to become a king of the Holy Roman Empire and in January 1254 (six months after Mindaugas) he was crowned king of Rus' (Regis Rusie). Historians believe that Daniel received offers of the crown starting in 1246 but turned them down since the coronation implied a conversion from Orthodoxy to Catholicism. It is unclear whether religious purity was the real reason for his hesitations, since Daniel closely interacted and established family relations with both Lithuanian pagans and Polish and Austrian Catholics. In any case, after the coronation, he did nothing to spread Catholicism in his lands.

Thus, two kingdoms emerged almost simultaneously on the ruins of the Rous' Lands—the Lithuanian and the Ruthenian kingdoms, formally belonging to the Catholic Holy Roman Empire and oriented toward an alliance with the crusaders. Accordingly, their common enemies became Jochi's Ulus and its vassal, Grand Prince Alexander Nevsky, whose title made him the master of Kyiv, which was still perceived as a symbol of domination in the Rous' Lands. The joint actions of the Lithuanian and Ruthenian kings against the Mongols soon led to their rivalry and a new breakup. The Mongols, anxious about the strengthening of their neighbors, wasted no time in exploiting the discord between the newly minted kings. In 1258, the Mongol army commander Boroldai (Burundai), the one who had obliterated the Vladimir-Suzdal army at the Sit River in March 1238, made Daniel of Galicia an offer that he could not refuse, that he join the Mongol military expedition against Lithuania. Despite his conflict with Mindaugas, Daniel refused to lead the Galician army personally and asked his younger brother Vasilko Romanovich to do it. Obviously, this was an attempt to downgrade the significance of the conflict: it was not the Ruthenian king who personally went to war against the Lithuanian king at the call of the Mongols. After the joint victory over Mindaugas, the next year Boroldai brought his troops to Daniel's own kingdom and demanded that the fortifications of several cities be torn down.

Boroldai used the traditional Mongol tactic of defeating opponents one by one, with subsequent attacks on a former ally. He succeeded in restoring the Ulus of Jochi's dominant position in the region, particularly given that at the same time, in 1257–9, with the help of Alexander Nevsky, the Mongols subjugated the rich Novgorod land as a formal vassal. However, even heavy defeats of the Lithuanian and Ruthenian kingdoms did not lead to absolutely catastrophic consequences: the kings retained their power (the prudent Daniel fled to Poland in 1259 at the time of the Mongol invasion), the lands were not completely devastated, and the Mongols did not leave behind their garrisons. Obviously, there were limits to the power (and appetites) of the Jochi's Ulus rulers when it came to exercising dominion over neighboring territories.

The End of the Grand Transition Period

The royal title did not help either Mindaugas or Daniel of Galicia. Their Catholic allies in the Teutonic Order or Poland did not come to their aid. The title was not useful in domestic affairs, and was even outwardly harmful in the case of Mindaugas, who

Local Polities to Hierarchical Statehood

soon discovered he had paid too high a price for it. Samogitia, which he ceded to the Teutonic Order in exchange for his coronation, refused to subordinate to the new masters. After several years of military confrontation, the Teutonic Order attempted to crush the Samogitian resistance and gathered an army of 3,000. The majority of troops were provided by the Curonians and Aesti, and the core of the army consisted of 200 knights, mainly members of the order, as well as Danes and Swedes. On July 13, 1260, near Lake Durbe (in the west of modern Latvia), crusaders battled with about 4,000 Samogitians, who were probably under the command of Mindaugas's nephew Treniota. At the beginning of the battle, the Curonians deserted and themselves attacked the knights from the rear. The rest of the auxiliary troops left the battlefield. As a result, the Teutonic Order suffered its most severe defeat of the thirteenth century: 150 knights were killed in battle, including the Teutonic land master in Livonia. Fifteen knights were captured, and eight of them were immediately tortured to death by the Samogitians.

After the crusaders' defeat at Durbe, the conquered Baltic tribes rebelled: the uprising of the Curonians was suppressed by the Teutonic Order only in 1267, by the Prussians in the 1270s, and by the Semigallians in 1290. The remarkable victory of the pagan Samogitians over the Teutonic Order also delivered a heavy blow to the Lithuanian King Mindaugas: he did not fight against the crusaders for Samogitia, which he voluntarily handed over under their rule, having accepted religion and the crown from the occupants. The alliance with the order that saved Mindaugas in 1251 now compromised his authority in the eyes of his subjects. In 1261, Mindaugas publicly renounced Christianity and hence his royal title, and began to energetically act against the order. Apparently, a new sharp political turn did not help him: in 1263, Mindaugas was killed in a palace coup. For a short time, one of the conspirators, the Prince Treniota of Samogitia held the title of the grand duke of Lithuania, which in 1264 was assumed by Mindaugas's eldest son Voishelk (Vaišelga in modern Lithuanian).

The Ruthenian king Daniel of Galicia did not outlive Mindaugas by much—he died the next year, in 1264, and his royal title did not pass to his immediate heir. In the interval between the deaths of Mindaugas and Daniel, on November 14, 1263, Grand Prince Alexander Nevsky died on the way home after visiting his Mongol suzerain Berke (brother and heir of Batu). Like Mindaugas and Daniel, he also tried to return the initial political weight of the old title of grand prince, which, as "prince of princes," was quite consistent with the title of king of the Holy Roman Empire. Soon, in 1266, Khan Berke died. He was the last ruler of Jochi's Ulus, who had personally participated in the Western campaign and was formally considered only a provincial governor under the supreme authority of the great khan of the Mongol Empire. The empire's disintegration was formalized in 1269, and Berke's successor, Batu's grandson, Mengu-Timur (Möngke Temür), became the first khan of the independent Golden Horde that emerged on the site of Jochi's Ulus.

With these leaders gone in the course of just a few years, the transitional period in the east of Europe ended. It had lasted for a quarter of a century, starting with the Western campaign of the Mongol Empire and the unification of the Teutonic Order with the remnants of the Order of the Livonian Brothers of the Sword. A completely new political arrangement formed on the ruins of the Rous' Lands and neighboring

154   *New Imperial History of Northern Eurasia*

formations—Volga Bulgaria, the Polovtsian Khanates, and the unions of the Baltic, Finnish, and pagan Slavic tribes that were partially drawn into their neighbors' sphere of influence.

The Golden Horde and Its Russian Ulus

When Jochi's Ulus gained independence from the great khan, it became Ulug Ulus (the great ulus), popularly known today as the Golden Horde. Popularized by Russian historical sources and historians, this name is usually applied more narrowly, to the European part of the former Jochi's Ulus that included Desht-i Qipchaq, Volga Bulgaria, as well as the steppe borderlands of the former Rous' Lands. With the elevation of the Golden Horde's status as an independent polity so rose the significance of their northern Russian vassals—the Vladimir-Suzdal principality and the neighboring northeastern territories of the former Rous' Lands. The Golden Horde could no longer count on help from Mongolia and itself was in dire need of military support from Russian princes. Russian troops participated in the Golden Horde's campaigns against the Ilkhanate in the 1260s, Byzantium (about 1270), Lithuania (1274), and the Alans in the North Caucasus (1277). The greater importance of the vassal Russian principalities contributed to their enhanced status. [2]

Elevation of the Russian Ulus

In 1262, after a series of town uprisings in Russian principalities, the would-be Golden Horde changed the old scheme of collecting tribute there. It was previously based on tax farming: tribute was collected by the "Besermen"—Muslim merchants from Central Asia, who paid the great khan in Karakorum for the right to act as the Mongols' fiscal agents. This was a universally accepted medieval practice: the tax farmer paid the expected amount of taxes to the ruler (be it a khan or a French king) from his own funds, and then compensated his expenses with some profit margin. After Great Khan Möngke's death in 1259 and the outbreak of civil war in the Mongol Empire in 1260, the expulsion of Central Asian merchants—natives of Chagatai's Ulus—from the rebellious Russian towns did not provoke harsh retaliatory measures from the rulers of Jochi's Ulus. Instead, Khan Berke entrusted the collection of tribute to the Russian princes themselves. This measure eliminated intermediaries from rival uluses on the fiscal territory of Jochi's Ulus, and also strengthened the princes' own treasuries and authority in the eyes of the population. When Mengu-Timur, the first khan of the independent Golden Horde ascended the throne in August 1267, he issued the first of the known yarlyks granting privileges to the Orthodox Church, including exemption from the payment of tribute. These decisions were instrumental in the consolidation of princely power in the vassal Russian lands as finally integrated into the political hierarchy of the Golden Horde. The church, which received the privilege of immunity from taxation, assumed a role as the most important political factor in the interprincely rivalry for the title of grand prince.

The elevation of northeastern Russia following the collapse of the Mongol Empire did not halt Mongol military expeditions against Russian principalities because the Russian princes themselves continued to resolve their political conflicts by military means, always soliciting the khan's assistance. From the moment of the independent Golden Horde's formation to the end of the thirteenth century, the Mongols carried out at least fourteen incursions on the territory of northeastern Russia, ranging from local raids to a large-scale invasion by the joint forces of virtually all the uluses of the Golden Horde in 1293. Almost all these attacks were carried out in response to the requests of rival Russian princes who appealed to the khan of the Golden Horde as their suzerain, the supreme arbiter in all matters, from petty territorial disputes to claims to the title of grand prince.

The Grand Duchy of Lithuania's Strategic Self-reliance

Integration into the Golden Horde was not the sole path to political survival under the changed circumstances. The choice of strategic "nonaligned" status was also possible, if only in cooperation with likeminded partners. Beginning in the 1260s, the fragments of the Rous' Lands that had preserved their independence—the Grand Duchy of Lithuania and the Grand Principality of Galicia-Volhynia—established an even more close interaction, through conflicts and cooperation. Having lost their status as kingdoms of the Holy Roman Empire, they kept their distance from both the Teutonic Order and Poland. In 1264, Mindaugas's son Voyshelk (modern Lithuanian Vaišelga), became the grand duke of Lithuania. He was an unlikely candidate for the office, having ascended to the throne after several years in an Orthodox monastery as an ordinary monk. But his sister was married to Shvarn, the son of Daniel of Galicia, whose troops helped Voyshelk to overthrow the conspirators—the killers of his father. Voyshelk ruled over Lithuania together with Shvarn, calling the prince of Volhynia Vasilko Romanovich (brother of the late Daniel of Galicia) his "father and lord"— that is, recognizing himself as Prince Vasilko's vassal. In 1267, Voyshelk categorically renounced power and retired to a monastery in Volhynia, so Shvarn became the sole ruler of Lithuania. Thus, the Grand Duchy of Lithuania and Galician-Volhynian principality became formally united under the common prince representing the Galician ruling dynasty. This arrangement did not last long: Voyshelk was killed soon thereafter, and Shvarn and Vasilko Romanovich died in 1269. The alliance of the rulers of Lithuania and Galicia-Volhynia, based on close family relations and religious solidarity, fell apart. Afterward, representatives of the Mindaugas clan and their opponents replaced each other as grand dukes of Lithuania, and their alliances with the rulers of Galicia-Volhynia alternated with sharp conflicts.

Only the role of the Grand Duchy of Lithuania as the Teutonic Order's main opponent remained constant. After the uprisings by Prussian, Yotvingian, and other Baltic and Finnish tribes of the Baltic region against the order were crushed, many of the tribes' members fled to Lithuania. On February 16, 1270, in the Battle of Karuse on the ice of the frozen Baltic Sea (off the coast of modern Estonia), the Lithuanian army defeated the combined forces of the Teutonic Order and Danish knights from Reval (Tallinn): 52 knights, including the Livonian land master and 600 foot soldiers,

156　　　　*New Imperial History of Northern Eurasia*

were killed. The order suffered even heavier losses on March 5, 1279, when its army was returning from a victorious raid in Lithuania. Once again, the Livonian land master of the Teutonic Order was killed, along with seventy-one knights. Despite these major victories, by the 1280s, after the Teutonic Order had suppressed the uprisings on the occupied territories, Lithuania's situation became more complicated. Starting in 1283, the struggle against the crusaders had to be waged simultaneously on two fronts, in Livonia and in the southwest, which was previously protected by the Yotvingians and the Prussians. In 1309, the headquarters of the Teutonic Order was moved from Venice to Marienburg at the mouth of the Vistula River in Prussia, and the Grand Duchy of Lithuania—the last predominantly pagan polity in eastern Europe—became the main target of the order's crusader expansionism.

The Golden Horde's Islamization as Protection against Sociocultural Convergence

The first decades of the fourteenth century were extremely stressful for all the political formations that had spontaneously crystallized on the ruins of the Rous' Lands, both the independent polities (Lithuania and Galicia-Volhynia) and the Golden Horde's Russian vassals. The Golden Horde itself was undergoing a profound transformation, reaching its heyday in the first half of the fourteenth century. In January 1313, after a palace coup, a new ruler ascended the throne of the Golden Horde: the previous khan's nephew with the Turkic name Uzbek, who had arrived from the city of Urgench in Central Asia (on the banks of the Amu Darya). Before it was captured by Chinggis Khan in 1221, Urgench was celebrated as "the heart of Islam," and a century later its Mongol rulers became thoroughly Turkicized and Islamized. Uzbek relied on the support of Central Asian clans and the Islamic party within the Mongol elite, so his ascendance to the throne of the Golden Horde had more profound consequences than the usual reshuffling of personalities within the ruling group.

In 1320, Uzbek adopted Islam as the official religion of Ulug Ulus (the Golden Horde). This was a revolutionary step because the compulsory imposition of one particular religion was inconsistent with the nomadic, fairly tolerant view of the spiritual sphere. Uzbek had to wait seven years before introducing his reform and breaking the fierce resistance of the nomadic aristocracy. According to a chronicler writing in the first half of the fifteenth century, members of the Golden Horde elite, including the ruler of the capital region, Sarai, were dissatisfied with Islamization and declared: "You [can] expect obedience and subordination from us, but why do you care about our faith and our confession, and how can we leave the law [*törü*] and regulations [*yasyk*] of Chinggis Khan and convert to the faith of the Arabs?" This attitude was quite typical of the Mongol Empire's ideology of domination, which distinguished political control and economic exploitation from cultural hegemony. This arrangement helped to consolidate Mongol power over conquered territories. With the empire's disintegration, however, strength turned into vulnerability: no longer representing the supreme power of the great khan in Karakorum and not enforcing cultural distance, the former Mongol uluses could be taken over by local indigenous elites through an assimilation process. This transformation was well under way in the Golden Horde,

Local Politics to Hierarchical Statehood

as manifested in the Kipchakization of the nobility and growing integration with the Russian principalities.

The intensive political involvement of the Golden Horde in the affairs of Russian principalities was complemented by cultural and personal ties. In 1261, its capital city of Sarai became the center of a new diocese of the Orthodox Church, which indicated that a large number of Russians were spending time there. Intermarriages among the Golden Horde and Russian elites were not infrequent in the second half of the thirteenth century. The prince of Beloozero and Rostov, Gleb Vasilkovich (1237–78), was married to Batu's granddaughter; the prince of Yaroslavl and the grand prince of Smolensk, Fyodor Rostislavich Cherny (ca. 1240–99), married Khan Mengu-Timur's daughter; the prince of Rostov, Konstantin Borisovich (1255–1307), also married into the Golden Horde in 1302. These marriages not only strengthened the ties between the Russian and Golden Horde aristocracies but also undermined the relationship of domination and subordination (of suzerain and vassal), since dynastic marriages assumed equality of the parties. Delegating the collection of tribute to the Russian princes provided them with powerful economic and political leverage and potentially posed a danger to the Golden Horde's hegemony.

Uzbek tried to stop this sociocultural convergence and hence the further strengthening of the Russian princes. This added political urgency to declaring Islam the official religion of the Golden Horde and it explained the eagerness to undermine the political legacy of the Mongol Empire. The chronicler reports that Khan Uzbek ordered the execution of 120 Chinggisids (aristocrats claiming direct descent from Chinggis Khan) who opposed the adoption of Islam.

Survival of the Weakest: The Rise of the Appanage Moscow Principality

Another priority was to prevent the political consolidation of the vassal Russian lands. Khan Uzbek modified the mechanism of tribute collection in Russian principalities: the tribute for the Golden Horde was still collected by the princes themselves only on the territories of neighboring (usually rival) principalities. To confirm his authority, each prince was accompanied by Golden Horde envoys and a military unit. Thus, in 1315, backed by the Golden Horde escort, the Tver prince collected tribute in Rostov and Torzhok; in 1317, the Moscow prince, with the support of the Golden Horde emissaries, raided Kostroma and attempted to make his way to Tver, but suffered a military defeat. This arrangement naturally intensified the mutual enmity among Russian principalities, but it also undermined the legitimacy of the princely power as depending entirely on the khan of the Golden Horde, as personified by his envoys and armed detachments. Between 1315 and 1327, historians count at least nine expeditions by Russian princes with the participation of the Golden Horde troops to collect tribute.

During this period, Tver became the strongest among the Russian principalities, so in 1318, Uzbek granted the yarlyk of the Russian grand prince (formally, the grand prince of Vladimir) to the weakest and least legitimate candidate—the Moscow appanage Prince Yuri (George), bypassing traditional political centers of the northeast such as Vladimir or Rostov. In 1326, under very dramatic circumstances, the yarlyk of the Russian grand prince was transferred to the Tver prince, and in 1327 Khan Uzbek's cousin Chol-khan (Shevkal or Shchelkan of the Russian chronicles) arrived in Tver with his retinue: apparently, collecting tribute from the grand prince remained the khan's prerogative. This fiscal procedure was carried out at the direction of Uzbek in the most humiliating form, emphasizing the subordinate position of the Russian grand prince as a vassal. Chol-khan moved into the palace of the Tver prince Alexander Mikhailovich, his retinue harassed the townspeople, to whose complaints Alexander Mikhailovich replied with the advice "to be patient." But the Tverians did not follow the advice: an uprising of the city commune broke out, and Chol-khan and his retinue were killed. The Moscow prince Ivan I Kalita rushed to take advantage of this crisis: he went to Khan Uzbek and returned in 1328 at the head of a punitive army consisting of five tumens (i.e., nominally numbering 50,000). Joined by troops from Moscow and Suzdal, this army devastated the Tver principality. In Tver, the Moscow prince confiscated the Spassky church bell—symbol of the veche power. Prince Alexander Mikhailovich fled the city, and Khan Uzbek divided the yarlyk of the Russian grand prince between Moscow and an even more insignificant Suzdal principality (which even got control over the capital city of Vladimir).

Surprisingly, that large-scale attack by the Golden Horde and the division of the grand-princely title between the two rulers only contributed to the political consolidation of northeastern Russia. Khan Uzbek's repressions weakened political competition among the rival principalities, eliminating the most powerful and ambitious rulers, except for the absolutely loyal Moscow prince. The next forty years became known as "the great quietness," as the Golden Horde did not stage a single raid of any significance on the lands of northeastern Russia. The Moscow prince Ivan Kalita (1283–1340 or 1341) took full advantage of the situation to elevate the status of his principality. A few years later, he managed to become the sole holder of the grand-princely yarlyk, authorized to collect the tribute for the Golden Horde in all the lands of Northeastern Russia. This was the next step in the direction of the political and economic consolidation of the Russian principalities, which Khan Uzbek had tried to avoid in the first place: now, of all the Russian princes, only the grand prince was allowed to collect tribute, so his title acquired even greater weight. Apparently, Uzbek's initial scheme, which envisioned the collection of tribute by rival princes with the support of the Golden Horde troops, proved too complicated and costly. Ivan Kalita succeeded in convincing Uzbek that he was able to cope with collecting tribute all by himself, delivering it in full and without reminders in the form of punitive expeditions. Under Ivan Kalita, Moscow became the permanent residence of the Metropolitan of Kyiv and All Rus', which was a factor of great political and economic importance.

From the 1330s on, a new political scenario took shape in northeastern Russia: the title of the grand prince of Vladimir began to convey the full representation of the Golden Horde's supreme power in the vassal territories. At the same time, the grand prince received additional endorsement from the Orthodox Church as a legitimate indigenous ruler, rather than an appointed foreign "viceroy." Securing the title of grand princes for the rulers of Moscow led to the foundation of a particular great-princely dynasty, elevated over the "ordinary" princes-Rurikids, and the appanage principality of Moscow de facto becoming the Grand Principality of Moscow.

Local Polities to Hierarchical Statehood   159

The Grand Duchy of Lithuania, Galicia-Volhynia, and Their Neighbors

Almost simultaneously, beginning in the mid-1310s, on the western outskirts of the former Rous' Lands, the Grand Duchy of Lithuania and Galicia-Volhynia were undergoing a qualitative transformation of their own. As in the relations between northeastern Russia and the Golden Horde, Lithuania's interactions with its Christian neighbors in the Baltics were not limited to the fierce confrontation with the Teutonic Order. The military alliance between the city of Riga (the former stronghold of the Livonian Brothers of the Sword) and the Grand Duchy of Lithuania, directed against the Teutonic Order, lasted an incredibly long time by the standards of that era (1298–1330). In turn, the Teutonic Order, despite its crusader proselytism, actively supported part of the political groupings within the Grand Duchy of Lithuania—paradoxically, usually siding with pagans and Orthodox Christians against Catholics. The case of the Grand Duchy of Lithuania vividly demonstrates that even in the era of medieval "religious fanaticism," political and economic rationality decisively prevailed in the relations between the Riga archbishop and Lithuanian pagans (or the Muslim Khan Uzbek and the Orthodox Moscow prince).

Gediminas: A Turn toward Reconsolidation of the Former Rous' Lands

One can note a certain asymmetric parallelism between the development of the former eastern and western Rous' Lands in the fourteenth century, each formation pursuing a different scenario of political self-organization. Thus, the Grand Dutchy of Lithuania experienced a period of political and territorial growth in the 1320s, at a time of harsh interprincely strife and unprecedented external pressure in northeastern Russia, but instead of "the great quietness" enjoyed by Russian principalities after 1328, the year 1329 marked the beginning of a long period of heavy wars for Grand Duchy of Lithuania. In 1316, Gediminas (1275–1341) became the ruler of Lithuania. His tenure as grand duke (historically, "grand prince") almost coincided with that of the Moscow prince Ivan Kalita and, like Ivan Kalita, Gediminas originated a new grand-princely dynasty. Unlike Ivan, however, Gediminas was not a vassal of a powerful, albeit distant suzerain, but an independent monarch who pursued an active expansionist policy.

In 1322, Gediminas sent letters to the pope and German cities announcing his desire to be baptized into Catholicism. In response, Pope John XXII insisted that the Teutonic Order suspend hostilities with the Grand Duchy of Lithuania. The opposition of pagans and Orthodox Christians in his entourage forced Gediminas to abandon this idea: in 1324, when the pope's envoys came to Gediminas, they were told that the whole story with baptism was merely a misunderstanding caused by the scribe's mistake. Nevertheless, at the insistence of John XXII the truce with the order lasted until 1328. This prolonged respite allowed Gediminas to extend his rule over most of modern Belarus and establish a protectorate over Smolensk and Pskov. The marriages of Gediminas's children strengthened alliances with all neighbors and even allowed

160 *New Imperial History of Northern Eurasia*

them to inherit important territories in the future. So, his son Algirdas (Olgerd) married the Vitebsk prince's daughter. Another son, Liubartas (baptized Dmitry), married the only daughter of the Galician-Volhynian King Andrei Yurievich. As a result, over time, Lithuanian princes became the rulers of Galician-Volhynian lands. One daughter, Aldona, became the wife of the heir to the Polish throne, the future king Casimir III the Great; the other, Maria, married the grand prince of Tver Dmitry Mikhailovich; the third, Aigusta (baptized Anastasia) married Ivan Kalita's son, the future grand prince of Moscow Simeon the Proud. Lithuanian princes had played an important role in the political life of Pskov since the 1260s, and in 1333 Gediminas's son Narimantas (Narimunt, baptized Gleb) was invited as a prince of Novgorod's northern territories in Karelia. In the first half of the 1320s (the exact date is contested), at the Irpen River northwest of Kyiv, the Grand Duchy of Lithuania's army under the command of Gediminas defeated the forces of Kyiv principality (probably supported by the Golden Horde troops) and occupied Kyiv and the cities on the left bank of the Dnieper bordering the steppe including Pereyaslavl, Putivl, and Belgorod. The Golden Horde struck back, and after this demonstration of force the two parties negotiated the status of the contested lands. They remained nominal vassals of the Golden Horde, so the khan's basqaqs remained in Kyiv, but direct administration was entrusted to the governors appointed by Gediminas. This expansionist policy reflected Gediminas's bold ambitions: in his 1322 letters, he had already introduced himself as "the king of the Lithuanians and many Russians, etc."

The truce with the Teutonic Order ended in 1328, and Gediminas had to put his ambitious plans on hold. After many years of preparation, in 1329, the Teutonic Order resumed the offensive against the Grand Duchy of Lithuania and occupied one key fortification in Samogitia after another. In 1337, in the middle reaches of the Neman River, crusaders founded Bayernburg (Bavarian castle), named after Henry XIV, duke of Bavaria, who participated in the campaign. Because the castle became an important foothold for further raids deep into the Lithuanian lands, the Lithuanians had tried unsuccessfully to destroy it for many years. During one such siege of Bayernburg, Gediminas was killed in 1341—almost simultaneously with the death of Khan Uzbek and Ivan Kalita.

Algirdas and Kęstutis: Alleviating Structural Contradictions by Dual Rule

After Gediminas's death, the vast territory of the Grand Duchy of Lithuania was divided by his brother and seven sons into eight parts. The seemingly inevitable disintegration of the principality was avoided thanks to the exceptional personal relations of Gediminas's sons and the political abilities of the two eldest brothers, Algirdas and Kęstutis. By 1345, with the general consent of all the Lithuanian princes, they formed a system of dual rule, echoing the division of nomadic confederations into left (senior) and right wings. Algirdas became grand duke, mainly administered the territory of the former Rous' Lands, and dealt with the Golden Horde, while Kęstutis ruled Samogitia and was responsible for the containment of the Teutonic Order. Algirdas was an Orthodox Christian, married first to a Vitebsk princess and then to a Tver princess,

Local Polities to Hierarchical Statehood 161

and Kęstutis remained a pagan. Complementing each other, the brothers built parallel hierarchies of service and cultural loyalty, uniting their multicultural subjects and converting personal qualities and relationships into political factors. As in many other similar cases, the flip side of the successful political system based on personal qualities and family ties was its complete dependence on specific historical figures.

Together Algirdas and Kęstutis managed to sustain the Grand Duchy of Lithuania as an independent political force, despite increasing pressure from powerful neighbors. On February 2, 1348, the Grand Duchy of Lithuania's army suffered a heavy military defeat by crusaders on the ice of the Strėva River near Kaunas; two sons of Gediminas (Narimantas and Mantvydas) were killed in the battle. Now the eastern Lithuanian lands of Aukštaitija became the battlefield. In the spring of 1362, the crusaders sieged and destroyed the Lithuanian stone castle in Kaunas. Over the next two decades, they conducted up to seventy campaigns against the Grand Duchy of Lithuania, gradually moving farther and farther east. Simultaneously, from the late 1340s, the Grand Duchy was involved in a protracted war with Poland over the "Volhynian succession." The Galician-Volhynian principality was inherited in 1341 by Gediminas's son Liubartas, but the Polish King Casimir III the Great (formerly married to Liubartas's sister, who died in 1339) occupied its capital city of Galich. In the course of the war, the Galician-Volhynian principality disappeared, being divided between the Grand Duchy of Lithuania (most of Volhynia) and Poland. On the third front of foreign relations, in 1362, in the Battle of Blue Waters (near the Synyukha River in the modern Kirovohrad region of Ukraine), the army under the command of Algirdas defeated the troops of three *noyons* (princes) of the Golden Horde. As a result, the Golden Horde's basqaqs were expelled from Kyiv and the former Rous' Lands along the steppe renounced their vassal subordination to the Golden Horde. In 1368–72, Algirdas conducted several campaigns against Moscow, intervening in another round of confrontation between the Tver and Moscow princes on the side of Tver. [3]

The impressive success of the Grand Duchy of Lithuania in absorbing the former Rous' Lands was largely explained by the deep political crisis in the Golden Horde, which caused its hold over the region to loosen. After the palace coup in 1359 and a series of political assassinations, the dynasty of Batu's direct successors was interrupted, and over the next thirty years the Golden Horde witnessed the succession of twenty-five khans. In some periods two "alternative" khans ruled at the same time, and the central government lost control over many uluses. The Moscow grand princes did not present a strong opposition to the Lithuanian expansion either. The Grand Duchy of Lithuania rulers in general were in alliance with Ivan Kalita's son and heir, Simeon the Proud (1317–53); another son of Kalita, who succeeded Simeon, Ivan II (1326–59) was a rather passive ruler; and the next grand prince of Moscow, Kalita's grandson Dmitry Donskoy (1350–89), ascended to the throne as a minor, after the death of his father. The biggest problem for the Grand Duchy of Lithuania was its own rapid expansion to the southeast: How could it reconcile the political tasks in the west (resisting the Teutonic Order, whose troops had already reached Vilnius) and in the east (becoming the main heir to the Rous' Lands and opposing the Golden Horde)? The Golden Horde was the Grand Duchy's main ally in the fight against the Teutonic Order, which, in turn, supported the opponents of the Golden Horde. The partnership between Algirdas and

162   *New Imperial History of Northern Eurasia*

Kęstutis as corulers made it possible to avoid this structural contradiction by political maneuvering, but in 1377, Algirdas died, and the title of grand duke passed to his youngest son Jogaila.

The Halt of Territorial Expansions and the Systemic Crisis of Legitimacy

Predictably, the transfer of power to Jogaila, bypassing Algirdas's eldest son Andrei, provoked a dynastic conflict that immediately escalated into a severe political crisis and complicated the country's relations with neighbors. Jogaila arranged the murder of Kęstutis, whose son Vytautas narrowly escaped death. The rival parties sought the Teutonic Order's support in exchange for territorial concessions, instead of resisting its further expansion. Soon the order occupied almost all of Aukštaitija, so that the Grand Duchy of Lithuania was confined to the territory of the former southwestern Rous' Lands. In northeastern Russia, Tver principality backed Jogaila as son of the Tver princess. Moscow, the old rival of Tver, supported his brother Andrei as a legitimate contender for the throne. When Jogaila finally prevailed over his rivals, his brothers moved to the Grand Principality of Moscow and recognized the grand prince's suzerainty. This meant that their appanages were, at least nominally, now subordinated to Moscow, which further weakened the Grand Duchy.

The profound political crisis of 1377–84 put the Grand Duchy of Lithuania on the brink of collapse as a sovereign polity, with no universally recognized legitimate ruler or a clear political course. Two alternative scenarios for saving the Grand Duchy of Lithuania were attempted at the same time. In 1384, Jogaila's mother, Princess Uliana of Tver, entered into an agreement with Grand Prince Dmitry Donskoy of Moscow that provided for Jogaila's marriage to Dmitry's daughter, the baptism of the Grand Duchy's population into Orthodox Christianity, and subordination to the grand prince of Moscow as suzerain. On August 14, 1385, without waiting for the implementation of the Moscow scenario, Jogaila signed the Union of Kreva with the Kingdom of Poland. Having been baptized a Catholic under the name Władysław, he married the eleven-year-old daughter of the deceased Polish King Jadwiga, promising to baptize the Grand Duchy of Lithuania into Catholicism and surrender his Lithuanian and Ruthenian lands to the Kingdom of Poland. Clearly, the Polish scenario was much more advantageous for Jogaila: he became a sovereign king rather than a vassal of Moscow's grand prince—himself an ulus vassal of the Golden Horde. But for the Grand Duchy of Lithuania as a polity, the two scenarios were not very different: both required baptism of the population and loss of sovereignty. It thus comes as no surprise that both options were considered simultaneously and quite seriously. [4]

Apparently, the Grand Duchy of Lithuania had reached a radically new level of political development and complexity. This vast and multicultural polity required the justification of statehood and the legitimacy of the government—both legal and ideological, as a conviction shared by the majority of the population—to be found within society, and not in some external and momentary political circumstances. For instance, there was a need to substantiate claims of the Lithuanian pagan princes to rule of the predominantly Orthodox population of the former Rous' Lands. The dynastic crisis and the loss of the ancestral Lithuanian territories of Samogitia and most of Aukštaitija just made this political task painfully evident. The possibilities for further territorial expansion were practically exhausted after the Grand Duchy's borders reached the territories of strong neighbors: Poland, Muscovy (the realm of the Moscow prince), and the Golden Horde, not to mention the Teutonic Order.

The purely "political," culturally neutral nature of the power projected by the rulers of the Grand Duchy of Lithuania ensured the rapid subjugation of vast territories with extremely diverse populations. The same cultural neutrality greatly problematized maintaining the country's unity when the active territorial expansion—which was both a major economic resource and a source of political authority—ended. There was a traditional medieval solution to this predicament: the adoption of a monotheistic religion as a common cultural and ideological code, which worked well for various eastern European polities in the first millennium CE. But in the late fourteenth century, the region reached such a high state of entanglement that the Grand Duchy of Lithuania could not escape the trap of blurring the boundary with the brethren in a neighboring rival country, and hence getting into cultural and political dependence on one or another spiritual "metropole." Adopting Catholicism meant subordination to Poland, Orthodoxy meant subservience to Muscovy, and a hypothetical conversion to Islam would mean surrendering to the Golden Horde.

The Reset of the Grand Duchy under Vytautas

At least in the short run, the Grand Duchy of Lithuania avoided complete incorporation into the Kingdom of Poland, as envisaged by the Union of Kreva, thanks to the preservation of the dualism of power. After a long struggle between Jogaila and his cousin, Kęstutis's son Vytautas, they reached an agreement in 1392. Under this agreement, Vytautas became the grand duke of Lithuania, and Jogaila, now the Polish king, received the nominal title of "Supreme Duke of Lithuania" (*dux supremus*). The informal division of powers by the corulers Algirdas and Kęstutis gave way, a quarter of a century later, to a formal division of jurisdiction between their sons. Preserving much of its independence, the Grand Duchy of Lithuania received uniform ideological, legal, and economic norms: Christianity, Magdeburg rights for the towns, and the extension of the privileges of the Polish gentry (*szlachta*) to the Grand Duchy of Lithuania's boyars who converted to Catholicism. The treaty of 1392 envisaged only temporary separation of the Kingdom of Poland from the Grand Duchy of Lithuania, until the end of Vytautas's life. But the new political arrangement proved to be so efficient that the actual unification of the Grand Duchy of Lithuania and Poland took place only many generations later, as a result of the Union of Lublin in 1569, which created a confederal state with a single monarch—the Polish–Lithuanian Commonwealth (Polish: Rzeczpospolita, the translation of the Latin "res publica").

Having overcome the dynastic and political crisis, the Grand Duchy of Lithuania under Vytautas reemerged as the foremost force in eastern Europe. In the second half of the 1390s, in alliance with the Teutonic Order, Vytautas attempted to crush the Golden Horde. The previous khan of the Golden Horde Tokhtamysh was defeated by the Central Asian emir-conqueror Timur (Tamerlane), lost his power, and in 1396 fled

164 *New Imperial History of Northern Eurasia*

to Kyiv under the protection of Vytautas. In 1397 and 1398, Vytautas led two campaigns to the steppe against the new khan Temur Qutlugh. He got as far as the Black Sea and the Crimea, returning with several hundred families of Tatars and Karaites loyal to Tokhtamysh and settling them in the Trakai principality near Vilnius. His 1399 campaign was given the official status of a crusade against the Golden Horde. Vytautas persistently strove to return the khan's throne to Tokhtamysh in exchange for his recognition of the suzerainty of the Grand Duchy of Lithuania. This legal and political arrangement would automatically have turned the Grand Principality of Moscow and other Russian principalities that were vassals of the Golden Horde into vassals of the Grand Duchy of Lithuania. These ambitious plans were ruined by the decisive battle of the Vorksla River—a tributary of the Dnieper just over 200 miles from Kyiv. The Golden Horde severely defeated the allied Lithuanian-Polish-Tatar-Teutonic army.

Ten years later, Vytautas joined the so-called great war with the Teutonic Order for the return of Samogitia to the Grand Duchy of Lithuania—which he himself had ceded to the order under the treaty of 1398, in preparing for the crusade against the Golden Horde (not to mention several treaties he and Jogaila had signed with the order during their struggle for power, as well as the treaty between Jogaila and the order of 1404, which also confirmed the transfer of Samogitia). On July 15, 1410, the decisive Battle of Grunwald took place near the German village of Grünfelde. In one of the largest and fiercest battles of the Middle Ages, the approximately 11,000-strong army of the order (which also included mercenaries from western Europe and the regiments of the Polish princes Konrad VII the White and Casimir V of Pomerania) were defeated by the allied army led by Vytautas (Grand Duchy of Lithuania), Jogaila (the Kingdom of Poland), and Tokhtamysh's son Jalal al-Din (the Tatar detachments). The allies outnumbered the forces of the Teutonic Order by about 50 percent. In the battle, 205 knights of the order, including its entire leadership, were killed, and many were taken prisoner. The Battle of Grunwald undermined the power of the Teutonic Order: in 1422, after many years of negotiations, the Teutonic Order completely withdrew from Samogitia. After new military defeats in the mid-fifteenth century, the order recognized itself as a vassal to the Polish kingdom. [5]

By reversing the direction of his expansionist policy from the southeast to the west, Vytautas did not completely abandon the idea of establishing his power over all the former Rous' Lands. His daughter Sophia was married to the grand prince of Moscow Vasily I, who in his 1423 will entrusted his wife and children to Vytautas's protection. In 1427, the widowed Sofia, in agreement with the boyars, transferred the Grand Principality of Moscow under the patronage of her father as regent during the minority of her twelve-year-old son, the future grand prince Vasily II. After that the princes of Tver, Ryazan, and Pronsk recognized themselves as vassals of Vytautas.

A Utopia of Political Unity and Cultural Tolerance: The Congress of Lutsk

The status of Vytautas as the ruler of a European great power was confirmed by the Congress of Lutsk—which represented for medieval Europe a truly unprecedented

Local Polities to Hierarchical Statehood 165

summit of monarchs. In January 1429, up to 15,000 people, counting servants and armed escorts, gathered in the Volhynian town of Lutsk, which had a population of several thousand people. The Kingdom of Poland was represented by King Władysław II (Jogaila), the highest clergy of the kingdom, and the heads of aristocratic families. From northeastern Russia, the Grand Prince Vasily II of Moscow and Metropolitan Photius, along with the grand princes of Tver and Ryazan arrived at the congress. The Teutonic Order was represented by the commander of its Balga branch (about 20 miles from Konigsberg), the Livonian Order—by Land Master Siegfried Lander von Sponheim himself, accompanied by the senior knights. From the Golden Horde came three ulus khans, who together controlled the lands from the Crimea to the Middle Volga. Envoys of Emperor John VIII Palaeologus arrived from the Byzantine Empire, and Pope Martin V sent his legate Andreas Chrysoberges (the future archbishop of Rhodes). The most important guests were the king of the Romans (i.e., the elected emperor of the Holy Roman Empire not yet crowned by the pope), the king of Bohemia and Hungary, Sigismund I of Luxembourg with his wife Barbara. In addition, the king of Denmark and Sweden, Eric VII of Pomerania, attended the congress. The participants were met and received by Vytautas, who was surrounded by representatives of the princely families of the Grand Duchy of Lithuania, Catholic, Orthodox, and Armenian bishops, as well as leaders of the Jewish and Karaite communities.

The agenda of the congress included building a coalition in opposition to the Ottoman threat in the south, settling trade conflicts in the Baltic, negotiating a union between the Catholic and Orthodox churches, and soliciting the title of king for Vytautas. Although the discussion of these topics did not lead to tangible results, the very fact that Catholic, Orthodox, and Muslim rulers gathered and spent several weeks together in negotiations, joint hunts, and feasts, is of great importance for our understanding of medieval Northern Eurasia. The numerous ideological and cultural barriers that divided them were real, but seem to have been greatly overemphasized by those whose task was to justify the policy of the sovereigns at that time, particularly in written documents. The Congress of Lutsk demonstrated that the rulers of the politically self-organized part of Europe—from the Danube to the Volga, and from the Baltic to the Black Seas—perceived themselves as members of a common political and cultural world. Fierce battles and fragile alliances, dynastic marriages and trade equally served as channels of interaction that were not yet identified with the collective interests of the "peoples." Even confessional disagreements, which seemed to be the basis of the medieval differentiation into "friends" and "aliens," did not manifest themselves in Lutsk: Catholics, Orthodox Christians, Muslims, Jews, and Karaites took part in official ceremonies and unofficial socialization on equal terms.

The Grand Duchy of Lithuania under the rule of Vytautas, who dreamed about the union of the Catholic and Orthodox Churches, was the ideal venue for an event such as the Congress of Lutsk as a demonstration of political unity and disregard for cultural differences: these were the principles that prompted the rapid rise of the Grand Duchy of Lithuania. However, in the fifteenth century, no political forms were capable of accommodating the cultural and religious differences of the population and a belief in the sacral nature of the supreme power (as bestowed by God) at the same time. This belief became the decisive factor in determining the legitimacy of a ruler in this era, and it marginalized other factors. As the Grand Duchy of Lithuania's political crisis of the 1380s made painfully evident, belonging to a local clan aristocracy was no longer enough to support one's claim to supreme power, particularly in a country with a multicultural population. Rule by the right of conquest remained a powerful argument in favor of one's legitimacy, but the hereditary transfer of power made this argument invalid in subsequent generations. The rudimentary political doctrines of the time and any elaborate claims to power were framed in categories of monotheistic religions—the dominant form of textual culture and abstract thinking. Therefore, hereditary rulers of large polities seeking to justify their legitimacy as part of the established worldview had to rely on the authority of an official monotheistic religion, which confirmed the divinity of their power in the eyes of all true believers. Pagan religious tolerance was becoming a vanishing anachronism—and Vytautas himself was the last European monarch brought up in paganism. The gradually increasing influence of the Kingdom of Poland contributed to the demise of the traditional tolerance for differences in the Grand Duchy of Lithuania, as this tolerance existed largely at the level of everyday practices and attitudes, rather than as formulated ideas.

After the Congress of Lutsk, there were periods when the Grand Duchy of Lithuania was almost completely independent of Poland (e.g., before his death in 1430, Vytautas planned to be crowned as a sovereign king of Lithuania), and also periods of closer integration of the two polities, but the general vector of development was their gradual converging. This was facilitated by the regime of personal union between them, making it possible for the grand duke of Lithuania to be elected king of Poland and for an heir to the Polish crown to become the grand duke of Lithuania. There was a systematic exchange between the Grand Duchy and Poland of nobility and clergy, ideas and practices. There was also the increasingly important factor of external threat. The strengthening of the Grand Principality of Moscow and its active expansionism pressed the Grand Duchy of Lithuania to develop its strategic alliance with Poland. At that time, the durability of such an alliance could be guaranteed only by the formal unification of the two countries.

The Grand Principality of Moscow and Its Neighbors: The First Attempt to Gain Independence

Whereas the Grand Duchy of Lithuania in the fourteenth century began its long transformation from most powerful polity in eastern Europe to junior partner in the Polish–Lithuanian Commonwealth, the Principality of Moscow followed the opposite historical course. The Grand Duchy of Lithuania was formed in the context of the Rous' Lands and in many ways was reworking the legacy of its political culture or at least was operating within its mental mapping. By contrast, the Moscow principality had already emerged as part of Jochi's Ulus (the Golden Horde): Alexander Nevsky's son, Daniel (1261–1303), was the first appanage prince of Moscow and the founder of the local dynasty. The center of a small appanage principality, Moscow first became the actual capital of the Grand Principality of Vladimir only in 1318, when Prince Yuri

Danilovich received the yarlyk of the Russian grand prince from Khan Uzbek. The yarlyk was withdrawn already in 1322, after which the Moscow princes were involved in a struggle for domination over the eastern part of the former Rous' Lands. Unlike the sovereign and independent Grand Duchy of Lithuania, the Moscow principality had always been an ulus of the Golden Horde and part of its political system. Therefore, Moscow rulers perceived their relations with neighbors and the very concept of domination as determined by their position in the intra-Golden Horde hierarchy.

When the Moscow prince Ivan Kalita was granted the right to collect tribute in all Russian vassal principalities on behalf of the Golden Horde, the ancient and still rather symbolic title of "Grand Prince" acquired a new weight. Besides control over the financial resources of neighboring principalities, this title gave the Moscow prince the political significance of a high-ranked representative of the Golden Horde's supreme power. The grand prince was no longer just "first among equals" of the Russian princes, but rose one step up: as a representative of the khan—and only in this capacity—he became "the prince of princes," that is, practically the king of the Vladimir-Suzdal land. The heirs of Ivan Kalita faced the double task of preserving this high political status of the dynasty while simultaneously dissociating themselves from the Golden Horde's khan, who could revoke this status on a whim. It was an internally contradictory task: the new status of the grand prince was bestowed by the khan's yarlyk and drew its political weight exclusively from acknowledging the khan's suzerainty—that is, it did not exist without the Golden Horde's political power. However, in order to secure the title for the dynasty of Moscow princes as hereditary and to further increase its status, emancipation from political dependence on the Golden Horde was required.

The Practical Usurpation of the Grand-princely Title by the Moscow Prince

The first step in this direction was taken by Ivan Kalita's sons and successors to the throne, Simeon the Proud and then Ivan II. Their main concern was to prevent the khan from being involved as the supreme arbiter in resolving intraprincely disputes. This was a customary practice introduced by Alexander Nevsky long before and used by Ivan Kalita himself, but now the Moscow grand princes began punishing attempts by Russian princes to solicit punitive expeditions from the Golden Horde against each other. The forty-year-long "great quietness" in the relations between the Russian principalities and the Golden Horde after 1327 testified to the success of the efforts to keep the Golden Horde at bay. The grand prince of Vladimir, which now usually meant the prince of Moscow, proved himself a full-fledged and effective representative of the khan's supreme power, one who was able to independently resolve local conflicts.

The palace coup of 1359 in the Golden Horde started the prolonged political crisis that eventually led to the collapse of this largest medieval state of Northern Eurasia. The growing autonomy of individual uluses further weakened the central power, while the kaleidoscopic change of khans meant that many of them lacked the time to issue yarlyks to vassal rulers (every new khan had to confirm or change all the appointments conferred by his predecessor). This led to a new paradoxical situation: a vassal (such as a Russian grand prince) possessed more legitimate authority than his nominal

168   *New Imperial History of Northern Eurasia*

suzerain—the khan of the Golden Horde—so the Moscow prince often retained his grand-princely title without the sanction of a new khan, sometimes even against his will. For the first time, the title of the grand prince of Vladimir acquired a certain autonomy from the supreme power of the Golden Horde.

The beginning of the crisis in the Golden Horde coincided with the accession to power of Ivan Kalita's grandson, Prince Dmitry Ivanovich (1350–1389), who later earned the nickname Donskoy. At the age of eleven, Dmitry had to travel to the Golden Horde, where he first received the yarlyk of Russian grand prince from khan Murad, who controlled the capital city of New Sarai (Sarai-al-Jadid), and then from Abdullah, an "alternative" khan who ruled in the western part of the Golden Horde. Ultimately, the support of the latter was more important because he was backed by Mamai (1335–80)—the most senior administrator and son-in-law of Berdibek, the last khan—a descendant of Batu, who was killed in 1359. Not of the Chinggisid lineage himself, Mamai could not aspire to become the khan, but he remained the most influential political figure in the Golden Horde throughout the crisis with the reputation of a kingmaker, holding control of its western part.

Khan Murad was offended by Dmitry's soliciting a sanction for power from his rival, so he revoked his yarlyk to Dmitry and gave it to the Suzdal prince. A little more than a week later, Dmitry's army expelled the Suzdal prince from Vladimir—the official capital of Vladimir-Suzdal principality, thus returning the title of grand prince to the ruler of Moscow by force. In 1365, Khan Aziz, who had replaced Murad, once again sent the yarlyk of the Russian grand prince to the Suzdal prince, but the latter voluntarily renounced his rights to the office. In 1371, Prince Mikhail of Tver secured the yarlyk for himself from another khan by bringing lavish gifts. The Moscow army did not allow Mikhail to enter the capital of the principality, and Prince Dmitry at the khan's headquarters arranged the return of the yarlyk to him by offering a much higher bid than what was paid for the yarlyk by the Tver prince. In 1375, faced with the unanimous support of Dmitry by other appanage princes of the Vladimir-Suzdal land, Prince Mikhail of Tver renounced his claims to the grand-princely title. As a result, in his will prepared in the spring of 1389, Dmitry Donskoy for the first time bequeathed his grand-princely title to his son as part of his inheritance. The title of grand prince of Vladimir that had been reinvented almost 150 years earlier as belonging to the ruler of the Golden Horde's Russian ulus, chosen and appointed by the khan at his discretion, now became the hereditary title of the Moscow princes.

Prince Dmitry Donskoy's Wars with Illegitimate Golden Horde Rulers

To symbolize his exceptional position among the princes of the Vladimir-Suzdal land, Prince Dmitry in 1367 began the construction of the white-stone Moscow fortress—the Kremlin—instead of the wooden one destroyed by fire. In 1374, when a fierce opponent of Mamai, Emir Cherkes, became the khan in New Sarai, Prince Dmitry stopped paying tribute to the Golden Horde. This decision was clearly connected with the growth of independence and power of the Moscow prince, but also with the collapse of legitimacy of the supreme power in the Golden Horde: in 1374–5, four khans replaced each other on the throne in New Sarai, and two of them seized power several times. The Moscow prince demonstrated his independence and military strength by a victorious raid against Bulgar—another vassal of the Golden Horde—rather than by an attempt to occupy Kyiv or some other former Rous' Land not subordinate to the khan. This choice speaks volumes about the mental mapping of Moscow's grand prince in the late fourteenth century and what he perceived as a natural political space for his activities. So, in March 1376, the united army of Moscow and Nizhny Novgorod defeated the Bulgar army. The Moscow prince appointed his governor (*daruga*) and customs officer in Bulgar and took a huge contribution of 5,000 rubles—the equivalent of the annual tribute paid to the Golden Horde by all Russian principalities. The contribution was distributed in such a way that the Moscow and Nizhegorod princes each received 1,000 rubles and the remaining 3,000 was distributed among the generals and soldiers. The Russian troops also brought artillery pieces from Bulgar to Moscow, which was probably the first encounter of Russians with firearms. This military operation became possible because the emir of Bulgar had by that time renounced the authority of the Golden Horde. Besides, he was a protégé of the New Sarai khan Aziz, an enemy of Mamai, who had long since been overthrown in yet another palace coup. Thus formally, the Moscow prince Dmitry acted as a loyal vassal of the Golden Horde (*ulusnik*) against an illegitimate separatist, and if not on the direct order of the sitting khan, then at least not against his will.

In 1380, the crisis that had been tearing apart the Golden Horde for many decades was overcome: its unity was restored, a direct descendant of Jochi, Tokhtamysh, became the new khan, and Mamai lost power and was killed. The grand prince of Moscow Dmitry played a significant role in these events.

From 1377 on, backed by the ruler of Mawarannahr, Emir Timur (Tamerlane), Tokhtamysh made one unsuccessful attempt after another to invade the territory of the Golden Horde and seize its capital New Sarai. Simultaneously, the situation of the Grand Principality of Moscow on the border with the Golden Horde escalated. The scarcity of reliable sources on the Golden Horde's policy during this period and the intentions of Prince Dmitry leave room for various interpretations. It is only known that on August 2, 1377, the Golden Horde army under the command of aristocrat Arab-shah Muzzaffar (Arapsha) defeated the united army of the Russian principalities on the Pyana River, just over sixty miles from Nizhny Novgorod, and then plundered the town. The location of the battle suggests two possible versions of the events. The princes of Nizhny Novgorod, who commanded the army, could have been preparing an attack on the Mordovian lands lying across the river. These territories were directly subordinated to the Golden Horde, so Arab-shah would have defended them, thus ruining Nizhny Novgorod as punishment. Or it could be that the Russian army was assembled to counter a punitive raid from the Golden Horde in retaliation for the campaign against Bulgar the previous year (but somehow only the junior partner in the raid on Bulgar, Nizhny Novgorod, was penalized). It is also unclear whether Arab-shah was already the khan in New Sarai at this time, owing the title to Mamai and fulfilling his will, or whether he was still an ulus ruler and acting on his own initiative.

In the spring of 1378 Tokhtamysh managed to put under his control the eastern part of the Golden Horde and entered the territory to the west of the Volga controlled by Mamai. Despite this direct threat, in the summer, Mamai found it necessary to dispatch five tumens (nominally 50,000 strong) under the command of Emir Begich against the Grand Principality of Moscow. Prince Dmitry did not wait for the enemy inside the new stone Kremlin and did not attempt to buy his way out of trouble, as was typical of Russian princes. He led his army toward the approaching Begich and met him on the Vozha River (a tributary of the Oka), not far from Ryazan. In the battle on August 11, the Moscow army defeated the Golden Horde troops, Begich and all five tumen commanders were killed. Unlike the encounter on the Pyana River in 1378, which resulted from a predatory raid by one or the other side, depending on interpretation, this time the conflict looked like a war in the narrow sense of a political confrontation (and not an economic enterprise). Mamai seemed to believe that the Grand Principality of Moscow's submission was crucial for victory over Tokhtamysh, even though Moscow was already the Golden Horde's vassal.

By April 1380, Tokhtamysh extended his power over almost the entire territory of the Golden Horde, including the capital, New Sarai. The territory controlled by Mamai decreased to the interfluve of the Volga and Don Rivers and the Black Sea steppes. The defeat on the Vozha River significantly weakened his military potential, and on September 8, 1380, he lost the decisive battle with the allied Russian army under the command of Prince Dmitry on the Kulikovo field (at the interfluve of the Don and Nepryadva Rivers, about 200 miles south of Moscow). Tokhtamysh became the undisputed leader of the Golden Horde, and Mamai fled to Crimea, where he was killed a few weeks later.

It is unknown who initiated the war between Mamai and Moscow. According to the traditional interpretation, Mamai gathered an army to punish the ambitious Moscow prince and subordinate the Grand Principality of Moscow. If so, he was acting incredibly slowly and neglecting to maintain any secrecy: his opponent must have known about these plans well in advance, so that he managed to gather an allied army to counter Mamai's prospective offensive. Practically all the northeastern principalities—vassals to the Moscow prince sent their troops to assist Prince Dmitry. Moreover, he received reinforcements from Moscow's traditional rivals—Suzdal, Tver, and Smolensk principalities. On the way south to the Don, the army of the Russian princes was joined by detachments of the Lithuanian princes Andrei and Dmitry (the sons of Algirdas), who were in conflict with their step-brother Jogaila and preferred to join the Moscow service, as well as the army from Novgorod, which was administered at the time by their cousin, the Lithuanian prince Yuri. The allied troops from all over northeastern Russia were scheduled to meet in Kolomna (sixty-five miles south of Moscow) on August 15. This means that the multiparty, long-distance negotiations concerning the joint actions, followed by the relocation of allied troops for hundreds of miles to a meeting point, should have begun many weeks earlier, and the news of Mamai's plans should have come to Moscow by the beginning of summer. From Kolomna, the allied troops marched for three weeks southward covering over 100 miles, crossed the Don River into the "wild field"—the domain of Mamai—and only then met his army. All these circumstances make Mamai a highly unlikely initiator of the new confrontation.

Mamai planned to strengthen his thinning forces at the expense of a mercenary infantry from the Genoese colonies in Crimea, as well as regiments of the Lithuanian grand duke Jogaila. However, it is definitely known that Jogaila's troops were too late to arrive by the beginning of the Kulikovo battle (unlike the regiments of the Lithuanian princes who supported Dmitry), and there is a reason to doubt that the Genoese managed to take part in the battle. Thus, it appears that Mamai not only wasted most of summer failing to prepare properly for the attack on Moscow (if he indeed contemplated it) but also was caught by surprise by the Russian forces that arrived on his own territory before his allies. The unexpected appearance of the Russian army in the steppe owed much to the fact that Dmitry led it not by the shortest route to the south but making a detour around the Ryazan principality. Ryazan belonged to the former southern Rous' Lands bordering on the steppe that had to sustain special relations with the Golden Horde and was systematically ravaged by Moscow raids. Keeping the united army's movement secret from the hostile Ryazanians meant making its arrival a surprise to Mamai.

The Battle of Kulikovo played a decisive role in the relations between Moscow and the Golden Horde, and its symbolic significance as a key episode of patriotic, and later Russian national historical mythology can hardly be overestimated. Given this symbolical importance, historians tended to reconstruct the circumstances of the battle on a scale absolutely inconsistent with the actual demographic and military potential of medieval societies. It was speculated that hundreds of thousands of soldiers fought on each side in the battle, which was depicted as a daylong combat. Recent studies by archaeologists and paleogeographers make it possible to reconstruct the alleged battle site. In 1380, it was a large forest glade sandwiched between ravines: no more than half a mile along the front and little over one mile in depth. This territory could accommodate forces large enough by the standards of that time—several thousand troops on each side. These were most likely professional warriors on horseback—members of princely retinues. The battle of a cavalry meeting engagement could last about half an hour.

Several weeks later, in September, the remnants of Mamai's troops met with the army of Tokhtamysh (either near the Dnieper rapids, or on the Kalka River in the Azov region) and, without fight, went over to his side and swore allegiance to the new khan. Having crushed Mamai, Tokhtamysh sent envoys to the Russian princes, thanking them for their help in defeating the usurper (Mamai) and informing them about the restoration of legitimate central authority in the Golden Horde. The grand prince of Moscow was reminded of his vassal obligations to the khan, including the regular payment of tribute, for which Tokhtamysh traditionally promised favors and protection from enemies. The princes recognized the authority of Tokhtamysh, sending his envoys back "with honor and gifts" and then dispatched their own missions to the khan with more gifts. The first to do this was the Moscow prince Dmitry—his envoys traveled to New Sarai already on October 29, 1380. They returned from Tokhtamysh "with much honor and benevolence from the Khan," which meant the confirmation of amicable relations.

The Post-Kulikovo Claim to Sovereignty and the Ensuing Backlash

Grand Prince Dmitry rushed to observe diplomatic conventions but not his vassal obligations. He did not send the mandatory tribute to Tokhtamysh, thus behaving not as a good ulusnik but more like Daniel of Galicia in relation to Batu: as a junior ally rather than a vassal. In the fall of 1381, he even started minting his own silver coin "denga" (from the Türkic *täŋkä*—coin). On one side, it depicted an armed warrior encircled by the inscription "Seal of the Great Prince" (the name of the prince was not indicated). On the other side was an inscription in Arabic script with the name of Khan Tokhtamysh. Very symbolically, the weight of the denga was equal to two-thirds of the Golden Horde dirham. Apparently, permission to mint coins for the first time in centuries was one of the khan's "favors" to the prince of Moscow, and the coin's design confirmed the sovereignty of Tokhtamysh and the dependent and impersonalized nature of the grand-princely power bestowed by the khan's yarlyk.

However, in the summer of 1382, the Moscow Mint changed the design of its coins. On the new coin, a figure holding a snake by the tongue or threatening a snake with cold weapons was added, and the inscription with the title of grand prince received the name "Dmitry." On the reverse side, the name of Tokhtamysh written in Arabic was replaced by the name of Uzbek. [6] This was a silent coup by means of political symbolism: coins were minted on behalf of a particular grand prince, Dmitry Donskoy, and the source of his power was identified not with the sitting khan of the Golden Horde Tokhtamysh, but with Khan Uzbek, who had died back in 1341. Uzbek was acknowledged not as Dmitry's sovereign but as someone who granted the yarlyk of grand prince to Dmitry's grandfathers—the Moscow princes Yuri Danilovich, and then Ivan Danilovich Kalita. As this symbolic gesture suggested, the title was granted to the dynasty of Moscow princes once and for all.

It is not known whether this symbolic action was accompanied by any practical political steps. It is clear, however, that this symbolic declaration marked a turning point in Moscow's relations with its neighbors. It soon became apparent that Tokhtamysh's discontent with demonstrative Moscow separatism was not Prince Dmitry's biggest problem. As it turned out, unlike the recent events of 1380 during the confrontation with Mamai, now he could not rely on the support of his neighbors or even his own vassals.

Back in the fall of 1381, Tokhtamysh had sent a splendid embassy to Moscow with the task of inviting Prince Dmitry to New Sarai. For an unknown reason, the embassy stopped in Nizhny Novgorod and then returned to the Golden Horde, and only a letter of invitation was sent to Dmitry. In August 1382, Tokhtamysh, at the head of a highly mobile force without siege weapons and infantry, attacked Bulgar, robbed the local Russian merchants of their boats, used them to cross the Volga River, and marched toward Moscow. Prince Dmitry moved his troops from Moscow to meet Tokhtamysh, as he had done more than once before in response to the threat from the Golden Horde. However, according to the chronicle, once already on the march,

> Prince Dmitry and other Russian princes, and generals [*voevody*], and advisers, and notables, and the senior boyars began to confer. . . . Disagreement emerged among the princes, [who] did not want to help each other, and brother did not want to help brother . . . because there was not unity among them, but distrust. When [he] understood, and comprehended, and considered this, the faithful prince became perplexed and contemplative and did not dare to stand up against

Local Polities to Hierarchical Statehood 173

the tsar himself [i.e., the khan]. He did not go into battle against him, and did not raise his hand to the tsar, but went to his city of Pereyaslavl[-Zalessky], and from there, past Rostov, . . . hastily to Kostroma.

Judging by the route of Prince Dmitry's hasty flight from his own army, disobedience and disagreement did not reveal themselves immediately, but they were apparent no farther than thirty miles from Moscow (one or two day's march): Dmitry did not dare make a detour on the road to Kostroma to pick up his wife and children in Moscow. They joined him later, fleeing from a city engulfed in turmoil and panic. Before the army of Tokhtamysh surrounded Moscow, a certain young Lithuanian prince Ostey arrived in the city and took it upon himself to establish order and defense. The chronicle's account is so vague that it is not possible to identify this figure or even to discern which camp of the warring Lithuanian aristocracy (Jogaila or Kęstutis and Vytautas) he belonged to.

On August 23, 1382, Tokhtamysh's vanguard appeared near Moscow. The scouts approached the city walls and, according to the chronicle, first of all asked the townspeople: "'Is Prince Dmitry here?' Those from the city answered from the fighting gallery: 'No.'"

Instead of chasing the grand prince to the northeast (as Batu's troops had during the 1238 campaign), Tokhtamysh besieged Moscow. The three-day siege of a stone fortress by horsemen who had crossed the Volga on merchant boats without any heavy weaponry could not be successful. The clear disinterest in Prince Dmitry's whereabouts and unpreparedness for the siege of Moscow calls into question the original goal of the 530-mile-long march from Bulgar. Then the sons of the Nizhegorod prince—Dmitry's brothers-in-law, who voluntarily accompanied Tokhtamysh, entered into negotiations with the besieged, promising them an honorable surrender. The townspeople opened the gates but were attacked, and the city was set on fire. According to the conventional historical narrative, 24,000 people perished as a result of the siege and the ensuing massacre. After that, the troops of Tokhtamysh raided the appanage principalities within a radius of about 90 miles from Moscow until they met the troops of Prince Dmitry's cousin, Vladimir Andreevich, who were stationed on the western border of the principality near Volok Lamsky. "Unaware of him and unknowingly, they ran into him," suffered a substantial defeat, and retreated southward to the steppe, along the way pillaging the Ryazan principality.

Tokhtamysh's raid is presented traditionally as a punitive expedition aimed to punish Prince Dmitry for the victory on Kulikovo field. The available historical information about these events is too scanty to reliably reconstruct Tokhtamysh's intentions, but it is quite sufficient to discard the traditional explanation as utterly inadequate. At this point, it should already be clear that the raid was not directly related to the Battle of Kulikovo, which enormously benefited Tokhtamysh, and for which, according to the chroniclers, he thanked the Russian princes. Moreover, the expedition initially did not target Russian principalities: Tokhtamysh attacked Bulgar, bypassing neighboring Nizhny Novgorod, and hastily moved on. When the prince of Nizhny Novgorod, on his own initiative, sent his two sons to Tokhtamysh, they did not find him in Bulgar and were forced to catch up, before voluntarily joining his campaign. After crossing the Volga, Tokhtamysh was met by Oleg, the prince of Ryazan, beyond the limits of his principality. Oleg personally showed Tokhtamysh convenient fords across the Oka River, so that the Golden Horde troops proceeded to Moscow not entering the territory of Ryazan.

The Difficult Choice between Power and Sovereignty

Everything in this story seems strange, particularly the complete lack of support (if not betrayal) of Prince Dmitry by those who had fought alongside him just two years earlier on Kulikovo field, and the unusual direction of the strike and the haste of Tokhtamysh's troops. Not only did the traditional rivals of Moscow, such as the prince of Tver, not come to Dmitry's aid; his father-in-law, the Nizhegorod prince, seemed to be acting against Dmitry of his own free will. Dmitry's cousin and closest associate, the Serpukhov prince Vladimir Andreevich, for some reason waited with his troops on the western border of Moscow principality opposite the invasion (which prevented him from defending even his own city of Serpukhov from ruin). The army hastily dispatched from Moscow to meet Tokhtamysh refused to obey Dmitry, thus making him "perplexed and contemplative." In Moscow, the civil authorities and even Metropolitan Cyprian could not calm the unexpected uprising that had flared up.

According to some accounts, on his way back, Tokhtamysh left the yarlyk of the Russian grand prince to the prince of Nizhny Novgorod, who did not dare to use it. Then the Tver prince paid a visit to Tokhtamysh to get the yarlyk for himself, and Dmitry Donskoy spent a lot of effort and money in order to retain his title. There was clearly deep mistrust of Dmitry Donskoy and disloyalty to him among the Russian princes, if not a coordinated conspiracy against the Moscow prince. Apparently no one was interested in a conflict with the supreme suzerain ("tsar" in the terminology of Russian chronicles), the khan of the Golden Horde Tokhtamysh, and no one was happy about the prospect of Dmitry Donskoy becoming a sovereign ruler. His independence by no means negated the vassal position of the other Russian princes, but instead of the distant overlord in New Sarai, who had no interest in annexing their territories, they would have been resubordinated to a neighbor with whom they had a rich history of personal conflicts and territorial disputes. Furthermore, at least theoretically, any prince could receive the yarlyk of grand prince of Vladimir from the khan, whereas Dmitry Donskoy was going to monopolize this title forever in Moscow. By the political standards of the time, Tokhtamysh was a legitimate ruler: quite possibly, it was in answering his call that Russian princes—recent rivals and even foes—joined forces to fight against the "usurper" Mamai. In his political aspirations, Dmitry Donskoy did not differ much from Mamai. He cherished the same ambitions of trading his status as an ulus ruler to that of a sovereign monarch, as it became clear from the design of his new coins.

Of course, Tokhtamysh more than anyone else was interested in crushing Dmitry's separatist ambitions, which were fraught with the loss of significant financial and human resources for the Golden Horde. Still, a wide gradient of dependence existed. The formal autonomy of the Galician princes in the thirteenth and early fourteenth centuries did not prevent them from paying regular "gifts" to the khans of the Golden

Horde and participating in their military expeditions. War was not the only option for keeping Moscow in the Golden Horde's orbit. If, nevertheless, Tokhtamysh decided to demonstratively punish the stubborn vassal and "reconquer" the Moscow principality, then it was more logical to bring a large army along the traditional route of raids from the steppes—from the south, rather than from the east. Dmitry Donskoy was a powerful opponent, and the distance from the Volga to Moscow (from Bulgar) is almost three times longer than from the Don. Instead, Tokhtamysh apparently crossed the Volga with very few troops: a typical Volga merchant boat of that time, of the *ushkui* type, held up to thirty people. Tokhtamysh, who, as the chronicle emphasizes, advanced very quickly (in "sudden attack"), had to ferry horses, at least two per warrior. The sources of that time rarely mention more than a hundred river vessels at one Volga pier, but even if several hundred boats were requisitioned in Bulgar, they could ferry hundreds, but not thousands of armed horsemen. The only skirmish with a local Russian military unit at Volok Lamsky ended in Tokhtamysh's defeat. Once he reached Moscow and discovered that Dmitry had left the city, Tokhtamysh made no attempt to find him. Instead of bringing the rebel prince to justice, he persistently stormed the stone fortress with clearly insufficient forces, until he reportedly tricked the townspeople out of the city and massacred them. Romantic historiography of the early nineteenth century saw nothing strange in this behavior of the "Tatars," but the known instances of mass-scale execution of civilians by the Golden Horde troops were rare and usually served as the punishment for treachery (such as the murder of envoys). Moreover, mass slaughter requires a lot of effort while, in the era of taking prisoners for slave trade, it was also economically counterproductive. Returning via the "usual" southern route, Tokhtamysh plundered the Ryazan principality, which was also strange, considering that the Ryazan prince voluntarily helped him cross the Oka River on the way to Moscow (for which Prince Dmitry devastated Ryazan the next year even more badly than Tokhtamysh had).

All these circumstances and the routes taken by the participants in the events suggest that Tokhtamysh's raid on Moscow was most likely impromptu. He went with a light force up the Volga River, from New Sarai to Bulgar, perhaps to expel Moscow officials and restore the direct jurisdiction of the Golden Horde over its northern ulus. Already in Bulgar he had made a sudden decision to urgently march to Moscow with the available troops, over half a thousand miles to the west. One can only speculate about the reason for this decision: Was it the acquaintance in Bulgar with the newest products of the Moscow Mint? Did he receive information about a plot against the Moscow prince? It is possible that Tokhtamysh was genuinely worried not about Prince Dmitry, who had proved his loyalty, but about the outcome of the political confrontation in the Grand Duchy of Lithuania—a most important regional player.

As was discussed earlier, after the death of Grand Duke Algirdas in 1377, his younger son Jogaila inherited his father's title. Jogaila began intriguing against Algirdas's coruler Kęstutis and his son Vytautas, seeking to consolidate full control over the Grand Duchy in his own hands. Kęstutis strategically allied himself with the Grand Principality of Moscow and the Golden Horde, so many years later, Tokhtamysh found refuge with his son Vytautas. In turn, in 1380, Jogaila supported Mamai against Moscow (and hence Tokhtamysh). The stakes were extremely high

176   *New Imperial History of Northern Eurasia*

for the neighboring countries in the confrontation between the anti–Golden Horde and pro–Golden Horde parties in the Grand Duchy of Lithuania. In the fall of 1381, Kęstutis captured Vilnius and displaced Jogaila. This event coincided with the aborted grand embassy of Tokhtamysh to Prince Dmitry. Given the dearth of information in the available sources, one can only speculate as to whether the embassy's goal was to encourage the Moscow prince to go on an expedition to help Kęstutis, and whether Kęstutis's victory made the costly embassy no longer necessary in the eyes of Tokhtamysh.

However, on June 12, 1382, Jogaila's supporters staged a coup in Vilnius. A few weeks later, Kęstutis and Vytautas were taken prisoners. Vytautas managed to flee, but Kęstutis was locked in the Kreva castle. Given the distance (over 1,000 miles), information about these events would have reached Tokhtamysh, who was in Bulgar at the time, sometime in July. It was logical for him to attempt to save Kęstutis, warning Dmitry to get his army ready or even begin moving toward Kreva. Moscow lay halfway on the direct route from Bulgar to Kreva (via Mozhaisk, Vyazma, and Smolensk). Whether ordered to march eastward against Tokhtamysh or westward against Jogaila, Dmitry's troops disobeyed, Moscow rebelled, and Dmitry fled to Kostroma. Tokhtamysh's vanguard arrived at the walls of Moscow on August 23, and Kęstutis was killed in the Kreva castle on August 15. It was possible for this news to have traveled 500 miles to Moscow in the course of eight to ten days. All Tokhtamysh could do now was to punish those conspiring against Grand Prince Dmitry among the Moscow elite, and retreat, giving his exhausted troops the opportunity to reward themselves for a difficult campaign with plunder. If so, Prince Dmitry was not the target of Tokhtamysh's sudden expedition and nearly lost his grand-princely status only because he failed to control his own capital city and his own troops.

This interpretation fits well the subsequent course of events. Immediately upon his return to New Sarai, Tokhtamysh dispatched a peace embassy to Moscow, and not the other way around, as would have been the case if Dmitry was concerned with appeasing the angry khan. The embassy restored the status quo in relations between Moscow and the Golden Horde: Dmitry treated Tokhtamysh's embassy with great respect but did not resume paying tribute. Dmitry's relationship with neighbors was a very different matter. The dramatic events of 1382 undermined his authority among the other Russian princes, who no longer recognized Dmitry as the unquestionable leader and hence the rightful holder of the khan's yarlyk of the grand prince. The growing opposition to the Moscow prince and attempts to take over his title convinced Dmitry that independence and power were not the same. On April 23, 1383, he sent his eldest son, eleven-year-old Vasily, to Tokhtamysh, and agreed to resume paying tribute to the khan. Legally and politically, this meant confirming his status as the Golden Horde's vassal. The change of political course was promptly reflected by a new design of Moscow coins: the image of the armed prince was replaced by what numismatists describe as a drawing of "a rooster and a small four-legged creature above him." The inscription mentioning "Grand Prince Dmitry" was preserved on the coin's obverse, but the name of Tokhtamysh replaced Uzbek's on the reverse. In exchange for publicly demonstrated obedience, Khan Tokhtamysh conferred upon Dmitry the title of grand prince of Vladimir, which was now officially transformed to grand prince of Moscow, as Tokhtamysh recognized the hereditary character of this title in the family of Moscow princes.

Thus ended the first attempt of the Golden Horde's ulus—the Grand Principality of Moscow—to free itself from vassal dependence. As it turned out, it was not that difficult to acquire practical independence and stop paying regular tribute to the khan as the supreme suzerain. The real problem was that the authority of the grand prince of Moscow was not recognized by his neighbors or even his own vassals (appanage princes), unless it was backed by the support of the Golden Horde. The most formidable challenge was to contemplate and formulate a radically new concept of legitimacy that would allow the grand-princely power to be recognized without the backing of the khan's authority or physical coercion alone. Spontaneous attempts to solve this daunting political and cultural problem continued throughout most of the fifteenth century.

Further reading

Crummey, Robert O. *The Formation of Muscovy, 1300–1613*. London: Longman, 1987.

De Hartog, Leo. *Russia and the Mongol Yoke: The History of the Russian Principalities and the Golden Horde, 1221–1502*. London: British Academic Press, 1996.

Frost, Robert I. *The Oxford History of Poland-Lithuania*. Oxford: Oxford University Press, 2015.

Halperin, Charles J. *Russia and the Golden Horde: The Mongol Impact on Medieval Russian History*. Bloomington: Indiana University Press, 1987.

Plokhy, Serhii. *The Origins of the Slavic Nations: Premodern Identities in Russia, Ukraine, and Belarus*. Cambridge: Cambridge University Press, 2006.

5

New Times

The Problem of Substantiating Sovereignty and Its Boundaries in the Grand Principality of Moscow (Fifteenth–Sixteenth Centuries)

Whither the Legitimacy of the Moscow Prince not Backed by the Khan's Authority

Such a detailed discussion of the vicissitudes encountered by the Moscow prince Dmitry in his relations with Mamai, Tokhtamysh, and neighboring Russian principalities is essential for understanding the logic of subsequent developments in the region. The events of the 1370s–1380s revealed the central problem faced by the Moscow princes: how to substantiate their claim to supreme power over the northeastern part of the former Rous' Lands if not by the supreme authority of the khan of the Golden Horde. Almost simultaneously, the rulers of the Grand Duchy of Lithuania faced a similar challenge to their authority in the former western Rous' Lands. Being pagans and culturally "foreign" to the Christian and Ruthenian-speaking majority of their subjects, the Lithuanian princes could not rely on the legitimacy much greater than that of the Golden Horde in the eyes of the population. Initially based on the right of the conqueror, the legitimacy of their power eroded with time after the normalization of rule, and required new and more lasting substantiation.

The Golden Horde never fully recovered after its prolonged political crisis of 1359–80. The restoration of the nominal order only made painfully clear the khan's inability to control the Principality of Moscow by force. Meanwhile, since the late 1320s, the princes of the appanage Moscow principality had effectively monopolized the title of the Vladimir-Suzdal grand prince. Prince Dmitry Donskoy stopped paying tribute to the Golden Horde in 1374, which meant renouncing his formal vassal status. Even the sacking of Moscow in 1382 by Khan Tokhtamysh, who restored the unity of the Horde, did not compel Dmitry to recognize the supreme power of the khan again and resume the payment of tribute. However, just as his ancestor, the Vladimir-Suzdal prince Alexander Nevsky, Dmitry discovered that only the power and military support of the Khan could secure the authority of the grand prince in the eyes of his peers—other Russian princes. Eventually, for the sake of confirming his status as the senior Russian prince, Dmitry voluntarily recognized the supreme power of the khan, but this could only be a temporary solution. The Golden Horde was on the wane and losing its former role as the region's dominant power and the supreme arbiter of the Russian princes.

The Disintegration of the Golden Horde

In 1395, Tokhtamysh lost in the decade-long conflict with the Central Asian ruler Timur (Tamerlane) over the eastern territories of the Golden Horde and fled to Vytautas in the Grand Duchy of Lithuania. Timur headed a devastating raid across the steppe regions of the Golden Horde, after which the Horde was no longer able to recover. For a brief period, the Golden Horde experienced its final renaissance in the early fifteenth century due to the exceptional personality of the skillful politician and talented military commander Emir Edigey (Edigu), who actually governed on behalf of several successive khans. In December 1408, Edigey even tried to seize Moscow in order to restore its strict subordination to the Golden Horde and the payment of tribute, which had stopped in 1395 after the fall of Tokhtamysh. Edigey besieged Moscow for three weeks with no success; he ordered the prince of Tver to assist in the siege, but the order was ignored. Edigey's troops plundered the vicinity, following the scenario of all military conflicts of that time, and retreated after having received a ransom of 3,000 rubles (formerly, the regular annual tribute was 5,000 rubles). Soon thereafter, the Golden Horde plunged into a new series of internal conflicts, and after Edigey's death in 1419, it disintegrated forever. The territories east of the Volga separated as the Blue Horde, which immediately continued splitting off further: in the early 1420s, the Khan of Siberia was proclaimed in Tyumen, and the Nogai Horde became autonomous in the steppes between the Volga and the Urals. The western part of the former Jochi's Ulus increasingly began being referred to as the Great Horde (or Volga Horde), its territory actually being reduced to the interfluve of the Volga and Don Rivers. The Kazan Khanate separated from it in 1438, mainly on the territory of Volga Bulgaria. In 1441, the Crimean Khanate followed suit, claiming control over the northern Black Sea region. Each of the new khanates presented a formidable political and military force, but even the Great Horde could no longer claim the former status of an empire, "the kingdom of kingdoms." [1]

The Crisis of Khan-Less Legitimacy in the Grand Principality of Moscow

Against this background of the former Golden Horde's fragmentation, in 1425–53, a severe political crisis erupted in the Grand Principality of Moscow. After the death of his father Vasily I, the ten-year-old grandson of Dmitry Donskoy, Vasily II, ascended the throne in 1425. From the very beginning, his power was challenged by various contenders for the Moscow throne and the title of the grand prince. They were all members of the same Moscow dynasty, all made extensive use of military force, frequently breached their oath, and treacherously poisoned and blinded each other, using all the tools available in the arsenal of political struggle in Northern Eurasia at that time (since older times, forced blindness had been perceived as a stigma disqualifying one as a potential ruler). Meanwhile, a capable and perfectly legitimate grand prince of Moscow, Vasily II, was present throughout the entire quarrel, and hence there was no apparent need for new candidates to the throne, so the acute vacuum of power was created not by the sudden interruption of the dynasty. Rather, just as Dmitry Donskoy had discovered back in 1382, the very office of grand prince as a sovereign ruler was in crisis after the breach with the khan as its undisputable source of legitimacy. Dmitry resolved the escalating crisis of his legitimacy by acknowledging the supreme sovereignty of Khan Tokhtamysh. Half a century later, with the crumbling Golden Horde, the traditional subordination to the distant powerful sovereign was no longer a feasible solution. The resulting conceptual void created room for competing scenarios of legitimacy of the grand-princely power. The crisis of 1425–53 was structured as a series of attempts to implement some of these scenarios.

Vasily II's Medieval Drama

At first, the young Vasily II's right to the throne was challenged by his late father's younger brother Yuri (Zvenigorod prince Yuri Dmitrievich). Uncle Yuri misinterpreted a clause from his father Dmitry Donskoy's will, evoking the "ladder" order of succession (i.e., power is transferred not to a son but to a younger brother of the deceased ruler). As can be seen in previous chapters, the ladder principle was rarely practiced in the Rous' Lands, and never before in the Moscow principality. The only explanation for bringing up this legendary legal norm in the fifteenth century was the need to find a new formula for the sovereign legitimacy of the grand prince that would not be conditioned by the supreme authority of the khan. To put it in modern terms, Vasily II's uncle Yuri was "inventing tradition" by appealing to some ancient, pre–Golden Horde norms.

The conflict between Vasily II and his uncle remained a purely legal dispute until 1430, when the grand duke of Lithuania Vytautas, the official patron of the young Moscow prince and his mother, died. In 1431, the khan of the Great Horde Ulugh Muhammad was asked to be the supreme arbiter in this dispute. Essentially, this was an attempt to revive the old practice of soliciting the khan's yarlyk as a patent to reign as grand prince. Now, however, it was not the rulers of different principalities who competed for the yarlyk, but members of one princely dynasty. Ulugh Muhammad judged in favor of Vasily II, but since the khan was no longer perceived as the almighty sovereign—the ultimate source of grand-princely power—his verdict did not resolve the quarrel.

It did not take long for the conflict to escalate. On February 8, 1433, Vasily II married the young princess Maria of Borovsk, thus increasing the chances of bequeathing the title to his future children rather than to the rival family line. At the wedding feast, his mother, Sophia, insulted Vasily's cousin—a son of his uncle Yuri—by tearing off his gold-plated belt. She recognized the belt as once belonging to Dmitry Donskoy and thus a rightful possession of Vasily II along with other grand-princely regalia. Her personal insult thus conveyed a statement about the patrilineal principle of power succession (from father to son): from Dmitry Donskoy to Vasily II's father to Vasily II, and not to his uncle. In response, the Zvenigorod prince Yuri went to war against his nephew Vasily II, defeated his army in the field, occupied Moscow, and exiled Vasily II to Kolomna. This episode resembled the old scenario of the transfer of power through conquest, when the city commune invited the winning prince to be the new ruler (see Chapter 3). However, Moscow did not have an autonomous city commune with the right to make seminal decisions at its veche, so one cannot speak of the population's voluntary acceptance of the victorious prince. Rather, the city elite—aristocrats (boyars) and senior servitors—voted with their feet in support of Vasily II by fleeing to Kolomna. Eventually, even the sons of Prince Yuri quarreled with their father and left Moscow. He had no choice other than to reconcile with his nephew and return the throne to Vasily II. After another surge of confrontation, Yuri of Zvenigorod once again defeated Vasily II and occupied Moscow, but he died suddenly in 1434.

Then Yuri's elder son declared himself grand prince of Moscow but was not supported by his younger brothers and Moscow boyars. They took Vasily II's side and resorted to another ancient scenario of power transfer by way of invitation to the throne. Since the city commune as a collective legal entity did not exist in Moscow, the invitation was formalized as a series of private agreements between Vasily II and lesser princes and boyars—members of the temporary coalition. Compared to an invitation by the veche, these private agreements were much less authoritative, which significantly reduced the prestige of the power thus obtained. As a result, a de facto regime of joint rule was established in the mid-1430s by Vasily II and his cousin Dmitry Shemyaka, the younger son of Prince Yury. The coins of the period simultaneously featured the names of both "Grand Prince Vasily" and "Grand Prince Dmitry." Unlike the Rous' Lands, the Mongol Empire, or the Grand Duchy of Lithuania under Algirdas, in the Moscow principality of the fifteenth century, there was no clear concept of the division of powers and territories between the corulers. The diarchy of the cousins only weakened the government by instigating mutual mistrust and disputes between the duumvirs.

The Sovereign–Vassal Relationships Rearranged and Inverted

This weakening revealed itself in an inability to sustain relations with Ulugh Muhammad, who in 1436 was ousted from power in the Great Horde, fled to the Crimea, and was then forced to flee even farther. At the end of 1437, with only 3,000 horsemen, he attempted to settle in the town of Belyov on the Oka River, on the border of the Grand Duchy of Lithuania and the Grand Principality of Moscow. Belyov was the territory of the Grand Duchy, which could be expected to strike against the occupants. Accordingly, Ulugh Muhammad pledged his friendship to Moscow. In response, of all possible actions or inaction, the Moscow government chose the least rational scenario. A large army was sent against Ulugh Muhammad. Moscow troops suffered a crushing defeat by the enemy, which was many times inferior in number. Ulugh Muhammad did not wait for a new attack of Moscow or Lithuanian troops and moved to the former Bulgar territory in the Middle Volga, where he founded the Kazan Khanate (1438). The compromised military capability of Moscow princes and their betrayal of Ulugh Muhammad explain why the new Kazan Khanate immediately took a very aggressive stance toward the neighboring Russian lands. Already in the spring of 1439, the Kazan khan sacked Nizhny Novgorod and burned the villages around the Moscow Kremlin. In 1444–5, Ulugh Muhammad launched another big raid on Moscow. Vasily II, who led the campaign against him, lost the battle near Suzdal on July 7, 1445, and was captured. [2]

Vasily II's coruler, Dmitry Shemyaka, showed no interest in rescuing his cousin from captivity. Instead, he declared himself the sole grand prince and minted coins sporting the ambitious title "Master of All Rus'," suggesting that he was no longer content with rule over the Grand Principality of Moscow alone. He sent a special envoy to the Kazan khan with a denunciation of Vasily II. Realizing that no one was going to pay ransom for his release, Vasily II vowed to Ulugh Muhammad to collect the ransom on his own. This was a strange arrangement: paying for one's freedom after already being free and in command of the army of a large principality. But Ulugh Muhammad agreed to this plan. On October 1, 1445, he let Vasily II go to Moscow accompanied by a military escort of 500 warriors.

At this point, we observe the resurgence of a political scenario of vassal relations, although it is difficult to say for sure who exactly played the role of vassal and who was suzerain. On the one hand, Vasily II expelled Dmitry Shemyaka from Moscow and began reigning with the sanction of the neighboring khan of Kazan (not even the Golden Horde). On the other hand, formal political dependence on the Kazan Khanate took the form of Kazan princes becoming vassals of the Moscow prince. The huge ransom for Vasily II was paid largely in-kind, by transferring various towns under their administration and taxation on behalf of the Moscow grand prince. Ulugh Muhammad's son Qasim was given the whole Meshchera land about 200 miles southeast of Moscow, where he founded the Qasim Khanate in vassal dependence on the Grand Principality of Moscow. Essentially, the Kazan khan used his military and political superiority to achieve the status of the Moscow prince's vassal.

Nevertheless, the contrast between Dmitry Shemyaka's demonstrative claims to autocratic rule over all the Rus' lands and Vasily II's formal concessions to the Kazan Khanate was striking. Dmitry Shemyaka began to spread rumors that Vasily II was preparing the transfer of the entire Moscow principality under the rule of the khan. He succeeded in securing the support of several appanage princes and some disgruntled Moscow boyars and carried out a coup d'état—a pure innovation in the Moscow political tradition. On the night of February 13, 1446, Dmitry Shemyaka's troops occupied Moscow without a fight. The next night Vasily II and his family were captured at the Trinity Monastery. He was blinded and exiled to Vologda, after swearing allegiance to Shemyaka as the legitimate grand prince.

The Reset of the Political Landscape

It would seem that Vasily II had lost any chances of regaining power. Nevertheless, just one year later, in February 1447, Vasily II ceremoniously entered Moscow—not secretly in the middle of the night and not after the city's takeover by conspirators, but as a legitimate ruler. It turned out that Vasily II enjoyed the wide support of the Moscow boyars and the populations of many towns. The prince of Tver, who had previously participated in Vasily II's overthrow, played a key role in his return. Vasily

II first moved from his exile to Tver, strategically located not far from Moscow, and his supporters from all over the land began to flock to him. At the same time, the appanage princes and boyars loyal to Vasily who had taken refuge in the Grand Duchy of Lithuania marched with their troops toward Moscow. At Yelnya, 200 miles southwest of the city, they joined forces with the army commanded by the Tatar princes Qasim and Yakub, the sons of the Kazan khan, who became vassals of Vasily II. While Dmitry Shemyaka was trying to blockade the enemy in the west of the Moscow principality, a cavalry squadron (of 100) sent by order of Vasily rushed into Moscow on Christmas (December 25) 1446. This small detachment met no resistance, occupied the Kremlin, and made the townspeople swear an oath of allegiance to Vasily II. Dmitry Shemyaka was forced to retreat to his family domain, lost several battles, and was left with only few supporters, but desperately fought for power until 1453, when, by order of Vasily II, he was poisoned on "neutral territory"—in Novgorod. Even the names of the characters in this political drama of Shakespearean proportion sound quite theatrical. The chef who poured arsenic into the chicken prepared for Dmitry Shemyaka was called Toadstool (Poganka), the name of the junior clerk who delivered the news to Vasily II and was immediately promoted to a higher rank was Vasily Trouble (Beda).

The Orthodox Church was a decisive factor in Vasily II's eventual triumph. On the way from exile to Tver, Vasily II stopped at the St. Cyril Monastery, whose abbot Tryphon released him from the solemn oath to Dmitry Shemyaka because the oath had been coerced. Soon after Vasily's return to Moscow, on December 29, 1447, all Orthodox bishops in the lands within Moscow's sphere of influence, along with several archimandrites and abbots, sent a letter to Dmitry Shemyaka. They substantiated Vasily II's right to reign and accused Dmitry of numerous sins, presenting him as an illegitimate ruler.

Upon regaining power, Vasily II concluded new agreements with all the main political subjects: the appanage princes of the Grand Principality of Moscow, neighboring Russian princes, as well as the grand duke of Lithuania and King Casimir IV of Poland. Essentially, this was a complex reset of the political landscape in the eastern part of the former Rous' Lands. Formally, the alignment of the main actors did not change, and the Grand Principality of Moscow only became weaker after the internal turmoil and ruin that had lasted for a quarter of a century. However, this prolonged civil war had the most important consequences for the rise of Muscovy as an independent state. To begin with, numerous appanage principalities within the Grand Principality of Moscow had been more closely consolidated. In the protracted conflict, it was impossible to maintain neutrality, so a series of treaties concluded and renegotiated by appanage princes with the contenders to the Moscow throne strengthened their ties with and dependence on the grand prince. Next, by the end of the political crisis in Moscow, its relations with neighbors had become clarified and formalized. The treaty of 1449 with the Grand Duchy of Lithuania delineated the border between the two polities in detail and resolved mutual territorial claims. It also restricted the interference of aristocrats of one country in the political affairs of the other country under the pretext of pursuing family or landed estate interests. Thus, the treaty gave priority to state sovereignty over princely private authority. The Kazan Khanate was a new powerful neighbor that emerged during the conflict, largely as its result. The Moscow prince ceded significant

New Times

territory for the creation of the Qasim Khanate but acquired loyal vassals in its khan and princes. Under the 1456 Yazhelbitsky treaty, Novgorod recognized its vassal subordination to the Grand Principality of Moscow.

Finally, and most importantly, amid the civil war and in the atmosphere of treachery and betrayal, a new formula of grand-princely power was spontaneously developed. Dmitry Shemyaka and Vasily II equally contributed to its formulation. By the 1450s, the norm of the hereditary succession of power by patrimony, from father to son, had firmly prevailed. The legendary ladder principle of succession and bequeathing of the title to other relatives were no longer considered legal options. It was recognized that the grand prince's power originated in his natural right to rule as a legitimate heir to his father; this power relied on the support of boyars and the servitor class, and it received supreme sanction not from any suzerain (such as the khan of the Golden Horde), but from the church. In turn, the church became dependent on the grand prince. In 1448, at the insistence of Vasily II, Bishop Jonah, who was born in a village near Kostroma, was elected Metropolitan of Kyiv and All Rus'. For the first time, the metropolitan was ordained not by the Patriarch of Constantinople, but by a council of Russian bishops, upon the grand prince's consent. This marked the beginning of the independence of the Russian Orthodox Church from the Patriarchate of Constantinople.

Thus, once it emerged as an appanage principality of the Vladimir-Suzdal Land—a vassal of the khan of the Golden Horde—by the second half of the fifteenth century, the Grand Principality of Moscow had acquired its own legitimacy as a sovereign polity. Even the church, which replaced the khan as the supreme authority sanctioning the rule of the Moscow prince, was "domestic" now, independent of external influences.

The Spatial Boundaries of Sovereignty

In the new political reality of the 1450s, the Grand Principality of Moscow's formal subordination to the Great Horde was already perceived as a redundant archaism. Sixty years earlier, even a ruler as ambitious as Dmitry Donskoy still needed the authority of the Golden Horde khan to secure his power over other Russian princes. But now this authority was of little practical use to the Moscow rulers, particularly when embodied by the much weaker and constantly disintegrating polity of the Great Horde. This explains why the Great Horde and its khan, Kichi Muhammad (r. 1435–59)—"Young Muhammad," who overthrew his predecessor, the "Elder" (Ulugh) Muhammad—played practically no role during the prolonged dynastic crisis in the Grand Principality of Moscow during the second quarter of the fifteenth century. Only at the very beginning, in 1431, when Ulugh Muhammad was invited to be the arbiter in the dispute between Vasily II and his uncle Yuri, did the Moscow authorities send the expected annual tribute to the khan. This was a political statement acknowledging the khan's suzerainty and therefore the legitimacy of his decision. Afterward, payments of the tribute once again became irregular. In any case, the real financial burden for Moscow was not the tribute to the Great Horde, but the ransom required to pay for Vasily II's release from captivity in Kazan. Meanwhile, the Great Horde had its own political problems: in 1453, an attempt to subjugate the Crimean Khanate that had seceded ended in a heavy military defeat on the Dnieper; in 1459 another ulus seceded from the Great Horde, forming the independent Astrakhan Khanate in the lower reaches of the Volga. In the 1450s, several raids against the Grand Principality of Moscow, intended as traditional reminders to pay the tribute, were successfully deterred by the Moscow forces.

Reinventing the Unity of the Rous' Lands

When Vasily II died in 1462, his son and successor, Grand Prince Ivan III (1440–1505), immediately changed the design of Moscow coins. Instead of the ruling khan's name, the reverse side of coins now featured the statement in Arabic script: "This is the Moscow denga." This claim of political independence from the Great Horde was not followed by any openly hostile political steps because the government of Ivan III was less interested in a final break with the khan than in the expansion of Moscow's control over the Russian principalities as well as the Ruthenian (former Rous') lands under the rule of the Grand Duchy of Lithuania. This was a new trend: back in 1395, Prince Vasily I, the grandfather of Ivan III, voluntarily handed Smolensk to the Grand Duchy of Lithuania under the treaty with his father-in-law, Vytautas. On the mental map of the Moscow political elite, which had formed in the context of the Vladimir-Suzdal land's vassal subordination to the Golden Horde, the former Rous' Lands did not belong to the perceived common political and cultural space of the Russian ulus. Smolensk and Kyiv were considered less related to Moscow than Vologda, which was located forty-five miles farther from Moscow than Smolensk, and for which Moscow rulers had started a fierce fight with Novgorod already in the late fourteenth century. However, in the fifteenth century, just as the Golden Horde's legitimacy was finally fading away, educated Moscow elites gradually rediscovered or even reinvented the pre–Golden Horde past as the period of legendary unity of all the Rous' Lands. So, in the most famous literary work of this period *Zadonshchina* (Beyond the Don River)— an epic tale about the 1380 Kulikovo battle—the Moscow prince Dmitry thus calls other Russian princes to a joint struggle with Mamai: "Brothers Russian princes, we are all [from] the nest of the Grand Prince Vladimir of Kyiv! We were born to suffer an insult from neither a falcon, nor a hawk, nor a gyrfalcon, nor a black raven, nor this infidel Mamai!"

The invention of a common past was part of constructing the sovereign political legitimacy as stemming not from Khan Uzbek (as in the time of Dmitry Donskoy) and not even from Batu, but from some authentic domestic tradition of statehood. Formed as a result of the political crisis of the second quarter of the fifteenth century, the image of the Moscow grand prince as a defender of Orthodoxy and all Russian lands corresponded well to the new historical myth. The central role in this myth was played by the figures of Vladimir Sviatoslavich ("the Baptizer") and Vladimir Monomakh (as a wise ruler connected with the Byzantine Empire), who often merged into one generic "Prince Vladimir." Moreover, Moscow literati and politicians imagined the Rous' Lands by analogy with the Grand Principality of Moscow of the second half of the fifteenth century: as a hierarchical polity striving for centralization with a single capital (in Kyiv).

Moscow as the Third Kyiv

This evolution of political and cultural imagination in Moscow inevitably led to a confrontation with the Grand Duchy of Lithuania, which itself claimed to be the direct heir of the Rous' Lands, and on much more solid ground: at least, Kyiv belonged to the Grand Duchy of Lithuania. The treaty of 1449 between the two polities should have minimized the possibility of any mutual territorial claims and conflicts in the future—but only as long as the traditional division of former Rous' Lands persisted into the Russian ulus of the Golden Horde and the territories that joined the Grand Duchy of Lithuania. Moscow's claim to the legacy of the Rous' Lands radically destabilized the relationships between the neighboring polities, far beyond any border disputes. By the early 1470s, the texts produced in Moscow had elaborated the narrative of Moscow as the new Kyiv. Following it, in 1471, Ivan III informed the Novgorodians who were trying to switch their vassal allegiance from Moscow to the Grand Duchy of Lithuania:

> You are my patrimony, oh people of Novgorod, dating back initially to our grandfathers and great-grandfathers, from the Grand Prince Vladimir, who baptized the Russian land—the great-grandson of Rurik, the first grand prince of your land. And from that Rurik and even to this day, you knew the only lineage of those grand princes, initially of Kyiv, up to the Grand Prince Dmitry-Vsevolod Yuryevich of Vladimir [who was also Prince of Novgorod, r. 1222–38]. Their lineage continues from that great prince to me; we own you and reward you and proscribe [certain activities] from here, and also we will execute you, if you start considering us not as in the old days. You have been subjects of no king or Grand Prince of Lithuania since your land formed.

In a 1490 letter to the emperor of the Holy Roman Empire Maximilian I, Ivan III announced direct claims to a big part of the Grand Duchy of Lithuania: "If, God willing, we begin to reconquer our patrimony, the Grand Principality of Kyiv, which is owned by the king of Poland Casimir and his children."

The idea of the state as a historical and cultural entity (both linguistically and religiously) was totally revolutionary in mid-fifteenth-century Europe. It undermined the foundations of medieval political legitimacy as constituted by the legally bound personal contract between the vassals and the sovereign, be it a prince or a king. The Grand Principality of Moscow itself was nominally considered a vassal of the Muslim Great Horde with a predominantly Turkic- and Kipchak-speaking population. In turn, the Qasim Khanate, with its predominance of Muslim Turks among the privileged strata, was a loyal vassal of mostly Christian, Slavic-speaking Muscovy. Thus, the elite of the Grand Principality of Moscow preferred to separate the rhetoric of religious and cultural purity from actual political practice in domestic affairs—no one perceived the Qasim Khanate as a hostile force or demanded the baptism of the Qasim Tatars. But after liberation from the Great Horde's suzerainty, the emerging phenomenon of the foreign policy as differentiated from domestic affairs encouraged the free rein of new ideas, which was fraught with far-reaching consequences.

The Grand Duchy of Lithuania and the Grand Principality of Moscow were formally in perfectly amicable relations, so the first cause of the confrontation between them was presented by a third party. Concerned about the Moscow government's efforts to strengthen its control over Novgorod, Novgorodians attempted to eliminate their political dependence on the Moscow prince and recognize the Grand Duchy of Lithuania as their new suzerain. In the old medieval political logic, this was possible, particularly given that the Grand Duchy could claim its historical rights over Novgorod as part of its Kyivan heritage. In response, the Moscow army marched against Novgorod in the summer of 1471. The Novgorodians were defeated, the "Lithuanian party" among the Novgorod notables lost its influence, and the Novgorod republic formally recognized its status as Ivan III's vassal.

The Ugra Standoff and Moscow's Symbolic Emancipation from the Hegemony of the Great Horde

At the same time, Khan Ahmed (Akhmat) of the Great Horde was establishing allied relations with the Polish king and grand duke of Lithuania Casimir IV. As part of his diplomatic effort, Ahmed officially supported the Grand Duchy's claims to Novgorod. Therefore, upon learning of Novgorod's formal subordination to Moscow, Khan Ahmed perceived this as a direct challenge to his authority and in the summer of 1472 staged a large-scale military campaign against Moscow. The government of Ivan III considered this illegal interference in Muscovy's affairs. The Moscow army marched against Ahmed's forces and did not allow them to cross the Oka River to the territory of the Grand Principality. Ahmed was forced to retreat, which in Moscow was considered a decisive victory over the Great Horde: the Moscow government officially refused to pay tribute to the khan and informed foreign powers about the termination of formal vassal relations with him as the suzerain.

In practical terms, this announcement had little consequence because, even before, the annual tribute to the Great Horde had been paid very irregularly if at all. The amount of the tribute, probably 7,000 rubles on behalf of the entire Grand Principality of Moscow, was more than two times less than what Novgorod alone had to pay Moscow under the treaty of 1471 as an indemnity (that is, what was considered a heavy, but quite feasible toll). The formal termination of the annual tribute did not stop quite regular payments to various khans of the polities that emerged on the ruins of the Golden Horde, as part of the political ritual of maintaining friendly relations, all the way through the sixteenth century. The amount of these payments varied but often reached several thousand rubles a year.

In 1476, Khan Ahmed began to systematically restore the former power of the Golden Horde, trying to subjugate its former uluses—Crimea, Astrakhan, and, in 1480, Moscow. In the summer of 1480, he once more moved his forces against Moscow. At the end of September, two armies stood against each other, separated by the border river Ugra (a tributary of the Oka): Ahmed came from the territory of the Grand Duchy of Lithuania. On October 26, the Ugra froze over, and on November 11, Ahmed ordered his troops to retreat since they were not ready for the winter campaign. Neither side dared to start the battle because too much depended on its outcome. Still, Ahmed's retreat tacitly suggested he had given up on subjugating Moscow, which ultimately led to the demise of his authority and to his murder in 1481. However, twenty years later, in 1502, Ivan III himself sent an envoy to Ahmed's son, the khan of the Great Horde, Sheikh Ahmed, pledging obedience and paying the annual tribute. This was a tactical maneuver that destroyed the alliance of Moscow's foes—the Grand Duchy of Lithuania and the Great Horde—and lulled the khan: at the same time, Ivan III and the Crimean khan agreed to attack Sheikh Ahmed. In the same year, the Great Horde fell under the attack of the Crimeans and ceased to exist. Thus, any date between 1462 (when Ivan III ordered that the design of Moscow coins be changed) and 1502 can be designated as the time of Moscow's renouncing of its vassal subordination to the Great Horde. In reality, this process of political emancipation dragged on for many decades, and its formal confirmation held low priority for the Moscow rulers, who were more interested in practical strategic results.

The war of 1472 with the Great Horde had a much more decisive effect on the political imagination within the Grand Principality of Moscow: in this sphere, radical changes followed immediately. For the first time, the historical chronicles and writings of important clergymen featured derogatory characteristics of "tsars"—the Great Horde khans. The previous khan, Kichi Muhammad, was now called "godless," the current khan Ahmed—"evil-minded." Scribes redacted the ancient chronicles inserting novel characteristics, so that even Khan Batu received the epithets "godless" and "accursed"— in the past, nothing of the kind was imaginable even in the most anti–Golden Horde texts. The supreme ruler was beyond criticism, since he personified the foundations of the social and political order. In the 1470s, the desacralization of the Great Khan's power led to the differentiation of the once syncretic figure of the supreme ruler into the person of a khan and the title of "tsar." As a result of the Grand Principality of Moscow's practical (political) and symbolic emancipation from the hegemony of the Great Horde, the position of tsar became vacant. Originally, the Byzantine emperors were called "tsars" in the Rous' Lands, but the demise of Byzantium under the blows of the Ottoman Turks in 1453 also left the Moscow elite without this mostly symbolic authority. It is not surprising then that after 1472 the grand prince of Moscow tried on the vacant tsar's role as a new "master of all Rus'." He claimed both the possessions of the Grand Duchy of Lithuania and the legacy of the Golden Horde, including the territories outside the northeast of the former Rous' Lands.

Ivan III: Marrying the Byzantine Legacy

In 1472, Ivan III married the niece of the last Byzantine emperor, Sophia (Zoe) Palaiologina, thus symbolically confirming changes in the Moscow political imagination and reinforcing his own identification as emperor (tsar). Sophia was the younger daughter of Thomas Palaiologos, Despotate of the Morea—the governor of the Byzantine province in the Peloponnese in Greece and the brother of the last emperor, Constantine XI. The very idea of Sophia's marriage to the widowed grand prince of Moscow was put forward by Pope Paul II in 1469. After the Turks occupied Constantinople (1453) and the Peloponnese (1460), Sophia's family converted to Catholicism and lived in Rome on a modest subsidy from the Vatican. Initially, there were plans for her marriage to King James II of Cyprus, then to the Neapolitan count Caracciolo, and finally, in an attempt to persuade the Moscow ruler to support the union between Orthodoxy and Catholicism, a poor but blue-blooded bride was offered to Ivan III.

Obviously, Ivan agreed to a dynastic marriage, which promised no practical diplomatic benefits, solely for the symbolic meaning of this act. It suggested parallels with the figure of Vladimir Monomakh, whose myth as the direct ancestor of the Moscow princes and the common ruler of all modern Russian and Ruthenian lands, had been actively cultivated in Moscow. Vladimir's mother was a niece of the Byzantine emperor Constantine IX, whereas Ivan was marrying a niece of Emperor Constantine XI.

At the same time, what was meant as a symbolic marriage turned out to have an immediate practical consequence for Moscow's politics. Most probably, Sophia became the reason for the Moscow government's open break with Khan Akhmed and the subsequent rethinking of the grand-princely status. According to the testimony of Dmitry Trakhaniot (Tarchaneiotes), who accompanied Sophia to Moscow in November 1472, as an aristocrat raised in Rome, she was shocked by the Russian diplomatic ritual of servile greeting of ambassadors from the Great Horde. Unlike Sophia, Muscovites viewed it as a mere formality, a survival from the thirteenth century that no longer irritated even the most independent grand princes. The diplomat from the Holy Roman Empire and traveler, Baron Sigismund von Herberstein, who interviewed Dmitry Trakhaniot's son, recorded the following story about Ivan III's decision after 1472 to cast away even the appearance of a respectful attitude toward the khan (which would have allowed the status quo to be maintained for several more decades):

> However, no matter how powerful he [Ivan III] was, he was still forced to obey the Tatars. When the Tatar ambassadors arrived, he went to meet them outside the city and listened to them sitting [on horseback] while standing [on his feet]. His Greek wife was so indignant at this that she repeated every day that she had married a slave of the Tatars, and therefore, in order to someday abandon this servile custom, she persuaded her husband to feign illness when the Tatars arrived.

Thus, the rise of a new image of the grand-princely power as sovereign and even "imperial" (tsar-like) caused an open break with the Great Horde. The ensuing confrontation with the Grand Duchy of Lithuania over Novgorod (and later over the Lithuanian territories proper, including Smolensk), as well as the symbolic identification with the political legacy of the Byzantine Empire, exacerbated the conflict with the Great Horde, something that, pragmatically speaking, Moscow would have preferred to avoid. Subsequent developments showed Ivan III's reluctance to shift from ideological declarations to military confrontation with the Great Horde. No decisive battles were fought during the escalations of political conflict in 1472 and 1480—on both occasions, the hostile armies limited themselves to the demonstration of force, standing on the opposite riverbanks. After the official refusal to pay tribute to the Great Horde in the mid-1470s, Ivan III still dispatched several reconciliatory missions to Khan Akhmed. In 1480, the Moscow elites were eager to make concessions to the khan's demands. The

New Times

Grand Principality of Moscow could not be defeated, much less subjugated, by military force, but pragmatically, it was much cheaper to sustain peace along the vast southern borders by periodically sending embassies with gifts to the khan and observing the ancient etiquette of obedience when receiving his ambassadors.

Indeed, the demise of the Great Horde in 1502 only exacerbated the strategic situation on the border with the steppe, rather than improving it. Ivan III's former ally, the Crimean khan, became the immediate neighbor and adversary. Moscow had no prior history of strategic partnership with the Crimean Khanate or the Nogai Horde of the kind that it had had for centuries with the Great Horde: although institutionalized in the form of nominal vassal subordination to the suzerain, it was comprehensively regulated by a ritualized tradition. With the elimination of these ritualized relationships as well as formal dependence on the Great Horde, military clashes and devastating raids from the south did not decline but only increased manifold, becoming the main security threat in the sixteenth century and retaining their severity in the seventeenth century. After 1507, the Crimeans raided the Grand Principality of Moscow almost every year. In 1521, they besieged Moscow, and in 1571, they captured, plundered, and burned the city. Nothing of the kind in terms of the intensity of aggression had been experienced from the Golden Horde since the beginning of the fourteenth century. But even earlier, the devastating attacks from the Golden Horde were mostly orchestrated by the rival Russian princes themselves. Maintaining traditional relations with the Great Horde was much more productive than constantly confronting its numerous successors.

Improvising the Tsar's Title

The dualism of pragmatic political practice and ideologically driven political rhetoric characterized the reign of Ivan III and his successors in the sixteenth century. Their attempts to substantiate claims for hegemony in the region were supported by references to incongruent political mythologies and thus were inherently contradictory. On the one hand, Ivan III posed as the direct heir to Vladimir Monomakh—the Orthodox sovereign of "all Russia." This led to a strategic confrontation with the Grand Duchy of Lithuania: first to the struggle over Novgorod, then to an undeclared border war for buffer territories in the upper reaches of the Oka River (1487–94). Eventually an open war took place (1500–03), and as a result, the Grand Duchy lost vast territories in the southeast, including Chernigov. The son and grandson of Ivan III continued the aggression against the Grand Duchy of Lithuania in an endless series of wars throughout the sixteenth century. On the other hand, Ivan III launched a political expansion to the territories that had never been part of the Rous' Lands and hence could not be claimed as his "patrimony," even fictively. In the early 1470s, Moscow began establishing its control over Great Perm in the northwest of the Urals (*Perämaa* in local Finnish languages can be translated as "borderland" or "the other side"). At the time, this was a distant colony of Novgorod, to which Novgorodians occasionally sent expeditions to collect tribute. From there, the servitors of the Grand Principality of Moscow began penetrating beyond the Urals, to the Yugra in the lower

192   *New Imperial History of Northern Eurasia*

reaches of the Ob River in what is now called Western Siberia, inhabited by the Khanty, Mansi, and Tatars. These lands had never entered the orbit of the Rous' Lands.

Even more significant was Moscow's systematic interference in the affairs of the Kazan Khanate. Quite a few Kazan aristocrats and hence pretenders to the khan's throne were enlisted in the Moscow service. As early as 1467, Moscow troops backed the vassal Qasim khan's attempt to become the ruler of Kazan. After a series of military conflicts, Moscow troops occupied Kazan (1487): they executed the leaders of the anti-Moscow party among the local elite and assisted a Tatar prince on the Moscow service to become the Kazan khan. Ivan III used this opportunity to add "Prince of Bulgaria" to his title. Volga Bulgaria was never part of the Rous' Lands, and therefore the conquest of the Kazan Khanate on its former territory could not be justified by the claim to Vladimir Monomakh's political heritage. Equally irrelevant in this case was the idea of continuity with the "Orthodox tsardom"—the Byzantine Empire, which was becoming an obsession of the Moscow elite. The Kazan Khanate was ruled by Muslims over the Muslim and animist populations, and the idea of forcefully converting this population to Christianity did not even occur to anyone in the fifteenth century. Unrelated to the Rous' Lands or the Byzantine Empire, Bulgar was formerly an ulus of the Golden Horde. Therefore, by adopting the title of Prince of Bulgaria, Ivan III appropriated a part of the Golden Horde's political heritage. The grand prince of Moscow did not claim either the territory of the Kazan Khanate, or the payment of tribute, but symbolically he acquired the same status in relation to Kazan as that enjoyed by the khans of the Golden Horde in relation to Bulgar.

Thus, the idea that the power of the grand prince of Moscow was essentially that of the tsar (the emperor or the great khan) was substantiated by references to three different, often mutually contradictory political legacies: pre-Mongol Kyivan Rus', the Byzantine Empire, and the Golden Horde. The emerging new status of the tsar arbitrarily combined different elements of these three distinct political scenarios largely on an ad hoc basis, under the influence of pragmatic concerns such as the question of succession to the throne or relations with appanage principalities and neighboring states. For example, in the treaty of 1481 with the Livonian Confederation (the heir to the old Livonian Order), Ivan III and his son and coruler Ivan Ivanovich called themselves "tsars"; in the treaty between Novgorod and Sweden (1482), Ivan III was referred to as the "Russian emperor" (*Rysse keysere*); in the treaty of 1487, as "the great king, Emperor of all Russians, Grand Duke" (*groten Koniinges, Keijser ower alle Rwslant, Grot Förste*). In June 1485, Ivan III used the title "Grand Prince of All Russia." During the coronation of his grandson Dmitry (1498), the grand prince and coruler, Ivan III officially used the titles "tsar" and "autocrat." The latter was another borrowing from Byzantine political practice, where *autokrator* meant the senior coemperor. The growing power and ambitions of the grand prince of Moscow prompted the Holy Roman emperor Frederick II to offer Ivan III the royal crown in 1489. In the thirteenth century, such a proposal would have been the ultimate dream of any ruler in the former Rous' Lands. Princes of Lithuania and Galicia-Volhynia greatly enhanced their authority by becoming kings. But Ivan III had already claimed the much higher status of tsar ("Caesar," i.e., emperor or great khan). He rejected the offer rather arrogantly, stating: "By the grace of God, we are sovereigns in our land from the beginning, from

New Times

our first ancestors; we are appointed by God, just as our progenitors . . . they wanted no appointment from anyone and neither do we now."

As was typical in the era of Ivan III, this declaration also contained an inherent contradiction: his "progenitors" during the pre-Mongol period considered the Byzantine emperor to be the "tsar" and perceived grand princes of the Rous' Lands to be equal in rank to European kings. Later, as vassals of the Golden Horde, the Vladimir grand princes ruled only when they had the yarlyk issued by the khan. But the claim of the divine origin of grand-princely authority made any references to hereditary rights and traditions unnecessary, especially since Ivan III himself systematically violated these traditions. Having formulated the eclectic ideal of the supreme ruler, in the 1470s, Ivan III focused on "gathering of the Russian lands": the Moscow principality absorbed the parts of the former Vladimir-Suzdal Land that still retained their independence (such as Yaroslavl and Rostov). In the 1480s, Moscow took over its old rival—the Tver principality and subjugated the Ryazan principality. Simultaneously, Moscow continued to consolidate its internal appanage principalities. Many of the local princes who lost their possessions joined the ranks of noble servitors. As a result of the military campaigns of 1471 and 1477–8, Novgorod lost its independence, and its veche bell and archive were taken to Moscow. Pskov lost its autonomy as well. In a series of wars, vast territories were annexed from the Grand Duchy of Lithuania. Ivan III also attempted, but failed, to reclaim the territories on the Karelian Isthmus that Novgorod had ceded to the Swedish king back in 1323.

Moscow as a Herald of Protonationalism

Acting on all these fronts simultaneously, Ivan III projected his vague ideal of "tsar" power on the real world, using military force as his main political instrument and achieving success where circumstances were more favorable. This is not to deny his indisputable political talent and the fact that he managed to identify a political program that resonated with many of his subjects and the residents of neighboring principalities. In the last quarter of the fifteenth century other regional powers were going through hard times: the Great Horde was consumed by confrontation with the khanates that had seceded, the Grand Duchy of Lithuania was impacted by growing tension between the increasingly widespread social and political institutions of the Kingdom of Poland as its counterpart in the political union and traditions of the Rous' (now Ruthenian) Lands. Ruthenian language (rus'ka mova), which developed on the basis of local dialects spoken in various Rous' Lands, remained the official administrative language of the Grand Duchy of Lithuania until the seventeenth century (it is also called "Old Belarusian" or "Old Ukrainian"). The majority of the population professed Orthodoxy. In 1458, the Metropolis of Kyiv, Galicia, and All Rus' was established in Vilna (Vilnius), which from 1470 was subordinate to the Ecumenical Patriarch of Constantinople. At the same time, the new leading political force in the land—the szlachta (nobility)—was a profoundly Polish cultural phenomenon. The Catholic Church enjoyed increasing prestige and power. The dualism between political "Polishness" and local "Lithuanian" patriotism made it difficult to resist the active expansionism of Moscow, which was carried out under the slogans of the return of the Rous' ("old Russian") heritage and the protection of Orthodoxy.

It should be added that the situation of the Grand Duchy would be much more desperate if not for the utter underdevelopment of literature and political writing in the Grand Principality of Moscow in comparison with the Grand Duchy of Lithuania or Poland. The ritualized language and the lack of experience in articulating complex ideas on social and political topics prevented Moscow from taking full advantage of the revolutionary discovery made in the era of Ivan III: when political boundaries coincide with the cultural (religious-linguistic) community and historical territory, they produce a special type of society. This is how intellectuals of the nineteenth century defined the "people," and this understanding prompted political mobilization, unprecedented in scale and intensity—the creation of national states that led to two world wars. Probably, only the Reconquista on the Iberian Peninsula, which concluded at the end of the fifteenth century, and which was also carried under the slogan of the return of historical territories, could be compared with the program of "returning the historical heritage" that was spontaneously formulated in Moscow. However, the conquest of land south of the Pyrenees from the Arab rulers was carried out simultaneously by several Catholic monarchies until the final stage; it was not so much about the reunification of the once divided population as about the expulsion of the "invaders" and, in fact, the recolonization of the peninsula. Neither the Kingdom of England, nor the Kingdom of France, nor the Holy Roman Empire, nor the Italian principalities and republics drew their legitimacy from the unique combination of religion, language, and statehood on the territory of some preexisting historical polity. The old medieval political system was based on personal relations arranged in the hierarchies of vassal subordination. In the context of this system's disintegration in the fifteenth century, the idea of reviving the fictional unity of the Rous' Lands under the rule of the Orthodox grand prince of Moscow was ahead of its time. It was probably even better for Ivan III that his entourage could not elaborate this concept into a consistent theory, because that would have made it extremely difficult to exploit two other alternative scenarios of power: the Byzantine legacy of the emperor's title and the legacy of the Golden Horde, inherited by its former ulus by the right of conquest and helping to legitimize the rule over the "non-Russian" and non-Christian populations. But even in its embryonic form, the theory of reviving the legacy of the Rous' Lands contributed to the demoralization of the Grand Duchy of Lithuania and its marginalization as the heir of ancient "Rus." This entailed a grandiose rethinking of the mental map of a large part of Northern Eurasia, from the Danube to the Urals.

The medieval spatial imagination had difficulty drawing insurmountable boundaries within the Christian world. The majority of the population was illiterate and was usually disregarded as a factor determining local specificity, while the aristocratic elites were quite "international," often moving from country to country in pursuit of new service opportunities or even a throne. Political borders designated not language communities or communities of shared ancient history, but landholdings formed by ruler-vassals' relationships. The Congress of Lutsk (1429) attended by many European rulers clearly demonstrated the utter plasticity of linguistic and even confessional boundaries. The Grand Duchy of Lithuania embodied the normality of the coexistence of Catholics and

Orthodox Christians, along with pagans and Muslims within common political borders (which did not necessarily mean that this coexistence was peaceful). A century later a similar congress of monarchs on the Lutsk model would have been unthinkable. By that time Europe was split by the Reformation. The wide spread of literacy in vernacular languages and the dependence of rulers and religious leaders on the mass support of the population made a thing of the past political arrangements such as in the Grand Duchy of Lithuania under Vytautas, characterized by the government's disregard for religious and cultural differences. In 1555, the Peace of Augsburg between German Protestant princes and Emperor Charles V proclaimed the principle "cuius regio, eius religio"—"whose realm, his religion," which was adopted Europe-wide. It became natural to perceive the state borders as demarcating cultures and peoples. Soon the Union of Lublin (1569) between the Grand Duchy of Lithuania and the Kingdom of Poland finally united the two states as a common political entity, the Polish–Lithuanian Commonwealth (Rzeczpospolita). Within the new dual state, the Grand Duchy of Lithuania preserved its administrative and judicial systems, its own army and money, but had to transfer vast territories to the Polish side, including Volhynia and the Kyiv principality. This arrangement was met with strong resistance in the Grand Duchy, but the only alternative to the unification was an even more aggressive takeover by the Grand Principality of Moscow. The new spatial and political imagination prevailing in the European part of Northern Eurasia had no place for independent countries that did not differ in language or religion from their neighbors. The accelerated Polonization of the Grand Duchy of Lithuania and the rising domination of the Catholic Church resulted in no small part from a conscious political choice and were used to create a more effective border with predominantly Russian-speaking and Orthodox Muscovy.

Defining Moscow as a Civilizational Other

Using a new idea of the political unity of cobelievers who speak the same language and share the common history of belonging to the same legendary polity in the past, Ivan III not only expanded his power but also created preconditions for the emergence of new, more solid cultural boundaries. In the mid-fifteenth century, these boundaries did not exist. The offer of the royal crown to Ivan III in 1489 suggested that the Grand Principality of Moscow and its ruler were not yet fundamentally differentiated from the princes of Galicia or Lithuania by their neighbors, even though the Moscow princes were less "cosmopolitan" in terms of their education, worldview, and language skills. A ruler of the Grand Duchy of Lithuania could be expected to be fluent in Ruthenian, Lithuanian, Polish, and German, while the Moscow princes, apparently, in addition to their native language, spoke only a dialect of the Turkic (Tatar) language. However, from the early sixteenth century on, a new myth was created and broadly disseminated, about the cultural and even "civilizational" otherness of Muscovy, whose inhabitants were alien to the Christian peoples even more than the Muslim Turks. The initiators and main propagators of this myth were Polish political writers, whose activity intensified with each new Moscow–Lithuanian war (1500–3, 1507–8, 1512–22, 1534–7, and the Livonian War of 1561–82), usually followed by concessions of new territories to the Grand Principality of Moscow. By the middle of the century, almost half of the former territory of the Grand Duchy of Lithuania passed to the authority of Moscow, and became the zone of closest contacts between the neighboring countries in peacetime and the launchpad for new attacks during military confrontations. It was the recently "Lithuanian" population of these lands that was presented by Polish authors as genuinely alien and barbaric, although these people in no way differed from the inhabitants of the lands still ruled by the Grand Duchy of Lithuania.

One of the most authoritative propagators of the myth was the Archbishop of Gniezno and primate of Poland (the most authoritative among the Polish bishops) and the former grand chancellor of the crown Jan Łaski. He participated in the Fifth Council of the Lateran in Rome on behalf of King Sigismund I, presenting in 1514 a report "On the Tribes of Ruthenians and Their Errors." The report paid special attention to Orthodox Christian faith. Specifically, Łaski revealed—as if speaking about unknown aliens from space, and not about the community of believers that made up the majority not only in Muscovy but also in the Grand Duchy of Lithuania: "Their priests fall into unrighteousness when they kill a sparrow or any other bird, and they do not achieve righteousness until that bird gets completely rotten under their armpits. Such is their punishment, which is not so severe if someone kills a Christian."

Whatever the real structural and cultural differences between the societies of the Grand Principality of Moscow and the Kingdom of Poland (and later, other European countries), the imagery of the alien or barbarian Other had its own logic and dynamics. It helped to consolidate and solidify political borders between kindred societies at the time when clear territorial boundaries could be only visualized between distinctive landscapes or private possessions. The crisis of medieval political legitimacy as based on vassal relations with individual rulers rather than territorial polities made it an imperative task to substantiate the limits of a country's sovereignty as stable and objective, independent of personalities and their private arrangements. The initial attempts to solve this problem by limiting the right of vassals to switch allegiances from one overlord to another—for example, in the treaties of the second half of the fifteenth century between the Grand Principality of Moscow and the Grand Duchy of Lithuania—proved fruitless in stabilizing territorial borders. It was much more effective to cultivate and propagate cultural and ideological stereotypes as the basis for a new understanding of state sovereignty of the entire country, not just its ruler. In any case, the Polish side mastered this instrument much better than Muscovy, due to greater literacy and the development of secular literature. Whereas the Moscow elite strove to redraw the mental map of the grand principality by claiming the historical legacy of the Rous' Lands, their Polish counterparts even more actively solidified the symbolic border with Muscovy through their ideological projections.

The Problem of "Otherness" in the Buffer Zones with the Former Golden Horde Uluses

Actively pushing the principality's western borders under the elaborated ideological pretext, Moscow rulers at the same time were not able to draw clear boundaries in the east and south, with neighboring fragments of the former Golden Horde. The process of Vladimir-Suzdal Lands' emancipation from the suzerainty of the khans dragged

New Times 197

on for a century and was accompanied by the creation of buffer zones between the Russian territories and the adjacent uluses of the Golden Horde. These buffer zones were inhabited by various peoples whom Russians indiscriminately called "Tatars," eagerly admitting them into the service of the Moscow princes. Thus, on the border with Bulgar, not far from Nizhny Novgorod, the so-called Kurmish Tatars—the Turkic-speaking descendants of the ancient local population (Bulgars, Burtas, Mordovians, and Chuvash)—lived and performed border guard duties. In the southeast, near the town of Kadom 150 miles east of Ryazan, another group of the Golden Horde population joined the Moscow service and became known as the Kadom Tatars. Aristocrats of the Golden Horde usually joined the service of the grand prince as individuals and were baptized in order to preserve or even enhance their social status. But the so-called service Tatars, who lived on their traditional territory, remained Muslims. Under Vasily II, buffer zones ruled by Muslims multiplied along the southeastern borders of Muscovy, so that the Qasim Khanate founded near Kadom as a vassal principality was just the most prominent example of them. Ivan III tried to achieve the same status for the Kazan Khanate that was an independent and originally hostile polity. As a result, regardless of this tactic's success in each case, the border with neighbors was becoming even more blurred, and so were the boundaries of the Moscow ruler's sovereignty. The power of the grand prince was gradually diminishing and becoming more conditional as distance from Moscow increased, from directly administered regions to appanage principalities, from there to dependent territories, then to vassal principalities and khanates, and finally to temporary allies.

Successful extension of the grand prince's authority over the borderland "Tatars" might have encouraged plans to take over all the former Golden Horde's possessions, or at least this is how modern historians sometimes interpret the Moscow rulers' expansionism. However, any attempt to reverse the previous relations between Moscow and the Golden Horde, with the grand prince taking the place of the khan and resubordinating other former uluses on approximately the same conditions on which Moscow had been subordinate to the Golden Horde under Dmitry Donskoy, was destined to fail. The old political system based on the personal relations of vassals with the suzerain had stopped working everywhere on the European part of the continent by the end of the fifteenth century. In some cases, for example, in the Holy Roman Empire, this led to the de facto independence of the princes of the empire, which increasingly resembled a loose confederation. Elsewhere, a consolidation of the central power was the response to the crisis: in England after the Wars of the Roses (1455–85), in France after the end of the Hundred Years' War (1453), and in Spain after the end of the Reconquista (1492). The Grand Principality of Moscow demonstrated the same historical dynamics after the resolution of the political crisis of the second quarter of the fifteenth century (1453). The grand prince of Moscow consistently demoted former independent principalities to the position of subordinate appanages and took over most of the old appanage principalities under his direct rule. He liquidated private armies of individual princes and appointed crown administrators to formally independent lands, such as Novgorod or Pskov. The remaining appanage principalities were preserved to be redistributed among the grand prince's family members as a share of his inheritance. On the one hand, although nominally autonomous, the appanage principalities served

198   *New Imperial History of Northern Eurasia*

a barrier to centralization and a potential source of political instability. On the other hand, they were ruled by members of the same family, and the general trend was a further reduction of independent appanages. In 1497, Ivan III authorized the code of laws that were enforced on the entire territory of the Grand Principality of Moscow, and coinage became the exclusive privilege of the grand prince. His authority was now communicated directly through the emerging state apparatus of crown representatives and officials, and not through personal agreements with local rulers.

Institutional Boundaries of Sovereignty: The Kazan Khanate and the Crisis of Vassal Relations

The ineffectiveness of formal vassal status as a means of political control was especially evident in relations with the Kazan Khanate. In the fifteenth century, it was no longer realistic to expect annual tribute to be received from vassal lands, as the relations of the Grand Principality of Moscow and the Great Horde had demonstrated. The collection of regular tribute could be ensured only by permanently stationing a large military contingent in the vassal territory, which would have undermined the very concept of "vassal" as a dependent but otherwise autonomous ruler. As it turned out, key to the preservation of vassal relations was not so much the suzerain's determination to impose his will as the vassal's eagerness to obey. The need to rely on medieval interpersonal power relations of rulers in the age of growing cultural and political polarization of whole countries confined the old power relations to a vicious circle: to rely on a loyal vassal, a ruler first had to install a loyal vassal. In the span of about seventy years, between 1484 and 1552, the Moscow princes succeeded eight times in making their candidates, usually natives of the Qasim Khanate, the khans of Kazan. At the same time, the khans openly hostile to Moscow and loyal to the Crimean Khanate occupied the throne in Kazan for almost as long as the khans who recognized themselves as Moscow's vassals. However, the policy of Moscow rulers toward Kazan remained unchanged for many decades. Ivan III and his son and heir Vasily III (1479–1533) continued to dispatch troops against Kazan: to support Moscow's candidate to the throne, to suppress a rebellion against him, or to repel an attack by a hostile Kazan khan. Many of these campaigns yielded no result or even ended in the defeat of the Moscow troops. Still, the idea of direct subordination of the khanate to Muscovy by incorporating it into the grand principality, once and for all, apparently did not even occur to the Moscow authorities. They continued to invest all their efforts in securing the next Kazan khan's personal loyalty to the grand prince.

Treating a Foe as a Vassal

This tactic did not immediately change even after Sahib Giray (Säxip Gäräy), the younger brother of the Crimean khan Mehmed Giray, came to power in Kazan in April 1521 as a result of a coup, and realigned Kazan from Moscow to the Crimea. Just a few months later, in the summer, together with his brother's huge army, Sahib Giray's troops invaded the Grand Principality of Moscow, capturing and ravaging Nizhny Novgorod

New Times

and Vladimir. The combined Crimean-Kazanian-Lithuanian forces besieged Moscow, plundered the vicinity, and retreated only after Vasily III signed a charter recognizing himself as a tributary and vassal of the Crimean khan! The only reason this humiliating debacle did not have the devastating political consequences that seemed inevitable was that the Ryazan governor—*voevoda*—Ivan Khabar tricked the Crimeans returning with the war booty into giving him the incriminating document. When Mehmed Giray, as Vasily III's new overlord, ordered the surrender of the garrison, Khabar pedantically demanded that a supporting document be presented. As proof, the khan's envoys showed the grand prince's charter, which Khabar seized, and then ordered his artillery forces to disperse the enemy.

The next crisis of relations with Kazan took place in the spring of 1523, when the Kazan khan ordered the execution of the Moscow ambassadors and merchants who had been arrested two years earlier during the palace coup in the city. In response, Vasily III organized a new military campaign to the east. Unlike many punitive expeditions in the past, in addition to devastating the lands of the khanate and clashing with its military units, this time the Russian troops used new tactics. In September 1523, they built a fortress (today, the town of Vasilsursk) at the confluence of the Sura River into the Volga, about halfway between Nizhny Novgorod and Kazan. The fortress was erected at the foot of the mountain, on which the capital city of the Mari people, Tsepel, had been located, now already ruined by the Russians because the Mari were subjects of the Kazan khan. Nearby was the sacred grove of the Mari, dedicated to the supreme God Kugu Yumo. For the first time, an outpost of Muscovy was established on the land of the Kazan Khanate, controlling part of the khanate's territory and population. [3]

Curiously, even this modest innovation of a tactical rather than a strategic nature drew wide criticism in Moscow: there were concerns that it would become more difficult to establish amicable relations with Kazan, which were still viewed as the ultimate goal. Vasily III gave two reasons to explain his 1523 campaign against Kazan: first, the murder of Moscow ambassadors and merchants, and second, the fact that Sahib Giray "became king without the grand prince's knowledge." In other words, the violation of his will as a suzerain was equated with direct hostile actions. In contrast to the political process along the western border, where vast territories of the Grand Duchy of Lithuania were annexed by Muscovy, nobody even considered the annexation of the Kazan Khanate. In the next year (1524), even larger forces were sent to Kazan, where they besieged the city but could not take it. The campaign was headed by Kazan's former khan Shahghali (Shah-Ali), overthrown by Sahib Giray in 1521: obviously, in the case of success, he should have regained the Kazan throne as a loyal vassal of Moscow.

Modernist Politics of the Centralization of Power

The traditional sovereign–vassal scenario pursued in relations with Kazan contrasted not only with politics along the western borders but also with Vasily III's "modernist" efforts to centralize power. At the beginning of 1510, he abolished the remnants of Pskov independence: the veche bell was taken away from the city, 300 families of local notables (boyars and merchants) were forcefully resettled to the inner regions of Muscovy, and Moscow residents came to replace them. These measures repeated the steps taken by Vasily III's father, Ivan III, in 1478, during the final liquidation of Novgorod's independence. At that time, the families of Moscow servitors replaced a thousand families of Novgorod's elite in the city. In another war with the Grand Duchy of Lithuania, in 1514, the Russian army captured Smolensk, and again Vasily III used the tactics of forced resettlement: the inhabitants of the Smolensk region were sent to the east, and residents of Muscovy's borderlands were settled in their place. This measure suggests that Vasily III did not completely trust the declared "primordial Russianness" of the population of Smolensk, which had become Lithuanian less than a hundred years earlier. Large-scale population displacements were not new to the region, but the organized exchange of whole categories of residents between the two regions seems to have been Muscovy's invention. In 1517, Vasily III summoned the prince of Ryazan to Moscow, arrested him, and seized his principality. He did the same with the Starodub appanage principality in the northeast and with the Novgorod-Seversky principality, recently taken from the Grand Duchy of Lithuania, in the southwest. The grand prince actively intervened in the affairs of the Orthodox Church, displacing and appointing metropolitans at will. As a result, the church became an even more loyal supporter and facilitator of the grand-princely power. Simultaneously, the state administration was also properly reformed. Whereas Ivan III appointed clerks specializing in particular tasks, Vasily III organized them into chancelleries with a permanent staff that became known as "offices" (*prikazy*).

These concerted efforts at centralization of the supreme power made the traditionalist policy toward Kazan particularly conspicuous. Vasily III projected his enhanced sovereignty inside the Moscow principality and in the form of westward expansion but did not even try to apply it to relations with Kazan. Meanwhile, recognizing himself as a vassal of the Crimean khan, and after 1524 of the Ottoman Sultan, the khan of Kazan demonstratively broke off the former vassal relations with the Grand Principality of Moscow. Of primary practical importance was Kazan's alignment with Moscow's most formidable enemy—the Crimean Khanate. Moscow's intervention in Kazan politics risked triggering a Crimean attack, while in the event of a new large-scale raid from the Crimea (from the southwest), Kazan could attack Muscovy from the rear (from the east, as in 1521). By the 1530s, the previous course to sustain indirect sovereignty over Kazan had proved completely inadequate.

The Kazan Dilemma

The Kazan Khanate partially relied on the Bulgar traditions of statehood dating back to the pre-Mongol period; it demonstrated bold political ambitions, and in general was too large and independent to be turned into another "internal ulus" like the Qasim Khanate or into a loyal vassal. No other models for dealing with culturally foreign polities were known in the Grand Principality of Moscow. From a military point of view, the conquest of Kazan was a practical possibility and had actually happened several times in the past. However, it was unclear what could be done to the conquered enemy other than making it accept another Moscow appointee as ruler. Unlike the annexed territories of the Grand Duchy of Lithuania with their culturally kindred

New Times

population, which Muscovy integrated almost effortlessly, the population of the Kazan Khanate was predominantly Muslim and pagan. These people had their own clergy and administration that could not be accommodated in the existing social system of the Grand Principality of Moscow.

Essentially, this was the dilemma of the accommodation of a multicultural population by an early modern polity built around the ideal of unification—centralized state institutions and the principle of the sovereign's divine power. A truly legitimate monarch could not rule the "infidels" who relied on their own administrative and religious institutions. In this regard, Moscow rulers theoretically could refer to two historical precedents. The Christian kings in the Iberian Peninsula pursued a policy of ethnoconfessional cleansing in the fifteenth century, expelling Muslims and Jews from newly conquered territories. As a result, in place of numerous multiconfessional kingdoms and emirates, a single Spanish kingdom emerged—a Catholic polity striving for monoculturalism based on the Castilian Spanish language. Simultaneously, the expansion of the Ottoman Empire at the expense of conquered Christian countries of Southern and Central Europe offered a different example. The diverse populations were allowed a high degree of autonomy as confessional communities, subordinate to their own spiritual leaders. These transterritorial confessional groups, later known as millets, also enjoyed the right of their own jurisdiction and collection of their own taxes. The system of taxation and dues generally discriminated against non-Muslim millets, but there was no forced conversion to Islam or direct repressions of "infidels." Millets of Muslims, Orthodox Christians, Catholics, Armenians, and Jews were expected to demonstrate loyalty to the sultan and obey all his orders. The ruling class of the empire, including senior officials, consisted largely of representatives of non-Muslim millets (Greeks, Armenians, and Jews). A Greek named Skinder was the Ottoman Empire's ambassador in Muscovy at the time of Vasily III. The millet system allowed the sultan to remain the true Muslim caliph, who could not be the ruler of the gentiles, and at the same time maintain state control over the non-Muslim populations. It was this complex structure of power that was making the Ottoman polity an empire, and not merely a vast confederation of lands, like the nominal possessions of the German emperor. A single political, economic, and largely legal and cultural space integrated various territorial and population groups that preserved their own religious, juridical, and everyday traditions, as well as self-government. In 1566, the French politician and philosopher Jean Bodin admitted that the Ottomans' vast polity was the only one legitimately called empire:

> This fact is obvious to everyone—if there is anywhere in the world any majesty of empire and of true monarchy, it must radiate from the sultan. He owns the richest parts of Asia, Africa, and Europe, and he rules far and wide over the entire Mediterranean and all but a few of its islands. . . . But he seized the provinces of the Christians and the empire of the Greeks by force of arms, and even devastated the lands of the Germans. . . . The way in which the Germans define a monarchy is absurd. . . . It is even more absurd that they think they hold the empire of the Romans. . . . How much truer it is of the king of the Turks, who took Byzantium, the capital of the empire, from the Christians, the region of Babylon, which is

discussed in the book of Daniel, from the Persians, and joined a great part of his dominion beyond the Danube, up to the mouths of the Dnieper, to the old Roman provinces?[1]

Bodin's critique of the Holy Roman Empire of the German Nation might have been influenced by political considerations, but his theory of monarchal sovereignty and truly imperial power reflected the general mindset of the time and was broadly accepted.

The New Imperial Policy toward Kazan

Perhaps not coincidentally, the Moscow government had radically changed its policy toward the Kazan Khanate only after 1547, when Vasily III's son and heir, Ivan IV, was crowned as tsar (i.e., Caesar, emperor) of all the Russias. Of the Moscow rulers claiming the legacy of the Rous' Lands, Ivan IV was the first to ascend the throne not as a grand prince but as a tsar. Already in the late fifteenth century, his grandfather Ivan III experimented with the title of tsar, as did his father, Vasily III. In 1514 Holy Roman emperor Maximilian I addressed Vasily III in a letter "by the grace of God, the emperor and lord of all the Russians" (*Von Gotes Gnaden Käyser unnd Herscher aller Rewssen*), which was the first time the arbitrarily appropriated title was recognized by a foreign power. But Ivan III and Vasily III were crowned as grand princes, and this symbolic moment of the divine sanction of power confirmed their grand-princely status. Sixteen-year-old Ivan IV became the first Moscow ruler to ascend the throne as the formally inaugurated tsar. The rite of anointing was developed by Metropolitan Macarius, since no one in Muscovy knew the details of the Byzantine emperors' anointing. As a result, due to some misinterpretations and misunderstandings, the ceremony of Russian tsars' anointment acquired important semantic differences not only from the western European but also from the Byzantine imperial traditions.

After the coronation in January 1547, Ivan IV's first action was marriage to a boyar's daughter Anastasia Romanovna, and the next was a major campaign against Kazan. The acquisition of the tsar's status, apparently, directly presupposed the subordination of the Kazan Khanate. After Vasily III's death (1533), when the real power in the realm belonged to rival boyar groups, relations with Kazan reached an impasse. Khan Safa Giray, who reigned from 1524, with short interruptions by the pro-Moscow khans, until his death in 1549, carried out daring raids on Murom and Nizhny Novgorod with impunity. Under pressure from the powerful Crimean Khanate, the Moscow government did not retaliate with military means and instead conducted negotiations with Kazan. Systematic raids served as an important auxiliary source of income for the Kazan nobility and warriors, especially in lean years, providing not only material loot but also captives to be used as laborers or sold as slaves.

The campaign had to be postponed for the winter due to the dramatic events of summer 1547—a big fire in Moscow and a large-scale revolt of the townspeople. In December 1547, the young tsar personally led his army from Vladimir to Kazan, accompanied by a large convoy of artillery required to storm the city. In February 1548, having passed Nizhny Novgorod, the army stopped for the night in the village of

Rabotki, some forty miles down the frozen Volga River. The cannons were left on the ice overnight. In the abnormally warm winter of 1548, the thin ice could not hold the weight of the cannonry and they sank to the bottom. Ivan realized that the successful siege of Kazan had become impossible and returned to Moscow. The troops continued their march to Kazan led by Ivan's generals, defeated the khan's army near the city, and plundered its vicinities for a whole week.

This failure did not discourage Ivan: apparently, the victory over Kazan was his absolute priority, connected with the very title of tsar. The new campaign in 1549 reproduced the previous one: the army set out from Vladimir on December 20, passed Nizhny Novgorod without major incident, and on February 12 approached Kazan. Once again, the weather ruined the ambitious plans. On the twelfth day of the siege, a strong sudden thaw and rain flooded the lowlands surrounding the fortress hill. Food and gunpowder got wet in the Russian camp, so the siege had to be lifted. The repeated failure showed that the advantages of the firm winter roads could not compensate for the challenging task of carrying heavy weapons for hundreds of miles all the way to Kazan. To capture Kazan, a base in the city's immediate vicinity was needed. The following winter, in the upper reaches of the Volga, near the town of Uglich, a complete fortress was built: walls, towers, a church, and some houses. Then all the structures were dismantled and delivered in May 1551 by timber rafting down the Volga River to the place where the Sviyaga River flows into the Volga, about twenty miles from Kazan. Under the Moscow cavalry's protection, in four weeks the fortress was reassembled in a new place and named Sviyazhsk.

The appearance of a Moscow fortress at a distance of a one day's travel by foot from the capital of the khanate had dramatically changed the strategic situation. The Mari and Chuvash tribes of the "mountain" (right) bank of the Volga renounced their subordination to Kazan and recognized the tsar's authority. The Sviyazhsk garrison blocked the delivery of supplies to Kazan by water. Now the Kazan elite expressed an acute interest in restoring the old vassal relations with Moscow. It was demanded that the leaders of the "Crimean party" leave the khanate, and about 300 of them attempted, unsuccessfully, to break through from the city to the Crimea. In August 1551, the remaining Kazan nobility recognized Qasim khan Shahghali as Kazan khan for the third time. The Moscow authorities also demanded the release of Russian prisoners being held in captivity in the khanate. According to the lists of bread allowance provided to former captives, in the course of just one week, 60,000 people were released.

However, the government of Ivan IV no longer counted on the seignior–vassal scenario. Judging by the available information, this time, Shahghali had the task of laying the groundwork for a hybrid system of rule. The Kazan Khanate was to be preserved as a highly autonomous administrative unit, at least on the territories inhabited by Muslims. The khanate's social structure was to remain intact, and the Muslim Tatar noblemen were expected to enjoy rights and privileges equal to those of their Russian peers in Moscow. But instead of the Turkic-speaking Muslim khan, the highest authority in the khanate was to be given to the tsar's viceroy (*namestnik*). This political structure was in many ways reminiscent of the Ottoman millet system: a large heterodox community that retained its self-government, including a legal system based on Islamic law, while remaining fully subordinate to the centralized state.

The plan was nearly implemented: on March 6, 1552, the residents of Kazan were summoned to listen to the tsar's charter declaring the elimination of khanship and the appointment of the military commander of Sviyazhsk as the Kazan viceroy. On March 7, the Kazanians took an oath of allegiance to the new government. On March 8, the interim government was sworn into office in Sviyazhsk. This fast and smooth political transition was facilitated by the Russians' taking of eighty-four Kazan aristocrats as semivoluntary hostages—a common practice in the region—which guaranteed the implementation of agreements. On the morning of March 9, the viceroy, the reinforcements for the Russian garrison in Kazan, the new government, and the hostages left Sviyazhsk for Kazan. As soon as the procession reached the city walls, several Tatar aristocrats staged an impromptu mutiny in Kazan: the insurgents locked the city gates, disarmed, and later killed the Russian garrison. The son of the Astrakhan khan Yadegar Mokhammad became the new khan of Kazan. The plan to create a Tatar "millet" failed, and the annexation of Kazan by military force became inevitable.

In the summer and autumn of 1552, Ivan IV and his generals planned and executed a military operation against Kazan that was exemplary for the time in terms of sophistication and coherence. The army marched for a month and a half in two parallel columns, about 120–130 miles apart. The two columns coordinated with each other, and reconnaissance and sapper units in the vanguard constructed bridges and roads. As a result, the troops synchronously approached the rally point near Kazan, having covered over 520 miles and in good physical shape, ready for combat. In contrast to previous campaigns, the army moved along Muscovy's southern border eastward in order to be able to repel the attack of the Crimeans. This decision was key to the success of the entire campaign. Back in 1551, the Ottoman Sultan Suleiman II the Magnificent had called upon the warring Muslim khanates that had formed on the ruins of the Great Horde, to rally in defense of Kazan. He appointed a new Crimean khan, Devlet Giray, who vowed to restore a single Muslim state from Crimea to Kazan that was capable of curbing Muscovy's expansion. Essentially, this was a plan to restore the political realities of the fourteenth century, subordinating Muscovy to the new Great Horde as its former ulus. As expected, the Crimean troops attacked from the south in the direction of Tula and Kolomna. The southernmost column of the Russian army played its role as a covering force, repelling the attack and capturing the artillery that the Ottoman sultan had given to the Crimeans.

On August 13, 1552, all the troops and supply trains gathered in Sviyazhsk. Ten days later, the Russian army surrounded Kazan and began a systematic siege organized by the standards of mid-sixteenth-century European military art. For a month, artillery bombarded the city from the ground and siege towers. Simultaneously, sappers were digging mines under the walls of Kazan, planting powerful explosive charges underneath. On September 30, a blast destroyed a section of the city wall, and the breach was immediately taken under control by the Moscow troops. However, further advancement was postponed until the elaboration of a detailed plan of attack. On October 1, the city defenders were offered the chance to surrender at their discretion. Upon their refusal, on October 2, the stubborn resistance was crushed, and Kazan fell. The khanate's former rulers were forced to leave Kazan. Safa Giray's fifth wife, Syuyumbike (Söyembikä), who ruled the khanate in 1549–51 as regent during the minority of her son Utamesh (Ötemish Giray), was compelled to marry Shahghali of the Qasim Khanate. Utamesh, who was six years old at the time, was taken to Moscow and brought up at the court of Ivan IV. He was baptized, died at the age of nineteen, and was buried with royal honors in the Archangel Cathedral of the Moscow Kremlin. Yadegar Mokhammad, the last khan of Kazan, was baptized Simeon in January 1553. He was given the city of Zvenigorod near Moscow to govern and use as a source of personal revenue. After a chain of uprisings in the Kazan region, in 1557, the Russian authorities evicted the remaining residents of Kazan to a settlement in the city's vicinity and resettled in their place 7,000 families from Muscovy's interior areas. To manage the territory of the former khanate, the Office of the Kazan Palace was created in Moscow—a nascent ministry of colonies of sorts that oversaw all the recently annexed lands in the east and south. Although the Kazan Khanate did not become a separate, albeit subordinate, entity within the Muscovite tsardom, it persisted in the political imagination. The office of the nonexistent "Kazan palace" remained a key government agency until the early eighteenth century, and Ivan IV added a new designation to his title—"Tsar of Kazan"—which was used by Russia's rulers until the end of the monarchy in 1917.

Reclaiming the Golden Horde's Legacy

Muscovy's annexation of the Kazan Khanate was perceived in the Crimean Khanate, in the Nogai Horde in the Ponti-Caspian steppe, in the Astrakhan Khanate along the Lower Volga, and probably in Moscow itself as a bold claim to the Golden Horde's political legacy by its former ulus. Right after the conquest of Kazan, in 1554, the 30,000-strong Russian army was sent down the Volga against the Astrakhan Khanate. Its central city Hajji Tarkhan (Astrakhan) was located not far from the ancient capitals of the great nomadic polities: Atil of Khazaria, Sarai of the Golden Horde. In its dealings with Astrakhan, the Moscow government went through the same stages as in the case of Kazan. The initial plan was to turn this remote territory located 875 miles from the recently conquered Kazan into a loyal vassal. Moscow's candidate for the Astrakhan throne was Dervish Ali, a grandson of the last khan of the Golden Horde, Ahmed. Dervish Ali had spent several years in the Moscow service, and his candidacy was also supported by the Nogai Horde, which occupied the territory between the Volga and the Urals. However, Moscow was far away, while the Crimean possessions were nearby, so under the influence of the Crimean khan, Dervish Ali soon expelled the Russian representatives. Then Ivan IV sent a second military expedition that defeated the Astrakhan troops. This time, the khanate was liquidated, and its territory subordinated to the Office of the Kazan Palace (1556). In 1558, the new city of Astrakhan was founded on the other side of the Volga, to be used as a barrier separating the new Russian possessions from the territory of the Crimean Khanate.

Muscovy's annexation of the Kazan and Astrakhan Khanates triggered a chain reaction of other regional polities switching allegiances to the tsar as the new sovereign. In 1557, the leader of the Great Nogai Horde, Ismail Bey, recognized himself as a vassal of Ivan IV. Southeast of the Ural Mountains, the khan of Sibir, Yadigar, was fiercely struggling with the contender to his throne Kuchum, a relative of the khan of Bukhara. In

206 *New Imperial History of Northern Eurasia*

search of an ally, in 1555, Yadigar hastened to pledge himself a vassal of the Moscow tsar and offered to pay the annual tribute in furs. Initially, he promised tens of thousands of pelts, but then proposed a more realistic amount of 1,000 pelts per year. Simultaneously, the Kabardian (Adyghe) princes in the North Caucasus established vassal relations with Moscow. Kabardian detachments took part in campaigns against Kazan and Astrakhan, and in exchange, Ivan IV provided military assistance to Kabardian princes fighting the common enemy—the Crimean Khanate. Moreover, after the death of his first wife (1561), Ivan IV married a Kabardian princess despite the fact that the Kabardians practiced Islam. One can even suggest that this significant spatial and cultural distance was precisely what predetermined the tsar's choice of a wife. He chose his first wife, Anastasia Romanovna, in 1547, after personally reviewing 1,500 eligible Muscovy brides. In contrast, the long-distance and completely depersonalized selection of Qochenay bint Teymour (baptized Mary) from distant Kabardia underscored Ivan's own distancing from Moscow "land" as only one of the territories under his rule.

The Construction of the Tsar's Power and the Problem of Absolute Sovereignty

Ivan IV's marriage to a Kabardian princess signaled his growing alienation from the Moscow elite and, more generally, a profound transformation of his attitude toward his subjects. Ivan had always been prone to severe punishments and could order the execution of high-ranking associates merely on suspicion of treason or even a lesser offense. In this regard, he differed little from his father, Vasily III, or the boyar government that ruled the country during his childhood. What changed in the 1560s was the gradual transformation of personal cruelty into the regime of a government based on systematic terror. Traditionally, historians have explained this transformation by Ivan's psychological breakdown after the death of his beloved wife Anastasia Romanovna, who was allegedly poisoned by conspirators (1560); by disillusionment with former associates and advisers; or by growing discontent with the Moscow aristocracy who resisted centralization of the tsar's power and elevation of the status of the service nobility.

Rationalization of the Government versus the Quest for Absolute Power

All these observations are absolutely correct. Indeed, a study of Anastasia Romanovna's remains (2000) revealed an abnormally high content of arsenic and especially mercury, which confirmed suspicions of her poisoning. Ivan IV believed that she was murdered by his closest associates: the confessor Archpriest Sylvester and Aleksei Adashev, an important statesman of humble origin. The political differences between the tsar and his associates were also growing.

Back in the 1550s, Sylvester and Adashev were instrumental in designing important reforms. The zemstvo reform recognized all peasant and urban communes as autonomous legal entities that were entrusted with electing the local administration and judges, as well as collecting taxes. Part of the tax revenues were used to finance crown officials who governed bigger territories and tried criminal cases in coordination with zemstvo officials. The military reform abolished the system of financing crown officials by "feeding" (*kormlenie*), which allowed administrators to raise the population's taxes indiscriminately. The Code of Military Service standardized the rules for manning the army by different categories of landholders, consolidating the class of the service nobility. These measures helped to create a modern standing army. The regular infantry—musketeers (*strel'tsy*)—were professional soldiers who subsidized their modest salary by economic activities as artisans, traders, and agriculturists. Service nobles (servitors) constituted the core of the cavalry. Their military service was remunerated by conditional landholding of about 180 acres per one fully equipped warrior, often at the expense of the hereditary aristocracy. The right to use the land depended on continuous military service. As the Code of Military Service put it, "those who hold the land but do not provide service [as expected] are liable to having money withheld [to compensate] for the recruits [not provided to the army]." Other major innovations included the promulgation of a new code of law and the final crystallization of the central government bodies—offices (*prikazy*): Office of Land Tenure (*pomestnyi*), Office of Ambassadors ("Foreign Office"), Office of Musketeers, Artillery Office, Robbery Office, Book Printing Office, Office of Petitions, and others. Together, these measures formed "normal" European early modern statehood in Muscovy.

Part of this "norm" was also the election of the Holy Roman emperor and the restriction of his power by the Imperial Diet (Reichstag)—a representative body of the imperial estates; or the election of the Polish king by the nobility and the limitation of his power by the Diet (Sejm)—the elected assembly of noblemen; or the rising importance of the parliament in England and the dependence of the French kings of this period on the aristocracy. Ivan IV appreciated the reforms that furnished him with a modern army, including probably the best artillery in Europe at that time, and an effective state apparatus. But he perceived any claims to political participation from the aristocracy or zemstvo (representatives of local self-government) as treacherous attempts on the tsar's power. Due to the erroneous interpretation of the rite of anointing, this power was deemed divine: instead of anointing with the Oil of the Catechumens, Ivan IV received a semantically very different anointing directly likening him to Christ, whom "God anointed . . . with the holy Spirit and power" (Acts 10:38). In response to Ivan's intensified promotion of his claim to absolute power, aristocrats and military leaders began fleeing to foreign rulers, which in the mid-sixteenth century already constituted treason. The most famous of these political émigrés was the celebrated general, Prince Andrei Kurbsky, who escaped to Lithuania in 1563. Thus, the death of Ivan IV's wife, the conflict with the circle of reformist statesmen, and betrayal by high-ranked associates were quite real factors that influenced Ivan's turn to the rule of terror.

Absolute Power that Was Unable to Express Itself

At the same time, for Ivan IV himself, nothing really changed in the early 1560s. He consistently implemented the ideal of imperial (tsarist) power, and the main problem was that nobody in Muscovy knew how this power was to manifest itself. The Byzantine Empire had fallen a century earlier, the emperor of the Holy Roman Empire only nominally held the title of "tsar," and it was inappropriate for a Christian monarch to openly imitate the Turkish sultan. The underdevelopment of specialized political and legal discourses in Muscovy, the absence of broad public discussions and political pamphlets in general made it difficult to articulate and clarify new ideas. Even two decades after Ivan's coronation as tsar, a developed rhetorical substantiation of his claims to the imperial title was nonexistent. In 1569 the Russian ambassador to Constantinople was instructed: "Should they ask him about the Tsar's title—why does your ruler call himself a tsar? Then he should answer: I am a young lad and know nothing about that. Anyone wishing to find [the answer] will have to travel to the realm of our ruler, and there he will find out." Thus, the only argument legitimizing Ivan's imperial title was personal and direct experience, a physical encounter with the manifestations of his special tsarist power. As a result, political practice has become the main sphere of ideological experiments and the elaboration of key concepts. The meaning and limits of a new, imperial sovereignty were determined through actions in various spheres: in personal life and domestic and foreign policy.

The Livonian War: When Guns Speak

Ivan IV began his reign with the subordination of the Kazan and Astrakhan Khanates, but he sharply disagreed with his advisers, who identified the Crimean Khanate as the next military goal. This would be a rational decision from the security perspective: devastating raids from Crimea presented an existential threat to Muscovy. Taking control over the entire Volga River provided the Russian army with a reliable transportation route facilitating the delivery of heavy weapons and supplies to the territory controlled by the Crimean khan. An alliance with Kabardia presented additional advantages for an attack on Crimea from the northeast. Ivan IV never forgave those who were making him yield to the pressure but conceded to his associates and authorized several attacks on Crimean possessions. In 1558, he sanctioned the raid of Cossacks led by Prince Dmitry Vishnevetsky to Azov, and the campaign under the command of General Daniil Adashev against the Crimean Peninsula at the beginning of 1559. Russian troops temporarily captured the port of Kezlev (Yevpatoria) in western Crimea. However, simultaneously (in January 1558), Ivan IV began a war with the Livonian Order, and from 1560 he concentrated entirely on this "western front," forsaking the assault on the Crimea. The Livonian War, which began with the defeat of the Livonian Order, dragged on for twenty-five years, soon evolving into Muscovy's confrontation with the Grand Duchy of Lithuania and the Kingdom of Poland (united in 1569 into a single polity) and Sweden. In the 1570s, Ivan IV orchestrated the creation of a vassal Kingdom of Livonia, installing as king the Danish duke Magnus of Holstein, who married Ivan's second niece. The result of hostilities that lasted for a quarter of a century was a return to the status quo ante bellum: Muscovy gave back all the conquered territories, almost exactly restoring the prewar borders, at the cost of ruining the country's economy. Traditionally, the Livonian War has been explained as Ivan IV's attempt to secure access to the Baltic Sea, but Russian documents of that era did not formulate or even mention

New Times

this idea. Economically and politically, Muscovy had no need to alter the system of Baltic trade via Novgorod and Livonia that had developed over centuries. Officially, the war began by demanding that the Livonian Order pay compensation for the use of an apiary in the disputed territory. The so-called Yuryev tribute was mentioned in fifteenth-century documents as the order's obligation to pay five poods of honey a year (180 pounds). From a practical point of view, the refusal to fight Crimea looked absurd, just as the decision to start a war in Livonia over a keg of honey.

Things look different when viewed from the vantage point of the early modern symbolic geography of power. Ivan IV was the first ruler of Muscovy in nearly a century who did not initiate a war with the Grand Duchy of Lithuania seeking to annex another part of it. Since the time of his grandfather Ivan III, the "Lithuanian" lands were considered the patrimony of the Moscow grand princes. But Ivan IV strove to acquire imperial power, which would be superior to the ancestral grand-princely power and require more than a hold over the lands "rightfully" belonging to him. The most obvious sign of a true tsar (Caesar) was the conquest of foreign kingdoms on a whim, simply to demonstrate superpower. The subordination of Kazan and Astrakhan, the recognition of vassal dependence by the Nogai Horde and the Siberian Khanate confirmed Ivan's status as a tsar but created completely undesirable and unambiguous historical parallels at a time when historical parallels were perceived as sameness. If Ivan III likened himself to Vladimir Monomakh and was preoccupied with assembling "Russian" (Rous') lands, it appeared as if his grandson, Ivan IV, was gathering the Golden Horde uluses. It only remained to conquer the Crimea and the steppes of the Black Sea and Azov regions it controlled to fully restore the political legacy of Batu. Apparently, the Crimean khan Devlet Giray understood Muscovy's policy in these very terms. Devlet Giray's own goal was the revival of the Jochi's Ulus, so after the conquest of Kazan, he saw Ivan IV as a direct rival. Devlet took full advantage of Muscovy's reorientation from the southern to the western front. After a series of raids and several unsuccessful attempts to return Astrakhan, in 1571, the Crimean army burned Moscow and captured tens of thousands of prisoners. Devlet Giray adopted the evocative sobriquet Taht Alğan (the one who captured the throne). The next year, he assembled an army that was three times larger than in 1571—from 80,000 to 120,000 soldiers, which must have embraced nearly the entire combat-ready male population of the khanate, and set off on a new campaign, announcing that he was "going to Moscow for the tsardom." The crushing defeat of the Crimean army forty miles south of Moscow at the Battle of Molody (July 30–August 2, 1572) by much smaller Russian forces ruined these plans and undermined the power of the Crimean Khanate for many years. But had the army of Ivan IV conquered the Crimea and its steppe uluses in ancient Desht-i Qipchaq, it would have been Ivan's turn to call himself "the one who captured the throne"—the throne of the khans of the Golden Horde.

It is possible that the Muscovite elite actually perceived their tsardom as the rightful successor to Jochi's Ulus, but Ivan clearly did not want to be identified with the Golden Horde khans. Likewise, he evidently prioritized the goal of achieving a "true" imperial power over securing the prosperity of the state, in the modern sense of economic growth and neutralization of external threats. He communicated these priorities in the language of political practice, for example, by choosing the object of conquest beyond his "hereditary" territories surrounding Muscovy, be it the former Rous' Lands in Lithuania or the Golden Horde's uluses. In the logic of political imagination of the time, the conquest of tiny Livonia, which had never before been part of any "Russian" state, gave Muscovy a truly imperial status and confirmed the autocratic nature of the tsar's power. In other words, this power and possessions owed solely to the divine will of God being communicated through the tsar's personality, and not to any historical or legal human tradition.

International Recognition

The tsar's title of Ivan IV was recognized in England already in 1554, and in 1557, he was addressed by Queen Mary Tudor as the "Emperor of all Russia." In 1560, the Ecumenical Patriarch of Constantinople Joasaph II confirmed Ivan's title using the term Basileus (Βασιλεύς), which had been reserved in the Byzantine Empire solely for its emperors. The patriarch declared that Ivan's name was to be included in the Sunday prayers in the Cathedral Church of Constantinople, just as the names of Byzantine emperors had been in the past, and that all the Orthodox dioceses were instructed to follow suit. Considering that members of the Orthodox clergy in the Grand Duchy of Lithuania were canonically subordinate to the Patriarch of Constantinople, this meant that the Orthodox residents of Lithuania (and later the Polish–Lithuanian Commonwealth) were obliged to venerate the Moscow tsar weekly as the supreme defender of the faith and the heir to the Byzantine emperors. Obviously, this presented a tremendous problem to the country, whose main adversary was Muscovy. In 1596, this conflict became one of the main reasons for the Union of Brest: the decision of some of the Orthodox bishops in the Polish–Lithuanian Commonwealth to come under the authority of the pope of Rome, establishing a separate Greek Catholic Church. The pope also refused to formally recognize Ivan's title, because the traditional concept of the Christian empire regarded it as the earthly counterpart of papal religious power and a reflection of unique divine authority. Accordingly, there could be only one true empire, and that was the Holy Roman Empire. Incidentally, the Holy Roman emperor Maximilian II was less adamant in protecting his monopoly on "empireness." Driven by pragmatic political considerations, in 1576 he offered Ivan IV the title of "the Caesar of the Orient," which should have preserved the uniqueness of his own empire as the "western" one. Since Ivan was interested only in being recognized as "the Caesar of All Russia," Maximilian eagerly complied, while his son and successor Rudolf II already addressed Ivan IV by the Russian title "czar." It would not be long before it was forgotten that "czar" (tsar) was just the Russian rendition of Kaiser (Caesar)—"emperor," and the title became perceived as a local peculiarity.

Cultural Distance as a Political Resource

The international recognition of his tsar status was important to Ivan IV, but it had little impact on enhancing his power within the country, where he was still perceived just as any another grand prince of Moscow. How should the power of the tsar differ from the power of the grand prince in relations with his subjects? Responding to this question in the language of political practice was even more difficult than answering the question "why does your ruler call himself a tsar?". Further increasing the arbitrariness of power was not a satisfactory solution. Many early modern European rulers resorted to tyrannical methods in response to the crisis of political legitimacy based on interpersonal relations between the suzerain and vassals. Already Ivan IV's grandfather, Ivan III, had earned the nickname "the Terrible" (the Fearsome), so personal cruelty and severe punishments could not really distinguish the first tsar from his predecessors—the Moscow grand princes—or from his European peers. A typical example was Mary Tudor ("Bloody Mary"), who ruled England in 1553–8 and became famous for executions of the aristocracy and high clergy, including the Archbishop of Canterbury—the highest priest in the land. In less than four years, about 300 prominent Protestants were burned at the stake, including at least fifty-six women. This was done in accordance with the accepted legal procedure, and this level of brutality was quite typical for the time. Therefore, executions could not set Ivan IV apart as tsar.

As was mentioned earlier, in 1561, the widowed Ivan married the Muslim Kabardian princess, gaining no additional symbolic or political advantage other than establishing a distance from Muscovy's aristocracy. The same desire to distance himself from the traditions and culture of the native land can be seen in the initiative to commission *The Book of Degrees* (of Imperial Genealogy), produced in 1560–3. This first official, systematic history of Muscovy traced the pedigree of the Moscow rulers to the legendary Roman "Prus, the brother of Caesar Augustus." As the result of a historical aberration, Prussia and even Livonia were declared the "homeland" of the Moscow tsar's ancestors. Around 1565, Ivan IV told a Münster merchant that he was of the Bavarian rulers' kin "and that the name of our boyars means Bavarians." In 1570, he confessed to the Danish duke Magnus: "I myself am of German origin and Saxon blood." What matters is not whether Ivan believed in his foreign ancestry, but the obvious fact that he deliberately distanced himself from the Moscow aristocracy and, more broadly, from the Russian aristocracy: the tsar's power could not be conditional based on descent in common with his subjects!

Oprichnina: The Apartheid Regime

Finally, Ivan IV took the most radical empirical step toward constructing a truly imperial power. He applied to his own country the same approach that he used to legitimize the imperial title in foreign relations: acting as a ruthless invader and triumphant conqueror. In early January 1565 the tsar left his residence in the Kremlin, accompanied by his courtiers. Taking with him the state treasury and the best Moscow icons, Ivan relocated to the fortified Alexander settlement (Aleksandrova sloboda) about eighty miles northeast of Moscow. This was the separate estate (*oprishnoe vladenie*) of his mother Elena Glinskaya, which she had inherited after the death of her husband, Grand Prince Vasily III. When he had arrived in Alexander settlement, Ivan declared his intention to abdicate. The Moscow boyars and clergy begged him to stay in power and Ivan graciously agreed, but on his own terms. First of all, he secured the right to execute the "disobedient" boyars and confiscate their property without interference from the clergy. He also divided the tsardom into the regular territory of the Russian land (*zemstvo*) and his extended separate estate (*oprichnina*), mostly in the northeast of Muscovy. The zemstvo was left to be ruled by the Moscow government of boyars through the existing system of administrative offices (*prikazy*). The oprichnina, a state within a state and apart from the regular state, was headed by the tsar himself. Literally meaning "something separate," oprichnina can most accurately be translated as "apartheid." Alexander settlement became Ivan's new residence and the capital of the new apartheid entity that was in all respects elevated over the regular Russian land and dubbing its social institutions. There was the apartheid, more prestigious class of service nobility, the oprichnina's own musketeers, the boyar counsels to the tsar, and the administrative offices. The apartheid standing army was recruited from oprichnina districts, eventually growing from 1,000 to 6,000 troops. The oprichnina servitors and officials were forbidden to communicate with their zemstvo peers, whereas the zemstvo residents were forbidden to enter the territory of the oprichnina. Even Metropolitan Philip, the top hierarch of the Russian Orthodox Church, had to issue a written promise to stay away from the oprichnina. In this system of political and social apartheid, the Russian land was unconditionally subordinated to the territory and social strata consolidated by Ivan IV as his separate estate—the oprichnina.

From the very beginning, Ivan unleashed a campaign of oprichnina terror against the Russian land. This was the mass terror that indiscriminately targeted petty servicemen and aristocrats alike, as well as the clergy: even Metropolitan Philip fell victim to it. A continuous escalation of terror became inevitable after Ivan had authorized the apartheid officers to find and eradicate "treason" on their own initiative: everyone was free to identify potential victims who could be killed and deprived of property without trial. Naturally, the settling of personal scores and enrichment were the main incentives of these vigilantes, so the scope of "treason" only increased as a result of the repressions—it did not decline. In January 1570, the apartheid army sacked Novgorod and subjected it to terrible devastation. Novgorodians were drowned in the river or shot with arquebuses, and their property was plundered. Ivan's men burned the goods and supplies that could not be hauled from the city. They robbed churches and even stole the famous gates of the St. Sophia Cathedral, which were then installed at the Assumption Cathedral in the Alexander settlement. The actions of apartheid servitors in Novgorod and other zemstvo localities have often been compared to actions of foreign occupiers, first of all the Mongols, but this comparison is misleading. Their exaggerated and clearly redundant cruelty resembled not any historical precedents but their greatly hyperbolized, fictional depictions in chronicles and stories about Christian martyrs. It is possible that the fantastic description of atrocities in these books had inspired attempts to implement them in reality in the first place. The sophistication of executions and torture conducted by Tsar Ivan's associates and the violence unleashed against Novgorod—which was clearly superfluous by the standards of the "usual" wartime massacres—betray the desire to indulge personal fantasies rather than punish, however cruelly, any specific enemies. Apparently, the symbolic meaning of the oprichnina terror, at least for the tsar himself, was more important than practical considerations such as the choice of victims, the substantiation of their sentences, or the methods of punishment.

New Times   213

Viewed from this perspective, the oprichnina terror conveys an elaborated ideological system centered on the symbolic conquest of the Russian land. The superiority of the tsar's imperial power over ordinary secular power revealed itself not only in uncontrolled and completely arbitrary violence but also in special ceremonies and rituals invented by Ivan IV. His inner circle of apartheid officers constituted a special military-religious organization. It was headed by the tsar, who called himself the oprichnina's "hegumen" (*igumen*—abbot, the superior of a monastic community). His closest associate, Prince Athanasius Vyazemsky, had the title of a cellarius (*kelar'*— the monastery butler in charge of economic matters). Grigory "Malyuta" Skuratov, a sadist who had earned a reputation as the oprichnina's chief executioner, held a low rank designated by the Greek word *paraklisiarch* (a sexton or a doorkeeper). During pauses between the bloody raids, the tsar maintained a strict regime of monastic piety. He woke up his warrior-monks for the midnight office that is dedicated to the Second Coming and the Last Judgment in the Byzantine rite, followed by matins and the liturgy. Ivan personally rang the church bells, prayed, and read the Gospel to his followers during the meal. Overall, religious services could take up to nine hours a day. The apartheid officers wore black, monk-style clothing and rode on horseback, strapping a broom and a dead dog's head to their saddles, which was supposed to symbolize their doglike devotion to the tsar and hatred of strangers, and their eagerness to sweep out sedition.

To a modern historian, the oprichnina may resemble other apartheid regimes usually introduced after a country's military occupation, be it the Norman conquest of England, the conquest of Prussia by the crusaders, or the Reconquista in the Iberian Peninsula. However, it is unlikely that Ivan IV had the necessary information and the analytical perspective to see these parallels as he designed his own apartheid regime. Besides, he brutally conquered not a foreign country but his own, where nobody openly opposed or even doubted the legitimacy of his rule. Perhaps Ivan did not have to look so far, since the northeastern Russian lands had relatively recently experienced the Mongol conquest. But actual Mongol rule had little in common with Ivan's terrorist regime. It was reinterpreted as such only retrospectively, after the old chronicles had been heavily edited in the sixteenth century.

What seems more certain is Ivan IV's conscious intention to imitate Catholic monastic and military orders—to the extent of his knowledge and understanding. It is no coincidence that the oprichnina was established after Muscovy had defeated the Livonian Order (dissolved in 1561). The Livonian War and temporary occupation of Livonia put Russians in close contact with the knights, so when Ivan IV established the oprichnina, quite a few Germans joined it, either as prisoners of war or by voluntarily changing their allegiance. Some of them had been directly associated with the Livonian Order. Even clearer was Ivan's mimicking of the monastic Dominican Order, which maintained high visibility in Livonia and the Grand Duchy of Lithuania. The Dominicans' coat of arms depicted a dog holding a burning torch in its mouth. The image referred to a play on words in Latin: "Dominicanus" sounds like "Domini canis"—"hounds of the Lord." On monochrome drawings and sculptures, the dog's torch with its forks of flame looks like a broom with long, loose bristles. So, wearing black and decorating their saddles with a broom and a dog's head, Ivan's apartheid officers reproduced the symbols of the Dominican Order. The imitation of the Dominicans was inspired by their established reputation as inquisitors: the first Grand Inquisitor of Spain, Tomás de Torquemada, and the authors of the famous treatise on demonology *The Hammer of Witches*, the German inquisitors Heinrich Kramer and Jacob Sprenger, were Dominican friars. This apparent symbolism conveys Ivan's intentions through the practical steps he had taken. Construing the oprichnina as an instrument for achieving and exercising the supreme power of the tsar, he defined this power by combining the images of the knights' grand master and the Catholic grand inquisitor, of the warrior-monk and the vicar of Christ, whose political authority was but a projection of God's divine power.

The Crimean khan's devastating and humiliating raid against Moscow (1571) dealt a heavy blow to the idea of the oprichnina as the embodiment of divine imperial power. Not only was the tsarist power incapable of defending the country, but the apartheid army proved to be worthless in the face of a strong enemy. Many apartheid officers evaded the call to arms, so only one oprichnina regiment participated in the war, in contrast to five zemstvo regiments. In 1572, Ivan IV dissolved the oprichnina: he ordered the execution of almost all high-ranking apartheid officers and prohibited the very mention of the oprichnina on threat of scourging.

A Method in Madness

The following year, the tsar insisted that the Qasim khan, Sain Bulat, an honored veteran of the Livonian War, be baptized under the name of Simeon Bikbulatovich. In his usual manner of articulating ideological innovations in the language of practical politics, in the fall of 1575, Ivan IV arranged for Simeon Bikbulatovich's official anointing as the tsar of Muscovy. The new tsar Simeon Bikbulatovich moved into the Kremlin, and Ivan IV once again abdicated the throne and retired to his appanage as "Ivan of Moscow." Less than a year later, Ivan returned to the throne as if nothing had happened and sent "Tsar Simeon" away, giving him the Grand Principality of Tver as compensation. This political masquerade, usually explained by Ivan's progressive mental disorder, makes quite a logical "statement": if the oprichnina, as the embodiment of divine and autocratic tsarist power, was overwhelmed by the Crimean khan—himself a vassal of the Turkish "tsar"—then the triumphant adversary's power must have been superior. To test this conclusion, Ivan appointed a new tsar of Muscovy, who was a Chinggisid and great-grandson of the last khan of the Great Horde. Thus, he demonstrated both the unprecedented absoluteness of his power, capable of appointing a new tsar and displacing him, and an interest in exploring the potential of the Golden Horde's political legacy as the foundation of the true tsarist power.

Every new political move of Ivan IV, both before the oprichnina's creation and after its formal dissolution, was accompanied by executions. It is difficult to separate the tsar's personal malice or mental disorder from political and ideological considerations as a motive for the murders. As a child, he entertained himself by throwing cats and dogs from the rooftop. As a fifteen-year-old, even before his anointment as the tsar and the beginning of his political activity, young Ivan routinely sentenced boyars to death on a whim. Thus, he was prone to murder well before ascribing any political urgency

New Times 215

to them. It is equally difficult to accurately assess the full magnitude of repressions unleashed by Ivan IV. Shortly before his death in 1583, he ordered that a memorial list of the oprichnina victims be composed; the list contained about 4,000 names and covered a period of about ten years. This number is not very informative: first, although exceptionally violent, the oprichnina period accounted for only a part of all the murders that had been committed on the tsar's order throughout his reign. Second, the list was most likely based on official records and is thus far from comprehensive even when it comes to the oprichnina era, given the magnitude of the persecutions, which did not always follow a formal trial.

Most importantly, the numbers alone are not very telling, and 5,000 or even 15,000 victims of repressions do not set Ivan IV apart from other European monarchs of his time. For example, during the St. Bartholomew's Day massacre of Protestants by Catholics in Paris on August 23, 1572, triggered by Queen Catherine de' Medici, several thousand people were killed just overnight. The total death toll of the hostilities in Paris and throughout the country in the next days and weeks is estimated to be from 5,000 to 30,000. According to some sources, Ivan IV condemned the massacre and insisted in a letter to the Holy Roman emperor that every Christian monarch should mourn the terrible loss of so many innocent victims. The era of mass religious wars was on the rise, driving the numbers of victims in each country to the tens of thousands. What made the oprichnina terror truly different was the fact that it was unleashed outside the context of a civil war, whether a religious strife or a peasant uprising. Ivan's terror targeted his own subjects, most of them completely devoted to him: the apartheid troops never had to suppress an open insurrection or even a protest against the tsar. Mourning the victims of the St. Bartholomew's Day massacre that had resulted from the escalation of mutual hatred and mistrust between the French Catholics and Protestants, Ivan IV preferred not to recall the devastation of Novgorod (1570) perpetrated entirely on his whim. Out of 30,000 Novgorodians, the apartheid army murdered between 5,000 and 15,000. The rest were doomed to starvation after their food supplies and property had been destroyed in the middle of winter.

What shocked contemporaries the most and distinguished Muscovy from other countries was not the number of people killed under Tsar Ivan's direct orders or with his indirect connivance, but the structure of and motives for the terror. Thousands of ordinary subjects of the tsar, aristocrats, and clergymen were murdered not because they did something wrong or even said something wrong in private. In other words, the terror was unrelated to its objects. Even if the man who unleashed this mass terror was psychologically unstable, there was a method in Tsar Ivan's madness. He consistently strove to emancipate his rule from any factors constraining the absolute power of the sovereign, be it political institutions, social environment, cultural traditions, or moral norms. For thirty-five years after his anointment as tsar, he was busy empirically constructing a "true" imperial power. Despite the obvious cultural and social specificity of Muscovy, this underlying ideological and philosophical concern was making Ivan IV a typical representative of the early modern political sphere, which prompted the killings of tens of thousands of people in the name of abstract ideas and theoretical disagreements.

The Crisis

Ivan IV died on March 19, 1584. In the morning, he asked to see the will that he had prepared in advance and reviewed it. Then he washed himself in the bathhouse for a long time. Emerging from the bathhouse, Ivan put on clean clothes and sat down at the chessboard. He died while playing chess and pondering the next combination. This thoughtfulness and preparedness at the hour of death presents a striking contrast to the life of the first tsar of Muscovy. When judged by regular moral standards, his life looked like a series of insane atrocities. If one attempts to connect the seemingly random dots and reconstruct the inner logic behind Ivan's unpredictable escapades, they begin to convey the story of a mystical search for the "true" imperial power of the tsar. This mystical quest continued throughout Ivan's long reign and resulted in a deep crisis that affected both the country, which probably did not interest him much, and the structure of power to which he devoted his whole life.

In a fit of anger or uncontrollable jealousy toward a potential successor to his throne, in November 1581, Ivan mortally wounded his son and heir Ivan Ivanovich (1554–81). By a cruel irony, this murder made Ivan's feeble-minded younger son Fyodor (1557–98) the only heir to the throne. Fyodor was physically incapable of embracing the extraordinary power of the tsar as constructed by Ivan IV over several decades. Leaving a successor who was no match for him as the absolute autocrat, Ivan IV also left a much weaker country. Its economy had been depleted by endless wars, by the devastating Crimean raid, and by the oprichnina regime of "internal occupation" that turned even regular tax collection into bloody raids accompanied by murders, arson, and confiscations of property. Muscovy's social order had been eroded by the endless confiscation of land and other property from the victims of political persecutions and the redistribution of estates among the service nobles as their conditional possessions. The systemic violation of any established norms by Ivan IV compromised the institution of landownership that had begun to take shape during the preceding decades. Economic hardship, wars, and epidemics had dire demographic consequences for the peasant population. To compensate for the deficit of farm labor and provide service nobles with populated lands that produced enough revenue to sustain their service, the government began to impose restrictions on peasant mobility. Traditionally, peasants were free to move to lands belonging to another landowner after the completion of the agricultural season late in the fall, during the week before and the week after St. George's Day. As of 1581, this right was periodically suspended with an announcement of "the forbidden years," which prevented peasants' relocations even after paying off all the dues they might have owed to their former landlord. This was a decisive step toward enserfing the peasants' and turning them into an attribute of the land. All the land in the country, in turn, was ultimately owned by the tsar but could be possessed, on his volition, by various landlords: boyars, service nobles, or autonomous peasant communes.

As to the political system, after decades of Ivan IV's experiments, it was in a state of complete decomposition: the direct heir to the throne was incapable of ruling by himself, while Simeon Bikbulatovich, the officially anointed tsar of Muscovy, was still around.

Ivan IV had demonstrated the exceptional nature of his power as fully autocratic—that is, not derived from any preceding authority—by making it strategically arbitrary. By doing so, he had deprived the tsar's status of any conventional legitimacy. Ivan IV proved to himself and to everyone that the tsar had to obey no rules; however, this also meant that there were no rules proving the new tsar's legitimacy. It was no longer possible to tell who had the right to the throne or why, so Muscovy went back to square one of the political process. It had to form virtually from scratch a new system of political relations, a new social structure, and the very understanding of why different population groups should be living in a common country controlled by a single state. This structural situation once again unleashed the forces of societal self-organization on a scale comparable to that during the formation period of the Rous' Lands.

Note

1 Cited from Jean Bodin, *Method for the Easy Comprehension of History*, translated by Beatrice Reynolds (New York: Norton, 1969), 293.

Further reading

Christian, David. *A History of Russia, Central Asia, and Mongolia*. Vol. 2. *Inner Eurasia from the Mongol Empire to today, 1260–2000*. Hoboken: Wiley Blackwell, 2018.
Frost, Robert I. *The Northern Wars, 1558–1721*. New York: Routledge, 2014.
Halperin, Charles J. *Ivan the Terrible: Free to Reward and Free to Punish*. Pittsburgh: University of Pittsburgh Press, 2019.
Kollman, Nancy Shields. *By Honor Bound: State and Society in Early Modern Russia*. Ithaca: Cornell University Press, 1999.
Romaniello, Matthew P. *Elusive Empire: Kazan and the Creation of Russia, 1552–1671*. Madison: University of Wisconsin Press, 2012.

6

The Transformation of Social Imagination

The Seventeenth Century

Scenarios of Transformation on the Region's Periphery

The end of the sixteenth century is often perceived as a turning point in the history of many societies in Eurasia, from the Atlantic to the Pacific Ocean. According to the classical historical periodization that was created in Europe at approximately the same time, this transformation corresponded to the transition from the Middle Ages to the modern period. These familiar labels have been long criticized for their arbitrary generalizations and for imposing a normative time frame. The numerous individual threads constituting the complex historical process are hardly ever synchronized in a way that produces a clear division between whole periods of human experience. More demonstrably, one can speak of changes in several of the many individual threads that opened new possibilities of societal organization at about the turn of the seventeenth century. On the one hand, the widespread use of firearms made the aristocratic heavy cavalry obsolete. On the other, this period witnessed the discovery of new, transpersonal principles and mechanisms of social cohesion—that is, beyond the traditional clan and tribal ties or the "feudal" hierarchy of vassals and suzerains. These two, possibly interconnected, developments inevitably changed the approaches to tackling age-old problems of effective control over multicultural populations and protection from encroachments by neighbors. Local solutions to these common problems were sought through experimentation and spontaneous self-organization. The relative defects and merits of these scenarios became apparent only retrospectively.

The Anational Qing Empire

In the east of the continent, usually designated simply as "China," in 1368, the Great Ming Empire came to replace the Great Yuan established and ruled by the Mongols. At the end of the sixteenth century, the Great Ming itself was on the decline. In its remote northeastern corner in Manchuria, dozens of different Jurchen tribes consolidated as the Manchus under the rule of the leader Nurhaci (1559–1626). He and his son Hong Taiji managed to overrun the Great Ming and create a new state that united the former lands of the Ming, Manchuria, and Korea, later expanding its territory at the expense of Mongolia, Tibet, and Xinjiang. This new polity was called the Great Pure State (Da Qing Guo) and is usually referred to today as the Qing dynasty. The rise of the Qing might seem a repetition of another cycle in "Chinese" history—if it is imagined as an unbreakable millennia-long continuity. The official Qing ideology also insisted on continuity with its predecessors, suggesting that the transition from the Ming to the Qing was merely a change of the ruling dynasty. However, the Qing project was a profoundly innovative one: it consciously built a multiethnic empire that was equidistant from all its constituent ethnoconfessional groups. [1]

The Manchu ruling elite neither hastened to assimilate into the Han culture nor posed as foreign invaders. They tried, in principle, to separate the political sphere from the traditional association with tribal aristocracy by proclaiming that the Qing Empire was superior to any other polity in the world and gradually introducing the regime of autarkic self-isolation. Ideological isolationism was reinforced through the system of education and implemented in practice with the help of border guards. To this empire that claimed to be absolutely unique in its preeminence, it did not matter whether its rulers were Manchu, Han, or Tibetans, or how they fared in comparison with other countries. Isolationism deemed any national specificity—cultural, religious, and linguistic—irrelevant, so the quite modern, efficient Qing state assumed an anational stance as a way to deal with the population's diversity. Today, to be sustained as an anational polity, a multicultural society requires a political regime of universal citizenship as well as a working model of common, secular and supraethnic, mass culture. The Qing rulers achieved a similar effect simply by isolating their power structures from the "tribal" logic of thinking and by closing the country to foreign influence.

This strategy proved effective for over a century: the rates of population and economic growth in Qing China outstripped other countries of Asia and Europe until the mid-eighteenth century or even the turn of the nineteenth century. Key to this success was maintaining the self-perception that provided cohesion to a society that was immune to external influences. But this same isolationism turned out to be the primary weakness of the Qing social system. The forceful break of Qing isolation by European powers in the mid-nineteenth century immediately triggered a radical transformation of the popular worldview in China. The ruling dynasty was rediscovered as "foreign" (Manchu), and growing national resentment sustained the nationalist movement that eventually overthrew the Qing dynasty (1912). The Republic of China that replaced the Qing Empire adopted the slogan "Five races under one union," but gradually evolved into the Han nation-state, which accommodated other ethnoconfessional groups as national minorities.

The Hybrid Mughal Empire

To the west of the Great Ming, the descendant of Emir Timur (Tamerlane), Jalal ud-din Muhammad Akbar (r. 1556–1605), managed for the first time to unite almost the entire Indian subcontinent and the adjacent territories of modern Pakistan and southeastern Afghanistan into one giant polity. The subordinate Muslim and Hindu principalities became inner provinces or dependent vassals of what is known today as the Mughal

Empire—as the British called this colossal formation in the eighteenth century. Its rulers referred to their state in Persian as Gūrkāniyān—"[the domain] of the khan's son-in-law." Timur married into the Chinggisid clan and thus acquired legitimacy as an Asian ruler. Akbar's giant polity was a typical medieval Eurasian confederation that was sustained solely due to the combination of the ruler's military prowess and cultural tolerance. Akbar, a Muslim ruler, was an ideal match for this role: he abolished Jizya, the tax on non-Muslims, and appointed them to the highest positions in the government. The scion of a Turkic-speaking clan, he nevertheless promoted Persian culture as a universal medium among different local cultures and even religions. Christian, Islamic, and sacred Hindu texts and poems were translated into Persian and circulated in the common public sphere. This remarkably inclusive regime was based solely on Akbar's personality rather than any institution or principle, be it clan ties, Turkic cultural solidarity, or Islam as the dominant religion. Accordingly, the delicate equilibrium between different regional, religious, and ethnocultural elites was not stable. It could easily upset by the Indian rajahs' demands for something more than mere tolerance of their religion; or by the Muslims' requests to stop indulging the infidels; or by the borderland separatists; or simply because of a dynastic crisis. Predictably, all these factors played out over time, and by the beginning of the eighteenth century the Mughal Empire had begun to disintegrate. [2]

The Monocultural Qizilbash Empire

The Qizilbash Kingdom (Safavid Persia) and the Supreme Ottoman State (traditionally called the Ottoman Empire) lay farther west. Unlike their eastern neighbors, by the end of the sixteenth century, these were long-established polities. However, they also faced the problem of formalizing their system of power, and responded to this challenge in different ways. [3]

The historical region of Azerbaijan was home to the Safavid dynasty of shahs (rulers), who spread their power over the entire territory of historical Iran in 1502. The language of the shah's court and the army was Azeri Turkic, while Persian remained the language of the administration. The city of Tabriz in Iranian Azerbaijan was the country's capital, and the shah's power relied on the support of the nomadic Turkic aristocracy of the Qizilbash ("the red hood") tribal confederation. Safavid Persia reached the peak of its power at the beginning of the seventeenth century under Shah Abbas I the Great (1571–1629), who, around 1600, carried out a radical political reform. He eliminated the ethnoconfessional "division of labor" that was traditional for medieval Eurasia, where specific tribal and regional groups often specialized in different social roles. One provided cultural figures, another crown officials, a third staffed the aristocracy and military leaders, and the rest represented the bulk of the taxable population. Abbas moved the capital in 1598 to Isfahan in the center of the country, and created a standing army and professional guards on a supratribal basis. To this end, he purged the Qizilbash elite, thus eliminating their overwhelming political influence and the regime's dependence on the military strength of the nomadic Turkic tribes. Although Turkic remained the language of the courtiers, Abbas recognized the official status of the Persian language and culture. As a result, the Qizilbash state lost its hybrid character (in contrast to the Mughal Empire) at the cost of identification with a particular—Persian—cultural, linguistic, and religious norm (in contrast to the "anational" Qing Empire). As it turned out, this was not enough to withstand pressure from numerous hostile neighbors, and in 1722, the Safavid dynasty fell under the onslaught of the Afghan Pashtun tribes.

The Stable Ottoman Empire

The Ottoman Empire had survived all the great powers of its time, finally disintegrating only after the First World War (1922). The primary difference between the Supreme Ottoman State and its neighbors around 1600 was its absence of any radical transformations. It had reached its peak of power only recently, in the 1560s, so it seemed that combination of centralization and recognition of local differences it had achieved was ideal and needed no further improvement. In contrast to most other countries, these differences were not just recognized but also legally formalized. Moreover, several alternative taxonomies of human diversity coexisted and intersected. For example, territorially, the empire was divided into four dozen eyalets (provinces) and a number of vassal countries. As a rule, each eyalet had a multitribal population, and an eyalet's borders did not coincide with those of any historical land or previous administrative unit. A judicial system based on Islamic law (Sharia) accommodated local common laws. In addition, other recognized confessions—Orthodox Christians, Catholics, Armenians, and Jews—enjoyed judicial and religious autonomy within the system of pan-imperial millets. In combination with the complex social and economic stratifications and groupings, these formalized divisions connected the Ottoman society rather than dividing it. The interweaving of different classification principles, none of which had absolute priority, relativized diversity and prevented it from providing the grounds for the country's disintegration. The Ottoman system for managing human differences required neither artificial isolation of the country in order to secure its subjects' "correct" perception of the supreme power, nor the forceful imposition of a single cultural norm for maintaining social unity. [4]

However, by the beginning of the seventeenth century, a discouraging downside to the enviable stability of the Ottoman regime became apparent: in the complexly intertwined Ottoman society, mobilizing human and material resources for effective and quick actions presented a major challenge to the central government. The formidable numerical superiority of the Ottoman army and its technically advanced military equipment still allowed it to defeat external enemies. At the same time, although empire's population had doubled in the second half of the sixteenth century, at the turn of the seventeenth century its expansion had come to an end. Despite short-term, albeit extremely impressive, offensives on several fronts, the territory of the Ottoman Empire no longer expanded, and only shrank. The Ottoman Empire was entering an era when stability was not always a synonym for political success.

The Reformation in the Holy Roman Empire

Compared to the vast multicultural polities mentioned above, the kingdoms and principalities of western Europe seemed small and almost homogeneous in terms of their populations. Except for an insignificant Jewish minority, these were purely Christian societies, much more culturally integrated than the empires of the Great Mughals or the Safavids. Only the Holy Roman Empire of the German Nation could match the great powers of the continent in population diversity and territory size. But even in the west and north of Europe, the onset of the seventeenth century was marked by a crisis of the old—"feudal"—political model and a search for new suprapersonal forms of societal consolidation. [5]

This crisis was triggered by the Reformation—the schism within the Catholic Church. On May 31, 1517, the Saxon theologian Martin Luther (1483–1546) nailed his "Ninety-Five Theses" to the door of the church at Wittenberg Castle. Styled as academic propositions, these theses invited a critical rethinking of the Catholic Church's doctrine and practices and contributed to the foundation of Lutheranism as a revisionist Christian confession. In contrast to the dissident movements of the past, Lutheranism and a number of alternative reformist currents that formed under its influence were supported by secular rulers. Despite fierce opposition from the Catholic Church, over several decades, the reformist Christianity (Protestantism) spread all over Europe, with the exception of the Apennine and Iberian Peninsulas. Nominally of purely religious character, the Reformation was a multifaceted phenomenon that resonated with different segments of society, which explained its outstanding success.

Luther sought to spiritualize Christianity by separating personal faith and righteous behavior from everything that had transformed the church into a political and economic institution: accumulating wealth, selling church offices and indulgences for sins, interfering with secular politics, and claiming possession of the highest, divine truth. It was not so much the theological position of Protestantism as its practical implications that became of decisive importance.

The very idea that believers must establish a direct relationship with God and read sacred texts, leaving to the church a purely logistical role or even eliminating its mediation altogether, exploded the old logic of social imagination. As discussed in Chapter 1, nothing was done directly in a feudal society that was held together by vertical hierarchies of mutual personal obligation and representation. It can be added that nothing was uttered directly in the texts or visual arts of that society without relying on the sophisticated system of allegories and metonymy. Thus, certain ideas and symbols were conveyed by using other symbols that belonged to another associative field. Monotheistic religion embodied the ideal model of social and political order. Hence, just as in the political domain, one's relationship with God as the "supreme suzerain" was mediated by his "representatives," the interpreters of absolute truth— the clergy. Without them, the Latin language of the holy books and church decrees remained incomprehensible to most of the laity in the Germanic principalities and in the kingdoms of England, France, and Sweden.

The indirect nature of feudalism and the old Catholic Church also manifested itself in the fusion of functions that today may seem completely disconnected, such as judicial authority and economic exploitation, or military service and serving God as his earthly representatives and mediators. By seeing in Christianity nothing more than faith and by demanding that individuals develop direct relationships with God, Protestantism staged a revolution in the old worldview. As a result, "power," "the court of justice," "war," and, later, "economy" became gradually dissociated from each other into separate phenomena. Furthermore, the Protestant conceptual revolution allowed individuals to conceive of their direct relationship with the supreme ruler of the land as subjects, eliminating the mediation of barons, counts, and dukes. This transformation created the preconditions for theorizing a new, hitherto inconceivable, social order based on pure ideas and abstract principles.

The Nationalization of Culture and the Social Imagination

On a more practical level, the required elimination of intermediaries between the believer and God brought to the fore the "technical" problem of comprehension. In a society formed as a network of personal contacts, linguistic and cultural barriers did not present serious obstacles. Everyone communicated with those who understood them, and individual communication circles overlapped, at least to some extent. The population of every province (and often every village) spoke its own dialect or even a language, but the chains of intermediaries connecting them compensated for the lack of a common language. Likewise, Roman Catholic Mass was celebrated in Latin, incomprehensible to the majority of parishioners, but sermons were permitted in local vernaculars. Priests used this opportunity to interpret the basic dogmas of Christianity in a language that was understandable to Swabian, Saxon, or Franconian villagers. But as soon as Luther proclaimed the priority of scripture over the practices and interpretations of the Catholic Church, he faced a formidable obstacle: the Latin text of the Gospel was simply inaccessible to the majority of Christians without intermediaries.

Therefore, in 1522, in the course of just a few months, Luther had already translated the New Testament into German, and in 1534 he published a translation of the entire Bible. At the time, there was no common or normative literary German language, so Luther took the first step toward its creation. While working on his translation at the Wartburg Castle in Thuringia, he visited towns and fairs in the castle's vicinity to listen to live spoken language so as to bring his translation closer to it. Thus, solving a purely theological problem, Luther unwittingly contributed to the formation of the standardized German literary language and unified German culture. Moreover, he helped discover a single national culture as a specific problem and political goal.

In the Middle Ages, the Catholic Church did not encourage translations of the Bible into vernacular languages. In some instances, such attempts were severely persecuted, whereas in others, they had no serious repercussions. Unlike these early translation experiments, which were of a purely academic or private nature, Luther intentionally addressed the broad audience of educated readers, mass-producing his translation using the printing press. The first edition of the New Testament in Luther's translation in September 1522 inaugurated a true publishing boom of Bible translations into vernacular languages: the first complete Dutch translation of the Bible and the Swedish translation of the New Testament (1526), the complete German Bible translated by Luther (1534), French translation of the Bible (1535), the first publication of the New Testament in Spanish (1543), in Finnish (1548), the Geneva Bible—the first complete translation of the Bible into English that was used by Shakespeare (1560), the Brest Bible in Polish (1563). Often, the translation of sacred texts became the first printed book in the local language, as was the case with the Catechism in Lithuanian (1547). Thus, by extracting Christian faith from the medieval entanglement of the relations of belonging and subordination, Protestantism simultaneously formed a new, even tighter combination of religion and national culture.

Formalizing Internal Divisions

Finally, in the sphere of politics, the Reformation's theological protest against the dogmas of the Roman Catholic Church resonated with those European sovereigns who sought a check on the power of the pope and his political allies (first of all, King Philip II of Spain). The reasons for the break with the Catholic Church greatly varied. The rivalry between the Holy Roman emperors and the papacy dated back to the twelfth century; the Seventeen Provinces of the Netherlands sought to liberate themselves from the foreign power of the Spanish king; and King Henry VIII of England wanted to divorce his wife and remarry against the will of the pope. Pragmatic considerations, such as trade competition, territorial aspirations, or claims to the throne, found in Protestantism a powerful justification for actions that otherwise lacked a legitimate pretext.

The German lands of the Holy Roman Empire became the first battleground in the growing confrontation between Catholics and Protestants. In 1555, the emperor and the Protestant and Catholic imperial princes concluded the Peace of Augsburg, which recognized the division into Catholic and Protestant lands according to the formula "whose realm, his religion" (*cuius regio, eius religio*). This meant that the imperial estates—secular and clerical princes, counts and barons, and free cities, directly subordinate to the emperor and represented in the Imperial Diet (Reichstag)—were free to choose religion for themselves and all their subjects. The latter either had to accept the faith of their sovereign or emigrate.

An even more radical compromise resulted from the Wars of Religion between Catholics and Protestant Huguenots in France that culminated in the St. Bartholomew's Day massacre (1572). In 1598, the first French king of the Bourbon dynasty, Henry IV, signed the Edict of Nantes, guaranteeing civic rights to the Huguenots. As in the case of the Peace of Augsburg, the edict was formulated in the medieval logic of corporate and communal privileges rather than individual rights and freedoms. The Huguenots, as a congregation, were granted an education system of their own, communal self-government and courts of justice, as well as special delegates to lobby for communal interests in the royal court. The Huguenots retained their control over 200 fortresses and castles, and the king pledged to finance their garrisons, which continued to obey the Huguenot leaders. In addition to autonomous duchies and provinces, often only nominally controlled by the crown, the edict created in France a supraterritorial parastatal entity that was largely beyond the king's control. Thus, the religious compromise did not soften internal divisions and contradiction—it strengthened and formalized them, thus creating a direct threat to the existing secular power.

The Catholic Counter-Reformation

The triumphant spread of Protestantism triggered the movement of the Catholic Counter-Reformation. Mobilized to defend the old theological principles and church institutions, the Counter-Reformation shared the new social imagination introduced by Protestantism. The movement used the colossal resources of the Catholic Church to disseminate it. The institutional reform transformed the old "feudal" church hierarchy, based on the partial delegation of "sovereignty" to lower ("vassal") clergy, into a centralized authoritarian structure. The traditional system of mutual personal obligations between the clerics of different ranks, which afforded a great degree of flexibility and undermined uniformity, was now perceived as corruption. The Counter-Reformation reforms fought this by formalizing relationships within the ecclesiastical hierarchy. By the seventeenth century, the medieval practice of direct transfer of knowledge and experience through the interpersonal communications of clerics became a thing of the past. It was replaced with absolute obedience to the pope, even of parish clergy, their subordination to local church authorities in daily routine, and standardization of the main theological principles and rituals. Every diocese now had to establish seminaries to train future priests, and the number of universities as centers of higher theological learning expanded. Founded in 1534, a new religious order, the Society of Jesus (Jesuits), created and propagated a new model of education and a new understanding of Christian piety. Taking vows of poverty, chastity, and obedience, the Jesuits did not live in monasteries but worked among the laity as professional missionaries. Their colleges offered the best education in Europe, combining subjects in the humanities with the teaching of theology that was modernized and devoid of excessive dogmatism. The Society of Jesus completely broke with the "feudal" political culture of monastic orders by introducing strict discipline within the organization, unquestioning obedience of junior members to their superiors, and subordination of private interests and ordinary morality to the higher interests of the Catholic Church and the pope. Essentially, the Jesuits formed a universal model of modern political power based on individual service to the concept of law and direct subordination to the supreme sovereign. Secular rulers at the time could only dream about such an arrangement.

The Predicament of Secular Rulers

The radical revolution of social imagination carried out by Protestants and their Catholic opponents could not be translated into political and social forms by merely demarcating spheres of influence. The old "feudal" social model could not accommodate the new emerging forms of solidarity and divisiveness. The Reformation promoted a factor of cultural—linguistic and religious—unity that hitherto had played no special role in European countries where all legitimate subjects were "Christian" and no one spoke a standardized national language. By the seventeenth century, the community of one's belonging did not necessarily coincide with the boundaries of a kingdom or a principality. Suddenly, the power of secular rulers was called into question: Who were they—the lords of vassals, the hereditary masters of certain historical "lands," the sovereigns ruling over the entire population within their jurisdiction or only over their coreligionists? If the sovereign and his subjects were expected to profess the same religion, did this mean that the residents of a neighboring country of the same faith were his potential subjects? How was one to comprehend, consolidate, and exercise the emerging new type of supreme power that no longer depended on the hierarchy of personal relations between suzerains and vassals, many of whom now could choose another religion?

These contradictions produced a deep ideological crisis and resulted in the long and extremely bloody Thirty Years' War (1618–48) that involved almost all European countries. Eventually, in many of them, the power of the ruler was consolidated on a new principle known as "absolutism." In other countries, disintegration along the new cultural-religious lines only intensified. The Polish–Lithuanian Commonwealth (Rzeczpospolita) presented a special case: in contrast to other complex polities such as the Holy Roman Empire, Rzeczpospolita preserved its territorial unity, but on different grounds from, for example, the Kingdom of France, and paying a fatally high price.

The Counter-Reformation in the Polish–Lithuanian Commonwealth as a Rejection of the "Common Cause"

On the eve of the Reformation, the population of the Grand Duchy of Lithuania and the Kingdom of Poland was unprecedentedly multiconfessional by the standards of western Europe: Catholics and Orthodox Christians, Jews and Muslims quite peacefully coexisted in close proximity. Therefore, the spread of Protestantism in the mid-sixteenth century added little to the already complex composition of Polish–Lithuanian society. Far more significant was the impact of the Counter-Reformation, whose ardent champion was the king of Rzechpospolita Sigismund III Vasa (r. 1587–1632). The political unity of the Polish–Lithuanian Commonwealth, often called "the gentry republic," rested on the strategic solidarity of its "citizens"—the Catholic and Orthodox noblemen (*szlachta*), whose property rights and political representation in the Diet (Sejm) were formally guaranteed regardless of their religion. The protracted military confrontation with Orthodox Muscovy and the high social and cultural prestige of Catholicism, which better suited the lifestyle and tastes of the elite, contributed to the Catholic Church's rising influence at the expense of Orthodoxy. However, for a while, this process did not directly affect the sociopolitical sphere. Sigismund III abruptly intervened in interfaith relations, transferring them to the political and economic plane. His main targets were not the Protestants, whose positions in the country had already been undermined by the end of the sixteenth century, but the Orthodox subjects of the crown. Their civil rights were protected by numerous legal acts ("privileges"), issued both before and after the 1569 Union of Lublin that had constituted the single Polish–Lithuanian state, but the Counter-Reformation's new social logic called their political loyalty into question. [6]

Canonically subordinate to the Patriarch of Constantinople and sharing a religion with the Muscovy tsars, the Orthodox noblemen could be suspected of treason just because the supreme power in Rzechpospolita came to be increasingly identified with Polish culture and the Catholic faith. Using the conflict among the Polish–Lithuanian Orthodox bishops, Sigismund played a key role in bringing about the Union of Brest (1596). Under its provisions, most of the Orthodox clergy of the Polish–Lithuanian Commonwealth adopted Catholic doctrine and recognized the supreme authority of the pope, thus forming the Ruthenian Uniate Church. Sigismund declared the Orthodox priests who did not recognize the union as outlaws, and until 1632, Orthodox parishes remained semi-underground.

The Split in the Political Class

What distinguished the Counter-Reformation in Poland–Lithuania from other European countries was that there was no need to restore the lost hegemony of the Catholic Church because it had lost nothing of its prior status. To the contrary, King Sigismund violated the order of things that had developed over the centuries and pushed for a radical sociopolitical transformation. Even though his policy did not primarily target Protestants, it was the epitome of the Counter-Reformation with its novel social imagination. The new social thinking disconnected religion from particular social groups and territories, recognized political power as a phenomenon in its own right, and developed the idea of a country as having "national interests" that were not identical with dynastic considerations. Sigismund III acted along all three of these political trends: he promoted the hegemony of the Catholic Church, tried to strengthen the royal power by limiting the rights of the nobility and the Diet, and sought to expand the country's territory in the Baltics. Choosing religion as the main idiom of new political thinking (and not Jean Bodin's theory of political sovereignty, for example), he succeeded only in his confessional policy. More precisely, Sigismund III achieved the monopoly of the Catholic Church in Poland–Lithuania at the cost of undermining the country's political stability and, soon thereafter, its territorial integrity. Most historians agree that his reign triggered the decline of the Rzechpospolita's political system.

The political unity of this vast multicultural country was secured by the privileged position of its multiconfessional nobility—the *szlachta*—which had the right to elect the king and even to propose a candidate for the throne. Nominally, all the noblemen enjoyed equal rights and privileges, but in reality, it was an extremely heterogeneous social group. Simple warriors who had no money to buy weapons for themselves, farmers who personally tilled the land, and even landless ragamuffins (*gołota*) constituted its lower strata. The top layer of the szlachta's elaborate hierarchy consisted of a few magnates—wealthy landowners and unofficial masters of whole provinces. As the history of the Polish–Lithuanian Commonwealth in the sixteenth century suggests, tensions between ordinary szlachta and magnates ran high. Under certain conditions, the petty noblemen could eagerly have supported the consolidation of the king's power in order to limit the magnates' omnipotence, as their peers did in other European countries. Sigismund III could have used this resource to strengthen the king's authority as the state power, but for this, he would have had to accept the fact that along with Catholics, Protestants and Orthodox szlachta were in his service. He chose to identify with the Catholics thus alienating many Orthodox and Protestant nobles in the Lithuanian and Ukrainian lands and the Cossack elite in the service of the crown, who anxiously clung to and protected their ancient privileges as the last guarantee of their status. Sigismund's ambitions to consolidate power while ignoring the will of the nobility eventually provoked the Sandomierz rebellion (1606–9). Legally, this rebellion qualified as a *rokosz*—the szlachta's armed opposition to the king justified by his tyrannical violation of their rights and privileges. The Sandomierz rokosz was joined by noblemen of all confessions and was led by Catholic and Protestant aristocrats, including the Lithuanian magnate Janusz Radziwiłł. The opposition outlined their demands in sixty-seven articles that stipulated the appointment of senior officials by the Diet and not by the king, the election of local officials by the szlachta rather than their appointment by the crown, the expulsion of the Jesuits from the country as the main champions of the Counter-Reformation, and the protection of the rights of non-Catholic denominations. Although Sigismund won against the rebels, he had to abandon some of his most radical reforms aimed at strengthening the king's power, creating a regular army, and completely banning the Orthodox Church. The nominal restoration of the status quo in the legal sphere could neither undermine the new normal that assumed the absolute preeminence of Catholicism and Polish culture nor compensate for the growing religious split within the szlachta.

The Split in Foreign Relations

No less disastrous were the results of Sigismund's foreign policy. He was a son of King John III of Sweden, so when his father died, Sigismund claimed his hereditary rights to the throne and in 1592 was crowned king of Sweden. The two strongest states in the Baltic region—the Kingdom of Sweden and the Polish–Lithuanian Commonwealth— were united by a common ruler into a potential superpower. This had been a common practice since the Middle Ages, and the history of Rzechpospolita itself began with the personal union between the king of Poland and the grand duke of Lithuania. However, such arrangements were successful only when founded on the old logic of dynastic legitimacy or a new practice of detailed treaties and constitutional acts. Sigismund wanted to operate within the old dynastic logic but while pursuing the modern policy of the Counter-Reformation. In other words, he insisted that his decisions were legitimate simply because he was the rightful successor to the throne, but these decisions actually disregarded dynastic law, the estates of the realm, and the new conflation of religion with culture.

It is no wonder that in Protestant Sweden Sigismund's fierce Catholicism soon raised growing concerns. The precedent of the Rzechpospolita proved that the union of multiconfessional polities was practically possible when pragmatic common interests prevailed, but Sigismund III opted to vigorously politicize and exploit religious differences. He was not just a Catholic king, but a Counter-Reformation crusader. The growing discontent with Sigismund in Sweden and the intrigues of his uncle, who acted as regent during the king's absence, prompted the Swedish parliament (Riksdag) to depose Sigismund III in 1599. Outraged, he started a war for the return of the crown, which dragged on intermittently until 1629. Sigismund achieved none

230 New Imperial History of Northern Eurasia

of his goals, instilled hostility in relations between the countries, and drew Sweden into a dispute over Rzechpospolita's possessions in the Baltics. Moreover, Sigismund's dynastic claims to the Swedish crown were turned against him: If the Polish king had the right to the Swedish throne, did the Swedish king not have the right to the Polish throne? Under the terms of the armistice concluded in 1635, hostilities ceased for twenty-six and a half years until the spring of 1652. When the armistice expired, the Polish–Lithuanian Commonwealth was no longer the country that started the war with Sweden in 1599. The Counter-Reformation consolidated one part of its society, creating a new supraregional cultural solidarity of Polonized Catholics while alienating another, very significant part.

The Rise of the Orthodox Christian Ruthenian Knighthood

By 1600, the Ruthenian Uniate Church had become the only legal Eastern rite in Rzechpospolita. It combined the Orthodox Church's liturgical practices and the Church Slavonic language with subordination to the pope. The crown's attack on Orthodoxy further boosted the ongoing gradual cultural Polonization of the Orthodox, mostly Ruthenian-speaking szlachta. The Reformation and Counter-Reformation impacted the ideal of chivalry, which was now being progressively associated not only with a title and military prowess but also with good education. In the Rzechpospolita, these were Catholic colleges and universities that provided modern types of high-quality education. The Polish language functioned as the language of prestige, culture, and administration across the Kingdom of Poland. Even in the Ukrainian lands, which were transferred from the Grand Duchy of Lithuania to the Kingdom of Poland under the 1569 Union of Lublin, Orthodox elites felt strong incentives to Polonize. Members of the Grand Duchy's aristocratic clans, such as the Vyshnevetski (Wiśniowiecki) and Sapeha (Sapieha) who identified as Orthodox Christians until the late sixteenth century, had converted to Catholicism by the turn of the seventeenth century. In general, the szlachta as a social category increasingly identified with Catholicism and Polish culture, while Orthodoxy was becoming the lot of peasants and Cossacks.

The Cossacks

The Cossacks' numbers and importance had significantly grown by the mid-seventeenth century. The earliest reliable sources on Cossacks date to at least the late fourteenth century, just when the Golden Horde began disintegrating and losing its control of the steppes. These sources register the presence of the settlements of free warrior-Cossacks in the steppe areas along the borders of the Kingdom of Poland, the Grand Duchy of Lithuania, the Grand Principality of Moscow, and the would-be Crimean Khanate. The word "Cossack" probably comes from the Turkic *qazaq*, meaning "free warrior." Cossacks occupied the socioecological niche once established by the Black Hoods—the communities of Turkic-speaking warrior-farmers on the fringes of the steppe along the Rous' Lands. There is no record of how the Black Hoods survived the period of Golden Horde hegemony, so one can only speculate as to whether they had any direct relation to the Cossacks of the time when the demise of the former Jochi's Ulus produced a growing vacuum of power in the steppe. The new political reality made the Cossacks visible to outside observers and contributed to the swelling of their ranks due to the continuous arrival of fugitive peasants, impoverished noblemen, defrocked monks, and *qazaqs* from various khanates that emerged on the ruins of the Golden Horde. The Cossacks settled in the lower reaches of the Dnieper, in a no-man's-land, and made a living by raiding neighboring territories from Moscow to Istanbul. They also eagerly became mercenaries for various rulers. In the lower reaches of the Dnieper beyond the rapids on the island of Khortytsya, the Cossacks established a fortress Zaporozhian Sich (literally, "an abatis beyond the rapids"). It gave a name to a primitive polity based on the principles of military democracy and commanded by elected chieftains—atamans. The word "ataman" is most likely of Turkic origin and means "the elder" (literally, "the great father"), so it is only natural that the steppe warrior-Cossacks borrowed the term as part and parcel of the broader culture and habitus of the steppe people. Curiously, a consonant word with an identical meaning that was also used by Cossacks at a later stage—hetman—had a different etymology, deriving from the German "Hauptmann" (headman). Whereas the German Hauptmann was an army captain, in the Polish–Lithuanian Commonwealth, a hetman was the commander of the crown army.

The commonwealth authorities contemplated two main strategies for dealing with their aggressive neighbor: the physical elimination or partial integration of the Zaporozhian Sich. The second option prevailed. In 1572, King Sigismund II invited 300 Zaporozhian Cossacks to join the service to the crown. This led to the emergence of the category of Registered Cossacks, who were listed in the official register and received a salary for their military service. Legally, Registered Cossacks were in the same category with the lowest, crestless szlachta. This status gave them the legal grounds to claim the same political rights as the rest of the Polish–Lithuanian nobility, which the Cossacks were deprived of. The king and especially the Diet treated the Registered Cossacks with suspicion and periodically closed the register. Nevertheless, by 1590, their number had reached 1,000, and by 1602, 4,000. In 1609, as a onetime temporary action, 50,000 Cossacks were included in the register.

The Cossacks varied greatly by origin and religion, with Orthodox Christians prevailing among them. The growing Polonization of the szlachta and the Cossacks' desire to raise their legal status as "knights" put them at the vanguard of the opposition to the Counter-Reformation, on behalf of the emerging stratum of Orthodox gentry. By the mid-seventeenth century, a fairly numerous hereditary Cossack *starshyna* (elite) had formed, providing cadres for captains (*sotniki*), colonels, and hetmans of the Zaporozhian Cossack army. Listed in the register as crown servitors and owning lands in the Dnieper region, the Cossack starshyna could be characterized as nobility and in fact substituted for the Polonized nobility in the Ukrainian lands. However, the Rzechpospolita did not officially recognize their high status. The Cossack gentry were not granted representation in the Sejm and were only superficially Polonized, so the szlachta looked at them with disdain and made no distinction between the peasants and the Cossacks. The deep social and cultural divides between the Cossacks and the szlachta reinforced each other.

Of Ruthenian Kin and the Polish Nation

The Counter-Reformation policy of Sigismund III exacerbated these tensions by promoting a nationalizing social imagination. The very term "nation" gained currency in the second quarter of the seventeenth century, when the bookish formula of a Polish author from the 1560s became widely popular among the szlachta in the former domain of the Grand Duchy of Lithuania: "gente Ruthenus, natione Polonus" (Latin, of Ruthenian kin and the Polish nation). The Ruthenian educated elite began modifying this formula in their writings, which initially served only a limited readership, into a more radical "populus Ruthenus"—the Ruthenian people. This development finalized the disintegration of the single "szlachta nation" of the sixteenth century. The initial political nation comprised all full citizens of the Polish–Lithuanian Commonwealth, who enjoyed equal political rights, used Latin as the lingua franca of the public sphere, and shared the "Sarmatian myth" of common origin from the warlike Scythians. That political community irrevocably split into two peoples-nations: the Polish-Catholic-szlachta nation and the Ruthenian-Orthodox-Cossack nation.

The crystallization of previously unorganized differences along the clear-cut divide between the two coherent "nations" (if not "peoples") within one polity was fraught with civil war. Such war could have been prevented by the king's active intervention, for example, by his equating the status of the Registered Cossacks with that of the szlacta or restoring the full rights of the Orthodox Church. But Sigismund III had wasted most of his royal authority on promoting the Counter-Reformation's cultural revolution. As a result, by the mid-seventeenth century, the king was not able to implement any measure that would not be supported by the Polonized szlachta. It was only a matter of time before the accumulating mutual irritation and demands would blow up the political situation. In early 1648, shortly before the end of the Thirty Years' War, which played a key role in shaping the modern European concept of politically and culturally unified nations, the long-brewing conflict in the Polish–Lithuanian Commonwealth exploded. The systematization of social and cultural differences by the Counter-Reformation had produced two opposing camps that started the civil war, usually called the Khmelnytsky Uprising.

Jesuit Schooling

Bohdan Khmelnytsky (1595–1657) was most likely born to a family of Orthodox petty szlachta, although some historians believe he was just a town commoner, and it is known that his mother was of simple Cossack background. His biography illustrates the profound influence of the Counter-Reformation on the Orthodox szlachta. Khmelnytsky began his education at the Kyiv Epiphany Brotherhood School, which had recently been founded based on the Jesuit model; he continued his studies at the Lviv Jesuit College.

The Jesuits played a key role in creating the modern school system as we know it: students were organized into stable groups (grades) for the duration of an academic year; each grade studied according to the same program in classes organized into regular periods. All colleges followed standardized curricula and teaching methods,

The content of education was not of decisive importance for Khmelnytsky, who later claimed that he had easily forgotten the Catholic theology taught by the Jesuits. But the concept of modern schooling shaped the very thinking of pupils. Liberal arts education, based on rhetoric and secular, primarily classical, literature, taught the skills necessary to understand everyday social reality rather than divine matters. When perceived through the prism of Greek and Latin texts, this reality appeared to fall short of the ideal social norm as presented in classical books. In these texts, the entire population of a country obeyed a common ruler and common law, and spoke a common language (that of the book's author). This was precisely the social ideal disseminated by the Counter-Reformation.

After completing his studies, Khmelnytsky took part in the war against the Ottoman Empire, spent several years in Ottoman captivity rowing a galley. There he learned the Tatar and Ottoman languages in addition to the Polish and Latin that he had learned at school. In the mid-1630s, he joined the campaign of the Polish–Lithuanian army against Muscovy and, according to some sources, was awarded a golden saber for saving the king's life. In 1637–8, at the high rank of general chancellor, Khmelnytsky participated in the Pavlyuk Cossack uprising.

Civil War between the Cossacks and the Szlachta

His own uprising against the crown began with a private conflict between two low-level administrators: Bohdan Khmelnytsky, a Registered Cossack, constable (*sotnik*) of the Ruthenian population, which was territorially organized into the Chyhyryn regiment, and Daniel Czapliński (Chaplinsky), a crown official of approximately the same rank but belonging to the szlachta. The conflict escalated when, in the absence of Khmelnytsky, Czapliński plundered his farm, kidnapped his concubine who later became his second wife, and flogged his son to death. Khmelnytsky tried to obtain justice in court, but the szlachta court treated him with disdain, awarding only 5 percent of the requested compensatory damages. As a loyal citizen of the commonwealth, Khmelnytsky turned to the king as supreme arbiter, but by the mid-seventeenth century the king was no longer in a position to intervene in szlachta affairs. Allegedly, King Władysław IV only complained in response that, carrying sabers on their baldrics, Cossacks still failed to defend their rights. This episode, along with other details, might be legend, but the general setup of the conflict with Czapliński accurately reflected the structural situation of the political and cultural confrontation between the Cossacks and the Polonized szlachta, which was further accelerated by the growing impotence of royal power.

In January 1648, a disappointed Khmelnytsky, along with some followers, headed to the Zaporozhian Sich, expelled the crown authorities, and was elected hetman of the Cossacks. Upon securing the Crimean khan's support, Khmelnytsky openly confronted the crown. Hastening to suppress the uprising at its inception, the king's top military commander, Grand Crown Hetman Mikołaj Potocki, dispatched his son Stefan at the head of a small force to disperse the rebels. In the battle at Zhovti Vody not far from the Sich, in early May 1648, the contingent of Registered Cossacks under Potocki's command abandoned him and went over to the side of Khmelnytsky. Potocki was killed in action and his force was destroyed. Marching along the Dnieper toward Kyiv, in mid-May, Khmelnytsky's army arrived at Korsun. In the ensuing battle, the Cossacks and Crimean Tatars destroyed the army under the command of the Grand Crown Hetman and his deputy, the Field Crown Hetman, and took both of them prisoners. This was a major blow to the Polish–Lithuanian Commonwealth. Turning westward to Lviv, in the fall of 1648, the united Cossack and Tatar forces obliterated the army of almost 40,000 of the commonwealth near Pyliavtsi in Volhynia, capturing huge trophies. They besieged Lviv and retreated only after receiving a big ransom. Riding the wave of success, Khmelnytsky began negotiations with the crown, which ended in 1649 inconclusively. Determined to crush the rebels, the Sejm announced a general mobilization of the szlachta, and the new crown army, led by the new king John II Casimir, headed to confront the Cossacks. In the battle of Zboriv in early August 1649, the Cossacks and the Tatars won another crushing victory, almost capturing the king himself.

From the outset, the hostilities were accompanied by massive looting and systemic violence against civilians, especially by the Cossacks and Crimean Tatars against Catholics and Jews. Numerous captives, including Orthodox Christians, were taken to Crimea and turned into slaves. Over the twenty years of the Cossacks' war with the crown (1648–67), thousands of Jews were killed. The total demographic losses of the Jewish population, counting those who died from epidemics and hunger or fled to other lands, are estimated at tens of thousands. The Cossacks despised the Orthodox Ruthenian peasants and treated them only somewhat better than Jews, robbing them and selling them into slavery. Over those twenty years, the total population of the Ukrainian lands was reduced by almost half. The brutality of the confrontation and colossal human losses on both sides were reminiscent of the Thirty Years' War that had just ended in the lands of the Holy Roman Empire.

The Autonomous Cossack State

Immediately after the Zboriv battle, negotiations between the two sides began. Despite the horrendous military defeat, the king negotiated from a strong position after Khmelnytsky's strategic ally, the Crimean khan, demanded that the Cossacks reconcile with the crown—most likely out of desire to preserve the balance of power in the region. As a result, the terms of the treaty concluded at Zboriv fell short of the Cossacks' initial expectations, but were nevertheless quite impressive. The hetman's control over the local administration was established in three provinces (voivodeships): Kyiv, Bratslav, and Chernigov. There, only the Russian Orthodox were

The Transformation of Social Imagination

235

allowed to hold administrative offices, while Jews and Jesuits were completely barred from these territories. The king pledged to increase the number of Registered Cossacks to an unprecedented 40,000. A testimony to the remarkable successes of Khmelnytsky, the Treaty of Zboriv simultaneously undermined his reputation as an uncompromising leader of the Orthodox Cossacks. Even the registry of 40,000 could not accommodate all those who wanted to remain Cossacks. The treaty provisioned the restoration of szlachta ownership of their former estates, which led to peasant discontent, and outside the three provinces—to mass executions of the participants in the uprising. Khmelnytsky himself was forced to participate in the suppression of protests by the Orthodox peasants against the Catholic szlachta, which damaged his popularity among the Ruthenian population.

Nevertheless, by the end of the 1640s, Khmelnytsky had practically created an autonomous Cossack state with its own taxation, administration, and foreign policy. The hetman's chancellery—headed by Ivan Vyhovsky, who was the general chancellor, intellectual, and future hetman—dispatched envoys to the Ottoman Empire, Muscovy, Transylvania, and Moldavia. Besides the general chancellor, the government (General starshyna) included the general quartermaster in charge of the material supply of the army, and two general judges who administered the hetman's court of law. Several other senior officers carried out the hetman's assignments. The next level of administrators was represented by the colonels of territorially defined regiments, who performed both administrative and military functions. Cossack regiments replicated the Mongol social organization into hundreds and thousands that designated a population capable of providing the stated number of warriors. Apparently, Khmelnytsky's ultimate goal was to create a separate principality for himself. During the 1649 negotiations, he declared to the king's envoys, "I am the monarch and autocrat," and later attempted to enter into a dynastic alliance with the Moldavian ruler Vasile Lupu by arranging the marriage of their children. He thus cared not only about the princely title as such—the ultimate dream of a medieval knight. Khmelnytsky saw himself as a hereditary ruler over a modern country whose population shared a common religion and language. Khmelnytsky's rhetoric betrayed a new social vision, essentially depicting his mission as a "national" war for liberation of the "Ruthenian people" from the Catholic Poles.

The war between the Cossacks and the crown resumed in 1650–1, after the Sejm refused to ratify the Treaty of Zboriv and allow the Metropolitan of Kyiv, Sylvestr Kosiv, to participate in its session. Once again, the Sejm announced the general mobilization of the szlachta, the territories controlled by Khmelnytsky witnessed a surge of violence against Poles and Jews, and the commonwealth army moved on against the Cossacks. In June 1651, Khmelnytsky's troops and the Crimean Tatars, led by Khan Islam Giray, were defeated. Soon the army of the Lithuanian hetman Janusz Radziwiłł (a distant relative and namesake of the Sandomierz rokosz's participant) captured Kyiv, forcing Khmelnytsky to conclude the Treaty of Bila Tserkva on extremely unfavorable conditions. Now the hetman's power extended only to the Kyiv province, and the crown's rule was restored in Bratslav and Chernigov voivodeships.

The country was devastated by the war. The only way to assemble an army comparable in size to the combined forces of the commonwealth was to enter into an alliance with a third power: either with the Crimean khan, giving him free rein to capture local residents and turn them into slaves, or with the Moscow tsar. In a region divided between the Polish–Lithuanian Commonwealth, Crimea, and Muscovy, there was no room left for the emergence of a fourth independent player, and the weakening of one of the regional powers was possible only by strengthening the other.

The Union with Moscow

In view of this predicament, Khmelnytsky chose to intensify contacts with Moscow. On October 1, 1653, the Assembly of the Land (*zemskii sobor*) in Moscow resolved to take hetman Bohdan Khmelnytsky "under the sovereign's high hand" (i.e., under patronage—the formula of subjecthood in Muscovy), arguing that otherwise the Cossacks could become subjects of the Crimean khan or the Ottoman sultan. Three months later, on January 8, 1654, the congress of the Cossack starshyna in Pereyaslavl (Pereyaslavs'ka rada) approved the decision to accept the suzerainty of Muscovy and thus formally secede from the Polish–Lithuanian Commonwealth. The terms of the deal were formulated by the Cossack starshyna and approved by the Boyar Duma in Moscow. The treaty signed at Pereyaslavl expanded the register of Cossacks on the crown's payroll to 60,000, confirmed the existing rights and privileges of the szlachta as well as those conferred by Polish kings. The document specified the monetary renumeration of various categories of the starshyna and the Cossacks' right to elect their hetman. The hetman was granted the right to communicate with foreign states, with the notable exception of the Polish king and the Ottoman sultan, which was an unprecedented concession on the part of the Moscow authorities.

However, Muscovy's flexibility had its limits, and the first conflict between the two parties occurred already in the church where the Cossack starshyna had gathered to take the oath of allegiance to the tsar. Khmelnytsky demanded that the tsar's ambassadors first take a solemn oath on behalf of their sovereign that the tsar would not hand over the Cossacks to the Polish king and would not violate their liberties. Vasily Buturlin, head of the Muscovy embassy, responded by declaring that in his country, the sovereign was not in the habit of taking an oath to his subjects. Khmelnytsky and the starshyna stormed out of the church and returned to take the oath only after a long consultation. This incident marked the clash of two different political cultures. For the Cossack starshyna, as members of the Rzeczpospolita political community shaped by the ideal of szlachta liberties, a contract with the monarch seemed natural. For Muscovy, the very idea of the tsar's contractual obligations in relation to his new subjects was unacceptable.

Civil War between the Lithuanian Protestants and the Crown, and the Swedish Invasion

By taking the Cossacks and the lands they controlled under "the tsar's high hand," Muscovy annexed a territory of the Polish–Lithuanian Commonwealth, which inevitably provoked a war between the two countries. Simultaneously, the 1635 truce between the commonwealth and Sweden expired. King John II Casimir and the Sejm had no interest in the old territorial disputes in the Baltics, but the Swedish ruling elite viewed the situation differently. Sweden emerged from the Thirty Years' War as a leading European power that had accumulated too many grievances against the Rzeczpospolita. Some members of the Swedish Council of the Realm agreed to support the former adversary against Muscovy, but only on the condition of territorial concessions in the Baltics and the Polish king's official relinquishing of his rights to the Swedish throne. John II Casimir was a son of Sigismund III and hence could theoretically claim his father's title as the king of Sweden.

The dispute over the Swedish crown was only one component of the ticking bomb planted by Sigismund III's Counter-Reformation policy under the Polish–Lithuanian Commonwealth. After the Cossacks claimed part of the commonwealth's territory to create a separate state for the Orthodox "Ruthenian people," the Protestants decided to follow their example. Khmelnytsky's nemesis, the Grand Hetman of Lithuania Janusz Radziwiłł (1612–55), the leading magnate of the Grand Duchy of Lithuania, was the main patron of Protestantism in the country. He subsidized Protestant parishes and financed the education of young people in Protestant universities in northern Europe. In addition, Radziwiłł dreamed of restoring the independence of the Grand Duchy of Lithuania under his rule and on the new principles of the post-Reformation era: as a state of one people and one religion. In late 1654, with a group of supporters, he began negotiations with the king of Sweden that apparently envisioned withdrawing the Grand Duchy of Lithuania from the commonwealth and entering a federation with Protestant Sweden. Thus, all the lands that were part of the Grand Duchy of Lithuania before the Union of Lublin were looking for a way to secede from the Kingdom of Poland. By marginalizing social groups, confessions, and cultures that did not fit the normative ideal of a Polonized Catholic szlachta society, the Counter-Reformation destroyed the Rzeczpospolita as a hybrid political entity based on tolerance and a balance of interests.

In December 1654, the Swedes offered assistance to the Polish king in the war against Muscovy in exchange for territories along the Baltic southern coast. John II Casimir refused any territorial concessions and in turn demanded compensation for his renouncement of claims to the Swedish throne. Then, upon securing the support of the Rzeczpospolita's Protestant vassal Duchy of Prussia and the Radziwiłł clan in the Grand Duchy of Lithuania, in July 1655, the Swedish army invaded the Polish–Lithuanian Commonwealth. The Deluge began—the rapid occupation of vast territories of the country, including Warsaw and Krakow. In August, Radziwiłł signed a treaty acknowledging the Kingdom of Sweden's protectorate over Lithuania, and in October, a "union" creating a Swedish–Lithuanian federation. Although these agreements were never implemented and the troops that remained loyal to John II Casimir managed, through extraordinary effort, to expel the invaders (1656), the Polish–Lithuanian Commonwealth suffered an irreparable blow. [7]

The Price of the Counter-Reformation in the Rzeczpospolita

Territorial losses after the Swedish Deluge and the protracted war with Muscovy (1654–1667) were relatively insignificant. Under the treaty of 1660 with Sweden, the Polish–Lithuanian Commonwealth formally renounced its authority over Livonia and

Riga, which had been lost to Sweden back in the 1620s anyway, and recognized the independence of its former vassal, the Duchy of Prussia. By the Truce of Andrusovo with Muscovy (1667), the commonwealth lost Smolensk, the Chernigov region, and Ukrainian lands on the left bank of the Dnieper under the rule of the Cossack Hetmanate. Much more devastating, especially in the short term, were the population decline and the economic collapse as a result of the war. But a truly irreparable damage to the Polish–Lithuanian Commonwealth was inflicted from within. The society and political order, once based on the ideas of compromise and solidarity transcending multiple partial differences, lost the ability to accommodate diversity. When Sigismund III was launching his Counter-Reformation policies, he strove to subordinate various "Others" and turn them into minorities within the same polity (for example, by imposing the Union of Brest on the Orthodox Church). The systemic crisis of the mid-seventeenth century transformed this approach from subordination to unequivocal rejection of everything that did not correspond to the szlachta-Polish-Catholic "monoculture."

In 1656, the crown army burned down the Polish Protestant town of Leszno accused of providing support to the Swedes; in 1658, the Sejm resolved to expel the Protestant congregation of Polish Brothers from the country; as of 1668, conversion from Catholicism to another religion was punishable by death. The transformation of social imagination triggered by the Reformation and Counter-Reformation had led to the reduction of the Polish–Lithuanian Commonwealth to the Kingdom of Poland, or more precisely, to the kingdom of the "Poles" in the sense of the cultural elite. In 1696, when the Ruthenian language (*rus'ka mova*, Old Belarusian) was replaced by Polish as the official language of administration and judiciary in the Grand Duchy of Lithuania, this move only formalized the transformation that had taken place decades earlier. While the Ruthenians in the Ukrainian lands, represented by the Cossack state, protected themselves from Polonization by seceding from the commonwealth, the Ruthenians in the Belarusian lands did not have this opportunity. There were no political institutions they could rely on to organize into a modern nation, now understood as a culturally distinct people-confession uniting representatives of all social strata but above all, the educated elite. The high Ruthenian (Old Belarusian) culture was inaccessible to most commoners, and the szlachta in the northwest of the Grand Duchy of Lithuania was forced to embrace the normative Polish-Catholic culture to preserve their privileged social status.

Liberum Veto and the Crisis of the Politics of Toleration

The most striking manifestation of the radical break with the tradition of a tolerant attitude toward diversity that so characterized the Grand Duchy of Lithuania could be found in the practice of *liberum veto*, which proliferated in the Rzeczpospolita precisely in the mid-seventeenth century. The list of the szlachta's ancient privileges that was formally codified in 1573 included the right of any deputy of the country's Sejm or a local Sejmik to a "free veto," blocking the discussion of a particular issue or the assembly in general. Paradoxically, despite the frequent conflicts and raving partisanship that occasionally culminated in armed confrontation (*rokoszh*), nobody exercised this right until 1652, when it was used to prevent extending a parliament session beyond the established time limit. Only in 1669, for the first time a deputy used his power of liberum veto to dissolve the entire Sejm. Subsequently, the use of liberum veto became routine. It was hailed as the epitome of szlachta liberties and the "szlachta republic" as such, a symbol of the rule of equals and only by common consent. The fetishization of liberum veto and the neurotic fixation on the cult of unanimity testified to the break with the Polish–Lithuanian Commonwealth's political culture of the sixteenth century. The Rzeczpospolita, which literally meant "common cause" (Latin "res publica"), provided full membership in the "szlachta republic" to any representative of the privileged class, from any lands within its jurisdiction, regardless of one's personal inclinations. It was this inclusivity that made the Polish–Lithuanian Commonwealth so attractive to the nobility of the region and, consequently, secured the commonwealth's status as Europe's largest polity, capable of keeping vast territories with multicultural populations under its rule. Nobody even considered using the right of a personal veto to block the joint work of the Sejm members, since the aim of this work was precisely to find a compromise that accommodated very diverse interests and was hence in the interests of every szlachta "citizen." By the second half of the seventeenth century, the very concept of szlachta citizenship changed, losing its prior inclusivity. The Orthodox, Protestants, Lithuanians, Ruthenians, and others now deemed marginal groups were no longer perceived as truly belonging to the new Rzeczpospolita. Instead of compromise, unanimity and homogeneity became the top political priorities. Therefore, everything that did not satisfy at least one deputy of the Sejm was doomed to the liberum veto.

The Ideal of Sociocultural Homogeneity and Its Political Implications

Homogeneity and uniformity were new social ideals forged in the process of the Counter-Reformation and the fierce Thirty Years' War in Europe. Aesthetically, the idea of confining diversity into a single framework elaborated on the basis of some formalized rational rules was expressed in the baroque—the dominant artistic style of the period. In the sphere of politics, this revolution of the social imagination usually resulted in the consolidation of crown power. No longer relying on the interpersonal "feudal" relations between the suzerain and vassals and eliminating all sorts of intermediaries and local deputies acting on behalf of the supreme power— dukes, bishops, city councils—the power of the crown began to acquire the features of a modern state as an impersonal mechanism for governing through professional officials.

The Polish–Lithuanian Commonwealth demonstrated the opposite trend: the powers of the king were only diminishing as one category of formerly equal participants in the "common cause"—the Polish-Catholic szlachta—established its hegemony over the rest. In the political system in which the king was elected, the partial disenfranchisement of some citizens benefited not the king but other citizens. They were ready to defend their privileged position and internal homogeneity against everyone, be it the Protestant szlachta, the Orthodox Cossacks, the peasants, or the king.

The growing frustration over the szlachta's stubborn resistance to any attempts at consolidating the king's power must have contributed to John II Casimir's decision in 1668 to abdicate and move to France, where he became an abbot. This gesture symbolically summed up the policy of the Counter-Reformation in the Polish–Lithuanian Commonwealth: in the end, religion prevailed over pragmatic politics.

Having lost cultural skills and political mechanisms for reconciling differences and managing diversity, the Polish–Lithuanian Commonwealth did not acquire a new centralized system of governance, which alone was capable of effective mobilization of the shrinking human and material resources. It was only a matter of time before the neighboring countries, emerging from the calamities of the Counter-Reformation with a renewed political system, would begin to pose a mortal threat to the vast but uncoordinated Rzeczpospolita.

The Crimean Khanate: From a European Power to the "Island of Crimea"

By the beginning of the seventeenth century, the Crimean Khanate had reached its heyday. This polity was no more despotic than Muscovy and no less developed economically than the Polish–Lithuanian Commonwealth. Its main strength, which gradually became its main weakness, was its ideal adaptation to a particular political-ecological niche. Another former ulus of the Golden Horde, the Crimean Khanate occupied a buffer zone in several aspects at once: between different regional powers, between the economy of nomads and the economies of sedentary societies, and between the economic and cultural areas of the Mediterranean and eastern Europe. The rulers of Crimea were vassals of the Ottoman Empire tightly controlled by the sultan, who appointed and deposed khans at his whim. Some khans ascended the throne and lost it twice or even thrice, following a change of heart in Constantinople. Vassal relations with the Ottoman Empire were of strategic importance to the khanate, but at the same time did not allow it to fully pursue its own interests, adapting to the changing realities in the region. [8]

The Last European Khanate

What an outside observer in Moscow or Krakow perceived as a single homogeneous "khanate of the Tatars," from the inside was experienced as a complex, extremely variegated social microcosm. The Ottoman traveler Evliya Çelebi, who journeyed all over Crimea in the second half of the 1660s, recalled that the people of the khanate spoke twelve different languages and often relied on interpreters to understand each other. In addition, the Circassians (Adyghe) in the Caucasus and the nomadic Nogais in the steppes north of the Black Sea recognized the Crimean khan's sovereignty. Tribal groups under the khan's rule were engaged in complex political relations with each other. Their aristocracies enjoyed a great degree of autonomy and privileges such as the right to vote for the next khan (who had to belong to the Giray family). Crimean khans ruled over Crimea, were masters of the former Polovtsian steppe, and periodically extended their power as far as the vicinities of Moscow, Kyiv, Lviv, and Krakow. However, they did not formalize their influence as a leading regional power institutionally by establishing a modern territorial state—at least outside the Crimean Peninsula proper. The reputation of a formidable rival of the Rzeczpospolita and Muscovy—the latter periodically paid tribute to the khanate until 1685—rested on the medieval practice of military raids. Crimeans devastated neighboring territories, bringing home rich loot, primarily livestock and prisoners. According to some estimates, in the course of the sixteenth and seventeenth centuries, three million captives were sold into slavery in Crimea, mainly at the slave market in Kaffa (Theodosia). This figure may seem inflated, but the reliable fragmentary information suggests that tens of thousands of captives could be brought to Crimea after a single big raid. Even at the beginning of the eighteenth century (1717), close to 20,000 slaves were sold annually in Crimea.

The second half of the sixteenth century witnessed forty-eight Crimean raids against Muscovy. After the Moscow tsars heavily invested in fortifying the country's southern border, the Rzeczpospolita became the primary object of Crimean raids that numbered seventy-five over the first half of the seventeenth century. Besides large "political" raids organized by the khan during wars or as a means to strengthen his power in the ancient logic of nomadic legitimacy, as well as when ordered by the Ottoman sultan, independent raids were staged by individual aristocrats for purely "economic" purposes. War booty was an important source of income for many Crimean cattle herders, or even their main income.

The Declining Economy of Raids

In the seventeenth century, much was changing in the Crimean society, but the new realities had almost no effect on the principles of the khanate's organization and administration. The sphere of its military and hence political and economic influence in the region was gradually shrinking. For many decades, Muscovy had been concentrating resources along its southern border, investing in regular border guards and the construction of grandiose defense lines stretching for hundreds of miles and blocking the usual paths of raids. Each new abatis line ran farther to the south than the previous one, reclaiming new territories of the forest steppe and steppe from the Crimean Khanate. After the incorporation of the Ukrainian lands along the left bank of the Dnieper, the Moscow government began building defense lines against the Crimean raids there as well.

Even more important changes developed within the Crimean society when former nomadic herders began switching to settled agriculture. The arable land expanded, reflecting the growing economy of orchards and vineyards, rice fields, tobacco, and melon plantations. Relatively few captives who were not sold overseas and remained in Crimea were changing their status from slaves to serfs. The share of agricultural products in the khanate's exports increased; it was formerly dominated by slaves and livestock products, such as leather, felt, and wool.

242 *New Imperial History of Northern Eurasia*

These developments testified to Crimea's ongoing transformation from a seminomadic polity based on raiding economy to a regular early modern European country. However, individual adjustments did not make the Crimean Khanate more competitive: overall, it failed to convert its former military dominance over neighbors into economic potential and to develop a more centralized political organization grounded in formal state institutions. The ability to project its military power far and wide did not prevent the gradual shrinking of the territory under the khanate's control. Eventually it narrowed down to the Crimean Peninsula. Even at the end of the seventeenth century, the Crimean Khanate remained a formidable adversary, but had lost its status as a leading power in eastern Europe. By that time, political weight and military might increasingly began to be determined by the effectiveness of a government that was capable of quickly concentrating material and human resources and directing them to where they were needed at the moment.

The Archaic Polity's Vulnerability

The Crimean Khanate's vulnerability was discovered in the last quarter of the sixteenth century, when it became a victim of the devastating raids by the Cossacks—inhabitants of the same political and economic niche of the steppe borderlands. Normally, the Cossacks and the Crimeans sustained neutral or even allied relations, but already in 1687 the Muscovy's regular army could reach the fortified Isthmus of Perekop—the gateway to Crimea. This and several subsequent campaigns were abortive for logistical rather than military reasons: crossing the arid steppe on foot with artillery and supplies required enormous organizational efforts. However, this purely "technical" nature of Muscovy's failures indicated that a full-fledged invasion of Crimea was only a matter of time.

Only the mighty patron, the Ottoman Empire, helped the Crimean Khanate to contain its strengthening northern neighbors, especially Muscovy. At the same time, Ottoman patronage was a factor weakening the khanate. Imposing political loyalty to the sultan, the Ottomans hindered the formation of a common Crimean, supra-clan political solidarity, similar to national solidarity that emerged in other European societies during the Counter-Reformation and the Thirty Years' War. Combined with a broad self-identification as Muslims, political orientation toward the sultan prevented the development of a specifically Crimean idea as a mobilizing factor, analogous to Polish-Catholic exclusive patriotism.

By the end of the seventeenth century, the army of nomadic pastoralist-cavalrymen had lost its former role as the most effective form of military mobilization, just as the steppe ceased to serve as a reliable barrier to the invasion of foot soldiers. The simultaneous demise of the economy of raids and slave trade, predicated on the ability to procure masses of captives, deprived the Crimean Khanate of its former advantages. They were compensated neither by the enhanced cohesion of the population that continued to speak a dozen languages nor by the more efficient administration, as the clan aristocracies retained their broad autonomy from the khan. The visibly shrinking sphere of political influence projected by the khanate gradually turned the Crimean

Peninsula into an "island"—large, still formidable and prosperous, but already peripheral to the region of Northern Eurasia.

Further reading

Basarab, John. *Pereiaslav 1654: A Historiographical Study*. Edmonton: Canadian Institute of Ukrainian Studies Press, 1982.

Frost, Robert I. *After the Deluge: Poland-Lithuania and the Second Northern War, 1655–1660*. Cambridge: Cambridge University Press, 1993.

Klein, Denise, ed. *The Crimean Khanate Between East and West (15th–18th Century)*. Wiesbaden: Harrassowitz Verlag, 2012.

Magocsi, Paul R. *A History of Ukraine: The Land and Its Peoples*. 2nd ed. Toronto: University of Toronto Press, 2010.

Plokhy, Serhii. *The Cossacks and Religion in Early Modern Ukraine*. Oxford: Oxford University Press, 2002.

7

The Tsardom of Muscovy in Search of an "Assembly Point"

Revolution of the Political Sphere

Back to Square One: Innovation Masked as a Return to Tradition

Decrepit and sick, the first tsar of Muscovy, Ivan IV, died on March 19, 1584. His death caused acute panic among his entourage: the boyars hastened to announce to the residents of Moscow that there was still hope for Ivan's recovery. At the same time, preparing for a possible urban riot, they ordered that the Kremlin gates be locked and summoned musketeers and gunners on the wall galleries. This was a typical reaction to the death of a dictator who, in pursuit of total control, had destroyed regular political institutions in the society. Ivan had composed his will at a young age and thereafter remained preoccupied with it. He regularly introduced new edits and detailed instructions regarding his heir. However, after three decades of radical political experiments, the entire edifice of authority hung on his personality and immediately began crumbling after his death. Ivan nominated his son Fyodor, who was considered "feeble-minded" and incapable of initiative, as the legitimate successor and appointed guardians to assist him. The regency council included members of the two hostile groups: former apartheid (*oprichnina*) officers, representing the tsar's court, and aristocratic boyars, representing the Russian land (*zemstvo*). A bitter power struggle between the two camps was inevitable and probably intended by Ivan as a substitute for institutional checks and balances. In the absence of a developed political system, this conflict was also destined to generate personal intrigues and armed skirmishes between the supporters of the competing parties.

Thus, it comes as no surprise that the confrontation between the "courtiers" and "zemstvo people" led to a riot in Moscow. Faced with the spreading anarchy, the ruling elite had to seek a compromise. They managed to negotiate the ousting of the most odious figures of the past reign, to exile and even execute some of the most influential and stubborn opponents, and to begin shaping a new political regime. On the surface, it resembled the old pre-oprichnina Moscow order: the council of senior boyars, retrospectively called the Boyar Duma by historians, regained its former influence. Now it included members of both rival parties. The seven-member boyar government (*semiboyarshchina*), which ruled Moscow and the whole country during the tsar's absence or illness, was restored too, along with the highest boyar office, the Master of the Horse (*koniushii*).

Historians have noted that any demonstrative "return to tradition" usually masks a break with the past and often hides a fundamentally new social arrangement. This holds true for the post–Ivan IV political regime. The more or less formal council of boyars formerly played an important role as adviser to the grand prince of Moscow but never aspired to doing more than underscoring the prince's legitimacy. In medieval Christian political thinking, the boyars' inner circle mirrored the apostles around Christ. Just as the apostles represented the foundation of the church around the exceptional figure of Jesus, the boyars represented the grand prince's authority over his subjects. But the political experiments of Ivan IV, driven by his obsession with discovering a truly imperial power, created an insuperable breach with the old political culture and institutions. Under Ivan's son, Fyodor Ivanovich, who was a weak if not nominal ruler, the Boyar Duma turned into an independent political body. Its members served on the council of guardians for Tsar Fyodor, and one of them, Boris Godunov, became the Master of the Horse with the hitherto unheard-of title of administrator (*pravitel'*). Boris Godunov (1552–1605) was a prominent apartheid officer of humble origin, who happened to be the new tsar's brother-in-law. He managed to survive the termination of the oprichnina and outsmart many powerful and dangerous rivals. Eventually, he acquired essentially the status of prime minister, which included the right to conduct foreign policy. Godunov was introduced to foreign ambassadors as the tsar's "portly and reasonable brother-in-law and administrator, servant and boyar Master of the Horse, the supreme commander, and keeper of the great [overlord's] possessions, [and] the kingdoms of Kazan and Astrakhan."

The formula "keeper of possessions" was a complete neologism, and had a sole parallel in the title "Lord Protector of the Realm and Governor of the King's Person," which was awarded in 1547 to Edward Seymour by the guardians ("executors") of the underage King Edward VI of England after the death of his father Henry VIII. In 1562, when Queen Elizabeth I contracted smallpox, she appointed her companion, Master of the Horse Robert Dudley, as Lord Protector. Intensive economic and diplomatic contacts between England and Muscovy were established early in the reign of Ivan IV, including the activities of the Muscovy Trading Company (est. 1555), as well as personal correspondence between Ivan and Queen Elizabeth. These contacts and the exchange of envoys continued after his death. Boris Godunov's title seems to reflect the influence of the diplomatic protocol and the need to find local equivalents for the translated foreign legal terms. Still more important is that this new title was recognized in Moscow and reflected a certain political reality. Godunov's political weight was confirmed and further strengthened by the proclamation, in May 1589, of the Moscow Metropolitan Job as the first Patriarch of Moscow and all Rus'. Muscovy thus acquired an autocephalous Eastern Orthodox Christian church of its own, autonomous from the Patriarch of Constantinople and claiming authority over other Orthodox dioceses in the region. This move directly prompted the 1596 Union of Brest in the Polish–Lithuanian Commonwealth as a protective measure against Moscow's confessional domination.

Defining the Domain of the "Political"

The functional differentiation of the hitherto syncretic figure of the ruler into the acting administrator (Godunov), on the one hand, and the legitimate holder of the supreme power (the nominal tsar), on the other, was the result not only of Tsar Fyodor's incapacity. It was the logical outcome of Ivan IV's political revolution. Ivan's experiments helped to extract the phenomenon of the "political" from the previously indivisible complex of domination-possession (of territory, property, power, subjects, slaves, etc.). Ivan IV differentiated this complex into "power" and "possession," albeit not legally or by creating new social institutions but through his "irrational" and destructive arbitrariness, which clearly demonstrated that "power" was separate from "economy," "ownership," and "hereditary privileges."

As was discussed earlier, a similar differentiation of the autonomous domain of the political was under way in many modern societies, further accelerated by the Reformation of the Catholic Church. In societies with a developed print culture, this transformation was becoming the subject of theoretical reflections. The Florentine Niccolò Machiavelli (1469–1527) penned one of the first and most famous treatises on the nature of power, *The Prince*, published posthumously in 1532, when Ivan IV was two years old, and Luther was finishing his complete German translation of the Bible. Machiavelli's attempt to rationalize the divine nature of power shocked his most enlightened contemporaries, so in 1559, his works were banned by the Catholic Church. Meanwhile, Machiavelli was only synthesizing the practical experience of the rich political life in the urban communes of Northern Italy. Their political sphere greatly differed from Muscovy's realities but still betrayed some fundamental parallels with other societies of that era. In particular, Machiavelli wrote about the predicament of the ruler who broke with the "customs of his ancestors":

A principality ["supreme rule" would be a more accurate translation of the original "principato"—a loan translation of Latin "principate"] is created either by the people or by the nobles, accordingly as one or other of them has the opportunity; for the nobles, seeing they cannot withstand the people, begin to cry up the reputation of one of themselves, and they make him a prince, so that under his shadow they can give vent to their ambitions. The people, finding they cannot resist the nobles, also cry up the reputation of one of themselves, and make him a prince so as to be defended by his authority. He who obtains sovereignty by the assistance of the nobles maintains himself with more difficulty than he who comes to it by the aid of the people, because the former finds himself with many around him who consider themselves his equals, and because of this he can neither rule nor manage them to his liking. But he who reaches sovereignty by popular favour finds himself alone, and has none around him, or few, who are not prepared to obey him. . . . It is to be added also that a prince can never secure himself against a hostile people, because of there being too many, whilst from the nobles he can secure himself, as they are few in number. . . . Further, the prince is compelled to live always with the same people, but he can do well without the same nobles, being able to make and unmake them daily, and to give or take away authority when it pleases him.[1]

248   *New Imperial History of Northern Eurasia*

Seemingly abstract, Machiavelli's political analysis was fully substantiated by the practice of Muscovite supreme rule. Besides bloody experiments with the greatest degrees of tyranny, Ivan IV's quest for a truly imperial power left his successors—Tsar Fyodor and the powerful "administrator" Boris Godunov—a legacy of a very different nature: assemblies of the land (*zemskie sobory*).

Assemblies of the Land: Autocracy without the Autocrat

This was the name given to congresses of delegates from all over the country. Representing different strata of free population, these delegates discussed important matters of governance. The very first congress of this type, called "the assembly of reconciliation," was convened in 1549 by Ivan IV, two years after he was crowned as tsar. Representatives of the land discussed the program of reforms proposed by the tsar's close associates, including the abolition of "feeding" (*kormlenie*) or the correction of the Code of Laws. The earliest known list of participants was composed for the assembly of 1566, which discussed the continuation of the Livonian War and had been convened already during the oprichnina period. Of the 374 participants, the groups of clergy, boyars, and clerks each accounted for approximately 8.5 percent. Different categories of nobles together constituted 55 percent of the participants, and merchants—another 20 percent. Overall, by the end of the seventeenth century, about sixty assemblies of the land had convened. Besides discussing various important matters, they had another vital function: every single tsar of Muscovy after Ivan IV, including Peter I, was formally elected by an assembly of the land. It seems paradoxical that the institution of popular assemblies was established almost simultaneously with the inauguration of the tsar's title, and by none other than the first and most authoritarian of all the Moscow tsars—Ivan IV. The same Ivan IV, who, in a letter to Queen Elizabeth I of England in October 1570, wrote contemptuously about the parliament as a body that belittled the monarch's dignity:

> And wee had thought that you had been ruler over your lande and had sought honor to your self and profitt to your countrie. . . . But now wee perceive that there be other men that doe rule, and not men but bowers and merchaunts the which seeke not the wealth and honour of our Maiesties, but they seeke there own profit of marchauntdize: and you flowe in your maydenlie estate like a maide.

So, why did the autocrat holding the title Lord of all Rus' needed the assembly of the land? This could not be a tribute to some ancient tradition: as we have seen, the princes of the northeastern Rousian lands persistently tried to suppress the institution of the city veche. Moreover, an assembly of representatives coming from all over a large country had nothing in common with a veche. Nor was the assembly of the land borrowed from Western Europe with its parliaments and estates-general representing the estates of the realm. Northern Eurasia east of the Carpathians had no stable self-organized corporations (legal estates) that enjoyed a degree of legal autonomy and represented their group interests before the crown. Therefore, there was no contradiction in Ivan IV's referring with disdain to "bowers and merchaunts" while regularly convoking

The late nineteenth-century Russian historian, Vasily Klyuchevsky, characterized the participants in the assemblies of the land as "agents for the execution of government orders": "The part of the 1566 assembly [members] who had at least some semblance of representation consisted of military governors, the noblemen from the capital serving as military marshals of the district nobility, and the top merchants from the capital, who acted as the government's financial managers." There was nothing autonomous about the social body represented at the assembly of the land.

It seems more plausible that the idea of zemstvo assemblies was borrowed from the somewhat misunderstood practice of the Muscovy strategic rival, the Grand Duchy of Lithuania. In the fifteenth century and the first half of the sixteenth century, whenever the need arose, the grand duke periodically convened the Valny Sejm, literally meaning "general assembly" (Latin: Comitia generalia). It considered approximately the same range of issues as the future Muscovy's assembly of the land, including the election of the monarch. The main difference between the two institutions was the Valny Sejm's aristocratic composition, which excluded the clergy and merchants.

Whatever the assembly of the land's historical roots, the key question is why Ivan IV and his successors needed it at all. Machiavelli wrote virtually nothing about the state as a distinctive system of government, a political machine: both because the state in the modern sense did not yet exist and because in the relatively compact Italian duchies the number of professional civil servants was very insignificant. But his abstract notion of supreme rule ("el principato") referred to governance as an institution independent of personalities, and hence captured the universal moment of crystallization of the modern state as a concept and a reality. Ivan IV did not read Machiavelli's treatise, but he faced the same predicament as the monarchs in northern Italy of the period: the stronger the autocratic power aspired to be, the higher the ruler's dependence on those who implemented that power in practice. Choosing between "the nobles" and "the people," Ivan chose "the people," or rather different categories of the population associated with the emerging service hierarchy. In his treatment of the nobles, Ivan IV was able not just "to make and unmake them daily, and to give or take away authority when it pleases him" (Machiavelli), be it the apartheid terror or the elevation of Simeon Bikbulatovich as tsar. He dismantled the old appanage system as the basis for administering a vast territory through the mediation of appanage princes (as a form of land tenure, appanages lasted much longer). Ivan achieved the absolute power of the tsar by avoiding the mediation of various lords—owners of autonomous territories. Instead, he relied on the appointed officials and servitors (nobles) who lived on the estates awarded for their service and represented the crown in their districts. Bringing together representatives of the boyars, government clerks, nobles, and merchants dependent on his administration, Ivan IV thereby asserted his supreme rule with the help of "the people"—only this was a special, "serving" people. The participants in the assemblies of the land represented not the magnate-aristocrats of their regions or the autonomous legal estates, but different sectors of the crown administration. Together, they embodied not yet the "state" as a ramified apparatus of professional civil servants, but "power" as a distinct phenomenon described in Machiavelli's treatise.

That is why, several weeks after Ivan's death, amid the acute confrontation between the parties of the "courtiers" and "zemstvo people," an assembly of the land was urgently convened. It confirmed Ivan's son Fyodor as the legitimate candidate to the throne and resolved the conflict between the boyars. The first formal election of the tsar by the assembly established a new political tradition. Taken most likely as a forced step to alleviate the political crisis, the convocation of the electoral assembly of the land validated Ivan IV's intuitive insight: for its stability, autocracy needed to rely not on a clique of aristocrats, but on the "serving people." Ivan IV had passed away and his heir and nominal tsar was unfit for the office, but this did not undermine the institution of supreme power (principate) itself. Boris Godunov became a full-fledged ruler with officially recognized status precisely because he was embraced by the sociopolitical base of autocracy. The primary source of "principate" had become not the belief in the divine origin of the leader's ancestral rights to the throne, and not the support of a group of influential aristocrats, but endorsement by collective executioners of "sovereign power"—the "serving people." Each of these people individually was merely a "tsar's bondsman" (as they publicly identified themselves), but together they constituted the very space of power.

Thus, a perfectly Machiavellian identification of power as a fully autonomous phenomenon took place in Muscovy. This power was separated even from the tsar's title, which Ivan IV temporarily bestowed upon the completely powerless Simeon Bikbulatovich. It was because of this revolution of political culture that the representatives of the "serving people" in the assemblies of the land did not object to the elevation of Boris Godunov. When Tsar Fyodor died in 1598, another assembly of the land elected Boris Godunov as tsar—a decision unthinkable half a century earlier. Not only was the new ruler elected by his subjects, but the fact that he was not a grand prince or even a Rurikid did not prevent it from happening.

Citizen Bondsman

The phenomenon of the "serving people" explicates a peculiar understanding of citizenship in political systems such as Muscovy. Citizenship is usually understood as the legal rights and obligations of a class of people who have a say in a country's politics, as well as their awareness of this role and hence a sense of responsibility for the country. The "serving people" of Muscovy were paradoxical citizens; they were fully aware of their central role in the construction of power but able to perform this role only on behalf of a truly autocratic ruler. The more arbitrary and unrestricted the ruler's power, the greater the sense of their civic status among the ordinary executors of the sovereign's will. The life of an ordinary servitor remained the same under any tsar: he had to participate in military campaigns and look after productivity on the estate awarded to him for the duration of the service. But as a member of the "serving people," he acquired an additional social prestige if performed his routine duties on behalf of the "great sovereign," whose "greatness" was evenly distributed among everyone enforcing the sovereign's power. Even if this involved humiliation and destruction of a part of the "serving people," the rest felt empowered and their service was validated, regardless of any material gains.

According to Jean Bodin's aforementioned theory of sovereignty (elaborated in his *Six Books of the Commonwealth*, 1576), the sovereign's power is absolute and indivisible. Judging by this standard, the power of the tsars was not fully autocratic (i.e., sovereign), as long as it relied on the collective endorsement of the serving people. Likewise, the theory of popular sovereignty that prevailed in the eighteenth century ("All political power is vested in and derived from the people" as per the US Bill of Rights) would consider the tsar's servitors not a people, but a bunch of bondsmen who took pride in the tyrannical rule of their master. But the Moscow aristocrat-boyars and particularly the "boyars' children" (service nobles) read neither Machiavelli, nor Boden, nor, of course, eighteenth-century authors. As has been already stressed, secular public polemics as a separate sphere was practically nonexistent in Muscovy, not to mention the sphere of professional social and legal theorizing. The idioms of Holy Scripture helped in describing political phenomena, and political practice served as the main format for contemplating social reality and developing schemes for its improvement. Unaware of the ongoing theoretical debates, the tsars nonetheless had designed a regime of complete sovereignty ("autocracy"): their power depended neither on some external political force, nor on a formal title, nor even on their following the Ten Commandments. At the same time, their "service people" in the aggregate functioned as the main guarantor of sovereignty and the source of legitimacy—something that no actual bondsmen or serfs were entitled to as individuals.

The paradoxical phenomenon of servile citizenship develops whenever conditionally dependent relations with the supreme power become the only opportunity to acquire political subjectivity—a political role and weight. "Independence through dependence" is an oxymoron that describes a historical moment when power relations have been fully differentiated from kinship and property but not institutionalized by the state as an anonymous and autonomous "system." The political subjectivity of the participants in the Valny Sejm in the Grand Duchy of Lithuania or the States-General in France was substantiated by their association with a political and economic resource that existed beyond the crown and autonomously from it: the private possessions of local aristocrats or the estates of the realm. In a modern state, even if it is an absolute monarchy, the citizen's political subjectivity is based on the legally formalized rights and obligations that are uniformly applied to a certain category of the population. The very phenomenon of the state is associated with universal logical principles—laws—that govern the sphere of public relations. Of course, rulers have issued laws from time immemorial, but one can speak of the modern state only if everyone related to the power—from rulers to ordinary executors of their will—turn into cogs in a coordinated political machine, which operates through formalized public rules-laws, rather than interpersonal and private relationships. The corruption and arbitrariness of individual officials and occasional uninformed laws issued by the ruler do not negate the very system in which the roles of administrators are formalized and thus are fairly independent of their holders. In such a modern political system, those who are recognized as citizens, even if these are only a few noblemen, acquire their citizenship due to formal participation in the state, rather than personal subordination to the will of a certain individual on the throne.

But what if the power of the sovereign is already clearly and effectively separated from the "feudal" personalized relations of mutual obligations and property rights, but there is yet no state to mediate and anonymize this power? Then "citizens"—participants in and conductors of power relations—have no choice but to associate themselves entirely with the figure of the autocrat. His power really depends on them; they create the body and the effect of this power, but only as long as they recognize themselves as the sovereign's "bondsmen." This peculiar understanding of citizenship, observable in sixteenth-century Muscovy, had formed a distinct political culture that resurged more than once over the next centuries during the periods of demise or underdevelopment of state institutions.

The supreme power in the form of tsarist autocracy relied on the numerous and rather amorphous "serving people," who collectively substituted for the state machine. What they had in common was neither a political program nor a bureaucratic ethos, but only loyalty to the tsar. This flexibility provided stability for Muscovy's political system under normal circumstances but could become a source of vulnerability in case of any uncertainty regarding the legitimate ruler. The "serving people" could not nominate their own candidate for the throne because when they were not in the service of a particular sovereign, they did not constitute a coherent group or an autonomous political force. This Achilles heel of the political system that began crystallizing behind the facade of Ivan IV's feats of arbitrary rule fully revealed itself during the first decades after his death.

The Realm's Inner Cohesion

A representative of the Muscovy Trading Company and diplomat, Jerome Horsey, who lived in Muscovy for almost twenty years with some interruptions (from 1573 to 1591), was surprised that Ivan IV's vast tsardom did not fall apart after his death:

> So spacious and large is now the dominions of this empeir as it can hardly be haeld within one regiment, but to be devided againe into severall kingdoms and principallites, and yet under one compleat monarcicall soveraintie, and then to over mightie for all his neighbor princis. This did he ayme at, was in good hope, and waye to make it feacable.

Indeed, it was only reasonable to expect that a vast country, held together by a mentally unstable tyrant through rule by terror, would disintegrate as soon as he was gone. And yet, after the death of the first tsar, Muscovy not only did not crumble but continued to expand. It was during this period that the real control over western Siberia was established: in 1587, near Isker, the capital of the Siberian Khanate on the right bank of the Irtysh, the tsar's officer Daniil Chulkov supervised the construction of the fort at Tobolsk. A chain of similar forts was built by Muscovite servitors along the Irtysh and Ob, until finally the Siberian Khanate practically ceased to exist after its khan Kuchum suffered a major defeat (1598). In 1604, Tomsk was founded on the eastern flank of Muscovy's possessions in Siberia, some 2,200 miles east of Moscow.

The Tsardom of Muscovy

In the course of two decades, much of the West Siberian Plain had been taken under control. [1]

Simultaneously, Muscovy expanded in the south, determined to keep in check the Crimean Khanate and establish control over the Cossacks on the Don and in the lower reaches of the Volga. In 1585, Voronezh was founded in the upper reaches of the Don. In 1586, the government began constructing a chain of forts that eventually comprised the Belgorod defense line, blocking the Muravsky Trail—a major caravan route connecting Crimea and Moscow and the path of systematic raids. In less than one decade, Livny, Belgorod, Oskol, and Valuyki were built as part of the Belgorod defense line. In 1599, Tsarev-Borisov was founded far into the steppe (on the territory of the modern Kharkiv region in Ukraine). At the same time, effective control was established over the entire course of the Volga: Samara was founded in 1586, Tsaritsyn (modern Volgograd) in 1589 at the portage between the Don and the Volga, and Saratov in 1590. The free Cossacks who settled in the Lower Volga preferred to move to the Yaik River in the Urals, away from the government troops and administrators. [2]

Even the westward expansion was a success during this period. In 1590, Muscovy went to war with Sweden and was able to regain the lands that had been lost as a result of the quarter-century Livonian War: the frontier districts of Ivangorod, Yam, Koporye, and Korela. As a defense measure against the Polish–Lithuanian Commonwealth, the grandiose construction of a four-mile-long Smolensk fortress wall was undertaken—one of the most ambitious infrastructure projects in the history of Muscovy (1595–1602). Earlier, in 1584–91, the six-mile-long white-stone wall of the White City was built in Moscow (along the modern Boulevard Ring) and an even longer wooden and earthen wall (along the modern Garden Ring).

Apparently, the "compleat monarcicall soveraintie," which prevented the vast tsardom from falling apart, did not wane after the death of Ivan IV. The fifteen-year nominal rule of Tsar Fyodor had confirmed the excessiveness of the extraordinary "imperial" despotism carried out by his father, as the Moscow tsardom's integrity could be successfully sustained without it. Of real importance was the readiness of the "serving people" to recognize themselves as the tsar's subjects and to carry on his power in the districts to which they were appointed. The new policy's success also owed to the fact that, despite heavy economic and demographic losses incurred during Ivan's reign, the country's economy was able to recover quickly. Just as three centuries earlier, in the wake of the Mongol invasion, a seemingly total disaster quickly gave way to new growth. The primitive organization of the economy and social processes meant that a rebound did not take much.

Unlike modern states, early modern societies lacked mechanisms of mobilization and rapid concentration of available resources—be it troops or food supplies. An extraordinary amount in tax collections or a single crop failure could easily ruin entire provinces. But they could equally quickly reinstate their humble norm after just a single plentiful summer or a onetime forgiveness of arrears. The vast tsardom always had potential recruits for the army and workers for ambitious construction projects, and the grain to feed them. The problem was not the lack of resources in the country but how to find them and then gather and deliver them to one place. However despotic, the tsar's will alone was insufficient for this task. Thousands of servitors scattered around

The Beginning of the Troubles

On February 19, 1600, in Southern Peru, on the opposite side of the globe from Muscovy, the Huaynaputina volcano erupted. This was the largest volcanic activity in the history of the South American continent. A huge amount of ash spewed into the atmosphere, producing the effect of volcanic winter. Resonating with the decreased activity of the Gulf Stream, it triggered the beginning of the third, coldest phase of the so-called Little Ice Age in Northern Eurasia, which lasted until the beginning of the nineteenth century. It is believed that the average temperature on the planet dropped by 1–2 degrees Celsius. Cooling did not happen synchronously everywhere, and the effects of climate change manifested themselves differently in different regions (a drop in temperature is only one of the multiple factors of complex weather processes). In Greenland, the peak of cooling was reached already in the first third of the fifteenth century, when glacier covered almost the entire territory of the former "green land." Very cold winters were noted in Muscovy from at least the mid-sixteenth century, and unusually severe winters were also registered much later, in 1656, 1778, and 1808. A direct result of the Huaynaputina eruption in eastern Europe was not so much the unprecedented winter frosts as cold and rainy summers. Year after year (1601, 1602, 1604), in the summer, a slowly moving cyclone would establish its hold over the region. Rains would fall for several weeks in a row, followed by frost: for example, on July 28, 1601, in Moscow, or on August 31, in Pskov. Large areas suffered crop failures. Given the low productivity of farming, a repeated crop failure led to an increase in the grain prices and a massive famine in 1601–3. The available fragmentary information indicates that in some areas rye prices had soared by twenty- to twenty-fivefold.

Meanwhile, the health of Boris Godunov, who had recently been crowned tsar, sharply deteriorated. In the fall of 1600, his condition was so bad that he was carried on a stretcher to a session of the Boyar Duma. Expecting his death was imminent, the boyars Mikhail and Fyodor Romanov assembled a private army of servitors on the premises of their Moscow residence, to support the claim of one of them to the throne. The Romanov brothers were nephews of Tsarina Anastasia, Ivan IV's beloved first wife, and hence somewhat related to the dynasty of Moscow princes. However, Boris Godunov recovered and on October 26, 1600, sent a musketeer regiment to storm the Romanovs' compound. The Romanov brothers were punished: Mikhail was imprisoned in a remote northern village, and Fyodor was compelled to become a monk in an equally remote monastery. Many of the nobles who served them were executed. Among those who escaped repressions was a musketeer captain's son, Yuri Otrepiev, who urgently took monastic vows and hid in a provincial monastery.

Famine and political instability prompted the proliferation of mass vagrancy and brigands. One band of brigands headed by a former military slave (*boevoi kholop*)—a personally dependent professional soldier, Khlopko Kosolap—grew to such a size that the government troops only with difficulty defeated it near Moscow in September 1603.

At that time, many perceived these events as God's punishment. The early nineteenth-century Russian intellectuals came to explain them on the basis of Boris Godunov's fatally bad luck. In the twentieth century, historians found such explanations naive and instead spoke of the Muscovite state's structural—political and economic—crisis. According to this newer interpretation, the autocratic regime had proved its unsustainability, along with the landholding conditioned by the crown service and based on the exploitation of serfs. However plausible, these explanations did not address the particular timing of the crisis. The sins of Boris Godunov and his subjects hardly exceeded those of Ivan IV and his Oprichniks, while the fifteen-year reign of Boris before coronation and the very fact that he became tsar, testified to his exceptional luck. As to the socioeconomic outlook of Godunov's Muscovy, it did not differ fundamentally from that of the previous and subsequent decades. What was truly unique and telling was not the crisis itself, but its manifestations, particularly the proliferation of impostors—claimants to the throne—and the reaction of different strata of the society to them.

The First Impostor

In 1603, five years after Boris Godunov, who was not even of princely background, became Moscow's first ruler elected outside the regular line of succession (1598), the first impostor in the history of the region appeared in the Grand Duchy of Lithuania, claiming to be Ivan IV's youngest son Dmitry. This name belonged to a real historical figure: in 1582, Ivan fathered a son Dmitry with his sixth or seventh wife. Since the Orthodox Church does not recognize more than three marriages, this son was considered illegitimate and could not claim the throne. After Ivan's death, Dmitry was sent with his mother and a small entourage to Uglich in the upper Volga, about eighty miles from Yaroslavl. There he died in May 1591: according to the official version, Dmitry, who suffered from seizures, was playing mumblety-peg with other boys in the yard when he was beset by a paroxysm and stabbed himself during the convulsions. The clan of Dmitry's mother, the Nagie boyars, who fiercely fought Boris Godunov for the throne, immediately accused Godunov of orchestrating the murder of the illegitimate prince. Either way, all agreed that Dmitry was dead. Yet, twelve years later a young man appeared in the Grand Duchy of Lithuania, and announced himself to be Prince Dmitry, who had miraculously survived the Uglich accident. He claimed that there was an attempt on his life by the assassins who had unwittingly killed another boy, while the real prince was secretly evacuated to the north of the country. Both versions—the organized political assassination and the organized rescue of Prince Dmitry—are extremely unlikely. Uglich was a small town with a population of barely 2,000 people, where everyone knew each other by sight and every stranger was immediately noticeable. The prince died in front of witnesses, and a large-scale investigation carried out after his death by a commission that included Godunov's supporters and opponents shows no sign that its results were falsified. Thus, the person who posed as the surviving prince has justly been called the False Dmitry. Most scholars agree that this was a servant of the Romanov boyars, Yuri (Grigory) Otrepiev, who managed to escape the 1600 crackdown on their followers.

Hitherto, there had been not a single instance of an impostor claiming a princely throne in the former Rousian lands, and it was unthinkable that someone would have come up with the idea of posing as a deceased prince's heir. Not that it was impossible in principle to deceive someone's relatives and friends, especially in an era before photographs and realistic portraits existed. In the late 1550s, in Languedoc in the south of France, an impostor successfully passed himself off as the peasant Martin Guerre who had disappeared eight years earlier. Guerre's sisters and even his wife "recognized" the impostor as the missing peasant; the wife bore him two children, and only three years later and with some difficulty was the impostor exposed. He lost his case in court only when the real Martin Guerre unexpectedly showed up. Modern historians argue about whether Martin Guerre's wife could have been sincerely mistaken when she acknowledged the impostor to be her husband—we will never know the definite answer to this question. But a structural situation that facilitated and even necessitated the appearance of an impostor was in place: as long as eight years after her husband's disappearance, Martin Guerre's wife could not remarry, since the death of her legal spouse had not been confirmed. Both she and the household needed a "head of the family," but only Martin Guerre, real or fake, could legally become one.

In contrast to the case of Martin Guerre (and False Dmitry), the tight, publicly visible princely circle simply left no room for the kind of uncertainty that an impostor could have exploited. The vacant office was immediately claimed by a well-known successor, even if he was not universally supported. False Dmitry appeared when the news of Godunov's ailing health made the prospects for a new tsar to succeed him on the throne both urgent and completely hazy. Godunov himself was going to transfer the throne to his son Fyodor, who in 1603 turned fourteen. But since Boris Godunov did not inherit the throne along patrilineal succession and became tsar solely by the assembly of the land's decision, his son's rights as heir apparent to the crown were far from self-evident. There were other, even more legitimate candidates for supreme power. These included the Rurikids, such as the boyar Vasily Shuisky, or the close relatives of Ivan IV's first three wives—for example, the boyar Romanovs, or even Ivan's youngest "illegitimate" son, had he survived. The novel situation of strategic uncertainty that resulted from Ivan IV's separation of pure power from traditional social hierarchies was reinforced by Boris Godunov's differentiation of the right to govern from the fact of belonging to the ruling dynasty. To this should be added the general acceptance of the idea of the tsar's election. Together these factors made the phenomenon of False Dmitry possible. In a sense, he was not a greater impostor than Godunov: he had no place in the regular line of succession but was able to substantiate his right to occupy the throne. In other words, False Dmitry possessed almost the same legitimacy as Godunov, because the very understanding of legitimacy of the supreme ruler had been profoundly transformed in Muscovy. The next decade went down in history as the Time of Troubles (*smutnoe vremia*). Originally this meant "the time of rebellions," but in modern Russian the old term sounds more like "the time of confusion" or "ambiguity," and these connotations seem much more appropriate.

This is how everything started. In the fall of 1604, just before the beginning of the season's thaw, False Dmitry crossed the Muscovy border at the head of several thousand mercenaries and szlachta volunteers. They brought almost no artillery with them. This

The Tsardom of Muscovy

was all the military support he could find in the powerful Rzeczpospolita in exchange for a promise, if he became tsar, to give up vast territories including Smolensk and Chernigov, provide military support in the war with Sweden, promote the spread of the Catholic faith, and make his supporters rich. Officially, King Sigismund III and the Senate (the upper house of the Sejm) of the Polish–Lithuanian Commonwealth did not support this campaign, given that the twenty-year armistice concluded with Muscovy in 1600 was in effect. All financial and organizational support for the expedition was provided by the powerful Grand Duchy of Lithuania's magnates Adam and Konstanty Wiśniowiecki, to whom the impostor revealed his tsarist origin, and their cousin Jerzy Mniszech, whose daughter False Dmitry fell in love with.

One can only guess now how seriously the Wiśniowieckis took False Dmitry's story and whether they actually believed in the success of his cause. It is only clear that they were extremely angry with Boris Godunov and were ready to aggravate him in any way they could. During Muscovy's southward expansion in the 1590s, the tsar's servitors reached the outskirts of Adam Wiśniowiecki's vast possessions. A series of border conflicts led to Boris Godunov's order in 1603 to burn the contested towns of Priluky (Prilutskoe) and Snetino, which were guarded by Wiśniowiecki's people. So, the Wiśniowieckis became instrumental in organizing False Dmitry's campaign, but also in keeping its scale down: they consistently resisted involving the crown troops in the operation. Finally, the geography of the invasion can indirectly testify to their plans. The troops crossed the border south of Chernigov, at a point located farther from Moscow than any other section of the long border north of Kyiv (500 miles), but directly adjacent to Adam Wiśniowiecki's possessions. Thus, it is possible that the Wiśniowieckis planned to use the impostor simply to get back at Godunov and force him to settle the territorial dispute in their favor. But events took an unexpected turn.

The military campaign began too late in the year and was only modestly successful. In three months, False Dmitry's followers had managed to advance only 150 miles through the poorly defended remote outskirts of Muscovy. It was still nearly 400 miles to Moscow and no money was left to pay the mercenaries. False Dmitry forbade looting, and apparently no one seriously expected to reach Moscow and be fully reimbursed there. On January 1, 1605, his troops rioted and most of the mercenaries retreated. A few days later, about 800 szlachta volunteers followed suit along with Jerzy Mniszech, one of the impostor's main supporters.

As the military potential of the movement was melting away, its political support among the local population surprisingly began to grow. The surrounding southwestern borderlands of Muscovy were recently annexed territories. The nobles serving there had little chance of advancing to the prestigious category of "Moscow noblemen and boyar children." Socially and culturally, they were much closer to the Cossacks, who became their neighbors after Muscovy's outposts advanced farther south at the beginning of the seventeenth century. These people were impressed by the treatment of prisoners after the invaders from the Rzeczpospolita captured the first several forts. False Dmitry behaved not like a conqueror, but like a kind tsar. He treated even the most resolved enemies generously and immediately freed the captured rank-and-file servitors and their commanders. Provincial nobles, who seemed destined to spend their lives in the middle of nowhere, suddenly saw a chance for rapid promotion by becoming close associates of the new tsar. More and more of them began to swear allegiance to False Dmitry. The garrisons located farther to the east from his path, in Sloboda Ukraine, such as the recently founded Belgorod and Tsarev-Borisov, began to go over to his side. Even the Don Cossacks supported False Dmitry: shortly after most of the Polish–Lithuanian troops abandoned him, 12,000 Cossacks arrived in his camp. By the end of January 1605, he had an all new army and was already halfway to Moscow. Then came the turning point of his enterprise.

From Impostor to Tsar

On January 21, 1605, the government army sent from Moscow clashed with the troops of False Dmitry not far from Sevsk, which was part of the Belgorod defensive line. The impostor's army was defeated and dispersed; he was nearly captured. The government troops unleashed merciless terror, murdering not only those who were captured on the battlefield but also the Cossacks, musketeers, and servitors who were simply supporting the impostor. Moreover, their families in local garrison towns were hanged. This brutality contrasted with the way False Dmitry treated prisoners, and many of Muscovy's "service people" were deeply appalled by it. Any split within the social base of the tsar's power meant the crush of its legitimacy and hence the demise of practical support. This was illustrated by a new paradoxical situation: over the next three months, False Dmitry remained completely passive, having taken refuge with the remnants of his troops in Putivl, 380 miles from Moscow. And yet his popularity and influence spread around the country. On April 13, 1605, Boris Godunov died unexpectedly, and the entire political regime collapsed. The government troops that were besieging the towns loyal to False Dmitry began going over to the side of the impostor; even prominent generals did the same. Not winning a major battle or even reaching Muscovy's inner territory beyond the outer defenses, False Dmitry found himself triumphant. He was so confident in the serving people's support that he did not hesitate to send his army under the command of Godunov's former generals to Moscow, while he was meeting with borderland servitors in Oryol. Then, in Tula, he waited for news about the fall of the government of Boris Godunov's son and, formally speaking, a legitimate heir. Thus, False Dmitry was not personally involved in the arrest and apparent murder of Godunov's widow and son. On June 20, 1605, he entered Moscow not as a conqueror, but as a legitimate sovereign returning to the capital after a long absence. On July 30, he was officially crowned as tsar.

In less than a year, an unknown fugitive from Muscovy had become the legitimate tsar. This amazing transformation—in the style of the early baroque rogue literature and Shakespeare's plays written during these years—became possible due to the peculiar distribution of power in Muscovy. But False Dmitry, now Tsar Dmitry Ivanovich, could not eliminate the structural situation of uncertainty about the rules of the new political system that remained largely unformalized. Nothing prevented new claimants to supreme power to come forward, under their own names and as impostors, potentially splitting the serving people's unity and thus undermining the old ruler's legitimacy.

The new tsar Dmitry Ivanovich apparently realized that his position depended on his popularity with the nobility, rather than on the military force. Learning from Godunov's mistakes and acting as a populist leader, he tried to appease the broadest possible strata of his "electorate"—the Muscovy servitors as de facto citizens of the established political regime. He ordered the rehabilitation of the boyars who were exiled under Godunov. Fyodor Romanov, now monk Filaret, was promoted to metropolitan of Rostov. The government raised the servitors' monetary compensation and the norms for conditional landholding. The southern borderlands, which were the first to recognize and support False Dmitry as the legitimate tsar, were granted a ten-year tax exemption and relief from the obligation to personally plow the "tithe tillage" (*desiatinnaia pashnia*). In an attempt to make the garrisons of remote defense lines more self-sufficient, Boris Godunov ordered Cossacks, musketeers, and even the noblemen stationed there to cultivate grain, which made them practically indistinguishable from peasants. Now they did not have to be self-sufficient. As to the real peasants, Tsar Dmitry outlawed hereditary bondage and decreed that bondsmen could serve only the people with whom they originally entered into the relations of indentured servitude.

These were very popular, if mutually contradictory measures. Inevitably, one group benefited at the expense of another and bred more discontent. The new tsar Dmitry Ivanovich did not last even a year in power. After his honeymoon with Muscovy's service people in the summer of 1605, by winter, tensions began to grow in different strata of society.

From Tsar to Rumored Impostor

Tsar Dmitry broke with many conventions of the preceding rule. He renamed the Boyar Duma the Senate and began calling himself emperor (apparently, he perceived this word purely phonetically, signing his title as "in perator"). At the same time, he dealt with the most important matters not by consulting the Senate, but through his personal, or "secret" council, staffed by his szlachta associates. The arrangement reflected the need to settle the old promises of lavish territorial and religious concessions and monetary awards, which legally constituted treason. The tsar surrounded himself with foreign bodyguards, and more and more foreigners were coming to Moscow. His demonstrative patronage of foreigners at the expense of natives irritated the Muscovy servitors. To compensate for tax breaks granted to the southern borderlands and payments to his Polish–Lithuanian allies, Tsar Dmitry imposed additional taxes on the Kazan territory and Siberia, thus stirring up more discontent among the local servitors.

Rumors that the tsar was an impostor began circulating at the highest and lowest echelons of the society. In the winter of 1605, in a secret letter to the Polish King Sigismund III, the boyars complained about his support of an impostor on the Moscow throne. At the same time, the authorities apprehended a monk of the Chudov monastery in Moscow, who publicly claimed that, in the new tsar Dmitry, he recognized a fugitive Chudov monk, Grigory (Yuri) Otrepiev. In the early spring of 1606 a band of Terek Cossacks was pondering where to head for raids that year: to the Caspian Sea, with the prospect of joining the Persian service afterward, or to the Volga

River. They chose the second option, and to protect themselves from the persecution of the authorities, they decided to declare the young Cossack Ileika "Little Ilya" Korovin "Prince Petr Fyodorovich"—the nonexistent grandson of Ivan IV and nephew of the no less fictional ruling tsar Dmitry. Having learned about the "nephew," the tsar did not publicly declare him an impostor and did not secretly order that his band of Cossacks be exterminated. Instead, he sent a messenger with a letter inviting "Petr Fyodorovich" to Moscow, where the newly emerged prince should either prove his case or "retire." This story demonstrates that by the beginning of 1606, the very concept of "impostor" had lost its original meaning of stigma. Although everyone knew that Ivan IV's son Fyodor was childless and hence no "Petr Fyodorovich" could exist, declaring the Cossack Ileika an impostor was like mentioning rope in the house of a man who has been hanged (to quote Sancho Panza from Miguel de Cervantes's famous novel published just months earlier). More importantly, the main problem was not that someone could be fooled by the impostor unless he was exposed by the authorities. It was the very ability of a random nobody to mobilize supporters that presented a central political challenge and signified the remarkable evolution of the Muscovite political system since Ivan IV's death.

Following the crystallization of "supreme power" as an autonomous phenomenon and its separation from the traditional ruling dynasty, a crude competitive political system emerged in Muscovy. If power was no longer the prerogative of one, it could be claimed by many. No institutional framework could accommodate this system, and not even some formal procedures and a political language capable of expressing the idea of competition among the candidates for the highest office in the land. And yet this competition was becoming a reality, just as the popular readiness to nominate new candidates. The theater of impostors was the only means to frame this new reality. Self-nominated candidates more or less convincingly posed as legitimate contenders for the throne, and were backed by their "constituencies." Followers believed the impostors' stories to the extent that individual candidates were meeting their socioeconomic aspirations. Autocracy based on unanimous support of the "serving people" gave way to the unstable rule of the majority candidate, with the prospect of the social base's further fragmentation.

Self-nominated "Candidates"

On April 24, 1606, the tsar's bride, Marina Mniszech, arrived in Moscow with her father Jerzy Mniszech, a longtime supporter of False Dmitry, accompanied by about 2,000 well-born szlachta and princes from the Rzeczpospolita with their servants and numerous troops. Tsar Dmitry received the long-awaited military reinforcement that was giving him an edge over possible opponents, but lost dramatically in mass support. The huge concentration of armed people in Moscow was a source of constant conflicts, and the fact that these people were foreigners did not help to ease the tensions, thus producing the general impression of a growing confrontation with strangers. Endless feasts and celebrations created a demoralizing atmosphere and undermined social order. On May 6, the wedding of the tsar and Marina Mniszech took place, on May 8, she was crowned as his consort, and on May 9, a multiday

The Tsardom of Muscovy

wedding feast began. There were reports of foreigners committing numerous assaults on locals in the streets and breaking into their houses. The behavior of Russian participants in the feasts was probably no different, but the foreigners were more visible, so the local residents found them much more contemptuous. On May 14, the boyar Vasily Shuisky organized a meeting of loyal supporters. They developed a plan of insurrection and composed a list of houses in which the important foreign guests were staying. The conspirators also must have plotted a palace coup in advance. For military support, they relied on a detachment of servitors from Novgorod and Pskov who were deeply discontent about the order to join an upcoming military campaign in the south.

The insurrection began at dawn on May 17, sparking a large-scale urban riot. The agitated Muscovites murdered more than a thousand foreigners. Amid the general chaos, the conspirators, led by Shuisky, surrounded the palace and killed the tsar. The massive riot provoked by the "Polish offense" was used as cover for a palace coup. Even if, as it is believed, most Muscovites did not want False Dmitry's death, at the critical moment there were not enough supporters around him to protect him from the conspirators.

Only two days later, an urgent meeting of Moscow notables proclaimed itself an assembly of the land and in this capacity elected the boyar Vasily Shuisky as the new tsar. Descending from the princes of Suzdal, the Shuisky clan was the second oldest among the Moscow Rurikids. In the mid-sixteenth century, a representative of this family would have been the most legitimate contender for the throne in the event of the Moscow princely dynasty's interruption. But at the beginning of the seventeenth century, their aristocratic Rurikid status already mattered little. Unlike his predecessors, Vasily Shuisky relied on "the nobles," not "the people" (to borrow Machiavelli's classification), which provided him with a very limited social base and hence limited power. On accession to the throne Shuisky took a special oath, vowing not to make important decisions without the Boyar Duma's general approval. It was said that the boyars manipulated him like a child. Meanwhile, a week after the murder of False Dmitry, rumors spread that amid the confusion of the riot, Tsar Dmitry had miraculously escaped death—again! A new impostor appeared, claiming the name of the first impostor.

Impostors as Systemic Politics

What is most surprising is that the growing political fragmentation did not lead to the disintegration of the country and borderland separatism. All new impostors—self-nominated politicians—came from the southern borderlands—the newly colonized chernozem zone of the former "wild field" in Sloboda Ukraine, the upper reaches of the Don, and the Chernigov and Ryazan regions. After recruiting an army of local servitors, Cossacks, and peasants, all the impostors headed to Moscow. This pattern suggests that the dramatic confrontations of the Time of Troubles involved the entire Muscovy tsardom as a single political space, with the center in the capital. Thus, despite the absurdity of each individual impostor's story, together they reflected a systemic political process oriented toward maintaining the common space rather than toward its fragmentation and rupture.

In the summer of 1606 in Putivl, where False Dmitry spent several months in early 1605 after his military defeat by the government army, a movement began to restore the rule of Tsar Dmitry Ivanovich, who had allegedly escaped death during the Moscow coup in May. At this stage in the political process, the personal presence of the impostor was no longer required: the rebels agreed to believe that the tsar was hiding in the Rzeczpospolita and would return when the capital again swore allegiance to him. The organizers of the movement were the governors of Putivl, Prince Grigory Shakhovskoy, and of Chernigov, Prince Andrey Telyatevsky. Shakhovskoy was a close associate of False Dmitry, so the new tsar Vasily IV Shuisky exiled him from Moscow to remote Putivl. Telyatevsky was a loyal servant of Boris Godunov and an opponent of False Dmitry. He was outraged when Vasily Shuisky, upon ascending to power, accused Godunov of murdering the young Dmitry of Uglich in order to discredit the assassinated Tsar Dmitry. Thus, political opposition to Tsar Vasily Shuisky took the form of a new impostor movement. Its army was headed by Prince Telyatevsky's former military slave, Ivan Bolotnikov, who called himself "[Tsar] Dmitry Ivanovich's supreme commander." Bolotnikov's army was a coalition of different social groups and political forces: there were Cossacks led by the already mentioned Ileika "Prince Petr Fyodorovich" Korovin; musketeers under the command of a Tula petty nobleman, Istoma Pashkov; nobles headed by the Ryazan "boyar's son" (a high-ranking servitor), Prokopy Lyapunov; and bondsmen and peasants, who saw Bolotnikov as their leader. Surprisingly, this most unlikely coalition, which included practically all social strata of Muscovy, held out for almost six months. Bolotnikov's army defeated the government forces and arrived at the walls of Moscow.

Failing to take Moscow's defenders by surprise, Bolotnikov had to launch a protracted siege. Time passed, but Tsar Dmitry did not show up, and the opposition coalition plunged into a political crisis. Without a real candidate to the throne, it was no longer possible to keep the existing conflict of interests at bay and maintain unity. Muscovites could rely neither on institutions, such as the parliament, capable of coordinating diverse group interests, nor on a developed political language and stable concepts that would allow them to discuss the political situation rationally, formulate group demands, and then look for an "interparty" compromise. All these structural underpinnings of modern competitive democratic politics were lacking at the time. Only a leader representing a certain political myth and claiming a high status could personally embody a compromise, but there was no such leader. In the middle of November 1606 the coalition collapsed: most of the noblemen and servitors left Bolotnikov and, in the absence of another leader, joined Tsar Vasily Shuisky. Despite this heavy blow, it took the government troops almost a year to cope with the remnants of Bolotnikov's army, which now represented a radical peasant-Cossack opposition to the "serving people."

In February 1607, Tsar Vasily Shuisky convened another assembly of the land in an attempt to solve the problem of False Dmitry once and for all. The assembly freed the population from the oath to Tsar Dmitry and exonerated those who had violated the oath to Boris Godunov's heirs. This legal measure was ineffective, because people's

The Tsardom of Muscovy

gullibility and blind obedience to the oath were not the roots of the crisis. It was promoted by the growing fragmentation of the "serving people" in the absence of a single popularly recognized candidate for the throne and hence a "program" capable of reconciling the main groups of interests. Ruling on behalf of aristocrats, Shuisky was not seen as such a unifying figure.

A Tale of Two Capitals: Coexisting Political Alternatives

This is why False Dmitry II appeared in the Ukrainian border town of Starodub, in the summer of 1607. He did not physically resemble False Dmitry I, whose erudition and manners he lacked. He may not even have been a Moscow nobleman. It is possible that he was a baptized Jew from the Belarusian town of Shklov in the Grand Duchy of Lithuania. This did not prevent local Muscovite servitors from crossing the border and swearing allegiance to the new self-nominated candidate for the throne. Starodub soon hosted an alternative Boyar Duma and attracted the remnants of Bolotnikov's troops and new volunteers from Muscovy's southern borderlands who formed the army of False Dmitry II. In early September 1607, this army marched to the aid of Bolotnikov, who was besieged by the government forces in Tula, but the army failed to arrive before he was finally defeated. After wintering in Oryol, the army of False Dmitry II headed to Moscow.

Repeating the pattern of Bolotnikov's campaign, the forces of False Dmitry II defeated the government troops, reached Moscow (in June 1608), made a failed attempt to capture the city, and then set up a camp in Tushino, about ten miles from the Kremlin. Only this time, the opposition army was headed by a nominally qualified contender for the throne. Therefore, instead of disintegrating, the Tushino Camp became the country's parallel capital. It featured a royal palace, where False Dmitry II received foreign ambassadors and his subjects; its own Boyar Duma; and even a seat of its own Patriarch of Moscow. Fyodor Romanov, who became the monk Filaret by order of Godunov and was promoted to metropolitan of Rostov by Tsar Dmitry, was declared patriarch by False Dmitry II. The coins minted under the Tushin government had a higher content of silver than the government money. Muscovy's northeastern territories from Kaluga and Kostroma to Velikiye Luki and Pskov swore allegiance to False Dmitry II, while the west (Smolensk) and the vast Kazan territory supported the Moscow government. This clear geographical demarcation was not yet a sign of the country's territorial split: the two alternative capitals were located just ten miles apart, as close as possible for two entities to occupy the same symbolic space without interfering with each other. False Dmitry II declared neither Oryol nor Pskov as his capital, and in his camp near Moscow, he reproduced the entire administrative and social structure of Muscovy.

A distinctive feature of the movement headed by False Dmitry II was its dependence on the military force from the Polish–Lithuanian Commonwealth and Cossacks. False Dmitry I had also begun his campaign with the Polish–Lithuanian mercenaries and szlachta volunteers, but most of them abandoned him halfway to Moscow. He owed his political and military success entirely to the "serving people" of Muscovy. By contrast, historians assess the share of Muscovites in the fall of 1607 at less than 10 percent

(2,000) of False Dmitry II's army. They were greatly outnumbered by 12,000 volunteers from the Polish–Lithuanian Commonwealth and 8,000 Zaporozhian Cossacks. After that the number of Rzechpospolita cadres only increased: numerous szlachta and even some magnates accompanied by hundreds of supporters who had participated in the Sandomierz rokosz (the armed opposition to King Sigismund III) and lost their cause, fled to Muscovy. In the spring of 1608, the ataman Ivan Zarutsky brought about 5,000 Don Cossacks to Tushino. In August 1608, the member of an important szlachta clan, Jan Sapieha, joined False Dmitry II at the head of 1,720 soldiers. In December 1608, a council of ten elected representatives of the Polish–Lithuanian troops became the real government in the Tushino Camp.

Vasily Shuisky's government was no less dependent on the foreign troops. In the summer of 1608 it reached an agreement with King Sigismund III, who promised to recall all subjects of the crown from the camp of False Dmitry II. When it became clear that the king did not have such power over the szlachta, the Moscow government took a radical step. On August 10, 1608, Vasily Shuisky sent a letter to the Swedish King Charles IX asking for military assistance. In February 1609, the two sides signed an agreement in Vyborg that stipulated the transfer to Sweden of the Korela fortress "and its district." In exchange, the Swedish king promised to send 15,000 mercenaries to Moscow, to be paid by the Shuisky government.

The latter detail is very telling, as was the accelerating "internationalization" of the political process in Muscovy in general. Private armies of foreigners fought on both sides because, with the important exception of the Don Cossacks, few people in Muscovy were willing to fight. In the spring of 1609, the Moscow government's general, Prince Mikhail Skopin-Shuisky, was able to recruit only 5,000 men in the Novgorod land. The 15,000 Swedish mercenaries were attached to this nominally Russian army to confront the nominally Russian army of False Dmitry II. Obviously, the Moscow government had the money to pay the soldiers, but almost no soldiers were left. The serving nobility—the backbone of Muscovy's professional army—did not just split into parties supporting different candidates for the throne. The noblemen "service people" began rapidly losing their social identity and motivation because their status as full-fledged "citizens" could be validated only through service to an undisputed autocratic ruler. During the period of *smuta*—confusion and ambiguity—the noblemen lost any reason to serve as well as the economic possibility of doing so. No longer representing the absolute supreme power, they had no authority to force the peasants to work for them.

Peasants fled from the estates or joined the impostors' armies, and neither the Moscow nor the Tushino government could prevent it. About ten "princes" of clearly peasant background had arrived at various times in the camp of False Dmitry II posing as his "relatives." All these "princes"—Avgust, Lavrenty, Martyn, Klementy, Semyon, Savely, Vasily, Eroshka, and Gavrilka—specialized in robbing rich landowners. To become a robber, there was no need to claim a high title or be recognized by the main impostor. Therefore, the pilgrimage of minor impostors to False Dmitry II was a clear political gesture on their behalf and a sign that the field of competitive politics had expanded so much that now it included self-nominated Cossack and peasant candidates. Simultaneously, the original main political class of servitors began to erode, being increasingly replaced by former marginals—foreigners and commoners.

In Search of an "Assembly Point"

The unprecedented expansion of the political sphere allowed even bondsmen and serfs to join it as full actors by nominating and supporting their own "candidates"—impostors. This revolutionary development took place in a vast tsardom, a political sphere that lacked mechanisms for mediating and coordinating group interests. At some point, the process of uncontrollable political self-organization had reached such a magnitude that most contemporaries (and many historians) began to perceive it as complete chaos. Nevertheless, this chaos still had systemic limitations, for it perpetuated a certain social framework even amid the dismantling old social order.

A new social order crystallizes around an "attractor" or an "assembly point" that serves as the cornerstone of an emerging stable social structure. Theoretically, there was a chance that a truly remarkable political candidate could emerge from the kaleidoscope of impostors, thus becoming an "attractor" for building a new stable political structure. But this scenario did not materialize in Muscovy. In a series of battles in 1609, the troops of the Moscow tsar defeated the forces of the Tushino tsar. Finally, on December 11, 1610, False Dmitry II was killed by the head of his bodyguards in Kaluga. Simultaneously, the Moscow boyars disposed of their protégé Vasily Shuisky, whose unpopularity made him a toxic asset. In July 1610, an assembly of the land convoked in Moscow declared Shuisky deposed and forced him to retreat to a monastery. The assembly elected the eldest son of King Sigismund III, Władysław, as the new tsar. Apparently, the Moscow boyars attempted to break out of the vicious circle of domestic impostors and acquire a guaranteed genuine royal. This, however, did not make Władysław any more legitimate in the eyes of the majority. The new tsar "Vladislav Zhigmontovich" (Władysław, Sigizmund's son) did not come to Moscow and was not officially crowned, in part, because he refused to convert to Orthodoxy. Thus, he was added to the list of impostors. The provisional boyar government in Moscow that ruled after Shuisky—the traditional seven-member *semiboyarshchina* of the interregnum period—discredited itself, too, by acting as a collective impostor. Almost immediately after False Dmitry II's death, at the beginning of 1611, False Dmitry III appeared in Novgorod, followed by False Dmitry IV in Astrakhan. The former was supported by the northwest of the country, and the latter by the entire Lower Volga region in the southeast. In March 1611, the acting governor of the Kazan region, boyar Bogdan Belsky, who believed that any Moscow government should be obeyed, was killed by a rioting crowd. The new head of the vast province, who had instigated the riot, the city clerk Nikanor Shulgin, insisted that the population swear allegiance to False Dmitry II, who had been killed three months earlier. Essentially, this meant refusing to recognize the authority of any acting central government. Indeed, Shulgin conducted an independent policy in relation to neighboring regions and refrained from any participation in Muscovy's common political space. He became the first powerful "politician" who was not interested in Moscow as the location and symbol of supreme power, and who deemed it unnecessary to legitimize his autonomous status in the form of an impostor.

Thus, in 1611, the first serious cracks appeared, running across Muscovy's common political space, which had never received a broadly recognized unifying leader. Apparently, there was no populist program or even a popular message that new political candidates could offer to their increasingly fragmented constituencies. When it seemed that the centrifugal forces had finally prevailed, the mechanisms of societal self-organization stumbled upon a new format for collective action, gradually abandoning the exhausted impostor paradigm. The shift was prompted by the changed political context that resulted when the invasion of foreign armies was no longer framed as supporting a legitimate domestic contender for the throne. In September 1609 King Sigismund III of Poland invaded Muscovy. He was outraged by the Vyborg treaty between Vasily Shuisky and Charles IX of Sweden, with whom Sigismund was waging a protracted war in the Baltic, and by the appearance of the Swedish troops in Muscovy as a potential "second front" in that war. The crown army besieged Smolensk. A year later, in the fall of 1610, after Shuisky was deposed and Sigismund's son Władysław was elected as tsar, a Polish–Lithuanian garrison was allowed into Moscow to maintain order in anticipation of the prince's arrival.

The Common Enemy as the Foundation for Societal Self-organization

The Swedish mercenaries plundering the northwest of the country and the occupation of Smolensk and Moscow by the Polish–Lithuanian army sparked popular indignation that united the hitherto polarized Muscovites. January 1611 witnessed the formation of yet another coalition of servitors from Ryazan, as well as the Volga and Siberian towns, including Tatar mirzas (aristocrats). This time, the base of the movement was Nizhny Novgorod in the Middle Volga, which had been little affected by the previous events of the *smuta*, and the goal was different compared to earlier marches on the capital. What united this league, known as the first People's Militia (*narodnoe opolchenie*), was not a common political candidate but a common enemy: the foreign troops. The People's Militia reached Moscow but failed to drive out the Polish–Lithuanian garrison. The coalition then convened a very inclusive assembly of the land that appointed a new government, representing the interests of various groups—boyars, servitors, and Cossacks. The coalition collapsed in the summer of 1611 due to rivalry between the Cossack and noblemen leaders.

As soon as the news reached Nizhny Novgorod in the fall of 1611, the second People's Militia began forming there. This time the initiative belonged to the Nizhegorod city authorities, supported by the merchants, servitors, and other townspeople. A tradesman and elected municipal official, Kuzma Minin, took charge of the campaign's logistics. He organized efficient mass-scale fundraising, which allowed him to pay high salaries to all the militia members. Prince Dmitry Pozharsky, a veteran of the first People's Militia, took charge of the military command. Nizhny Novgorod had avoided economic ruin during the protracted *smuta*, so it had the money for a military campaign but lacked the manpower. In the city, Minin was able to hire only 700 professional soldiers, of whom 200 were prisoners—"Germans, Lituans, and Tatars." The accumulated funds allowed him to attract more than 2,000 additional servitors from other lands. In contrast to earlier campaigns, militia members received compensation for their service from the leaders of the militia rather than acting on behalf of autonomous military formations with their own additional interests. At the end of winter 1612, the second People's Militia set out from Nizhny Novgorod and moved up the Volga. They stayed until midsummer in Yaroslavl, 150 miles northeast of Moscow, formed a new government, and began an active publicity campaign by conducting energetic diplomatic and domestic correspondence. In this regard, the story of the second militia repeated the story of False Dmitry, who had spent several months in Putivl avoiding military engagements with the enemy: in both cases, political authority and popular recognition were the results of the moral authority of the movement and "propaganda by deed" rather than military victories. In the fall of 1612, the militia forces succeeded in expelling the Polish–Lithuanian garrison from Moscow, deposing the seven-member boyar government, and driving the regular troops of Sigismund III, numerous gangs of robbers, Cossacks, and other armed people from the central regions of the country. In the winter of 1613 a large-scale assembly of the land was convened, which elected the new tsar: Mikhail Fyodorovich Romanov, the sixteen-year-old son of the boyar Fyodor Romanov, now Patriarch Filaret.

Lessons of the Crisis and a New Political Beginning

The restoration of the country's political and economic stability and the settlement of relations with neighboring countries took several years, but the systemic integrity of Muscovy's political space was restored in a relatively short time. Although still happening, the popular uprisings and Cossack raids had lost their political nature and the ability to mobilize wider population besides those immediately involved in the action. Impostors, as self-nominated candidates to supreme power, had disappeared from the public arena. Autocratic (sovereign) supreme power was restored in a new format: in 1613–1622, three assemblies of the land succeeded one another, each convened for a three-year term. They were almost permanently in session, so the new tsar, Mikhail Romanov, could discuss important political matters with the assembly and present the most important decisions for its approval, especially the unpopular ones, such as new taxes. This arrangement visualized and implemented a dual mechanism of autocratic supreme power, embodied by a tsar relying on his loyal "serving people." The unusually protracted assemblies of the land helped to rebuild the coherence of the monarchy's social base after almost a decade of sociopolitical turbulence, and gradually restored the legitimacy of the tsar as the absolute ruler recognized by all social groups and all territories. During the transitional period, assemblies of the land helped to reconcile disagreements and allay discontent, allowing the tsar to remain above the conflicts. After 1622, assemblies of the land were convoked after increasingly long intervals, for shorter periods, and only on especially important occasions, in full accordance with the political model set by Ivan IV.

The successful restoration of the Muscovy tsardom's political "constitution" did not mean that the Time of Troubles was merely a brief hiatus in the normal operation of the system, as can be assumed by looking at the formal results of the smuta. Assemblies of the land did not acquire autonomy as a distinct branch of power, and the tsar's unlimited authority was restored. However, one can see that the very understanding of power had changed, and the profound political crisis of 1604–13 was both a result of this change and a mechanism of its collective comprehension by "living through it." The bloody practical experience of the smuta substituted for whole libraries of treatises and political pamphlets, and spontaneously formed a new political culture that compelled Muscovites to think about the institutionalization of power—that is, about the creation of a state in the modern sense. Most immediately, the systemic crisis taught its observers and participants several important lessons about early modern politics.

First of all, it publicly revealed the anatomy of supreme power. Assemblies of the land in their solemn resolutions as well as the patriarchs of Moscow in their epistles tried hard to sacralize individual rulers as "chosen" exceptional personalities. Despite these attempts, practical life experience between the election of Ivan IV's legitimate heir, Fyodor Ivanovich in 1584 and the pledging of allegiance to False Dmitry IV or Prince Eroshka almost two decades later, had proven otherwise. The tsar's sacral power was an attribute of the office and not of a particular individual, much less of a family (dynasty). This did not necessarily mean the desacralization of supreme power. To the contrary, the very differentiation of power as an autonomous phenomenon, separate from clan seniority or property, only reinforced its mysterious nature. Perhaps it was precisely faith in the divine origins of true power that explained why there were so many impostors of all ranks during the Time of Troubles. Their titles and stories might have been totally incredible and ridiculous, but the people still took a chance on them, displaying irrational trust in God's ways.

Second, it became clear that whatever the origins of this mystical phenomenon, power was not acting by itself. Power was subject to a deliberate application and could be used wisely or wasted hopelessly. Boris Godunov's reign is a case in point. According to the traditional view of the tsar as merely a conduit of divinity, Godunov's failure could be explained only by his bad luck or grave sins (such as the alleged murder of Prince Dmitry in Uglich). But the Time of Troubles demonstrated on many occasions that in the end, the good judgment and responsible decision making of the people in power determined the outcome of political struggle. Thus a new type of thinking about politics emerged involving rational planning and the anticipation of various possible consequences. Moreover, for a brief period, far ahead of its time, a sphere of competitive mass politics even emerged. At the beginning of the seventeenth century, there were no institutional and cultural prerequisites for sustaining this phenomenon, which threatened to dismantle the very foundation of Muscovy's social order. However, the explosive political situation was masterfully defused in the end by the leaders of the second People's Militia and by a general readiness to restart the political system from zero, by electing a teenage tsar with no political past and obliging him to rule in cooperation with the assembly of the land. The events of 1612–13 demonstrated a genuine art of politics that was applied quite consciously and skillfully. This was the main result of the Time of Troubles' "political education."

The first People's Militia took a radical step in 1611 by rejecting the pattern of political mobilization around the figure of an impostor, even though its leaders had been personally associated with various impostors in the past. The second People's Militia (1612), organized by Minin and Pozharsky, took this new political strategy one step farther by relying, as a unifying factor, on a clearly formulated political program—liberation of the country from foreigners—rather than on a charismatic leader. The second People's Militia also established its legitimacy by state-building rather than through battles. The movement's leaders themselves were little known, and they publicly stated their goal from the outset: to elect a new tsar at the assembly of the land, taking into account the interests of various groups. In other words, this movement fought for the restoration of supreme power as an anonymous institution. The significant role of the modest Nizhegorod entrepreneur and local official, Kuzma Minin, and his popularity among his contemporaries are quite telling in this regard. Minin neither posed as a fake prince nor sacrificed his life to save the legitimate tsar— the usual path to glory for a commoner. Neither a boyar nor even a nobleman, all he did was fundraising for the military campaign and supervising its logistics. The fact that Muscovites were capable of appreciating the importance of this inconspicuous role, which would have been hard to imagine just ten years earlier, testifies to the spread of a new understanding of public service as state-building.

The role of impostors as political candidates became redundant in a society that accepted a vision of power as an anonymous institution that was formalized through the assemblies of the land and nascent bureaucratic apparatus. Now the ruler's identity, true or false, mattered less than the procedure that led to the highest office. Likewise, the transformation of the assemblies of the land into a permanent political body during the period of transition was a truly unprecedented political decision. Its matter-of-fact acceptance at the time suggests that no matter who proposed this idea, it must have received broad support and understanding.

The third immediate result of the Time of Troubles was the explication of the country's internal cohesion and external borders as dissociated from the dynasty. Contrary to Jerome Horsey's reasonable expectations, it turned out that Muscovy's unity rested not solely on the will of a powerful ruler. The impostors' attempts to occupy Moscow showed that they apparently perceived Muscovy's political space as one whole, controlled from the capital. Even at the peak of political chaos, with several equally legitimate governments simultaneously ruling the country, no borderland region seceded.

Besides the new political imagination, patriotism played a role in maintaining Muscovy's territorial integrity. This patriotism did not necessarily imply solidarity with coreligionists and fellow Russians and the xenophobic rejection of foreigners, as can be discerned in the rhetoric of the period's literary texts and in modern historical studies. Indeed, since the outbreak of the crisis in 1604, private armies of foreigners, primarily subjects of the Polish–Lithuanian Commonwealth, had raided Muscovy on behalf of various impostors. This was a destabilizing factor greatly irritating the local population, but it is unclear how much the popular perception of foreign troops differed from their perception of various domestic military formations, at least until King Sigismund III's intervention and the occupation of Smolensk and Moscow. Shuisky's murderous riot against the foreigners who came to Moscow for Tsar Dmitry's wedding in May 1606 was hardly a manifestation of some systematic Russian xenophobia. No such xenophobia prevented mass support of False Dmitry II, who relied almost exclusively on the szlachta army. Any clear-cut opposition between the locals and foreigners was problematic, as even religion and language could not serve as clear markers of groupness. A significant part of the szlachta participating in Muscovy's political crisis were Ruthenian-speaking Orthodox Christians, and thus not significantly different from the local population in cultural terms. Among the "patriotic" forces, the Tatar mirzas from the Qasimov Khanate and the Kazan territory played a prominent role, and there is evidence that Kozma Minin might have been the son of a baptized Tatar. Irrespective of the real or imagined cultural distance, the marauding Cossacks or servitors were hardly more cherished by the Muscovite population than the marauding "Poles" or "Swedes." On the other hand, even the leaders of the second People's Militia, who deliberately used the rhetoric of patriotism to mobilize supporters, saw nothing wrong in inviting foreign princes to the Moscow throne. During their four-month stay in Yaroslavl, they negotiated with the Swedish king the possibility that his brother Prince Charles Philip might become the next tsar, and with the Holy Roman emperor the prospect that his cousin might be the candidate for the throne. After Mikhail Romanov was elected tsar, his father, Patriarch Filaret, attempted to arrange his marriage first to a Danish princess, then to a Swedish one. So "patriotism" did not necessarily imply the xenophobic rejection of foreigners and exceptional love for everything domestic. Rather, this vaguely defined term referred to the completely new experience of rallying around a state as a political institution, instead of around the ruler's personality. No available language was capable of expressing this form of modern solidarity, hence familiar if misleading categories of commonality were used, such as the "Orthodox faith" or "Russian land."

The factor of mutual economic interest manifested itself much more clearly. Representatives of the southern borderlands—the Sloboda Ukraine, Chernigov, Ryazan, and the Don regions—had played an exceptional role during the Time of Troubles. Their mass discontent fueled the crisis, carrying a double message: utter dissatisfaction with the Moscow government and eagerness to support a new one that would understand their concerns. Living under the constant threat of raids from the Crimean Khanate, these people needed economic support and protection from the rest of the country. The Don and Terek Cossacks also viewed Muscovy's inner regions as an important economic resource, albeit in a different sense: as an object of looting. The story of "Prince Ileika" is very telling in this regard. When pondering the direction of the next campaign—to the south or to the north, to the Caspian Sea or up the Volga River—the Cossacks decided that it was more profitable to rob Muscovites than Persians. This perfectly rational choice must have been made for reasons that Nizhny Novgorod became the champion of the movement for state-building and unification. After the Muscovite servitors had established control over Western Siberia, the first decade of the seventeenth century witnessed the emergence of a steady flow of precious Siberian furs across the Urals, which galvanized the Volga trade route. The Makaryev fair fifty miles down the Volga from Nizhny Novgorod became Muscovy's main marketplace and a key intermediary in the transcontinental trade between India and Persia in the southeast and England and continental Europe in the northwest. The furs, reaching the Volga along the Kama River or via alternative northern paths, were traded in both directions. In the financial year 1611–12, during the preparation and dispatch of the second militia, 6,500 rubles in customs duties and taxes were collected in Nizhny Novgorod. In 1614, after relative political stabilization, this amount exceeded 12,000 rubles, and by 1619–20 had reached 17,000 rubles. The Volga fur trade attracted the predatory Cossacks, generated high revenues for the Volga cities, and made them vitally interested in maintaining political stability and economic security across the entire Muscovy. Units of armed men raiding on behalf of domestic impostors or foreign kings in the vicinities of Astrakhan, Novgorod, and Smolensk obstructed trade with Persia, Northern Europe, and the Polish–Lithuanian Commonwealth. The economic interests of the Volga cities, large monasteries, landowners, and servitors coincided: without the restoration of the central government in one form or another, it was impossible to conduct trade, return peasant laborers to the ruined estates, or receive salaries from the government.

The Time of Troubles became a turning point in the political self-organization of the region. It formed a new understanding of power in Muscovy and explicated the need for its institutionalization in the form of a "state" as an autonomous institution largely unaffected by the personality of a ruler, whether a legitimate one or an impostor.

The Beginning of Northern Eurasia's Integration

The Discovery of Siberia

Northern Eurasia had never been a single political or socioeconomic space. Perhaps only the Mongol Empire's Western campaign for a short time extended the power of the Great Khan from eastern Siberia to the Carpathians, but even this mostly nominal political unity almost immediately disintegrated into hordes, khanates, principalities, and other vassal and independent political formations. After that time, nobody had enough power (or desire) to repeat the Mongol conquests. However, it turned out that the exploration and conquest of thousands of miles in the continent's heartland did not require a mighty empire with a huge army or even the determination of an ambitious supreme ruler. In the late sixteenth and early seventeenth centuries, in the course of just a few decades, Muscovy managed to establish control over vast territories to the east of the Ural mountain range, which later became known as Siberia. This was possible due to a combination of several factors, of which the tsar's power played the least role.

After the annexation of the Kazan and Astrakhan Khanates, Muscovy assumed the political niche previously occupied by the Golden Horde. At least this is how the changing political landscape was perceived in the Trans-Ural khanates. Officially, as in the case of the Siberian khan Yadigar in 1555, and unofficially, Moscow was recognized as the suzerain and senior ulus of the former Great Horde. This status gave the newcomers from the European part of the continent the aura of legitimate conquerors. They were attracted by Siberia's rich natural resources—first of all, furs—and the archaic political organization of a relatively small population. Soldiers, who had been seasoned in battles with regular armies in Livonia or at Smolensk, did not even need a centralized command for successful military operations as bands of volunteers in breaking the resistance of local tribal militias. It was of no less importance that the colonizers had not been exposed to the Reformation (and the Counter-Reformation)—that is, to the new social thinking that manifested itself in these religious movements. Unlike the

Spanish, French, and British colonialists in South and North America, who perceived the world through the polarizing confessional prism of the Counter-Reformation and Reformation, the Muscovites in Siberia did not draw clear boundaries between themselves and the Other. This did not make their colonization any less brutal or force them to close their eyes to their differences from local peoples. They just did not systematize or politicize these numerous differences, which left room for pragmatic alliances and cooperation.

There were other important differences between the colonizations of Siberia and the New World. First, unlike in the Americas, Muscovite Cossacks and servitors did not find completely unfamiliar and fundamentally alien societies, languages, or religions beyond the Ural Mountains. For them, the peoples of Siberia were part of the post–Golden Horde world, to which Muscovy itself belonged. Furthermore, in the seventeenth century, the primary purpose for pursuing Siberia's conquest and political control was its thin population, rather than its territory, insofar as the agricultural technologies of the day made the use of central and eastern Siberia's land resources difficult. The natives of Siberia were indispensable for their skills as hunters of valuable fur animals. Making them pay the *yasak*—the annual tribute in furs—was the main goal and key economic driver behind Siberian expansion and the institution of a special regime for governing the conquered peoples. Under this regime, the native elites preserved much of their administrative authority and judicial power. It was unprofitable to destroy the local populations and drive them from their lands. On the contrary, the crown authorities in Moscow were extremely concerned about protecting the natives from overly zealous, greedy colonialists.

The largely spontaneous colonization of lands beyond the Urals expanded Moscow's nominal sovereignty to the taiga and tundra belt of Northern Eurasia, turning Muscovy from a regional eastern European power into a continental empire and bringing it into contact with the Qing Empire, as well as with numerous steppe polities of the Kyrgyz, Kazakhs, Dzungars, and the Altan Khans in Mongolia. By the mid-eighteenth century, Siberian expansion would lead to the establishment of Russia's colonies in North America and advancement into the steppe zone of Central Asia. Of no less importance was Siberia's economic significance as a reservoir of natural resources, primarily expensive furs. In the seventeenth century sable pelts became the hard currency of Muscovy, which lacked known sources of precious metals of its own. Since the first decade of the seventeenth century, western Siberia became a destination for peasant colonization, which eventually reached a scale of mass resettlement. The very vastness of Siberian expanses served as an important territorial resource, making it an almost inexhaustible rear of Moscow.

Siberian Encounters: The Stroganovs, the Siberian Khans, and the Cossacks

The conquest of what would later be called "Siberia" began as an outreach of commercial activities by the Stroganov family, who controlled the production and trade of salt in the northeast of the Moscow lands. The Stroganovs apparently came from Novgorod and its northern colonies. In the fifteenth century, they settled in Solvychegodsk, about

The Tsardom of Muscovy

400 miles southeast of Archangelsk. In the sixteenth century, Ivan IV granted the Stroganovs territories along Muscovy's farthest eastern flank, in the upper reaches of the Kama River and along the Chusovaya River. According to the 1558 charter, in these lands, Grigory Stroganov was instructed

> to start a town in a safe and secure location, placing canons and handguns on the walls and having gunners and gatekeepers to arrange for protection from the Nogai people and from other hordes. He should clear forest around that town, along rivers and lakes, and up to the summits; plow the fields in the town's vicinity; build houses; and people who were unregistered [as heads of households] and did not carry service obligations should be broadly invited to this town.

As soon as the Stroganovs established themselves in the western Cis-Urals, their commercial empire immediately came into contact with the Siberian Khanate, one of the heirs of Jochi's Ulus. The khanate was ruled alternately by representatives of the Shaybanid clan—descendants of Jochi's fifth son, Shaybani, and the Taybugids—who were most likely representatives of the non-Chinggisid aristocracy of the steppe. In the mid-sixteenth century, the Taybugid khan Yadigar was fighting for power with Shaybanid rivals, in particular with Kuchum, the son of Khan Murtaza II of Bukhara. Kuchum's frequent raids forced Yadigar to seek Muscovy's protection by sending tribute and a letter pledging a vassal oath to Moscow. This did not help him much, and in 1563, Kuchum seized the Taybugid capital Isker and killed Yadigar. The Bukharan Shaybanids established their rule of Siberian Khanate. [3]

Judging by the available fragmentary information, the Shaybanid Khanate was a typical steppe polity. The khan of Chinggisid descent relied on the Turkic-speaking aristocracy from all over the former Jochi's Ulus—the Kazakh and Nogai hordes, Bashkir yurts, and emigrants from Bukhara, Kazan, Astrakhan, and even Crimea. The khanate's main economic resource was the tribute in furs collected from the subordinate Mansi, Khanty, and Turkic-speaking peoples. The furs were sold through Astrakhan and, after its conquest by Ivan IV, through Bukhara, whose merchants were active in Siberia. Essentially, the Siberian Khanate performed as a commercial enterprise aimed at the most cost-efficient and sustainable extraction of precious furs for sale. The political-economic mechanism worked regardless of the ruling clan, be it the Taybugids, the Shaybanids, or later the Muscovite administrators.

After Yadigar had recognized Muscovy's suzerainty, his rival Kuchum began attacking other territories ruled by the tsar—the Perm land and the Kazan territory. The extension of the Stroganovs' commercial empire to the western Urals region made their towns and salterns the primary target of Kuchum's raids. Apparently, in order to stop these raids, the Stroganovs organized a military expedition against Kuchum's nomad camps along the Tobol and Irtysh, hiring a group of Cossacks led by the Livonian War's veteran Yermak (?–1585). Having received general instructions and supplies, the Cossacks were left to their own devices in the vast and unexplored expanses of Western Siberia. Finding and defeating the natives of this region was possible only with the help of other locals. The available historical sources suggest that Yermak's team of Cossacks included Tatars, Bashkirs, "Germans" (most likely Swedish prisoners of war), and

274 New Imperial History of Northern Eurasia

"Lituans," that is, previous subjects of the Polish–Lithuanian Commonwealth. They were supported by Yadigar's former allies among the local Tatars, Khanty, and Mansi. Who Yermak was remains a mystery. According to one version, he was of Don Cossack origin, according to another, he came to the Urals from the Novgorod colonies near Arkhangelsk, and according to a third, he was a baptized Kama Tatar. Theoretically, the name Yermak can be derived from the Russian name Yeremey (Jeremy), although he was never mentioned under this full name. It seems more plausible that his was the widespread Turkic name Yermek or the Alan name Yrmag, common in the Don steppes.

Siberia's Active Conquest and Resistance

In the fall of 1581, Yermak's motley party of about 800 soldiers went up the Chusovaya River on the western slopes of the Urals, overwintered at the Tagil mountain pass, and in the spring of 1582 descended the Urals' eastern slopes along the Tagil River to find themselves in western Siberia. During the spring and summer of 1582, Yermak's troops moved eastward down the Tura River across the Siberian Khanate, successfully repelling the attacks of its minor begs (chiefs). On November 4, 1582, in a decisive battle with Kuchum's main forces—mostly from Bukhara, along with local tribal militias of Mansi and Khanty—the Muscovites took over and Kuchum fled to the steppe. During the battle, local warriors abandoned Kuchum, which indicates the weakness of the Shaybanid power. On November 8, Yermak seized the khanate's capital Isker (also known as Sibir and Qashliq) at the confluence of the Irtysh and Tobol Rivers, not far from modern Tobolsk.

Given the loose political organization of the Siberian Khanate, military success and even the occupation of the capital did not yet mean the khanate's complete submission. In 1583, Yermak continued military operations, subjugating numerous Tatar mirzas and Mansi and Khanty princelings. Their submission followed a standard procedure. The armed people acting on behalf of the tsar forced the local population to pay annual yasak in furs. The "best people"—begs and princelings—swore allegiance (*shert'*) to the tsar, which was worded according to local customs. The loyalty of subordinated peoples was ensured by taking representatives of local elite hostages (*amanats*).

After defeating Kuchum, Yermak dispatched a Cossack ataman, Ivan Koltso, to Moscow with the collected yasak, and asked Ivan IV to accept the newly conquered territory and appoint a governor to administer it. The tsar appreciated this initiative: he pardoned all past crimes committed by the members of Yermak's team and sent Prince Semyon Bolkhovsky as the governor to Isker, accompanied by 300 musketeers. They brought salaries for Yermak's people and ammunition, but apparently no food supplies. Reaching their destination in November 1583, Bolkhovsky's detachment did not survive the winter. Although stationed in the forest area, all of them allegedly died of hunger and cold. Soon Yermak was killed in a skirmish on August 6, 1585, and the remnants of his team left Isker and returned to the Stroganovs' territory. But already in 1586, a new unit of 300 musketeers under the command of Vasily Sukin and Ivan Myasnoy arrived from Moscow. They set up a fort in Tyumen on the site of the Tatar settlement Chingi-Tura. A year later, Tobolsk was founded ten miles from the old Isker, followed by the forts of Surgut, Obdorsk, Tomsk, and Mangazeya, which became the northernmost outpost of Siberia's initial colonization. [4]

During the first decade of Siberia's active conquest, just over a thousand volunteer colonizers and even fewer government troops were operating on a territory of almost one million square miles. They were able to cover huge distances and exercise significant political influence due to Siberia's advantageous geographical characteristics: forty major rivers, including the Irtysh, the Yenisei, and the Lena, flow northward, with their often adjacent tributaries forming a network of waterways. Relatively small teams of Cossacks, servitors, and trappers used these waterways to move from one river basin to another across portages. Along the way, they founded new forts and imposed yasak on local tribes scattered along rivers. Already in 1619, the Tobolsk Cossacks founded the Tunguska fort (subsequently Yeniseisk) over a thousand miles away. By the 1630s, operating from bases such as Yeniseisk and Mangazeya, moving along Siberian rivers, Cossacks and servitors founded Bratsk, Irkutsk, and Yakutsk in eastern Siberia. In 1648, the Yakut Cossack Semyon Dezhnev, who built the first fort at the Kolyma River, sailed down the Kolyma into the Arctic Ocean and, circumventing Chukotka, reached the Anadyr River via the Bering Sea. Thus, in just over half a century, small groups of Cossacks and servitors had extended Muscovy's rule to the Pacific coast of Northern Eurasia. This rule was mostly nominal or enforced only within the immediate vicinities of forts separated by hundreds of miles of wilderness. The modern concept of a territorial state prevailing in the European part of Muscovy could not be applied to Siberia in the seventeenth century. Siberia's political space could be compared to that of the early medieval Frankish kingdom: as a set of discrete points—towns, forts, and winter huts—and the waterways connecting them. Cossacks and servitors contacted most local peoples only once a year when collecting the yasak. For some groups, such as, for example, the Yenisei Evenks (Tungus), the arrival of Muscovites only changed the addressee of the yasak payments: they had formerly sent the yasak to the Buryat princelings, but now it was collected on behalf of the tsar. The conquest of Siberia by Muscovy also little affected the lifestyle of nomadic Evenks, although with time this was to change with the proliferation of new goods, especially firearms, alcohol, and bread.

After the defeat of Kuchum, no large polity stood on the path of Muscovite colonization. The fall of the Siberian Khanate created a power vacuum in the forest-steppe zone of the region. The sedentary and nomadic tribes of the Turkic and Samoyedic peoples became the object of the systematic expansion or raids of the Yenisei Kyrgyz, the Dzungars, and the Altan Khans in Western Mongolia. The princelings of smaller tribes and clans themselves often sought the protection of distant Moscow against the raids of nomads. For example, the foundation of the Tomsk fortress on the lands of the Eushta Tatars followed the Eushta prince Toyan's mission to Moscow. In 1603, he petitioned Boris Godunov to accept his clan "under the sovereign's high hand," to build a fort on the Tom River and staff it with the tsar's servitors. In exchange for protection and patronage, Toyan promised to pay the yasak. He also tried to interest Moscow in the area with stories about numerous neighboring tribes and clans that could become a source of even greater yasak.

The foundation of Tomsk in 1604 led to new contacts and clashes between Muscovites and the Yenisei Kyrgyz. Over the next two decades, their camps became the target of repeated campaigns by Tomsk servitors and Cossacks. Aimed at subjugation of the Turkic and Samoyedic peoples of the region, these campaigns were accompanied by systematic plundering and violence. Local peoples retaliated. For instance, in 1614, the Yenisei Kyrgyz devastated the vicinity of Tomsk. Although elites of the Turkic and Samoyedic tribes were often baptized and joined the ranks of Muscovy servitors, during the seventeenth century, Siberia remained a giant battleground. Small groups of Cossacks and servitors regularly raided the camps of nomads, returning to their forts with the yasak that they regarded more as their personal loot than regular tribute to the government.

Colonization: Collaboration, Violence, and Tensions between the Tsardom and Its Colonial Agents

In the 1620s, the servitors and Cossacks from Yeniseisk and Mangazeya began to explore the basins of the Kamennaya Tunguska and Vilyui Rivers, and by the 1630s—the Angara and Lena Rivers. They received information about new lands from the conquered tribes. So, in 1621, the Yeniseisk servitors heard from an Evenk princeling about the river Ilin (Lena): allegedly, it was navigated by ships armed with guns, and prosperous cattle breeders Yaka (Yakuts) lived along its banks. Just a decade later, in 1632, the team of Petr Beketov, one of the most famous Siberian conquistadors of the seventeenth century, founded the Yakutsk fort on the Lena River. Operating from this new outpost, the Cossacks and servitors began to establish winter huts for collecting the yasak from the Yakuts and Evenks, and later, in the 1640s and 1650s, from the Buryats. Here, in eastern Siberia, the colonialists encountered larger peoples: the Yakuts and the Buryats numbered 20,000–25,000 people and could put up serious resistance. The Yakut toyons (princlings) systematically attacked yasak collectors and several times sieged Yakutsk (during 1633–4 and 1638–9). This stubborn resistance was partly explained by the arbitrary violence that followed the founding of Muscovite forts: in the absence of proper coordination, expeditions from Tomsk, Mangazeya, and Yeniseisk often targeted the same settlements requesting the yasak several times a year. Specific norms for the yasak collection and serious control over the legal share to be withheld by collectors and governors were lacking. In the absence of institutional political control, the obedience of the local population was ensured by means of the ancient steppe practice of taking amanats: relatives of the "best people" were taken to Muscovite forts to guarantee the loyalty of their kinsmen. Amanats spent many months and even years in forts and often died there, which triggered uprisings of their fellow tribesmen and attacks on the yasak collectors.

The escalating conflicts with the local population forced the tsarist government to take measures to regulate the yasak collection and appease the subjugated peoples. These measures contradicted the interests of the governors and servitors, who behaved as self-appointed lords in the conquered lands, only nominally obeying the supreme suzerain in faraway Moscow. The history of Siberia in the seventeenth century is the story of the tsarist government's attempts to curtail the oppression and plunder of local

The Tsardom of Muscovy

peoples by its agents in Siberia. Besides taking severe disciplinary measures against the most outrageous abuses of power, the government elevated the political status of local elites to restrict the legal sphere of Siberian governors' competence. For instance, in 1676, three princelings of Yakut's largest clan unions (uluses) traveled to Moscow, asking for the right to judge their tribesmen and administer the yasak collection. A tsar's decree confirmed their status as princelings and their right to try petty crimes. By the end of the seventeenth century, the Muscovy state recognized a group of hereditary aristocracy of East Siberian peoples and practically integrated this group into its sociopolitical structure. Local princelings enjoyed broad authority in collecting the yasak, conducting trials for misdemeanors, and administering their tribesmen.

In this respect, there were significant differences between western and eastern Siberia in the seventeenth century. In the west, colonists from the European part of Muscovy arrived in ever-increasing numbers and founded villages and towns, thus making the region virtually indistinguishable from the heartland provinces. In the east of Siberia, the newcomers from the west comprised a tiny fraction of total population. Even in the nineteenth century, settlers from the European part of the country comprised about one-tenth of the indigenous population in the Yakutsk region. Western Siberia could boast an archbishopric and even a metropolia (1688), whereas in eastern Siberia, the first bishopric was established in Irkutsk only in 1706 and remained the only one until the mid-nineteenth century. Demographically and culturally, eastern Siberia was more "indigenous." The government attempted to introduce compulsory cereal farming to provide the forts of east Siberia with locally produced grain, but the harsh climate made peasant techniques of land cultivation totally unsuitable in the new place. The not so numerous peasants who were resettled to the region had to adopt pastoralism from the local population and eventually their entire way of life. By the early eighteenth century, many Russian peasants in eastern Siberia became thoroughly assimilated into the Yakut and Buryat cultures, so, as late as the mid-nineteenth century, the Yakut language was used in the high society of Yakutsk on a par with Russian. For more than a century, eastern Siberia remained a remote and dramatically undergoverned borderland.

Finding Siberia's Boundaries: The Amur Expeditions and the 1689 Treaty of Nerchinsk

Muscovy's spontaneous territorial expansion found its limits after reaching the Pacific Ocean in the east and the Amur River in the south, in Outer Manchuria, which became the object of the Qing Empire's simultaneous northward expansion. In 1643, a servitor, Vasily Poyarkov, headed an exploratory expedition from the newly founded Yakutsk to the Amur River, populated along its upper and middle reaches, respectively, by the Mongol-speaking Daurs and Manchu-speaking Duchers. Poyarkov demonstrated a notoriously ruthless attitude to both the Daurs and the Duchers, as well as to his own subordinates. His actions provoked such fierce resistance among the local population that Poyarkov was forced to sail down the Amur avoiding land all the way to the Sea of Okhotsk and returning to Yakutsk through the territory of the Okhotsk Evenks (Tungus). In 1649, Poyarkov's attempt to reach the Amur was repeated by Yerofei Khabarov, one of the most colorful figures in Siberian history of the seventeenth century. Khabarov was born to a peasant family in the European north. Having accumulated excessive debt, he left his family and moved to Siberia. He became a trapper and a trader in western Siberia, traveling from Tobolsk to Mangazeya, before moving east to the Lena River. There, Khabarov founded the first saltworks in the region in what would later become Ust-Kut, and then built a mill about 150 miles down the Lena River. He successfully experimented with cultivating cereals, sowing twenty-eight acres in 1641. His ambitions and growing wealth brought him into conflict with the corrupt and arbitrary Yakutsk governor, Petr Golovin, who jailed Khabarov for several years. In 1645, Golovin was arrested and brought to Moscow for investigation, and Khabarov was released. Apparently, instead of restoring his ruined business, he persuaded the new governor, the Baltic German Dmitry Frantsbekov (Fahrensbach), to provide government funding for an expedition to the Amur, which took place in 1649–54. During this period, with a detachment of 70 and later 200 volunteers, Khabarov moved down the Zeya River south until its confluence with the Amur, plundering the Daurian and Ducher villages. At some point, disagreements among his men led to an open rebellion, and part of the Cossacks deserted. As a result of robberies and atrocities committed by Khabarov's people, the Daurs and Duchers began to move beyond the Amur under the protection of the Manchus, making the yasak collection impossible. All these became the source of complaints against Khabarov and provoked a standard response from the central government: a plenipotentiary investigator sent from Moscow arrested Khabarov and brought him to the capital to stand trial. Eventually, Khabarov was partially acquitted and promoted to the higher rank of a boyar's son. According to some sources, he was appointed as the administrator of Ust-Kut fort and its county. [5]

Initially, the Manchus showed little concern about the Amur campaigns at the hands of the Muscovite servitors. They were busy establishing the Qing dynasty and spreading its power over the former Ming territories. But in 1685 the Qing emperor sent a significant army of 3,000 to 5,000 with artillery against the fortress of Albazin, a distant Cossack outpost on the Daur territory. After a devastating siege, the fortress commander, Aleksei Tolbuzin, negotiated with the Manchus the garrison's safe retreat to Nerchinsk—Muscovy's main stronghold in the region. Having burned the remaining fortifications, the Manchu army also withdrew, leaving the crops planted around the fortress largely intact. Soon, a detachment of reinforcements from western Siberia arrived in Nerchinsk, but too late to help the Albazin garrison. These troops were commanded by Athanasius von Beyton, a Prussian officer, who entered the Muscovite service and converted to Orthodoxy. He and Tolbuzin decided to restore Albazin. By the summer of 1686, the restored Albazin had a garrison of up to 1,000 troops with enough artillery and provisions to withstand a major siege. The new fortifications designed by von Beyton presented a modern European star fort built of massive earth ramparts. The Manchu army returned to reconquer Albazin, but this time the siege was unsuccessful: the Qing artillery was unable to destroy the sophisticated earthworks, and the siege was lifted in 1687. [6]

In 1689, the 15,000-strong Manchu army approached Nerchinsk, where negotiations between the tsar's ambassador Fyodor Golovin and the Qing representatives took place. The special importance that the Qing emperor attached to these negotiations is evidenced by the fact that they were entrusted to Minister Songgotu, an uncle of the emperor's primary spouse. The Qing delegation also included Jesuit missionaries as experts on Muscovy and interpreters: the Portuguese Tomas Pereira and the Frenchman Jean-Francois Gerbillon. The Nerchinsk treaty of 1689 became the first diplomatic act between the Qing Empire and a European state and the first document formally recognizing Muscovy's Siberian possessions from the standpoint of international law.

The Qing were interested in securing the Amur region from Muscovy's encroachments. Drawing a border where no territorial statehood had ever existed before was a formidable task further complicated by the regular migration of local tribes. The Manchu government was particularly irritated by the Buryat and especially the Hamnigan Buryat clans' accepting the rule of Muscovy despite having traditionally been tributaries of the Manchus. Thus, in 1667, Gantimur (Mongolian Gyn Temor— "iron inside," baptized Petr) and his clan pledged allegiance to the tsar. He became the founder of the Russian princely family of Gantimurovs—a unique case in Siberian history. Gantimur's Hamnigan Buryats formed the core of the Tungus Cossack regiment. The Qing government repeatedly tried to return the baptized Gantimur and insisted on his extradition. During the Nerchinsk negotiations, it was decided "not to discuss the various old cases that had taken place before. The Russian people living in the Middle Kingdom and the Chinese subjects who are in the Russian state should be left to live in the same place." Golovin had to agree to the evacuation of all Muscovite settlements along the Amur and the right bank of the Argun River. The northern line of the Amur watershed (Stanovoy Range) became the border between the two states. Taking into account the very limited geographical knowledge of that time, in practice this meant the creation of a vast buffer zone along the northern bank of the Amur. [7]

The Treaty of Nerchinsk stopped Muscovy's expansion along the Amur, and changed its direction to the northeast. At the beginning of the eighteenth century, the Yakut Cossacks led by Afanasy Shestakov began the brutal conquest of the Kamchatka Peninsula, virtually annihilating the local population. Until the first half of the nineteenth century, the Chukchi in the extreme northeast of Eurasia resisted Russian colonization. They categorically refused to pay the yasak and successfully repelled attempts to establish Russian administration, destroying one military detachment after another. In the eighteenth century Siberian expansion continued southward, to the lands of the Kazakhs. In the mid-nineteenth century, taking advantage of the Qing Empire's weakness, the Russian Empire revised the Nerchinsk treaty and annexed the Amur region.

"Archaic" Colonization, the Integration of Northern Eurasia, and the Construction of Siberia as a Region

At the time when the Rzeczpospolita was disintegrating along ethnoconfessional divides, and the Crimean Khanate was steadily losing its sphere of political control, its neighbor and rival, Muscovy, had tremendously expanded its territory at virtually no cost to the treasury. The main contribution of tsarist power to the expansion was that it refrained from any decisive role in this process. The government did not impose an ideological regime on the annexed territories and only tried to limit the arbitrariness of its official and self-appointed agents. In exchange for the modest sums spent on military equipment and the dispatch of few hundred to several thousand servitors, the crown acquired a colossal material resource. Siberian furs served as a universal currency, the exchange rate of which only increased with global cooling in the seventeenth century. This currency allowed the country to survive the devastation of the Time of Troubles, preserving economic ties and territorial integrity, as well as to finance the creation of modern state institutions. Last but not least, Siberian furs apparently played a role in Muscovy's ability to annex the Cossack Hetmanate, which required putting the incredible register of 60,000 Cossacks on the government's payroll, and brought about another major war with the Polish–Lithuanian Commonwealth.

After Muscovite servitors and Cossacks had claimed the vast territories between the Urals and the Pacific Ocean for the tsar of Muscovy, the process of integrating Northern Eurasia into a single social and economic space began. Integration was accomplished by synthesizing multiple pockets of local knowledge into a single mental map, substantiated by the emerging new transcontinental social and political ties. Siberia acquired spatial boundaries as its expanses were explored by spontaneous colonizers—people of different ethnocultural backgrounds in the service of the tsar. Initially, Siberia was the name of the region just beyond the eastern foothills of the Urals. Soon its application was expanded to the territory all the way to the Irtysh River. Then Siberia came to refer to the entire landmass east of the Urals, to the shores of the Pacific Ocean or the political borders with the Qing Empire and Central Asian Khanates. A word of unclear origin, "Siberia" symbolizes the process of a region's formation through colonization, turning the imagined geography into a real map of connections and contacts, and the mental integration of disparate territories into a single "tsardom." This process, sustained through negotiations with various local groups and borrowing their local knowledge, preceded practical territorial colonization and secured its success.

That is why, in addition to material resources, the exploration and annexation of Siberia gave Muscovites an important cultural advantage over their formidable old rivals—the Polish–Lithuanian Commonwealth and the Crimean Khanate. The political cataclysms and civil wars of the Counter-Reformation proved that the Rzeczpospolita had lost its former ability to accommodate and integrate multicultural populations. Simultaneously, the multilingual Crimean Khanate was gradually transforming into a small Muslim principality. By contrast, throughout the seventeenth century, parallel to the exploration of Siberia, Muscovy had been developing the institutions of the modern state as an anonymous bureaucratic administrative apparatus. Inevitably, Muscovy's state-building incorporated the archaic medieval practices of indirect rule and delegation of powers to local elites: decidedly rejected by other European societies, these practices were a staple of Siberia's administration by the central government. If it were possible to include the Buryat tribes in the system of centralized government without turning them into "Russians" and forcefully baptizing them into Orthodoxy, the same could be done to the populations of Crimea or the Polish–Lithuanian lands, and on the same grounds. Conversely, by the end of the seventeenth century, neither the Rzeczpospolita nor the Crimean Khanate could even hypothetically guarantee the

Muscovy elite the preservation of their former status, lifestyle, and culture if part of their country was annexed. For a while, this remained a purely hypothetical asymmetry between the region's main powers. Only a readjustment of Muscovy's political goals and strategy in Eastern Europe could turn its Siberian experience into a practical advantage.

The Church Schism as a Step toward Unification

The sixteenth century's revolution of social imagination that had been brought about by the Reformation and Counter-Reformation was not limited to purely religious matters. Muscovy participated in this transformation, as can be seen in the final differentiation of "power," "property ownership," "religious authority," and "cultural solidarity" during the Time of Troubles. Curiously, the evolution of the religious sphere in Muscovy followed a reverse order to that in European countries: first, the local version of the Counter-Reformation took place, triggering in response a popular Reformation movement of sorts.

The Zealots of Piety

In 1652, the Metropolitan of Novgorod Nikon (1605–81), a talented and ambitious priest, was elected Patriarch of Moscow. Earlier, he had joined the circle of so-called Zealots of Piety, alongside Stefan Vonifatiyev, the confessor of the second tsar of the Romanov dynasty, Alexei Mikhailovich; protopope (archpriest) Avvakum; as well as Fyodor Rtishchev, a close associate of Tsar Alexei and the top administrator. They sought a regeneration of the church that would draw it closer to the word of God and purify it from earthly vices, errors of individual priests, and liturgical inconsistencies. This program reflected a new perception of social phenomena as representing certain general principles rather than reflecting idiosyncratic individual circumstances and experiences. Following this new logic, any typographically produced, identical copy of the book was seen as representing the same book, unlike a unique manuscript copy that was only a variation of the original text. Similarly, each military governor—*voevoda*— was expected to represent the tsar's will and the law of the land, instead of acting as a regional lord. In any case, this was the social ideal that was gaining increasing currency throughout the seventeenth century.

When the Zealots of Piety applied this perspective to the familiar practices of the Orthodox Church they were dismayed. It appeared that the church rites varied across the country and needed standardization, the priests lacked systematic training, and the entire church hierarchy seemed messy. The vague idea of improving the church that the Zealots of Piety had in mind would be called "modernization" today, while historically it closely resembled the program of the Catholic Counter-Reformation. The main stumbling block was the reference point for the desired transformation. According to Avvakum, it was to be found in the past: in the decisions of the Council of One Hundred Chapters (*Stoglavyi Sobor*, 1551), and in old icons and manuscripts. Unlike him, Nikon and other members of this intellectual circle prioritized the contemporary norms of the Ecumenical Patriarchate of Constantinople. They had been adapted to the realities of the former Rous' Lands by Ukrainian clerics in the Polish–Lithuanian Commonwealth, subordinate to the Patriarch of Constantinople. Hence, in 1648, when Rtishchev founded the "educational" (*uchilishchnyi*) monastery of the Transfiguration, he invited several dozen Ukrainian monks as the instructors. They were graduates of the Kyiv Collegium, a school created by Petr (Petro) Mohyla according to the Jesuit model. Later, Rtishchev's monastery served as the basis for the Slavic Greek Latin Academy, the first higher education establishment in Muscovy.

The Model for the Ideal Church

The real problem was that the ideal church as envisioned by the Zealots of Piety existed neither in Muscovy's past nor in the contemporary Orthodox Christian millet of the Ottoman Empire. Over the sixteen centuries of its existence, institutionalized Christianity had produced numerous pronouncements regarding religious norms but rarely codified the kind of formalities that both Nikon and Avvakum were looking for. The very idea of standardization and its value was as novel as baroque architecture or the concept of military uniforms.

In 1654, Patriarch Nikon sent a list of twenty-seven questions pertaining to the minutiae of worship to the Patriarch Paisius of Jerusalem. The best-known questions or seemingly the most important ones concerned the direction of church processions (clockwise or counterclockwise) and how many fingers to use in crossing oneself. These questions had little to do with proper theological issues. Moreover, it seems that Patriarch Paisius simply could not understand Nikon's "Counter-Reformation" fixation on formal liturgical matters. Perhaps, the Moscow Zealots of Piety were simply too much ahead of the Orthodox authorities in Constantinople and Jerusalem, who continued thinking in particularistic medieval terms. Be that as it may, Paisius did not know how to respond. He wrote to Nikon that the "Greek Church" did not perceive the ritual aspect of religion as truly important and that rituals could vary. Naturally, this was not true. The "Greek Church" was very prescriptive and had a long record of imposing its norms by force through violent conflict. But these norms were neither formalized nor systematically codified. They were transmitted through personal communication and socialization, and hence multiple lacunae and discrepancies were unavoidable. What Nikon wanted was a formalized and detailed "constitution," which none of the top Orthodox hierarchs had thought of.

Nikon's Reforms

As a result, Nikon and his associates resolved to systematize the "church rites" according to their own ideas. They decided that the compulsory norm required using three fingers to make the sign of the cross, and rejected the two-finger custom prevailing in Muscovy. The Moscow reformers also borrowed the Constantinople clerics' clothes and hairstyle, as presumably reflecting the true norm. This was how the *kalimavkion* (Russian *kamilavka*), a stiff cylindrical head covering worn by Ottoman Orthodox Christian priests and monks, became a mandatory element of Muscovite clerical attire, together with a long haircut. The proclaimed goal was to bring the Russian Orthodox Church into compliance with the Byzantine standard, but the identification of this ideal with contemporary practices of the "Greek Church" caused numerous misinterpretations. At the time when Christianity was adopted in the Rous' Lands, the Byzantine church practiced a two-finger sign of the cross, which later evolved into a three-finger sign but had apparently started as a one-finger sign: all these gestures were equally "Byzantine." The kalimavkion headdress was just a version of the Ottoman fez hat. As regards the hairstyle, before the Ottoman conquest, the Byzantine priests cut their hair short and shaved off the tonsure on the top of the scalp, just as their Catholic counterparts. Civic authorities, on the contrary, were distinguished by their long hair. But when the Orthodox Christian millet was created in the Ottoman Empire as a self-governing, fiscally and judicially autonomous entity, the priests became the millet's chief agents. In their capacity as civic officials, they changed the hairstyle. Nikon was aware of none of these important nuances. He vigorously enforced uniformity pursuing the ideal of the "regular Church" as the forerunner of the "regular state," just as the Jesuits created a model of the modern secular state in the Catholic world.

Between 1651 and 1656, Nikon and his supporters carried out several important reforms. For example, they banned polyglossia during the church service (the practice of several priests conducting the service at the same time, thus making it difficult for the congregation to follow); edited liturgical books according to the Greek standards; introduced the three-finger sign of the cross; replaced full earth-low bows with belt-low bows; changed the direction of the religious procession to counterclockwise; ordered that three alleluias be sung, whereas Moscow tradition called for two; and so on. One of the most radical of Nikon's decrees was the removal of old icons depicting the two-finger sign of the cross from churches and private homes. The Moscow Orthodoxy considered icons sacral, and their violation and the drastic break with the canon in icon-painting provoked harsh resistance both among lay believers and the clergy.

The Schism

The archpriest Avvakum, formerly in the circle of the Zealots of Piety with Nikon, and the Kolomna bishop Pavel led the resistance. The Moscow Synods of 1656 and 1666–7 confirmed Nikon's reforms and anathemized all those who remained true to the old liturgical customs as heretics and dissenters. They became known as the Old Believers. The Old Believers were exiled to remote monasteries, where they were imprisoned in dungeons, and the most persistent among them risked being burned alive, which was an obvious borrowing from the Catholic Inquisition.

Nikon's main opponent, the archpriest Avvakum, did not advance an alternative religious doctrine that would have made his protest against the official church comparable to Luther's original Ninety-Five Theses. Not unlike Nikon, Avvakum was interested in the standardization of worship, but he wanted to do it according to the old Moscow ways. Avvakum's ancient Moscow "norm" was as ephemeral a construct as Nikon's norm of the "Greek Church." Had Muscovy had a developed domestic theological scholastic tradition, Nikon and Avvakum might have pioneered the Orthodox Reformation as a theological revolution. But the formalized language of logical textual analysis and abstract theological theorizing was not yet available to them. Therefore, any discontent with the Orthodox Church was framed in the polemic over rituals and other formalities. This attitude revealed the shared goal of bringing the church to the ideal of a "regular"—rationalized and standardized—social institution.

Nikon's Challenge to Secular Power

This attitude eventually brought Patriarch Nikon into conflict with Tsar Alexei, which became as irreconcilable as the confrontation with the "schismatic" Avvakum. Luther's success owed a great deal to the fact that he was first and foremost a theologian and thus he did not directly challenge the lay authorities. His Reformation even helped those rulers who needed a pretext for escaping the grip of the pope and the Catholic Church on their power. By contrast, the Moscow circle of the Zealots of Piety did not include a single original theologian. Already perceiving social reality in a new light, they promoted the church reform because religion remained the main idiom for conveying one's worldview. As will be discussed in Chapter 8, important political and economic reforms were being implemented simultaneously with the church reform, but unlike the latter, the former received no rhetorical elaboration. In the 1660s and 1670s, there were still neither political treatises and pamphlets nor journalism in Muscovy to communicate political and economic ideas. Abstract thinking and written culture proliferated exclusively within the religious domain. Therefore, the support of the church reform by the tsar and his government did not mean that they prioritized liturgical matters over politics. This was just the only sphere they were able to discuss theoretically.

Similarly, having initiated the church reform, the Patriarch Nikon did not view it in isolation from other spheres of public life. Quite to the contrary, being the architect of the "regular church" greatly elevated his political status. Nikon behaved as if he had some symbolic advantage over the tsar. Born to a humble family of Mordovian peasants, Nikon was not content with becoming the first priest in the land, and included in his title of patriarch the clause "the Great Sovereign," which was formerly the tsar's prerogative. In the past, only Patriarch Filaret, the father and regent of the young tsar Mikhail Romanov, who once aspired to the throne himself, used this formula in his title. In this regard, Nikon continued the tradition of impostors as political candidates for supreme power, but he did not pretend to be someone else—a "real" tsar—he only appropriated new status as the patriarch of the reformed church.

The recently promulgated Conciliar Law Code of 1649 assigned the vast monastery landholdings to the purview of the special "ministry"—the Monastery Office—but Nikon energetically resisted the government's attempts to implement this policy. He insisted that the reformed church should remain completely autonomous and, moreover, above the government. In 1658, Nikon challenged Tsar Alexei to make a choice: either accept the patriarch's sovereignty or fight his authority. He publicly stripped himself of his patriarchal vestments and retreated to a monastery, where he spent several years testing the tsar. Alexei Mikhailovich did not yield to Nikon's pressure and, in 1666, with the help of Ukrainian clerics and two "patriarchs of the East," Paisius of Alexandria and Macarios III Zaim of Antioch, succeeded in deposing

Nikon. Personal conflict with Nikon, however, did not affect the project of building a "regular Church." It was left intact, but instead of accepting the church's leadership in societal transformation along the ideals of centralization and standardization, the tsar reserved this role for himself. He relied on the reformed church as a ready element of the future regular social order.

Little, Great, and White Russias: An Invention of Tradition

It was not a coincidence that the church reform and the dramatic schism it produced unfolded simultaneously with the civil war in the Polish–Lithuanian Commonwealth and the reorientation of its Orthodox population toward Muscovy. To a large degree, this reorientation was prepared by Kyivan Orthodox clerics, who had given up on restoring the former confessional equality in the Rzeczpospolita. The triumphant Counter-Reformation turned the nominal Republic of Two Nations into the Polonized Catholic kingdom that harassed its former loyal Orthodox Ruthenian subjects. In response, Ruthenian intellectuals came out with a vision of the great Orthodox kingdom under the Moscow tsar's rule. To be sure, Muscovy was a country not of Ruthenian people but of "Russian" people, which was the spelling used in the Conciliar Law Code of 1649. Local traditions and dialects in Kyiv and in the Moscow lands were many and diverse. However, their high bookish cultures were close, which made it possible to imagine the projected united, rationalized Russian Orthodox community as even more integrated than the existing Polish one. To substantiate this ambitious project, Ukrainian clerics and church polemicists developed the new concept of Little and Great Russias as two parts of a single "Slavic" people—similar to the way in which the Polish–Lithuanian szlachta claimed a common origin from another, Sarmatian, ancient "tribe."

The terms "Little Russia" and "Great Russia" became current in the fourteenth century. These were translations from the Greek language and referred to the differentiation accepted in Constantinople between the Galich (Halych) Metropolia (established in 1303) and Kyiv Metropolia. This happened after Metropolitan of Kyiv and all Rous' Maximus moved his official seat to Vladimir in the northeast of the Rous' Lands in 1299. In the traditional Greek usage, the designations "little" and "great/big" in relation to a territory indicated chronological precedence. For example, it was not the core territory on the Balkan Peninsula but later colonies of the Greek poleis across the Mediterranean that became known as Great Greece (Megali Hellas in Greek; Magna Graecia in Latin). Conversely, the region of Anatolia, which had originally been associated with "Asia" in early antiquity, became known as Little Asia or Asia Minor. The name signified the initial territory before Aisa's multifold extension on the mental map of Greek culture. This explains why, in the mid-seventeenth century, the Ukrainian literati decided to combine the old church concept of the Little and Great Russias (meaning: internal/external, initial/that which came after) with the new Slavic origin myth. They thus laid the foundation for the ideology of the new united polity. The implications of their creative act as well as the possible interpretations of their ideological design would transpire decades later.

In 1674, the archimandrite of the Kyivan Caves Monastery, a radical Prussian Protestant turned Orthodox monk, Innokenty Gizel (Innozenz Giesel), published *Synopsis*, the first general history of the Rous' Lands. This treatise formulated the archetypal modern narrative of the common Rus' statehood in the past and of the single "Russian Orthodox" people currently populating the lands of that former all-embracing state. Belarusian lands of the Grand Duchy of Lithuania were considered, canonically, as part of Little Russia. *Synopsis* interpreted Belarus as White Russia on a par with Little Russia and Great Russia, thus forming the triad of the tripartite Russian nation. The Moscow tsars of Great Russia—descendants of Prince Alexander Nevsky—were declared the only legitimate rulers of the composite Russian people. Gizel's model reflected the emerging conceptualization of German unity by intellectuals in various lands and sovereign states who, in the wake of the Thirty Years' War, observed the increasing disintegration of the Holy Roman Empire of the German Nation compensated by the growing coherence of high German culture. The application of this vision to Russian and Ruthenian lands was both revolutionary and completely arbitrary. In the eighteenth century, a further development of Gizel's model would lead to the reconceptualization of Muscovy as just a part of the new composite state, the Russian Empire.

Ukrainian Clerics and the Moscow "Counter-Reformation"

The mid-seventeenth-century intellectuals who politicized the church notions of Little and Great Russias hardly anticipated all the consequences of their conceptual innovation. Meanwhile, the specificity of Russian-language semantics soon resulted in changing the original Greek connotations of the terms "great" and "little." Great Russia came to be associated with preeminence, and Little Russia with junior status and deficiency (just as the Bolsheviks and Mensheviks in the twentieth century). Parallel to this development, in the wake of the civil war in the Rzeczpospolita and the Cossack state's secession, the initially polysemous concept of Ukraine acquired a main meaning connoting a periphery. This was not necessarily the case in the sociopolitical and linguistic context of the Grand Duchy of Lithuania in the fifteenth and sixteenth centuries, when Ukraine was usually understood as "krai" and "kraina"—the land and the motherland, the main forms of commoners' self-identification. In the mid-seventeenth century, nobody could have expected that a hundred years later, Kyiv's absolute cultural domination over the bleak Muscovite cultural scene would come to an end. The rise of scholastic theology and secular literature in the modernized Russian language reversed the relations of cultural dependance in the second half of the eighteenth century and redefined the *Synopsis*'s origin myth by marginalizing the historical role and cultural achievements of the Ruthenian elites.

Back in the seventeenth century, Kyiv's cultural hegemony looked solid. The educated elite from the Ukrainian lands enjoyed ever-growing influence in Muscovy due to its outstanding education received in Jesuit colleges or the Orthodox schools modeled after them. Ukrainian clerics' central role in the preparation of Nikon's reform, including editing liturgical books according to the "Greek norm," contributed to the reform's distinctive Counter-Reformation spirit. The structural transformation

The Tsardom of Muscovy

of the worldview and social thinking conveyed by the reform's general design was complemented by the distinctive style of its implementations that took the form of a ferocious culture war. Echoing the uncompromising hostility of the Orthodox Cossacks toward the Catholics and the Jews during Khmelnytsky's Uprising, the violent persecutions of the Old Believers after the Moscow Synods of 1666–7 looked like a slow-going civil war. In 1682, Archpriest Avvakum and his associates were burned alive in a log house. Many other leaders of the Old Belief, such as Nikita Dobrynin (Pustosviat), along with thousands of ordinary Old Believers fell victims of the government's war on the tsar's loyal subjects who were suddenly recognized as religious dissidents.

As will be discussed in Volume 2, it was educated Ukrainian clerics who spearheaded the assault on the Volga Muslims in the 1740s on behalf of the Russian imperial government. Despite the prevailing rhetoric of "Orthodox tsardom," in Muscovy, Muslims experienced no systemic pressure to convert and no legal discrimination. This was not because of some greater tolerance of Muscovy's religious and government authorities but because of their lack of ideological determination and assimilative skills. Unlike them, Ukrainian ideologists of the renovated Russian tsardom were inspired by the Counter-Reformation's social ideal of a well-ordered and homogeneous population and followed the Rzeczpospolita's example of rejecting any cultural hybridity. From this perspective, the tragic religious schism was an acceptable price to pay for a modern regular and hence universal Orthodox Church, open to all who were ready to accept its clearly articulated "constitution." Transcending Muscovite parochialism, such a reformed church could eagerly accommodate the brethren from the Polish–Lithuanian Commonwealth or, in the long run, the Ottoman Empire. The schism thus appeared to be a necessary precondition for the subsequent integration of different Orthodox communities into a well-governed, internally uniform community of the church and the state.

The Old Belief

The Old Belief also evolved toward universalism, but in a different sense. Initially possessing no elaborated theological doctrine and being split into a number of significantly diverging "sects," the Old Belief was an umbrella term uniting various forms of cultural, social, and political dissent. Given the underdevelopment of the rhetorical sphere in Muscovy, the Old Belief served as a social language of sorts to frame and communicate discontent, especially for the lower classes. During the first century after Nikon's reform, almost all popular uprisings involved Old Believers. Initially, they attacked churches and monasteries, but eventually social self-marginalization became their main form of protest. They tended to occupy all possible marginal social niches, from abandoning the world and living in isolation to self-immolation in remote sketes. They experimented with sexuality in a diapason from celibacy and self-castration to mass orgies. With time, intensive economic activity, viewed as a form of spiritual service—worldly asceticism—became an accepted form of practicing the Old Belief. The magnitude of the Old Belief movement is hard to access, especially since many Old Believers masked their identity by formal adherence to the official church. Peasants and merchants, who formed the social basis of the movement, often remained below the radar of the authorities, while consuming extensive literature and maintaining the underground religious hierarchy. Some currents of Old Belief were legalized in Russia only by the end of the eighteenth century.

Patriarch Nikon's church reform and the Old Believers' resistance to it can be productively compared to the original Reformation and Counter-Reformation only as a way to elucidate their systemic characteristics, without identifying completely with one or the other. In practice, the opposing religious camps in Muscovy could borrow from the repertoire of both the Protestants and the modernized Catholics. Thus, although quite "Counter-Reformative" by its goals, Nikon's reform fostered the revival of the almost forgotten practice of the sermon, which historically was a major contribution of the Reformation. On the other hand, in their revolt against the official church, the Old Believers demanded not a reform but the preservation of old liturgical ways, which formally disqualified them as a Reformation movement. Finally, both uncompromising camps accepted the possibility of condensing the entire religious experience and church organization to a single code of logically arranged principles and rules. This agreement reflected the fundamental transformation of the social imagination in Muscovy. What used to seem "natural" and "self-evident" transformed into objects of formal and hence rational reflection and, eventually, improvement.

Unification and Hybridity in Northern Eurasia

What social mechanism enabled the revolution of social imagination to occur in different societies across Northern Eurasia during a rather brief historical interval of just over a century? Was it the same mechanism, or did a unique constellation of factors and local structural conditions play a role in each case? Regardless of the answer, the very proliferation of the new perception of social institutions as autonomous and functionally differentiated, be it the church or the supreme power, testified to the ongoing consolidation of the region. Despite their multiple differences, individual societies began to share a common understanding of social processes. This was not a shared culture but just a common way of thinking about cultural and social phenomena. The individual results of a uniform thinking process could greatly vary depending on many factors, including the local distribution of power in a society.

The Counter-Reformation split the hybrid society of the Rzeczpospolita. It led to the cultural, but not political, consolidation of the Polish-Catholic szlachta as the core of the new nation and to the alienation of the Protestant and Orthodox communities. In Muscovy, the echo of the Counter-Reformation produced a split too, although different in nature and consequences. The reformed Orthodox Church did not treat any social group as a privileged community, functioning as "no one's" institution, which was equally open to everybody who accepted its "constitution." Marginalizing the advocates of Muscovy's particularism and isolationism, the reformed church became the first truly "imperial" institution capable of accommodating different local traditions into a single community of formalized principles.

Simultaneously, colonization beyond the Urals was constructing Siberia as a single region under the power of the tsar. The traditional and even archaic practices of colonization were the main factors of its success. The colonization primarily relied on informal personal agreements and the system of personalized relationships of loyalty, dependency (including hostage taking), and mutually beneficial exchanges of goods and services. It was the hybridity of its political practices that secured Muscovy's central role in the region's consolidation. The Moscow government alone was able to reconcile the post-Reformation new logic of social thinking with the ostensibly medieval system of political domination in Siberia. The Polish–Lithuanian Commonwealth and the Crimean Khanate could embrace only one of these elements but not the other. The ability to find a common language with the Cossack and Ruthenian Orthodox elites that had been rejected by the Rzeczpospolita proved the autochthonous character of Muscovy's revolution of social imagination. The Time of Troubles was an important episode in this conceptual revolution. Formally trained in liberal arts, Ukrainian clerics helped the new social thinking that was already emerging in Muscovy to acquire its rhetorical means of expression (the "language"). After that, it became possible to extend the sphere of rationalization from reforming the church to transforming the entire society, reinventing the country, now stretching from the Dnieper to the Amur. Instead of a hodgepodge of historical lands, an amalgamation of dynastic possessions, peoples, and religions, this country could be conceptualized in the abstract and universal categories of the state and empire.

Note

1   Niccolò Machiavelli, *The Prince*, translated by W. K. Marriott (London: E.P. Dutton & Company, 1908), 77–9.

Further reading

Dunning, Chester S. L. *Russia's First Civil War: The Time of Troubles and the Founding of the Romanov Dynasty*. University Park: Pennsylvania State University Press, 2001.

Forsyth, James. *A History of the Peoples of Siberia: Russia's North Asian Colony, 1581–1990*. Cambridge: Cambridge University Press, 1992.

Gruber, Isaiah. *Orthodox Russia in Crisis: Church and Nation in the Time of Crisis*. DeKalb: Northern Illinois University Press, 2012.

Perdue, Peter. *China Marches West: The Qing Conquest of Central Eurasia*. Cambridge, MA: Harvard University Press, 2010.

Perrie, Maureen. *Pretenders and Popular Monarchism in Early Modern Russia: The False Tsars of the Time of Troubles*. Cambridge: Cambridge University Press, 1995.

Index

Abbasid Caliphate   24–6, 46, 120
Aesti   131, 133, 136–7, 139, 141, 153
Ala ad-Din Muhammad II   116–17
Alans   18, 83, 116, 122–4, 127, 154, 274
Alexander Yaroslavich   145, 147, *see also*
    Nevsky, Alexander
Alexei Mikhailovich (Tsar Alexei)   281,
    284
Algirdas (Olgerd)   160–3, 170, 175, 182
Almysh   20–1
Altai Mountains   6, 113, 120
Amu Darya   25, 94, 156
Andrei Yaroslavich   148, 151
Ani Kingdom   25
animists   17–18, 192, *see also* Pagans
Armenia (Arminiya)   24–6, 116, 120
Armenians   28, 165, 201, 222
Ashot Bagratuni   24–6
assembly of the land   236, 248–50, 256,
    261–2, 265–9
Astrakhan   205, 209, 265, 271
Astrakhan Khanate   186, 188, 204–6,
    208–9, 246, 271, 273
Atil   15–18, 45, 205
Aukštaitija   131–3, 139–41, 161–3
Avar Khaganate   13, 14, 94, 112
Avvakum, archpriest   281–4, 287
Azerbaijan   24, 116, 221

Baghdad   20, 23–5, 40, 52, 72, 120
Baltic
    region   3, 38, 43, 52, 58, 111, 130,
        133–8, 140–1, 143–4, 155, 159,
        165, 228–30, 236–7, 266
    Sea   9, 23–4, 37–40, 49, 51, 55, 58, 67,
        130, 139, 155, 165, 208
    Balts   39, 41, 43, 47–9, 74, 82, 86, 90, 110,
        111, 130–1, 135–7, 139–41, 143,
        153–5
Batu   121–6, 129, 146–8, 172, 189, 209
    descendants of   152–3, 157, 161,
        168

Belarusian lands   238, 263, 286
Belarusians   140, 193, 238
Berke   153–4
Black Sea   24, 44, 46, 49, 51, 55, 57,
    164–5
    northern region of   6, 11, 13, 15,
        18, 49, 53, 89, 112, 122–3, 170,
        180, 209, 240
Boris, prince of Rostov   99, 100
Boyar Duma   236, 245–6, 254, 259, 261,
    263
boyars   46, 60–1, 72, 80, 107, 163–4, 172,
    182–5, 199, 202, 206, 211–12,
    214, 216, 245–6, 248–51, 254–6,
    259, 261, 265–7
Bukhara   25, 205, 273–4
Bulgar   20, 40, 44–5, 52, 72, 169, 172–3,
    175–6, 197
Bulgaria
    on the Danube (Kingdom of)   13,
        70, 80, 84, 93, 126
    Great   13, 19
    Volga   19–23, 44, 52, 57–8, 61,
        70–1, 85, 87, 89, 93–4, 120–3,
        125, 127, 129, 146, 154, 180,
        182, 192
Bulgars   18–24, 39, 40, 52, 79–81, 84–5,
    87, 89, 116, 121, 124, 197
Byzantium (Eastern Roman Empire)
    and its emperors   8, 9, 11–13,
        15–16, 18, 23, 25–8, 31, 34,
        45–7, 49–50, 53, 55, 57, 59–61,
        63–5, 68–9, 72–3, 79–80, 83,
        85, 88–9, 93–4, 101, 108–9, 111,
        113, 118, 130, 132, 140, 154,
        165, 186, 189–90, 192–4, 201–2,
        208, 210, 213, 283

Carpathian Mountains   2, 6, 8, 14, 19,
    23–4, 38, 53, 100, 112, 124–6,
    138, 145, 248, 271
Casimir III   160–1

Index

Caucasus 6–8, 13, 117, 123, 127, 240
    North 11, 15, 22, 116, 123, 126,
      146, 154, 206
    South 7, 12, 13, 18, 24, 25, 113,
      116, 120, 123, 127, 129
Chagatai's Ulus 121, 123, 127, 154
Charlemagne (Charles the Great) 18,
    29–32, 45, 91, 95
Charles IX 264, 266
Charles the Bald 29–30, 32–3
Chernigov 48, 56, 59, 61, 63, 102, 104–7,
    111, 121–4, 128, 139, 146, 150,
    191, 234–5, 238, 257, 261–2, 270
Chersonesus (Korsun) 64, 72, 84–5
Chinggisids 157, 168, 214, 221, 273
Chinggis Khan (Temuchin) 112, 115–22,
    124–6, 135, 146, 156, 157
Christianity (Christians) 8, 16–17, 20,
    23, 25–7, 29–31, 34, 47, 50,
    64, 68, 79, 83–6, 88–91, 93–4,
    101, 110–12, 120, 131, 134–8,
    140–1, 144–5, 151, 153, 159,
    160, 162–3, 165, 179, 187, 192,
    194–6, 201, 208, 210, 212, 215,
    221–7, 230–1, 234, 246, 270,
    282–3
Chuds 37–40, 47, 59, 181
coins 33, 40, 50–2, 58, 101–2, 104, 125,
    172, 174, 176, 182–3, 186, 189,
    198, 263
colonization 12, 38, 74, 111, 135, 145,
    194, 272, 275–6, 279–80, 288
commune, urban 95–100, 102–10,
    130–1, 133, 149, 158, 182, 206,
    247
confederation 135, 140–1, 192, 197, 201,
    221
    Prussian 131, 136–7
    Slavic-Finnish (of pactiots) 44,
      47, 49, 52, 58–60, 62, 68, 70, 73,
      82, 95–6
    steppe (of nomads) 89–90, 94,
      114–15, 117–19, 126, 128–9
Constantine the Porphyrogenitus 50,
    55–8, 61, 75
Constantinople (New Rome) 15, 26–8,
    44–7, 55, 57–61, 63–4, 68, 72,
    75, 82, 132, 189, 208, 210, 240,
    282, 285

corulership (dual rule) 17, 28, 77, 97,
    99, 102–3, 147, 148, 160–3, 175,
    182–3, 192
Cossacks 230, 264–7, 270, 272–3
    Don, Terek, Siberian, and
      Volga 253, 258–66, 270–1,
      274–6, 278–9
    Zaporozhian 112, 208, 229–38,
      240, 242, 264, 280, 286–7, 289
Counter-Reformation 226–33, 237–40,
    252, 271–2, 280–2, 286–8
Crimea 13, 15, 17, 18, 53, 84–5, 123,
    164–6, 170, 180
Crimean Khanate 182, 185, 188–9, 191,
    198–200, 202–6, 208–9, 214,
    216, 230, 234–6, 240–2, 253,
    270, 273, 279–80, 289
crusaders 120, 133–41, 143, 150–3, 156,
    159–61, 164, 213
Curonians 130, 139–41, 151, 153

Daniel (Danil) of Galicia 128–9, 146–8,
    151–3, 155, 172
Danube 8, 13, 23, 53, 61, 70–3, 75, 80–1,
    84, 93–4, 112–13, 118, 124, 165,
    194, 202
Daugava 131, 134–6, 138, 140–1
Demark 29, 139, 165
Desht-i Qipchaq (Polovtsian
    steppe) 113, 120–2, 124–6,
    128, 138–9, 143, 146, 154, 209,
    241
Devlet Giray 204, 209
Dmitry, son of Ivan IV 255, 262, 268
Dmitry Donskoy 161–2, 168–76,
    179–81, 185–6, 197
Dmitry Shemyaka 182–5
Dnieper 23–4, 37–9, 44–53, 55–9, 66,
    71–3, 82, 89, 98, 105–6, 118,
    123–4, 160, 164, 171, 186, 202,
    231, 234, 238, 241, 289
Dnieper trade route 44, 62, 70, 98,
    131
Don 13, 15, 18, 45, 53, 112, 118, 121,
    170, 175, 180, 186, 253, 261,
    270, 274
Drevlian land 76, 78, 100
Drevlians 50–1, 54, 57, 59, 62, 64–6,
    75–8, 80, 87

Edigey (Edigu)   180

False Dmitry   255–63, 267, 269, *see also* Otrepiev
False Dmitry II   263–5, 269
Fergana   25–6
Filaret, Patriarch, *see* Romanov, Fedor
Finnish language   38–9, 81–2, 107, 191, 224
Finns (Finno-Ugric peoples)   8, 22, 38–44, 47, 49, 62, 67, 74, 82, 86, 88, 90, 96, 110–11, 131, 135–6, 145, 154–5
Frankish Empire   18, 31, 41, 45
Frankish kingdoms   29–32, 42, 45, 53, 63, 74, 101, 275
Franks   29–32, 34–5, 39, 45, 57, 74, 94
Fyodor Ivanovich   246, 268

Galich (Halych)   124, 146, 161, 285
Galicia (Halychyna)   106, 111, 151–2, 193, 195
Galician-Volhynian principality   106, 124, 129, 139–40, 146–7, 149–51, 155–6, 159–61, 192
Gantimur   279
Gediminas   159–61
Godunov, Boris   246–8, 250, 254–9, 262–3, 268, 275
Goryeo, Kingdom of   119–20
Great Ming Empire   219–20, 278
Great Yuan State   120, 126–7, 219
Grodno   131–2, 139
Güyük   123, 126, 147–8

Halych, *see* Galich
Halychyna, *see* Galicia
hetman
        Grand Crown   231, 234
        of Lithuania   235, 237
        of the Zaporozhian Sich   231, 234–6
Hetmanate, Cossack   238, 280
Holy Roman Empire   124, 126, 136–7, 143–4, 151–3, 155, 165, 187, 190, 192, 194, 197, 202, 207–8, 210, 215, 223, 225, 227, 234, 270, 286

Horde, Golden   127, 129–30, 145, 147, 149, 153–72, 174–7, 179–81, 183, 185–9, 191–4, 196–7, 205, 209–10, 214, 230–1, 240, 271–2, *see also* Jochi's Ulus and Horde, Great
Horde, Great   180–2, 185–91, 193, 198, 204, 214, 271
Hulagu   120
Hungarians   18, 19, 23, 53, 72, 81, 83, 93–4, 100, 108, 111–12, 124–5, 131, 138
Hungary, Kingdom of   14, 53, 70, 93, 111, 123–6, 138, 145–6, 165

Ibn-Fadlan, Ahmad   20, 44
Igor   47, 56, 59–62, 64–7, 72–3, 75, 77
Ilkhanate   127, 154
Ilmen   37–42, 44, 89
Islam   12, 15–17, 19–23, 26–7, 34, 52, 84–5, 87, 89, 94, 156–7, 163, 201, 203, 206, 221–2, *see also* Muslims
Ivan I Kalita   158–61, 167, 172
Ivan III   186–95, 197–8, 200, 202, 209, 211
Ivan IV (Terrible)   202–17, 245–50, 252–6, 260, 267, 273–4
Iziaslav Yaroslavich   102–3, 108, 132

Jebe   116, 123
Jesuits   226, 229, 232–3, 235, 279, 282–3, 286
Jews   16, 17, 83, 165, 201, 222–3, 227, 234–5, 263, 287
Jin, Great   115–17, 119
Jochi   121, 169
Jochi's Ulus   123, 126–7, 129, 144–7, 152–4, 166, 180, 209, 231, 273
Jogaila (Władysław II)   162–5, 170–1, 173, 175–6
Judaism   16–19, 21, 23, 39, 83–4, 88–9
Jurchens   114–17, 119, 130, 219

Karaites   164–5
Karakorum   127, 147–8, 154, 156
Kazan   6, 192, 203–5
        Khanate   180, 182–5, 192, 197–206, 208–9, 246, 271, 273

Palace, the Office of 205
    region 259, 263, 265, 270, 273
Kęstutis 160–3, 173, 175–6
Khabar, Ivan 199
Khabarov, Yerofei 278
khagan, title of 13–17, 20, 45, 57, 77, 88,
    90, 95
Khazaria (Khazar Khaganate,
    Khazars) 13–20, 22–4, 39,
    40, 44–7, 49, 50–3, 57–8, 70–2,
    77, 79, 81, 83–4, 87–90, 94, 98,
    205
Khmelnytsky, Bohdan 232–7, 287
Khwarezm 20, 25, 116–17, 119, 127
Kichi Muhammad 185, 189
Kipchaks 113, 121, 157, 187
Kolomna 122, 170, 182, 204, 283
Korsun, *see* Chersonesus
Krivichians 37–8, 40, 47, 56–7, 59, 61,
    74, 81
Kuchum 205, 252, 273–5
Kulikovo battle 170–1, 173–4, 186
Kurbat 13
Kurbsky, Andrei 207
kurultai 115, 119–21, 126, 128
Kyiv 23–4, 37, 46–50, 52–4, 56–9, 61, 63,
    66, 70–1, 73, 75–6, 78–9, 81–5,
    87, 96, 99, 103, 105, 111, 116,
    123–4, 128, 131, 160–1, 164,
    186–7, 234–5, 241, 257, 286
    Collegium 282
    Epiphany Brotherhood
        School 232
    principality 57, 60, 62, 64–5, 67,
        70, 72, 75–8, 80, 85–6, 88, 90,
        94–109, 112, 122, 128–9, 132,
        135, 146–7, 152, 160, 169, 187,
        192, 195
Kyivan Metropolitan 158, 185, 193, 235,
    285

Ladoga, Old 39, 42, 56, 58, 71
Ladoga Lake 37–9, 42–5, 48–9, 52, 58
Latgalians 47, 49, 136–7, 139, 141
Lithuania
    Grand Duchy of 130, 144, 150–1,
        153–6, 159–67, 175–6, 179,
        181–2, 184, 186–96, 199–200,
        207–10, 213, 227, 230, 232,

    237–8, 249, 251, 255, 257, 263,
        286
    lands of 130–6, 139–41, 145, 147,
        149–50, 152
Lithuanians 131–2, 135, 150–2, 155,
    159–62, 164, 170–1, 173, 179,
    182, 229
Lituans 111, 132–4, 136–7, 139–41, 145,
    150, 255, 274
Livonia 133–4, 138–9, 144, 146, 151,
    153, 156, 192, 209–11, 237
Livonian Brothers of the Sword 135,
    137–8, 140–1, 149–51, 153,
    159
Livonian War 195, 208–9, 213–14, 248,
    253, 271, 273
Livs 49, 131, 133–7, 139, 141
Luther, Martin 223–4, 247, 283–4
Lyubech 47–8, 56, 59, 105, 106
    conference 105–9, 131

Macedonian dynasty 27–8
Magyars, *see* Hungarians
Mamai 168–72, 174–5, 179, 186
Manchuria 11, 114–15, 219, 277
Mari 199, 203
marriage patterns 10, 51, 73, 83–4,
    108–9, 133–4, 148, 151, 157,
    159, 162, 165, 189–90, 202, 206,
    235, 255, 270
Marwan II 15
Mawarannahr 25–6, 40, 94, 121, 127,
    169
Mazovia 131–2, 137–8
Mehmed Giray 198–9
Mengu-Timur (Möngke Temür) 153–4,
    157
Merians 37–8, 40, 47, 54, 59, 82, 85, 107
Merv 25
Mikhail Fyodorovich (Tsar
    Mikhail) 267, 270, 284
millets 201, 203–4, 222, 282–3
Mindaugas 149, 151–3, 155
Ming, *see* the Great Ming Empire
Möngke 120–1, 123, 126, 148, 153–4
Mongol empire (Yeke Mongyol
    Ulus) 112, 119, 126, 127,
    129–30, 146–9, 153–7, 182,
    271

Mongols 9, 14, 21, 48, 90, 94, 111, 113–
30, 135–6, 141, 143, 145–57,
212–13, 219, 235, 253, 271
Monomakh, *see* Vladimir Monomakh
Moscow, Grand Principality of 157–8,
162, 164, 166–77, 179–201,
230, 246, *see also* Tsardom of
Muscovy
Mstislav, prince of Kyiv 109, 132
Mughal Empire 220–3
Muscovy 163, 184, 187, 188, 195–202,
204–17, 225, 227, 233, 235–8,
240–2, 245–73, 275–89, *see also*
Grand Principality of Moscow
and Tsardom of Muscovy
musketeers 207, 212, 245, 254, 258–9,
262, 274
Muslims 14–15, 17–20, 23, 27, 85–6,
154, 159, 165, 187, 192, 195,
197, 201, 203–4, 211, 220–1,
227, 247, 280, 287, *see also* Islam

Neman 131, 140, 160
Neva 37, 39, 44, 131, 145, 148
Nevsky, Alexander 129, 145, 147–9,
151–3, 166–7, 179, 186, *see also*
Alexander Yaroslavich
New Sarai (Sarai-al-Jadid) 168–72,
174–6
Nikon 281–8
Nizhny Novgorod 169, 172–4, 183,
197–9, 202–3, 266–7, 269–70
Nogai Horde 180, 191, 205, 209, 240,
273
nomads 6–22, 26–7, 48, 50–1, 53–4,
72, 81, 83, 88–90, 94, 99, 100,
102–3, 111–20, 124–8, 135,
146–7, 149, 156, 160, 205, 221,
240–2, 273, 275–6
Normandy 41–2
Normans 28–30, 32, 38, 42, 45–6, 62, 77,
80–1, 213, *see also* Vikings
Norway 24, 74, 79, 93–4
Novgorod 38–9, 41–2, 44, 46–50, 52–4,
56–8, 60, 66–7, 70, 75–6, 79–81,
85, 87, 96, 99–105, 107–11, 122,
132–4, 136, 139–41, 144–5,
147–9, 152, 160, 169–70, 172–4,
183–8, 190–3, 197–200, 202–3,

209, 212, 215, 261, 264–7,
270–2, 274, 281

Ögedei 121, 123, 126
Oghuz Turks 94, 112
Old Belief 283, 287–8, *see also* Schism
Oleg, prince of Kyiv 47–51, 55–6, 59–62,
77, 87
Oleg Sviatoslavich, prince of Drevlian
land 73, 75–8, 80
Olga 66–73, 75–9, 82–4, 97
Onon River 113, 115, 119
oprichnina 211–16, 245–6, 248
Orthodox Church 30, 84, 110, 136, 140,
154, 157–60, 162, 165, 184–5,
195–6, 200–1, 210–12, 222,
227–32, 234, 238, 246, 255,
281–5, 287–8
Otrepiev, Yuri (Grigory) 254–5, 259
Ottoman Empire 3, 138, 165, 189,
200–1, 203–4, 221–2, 233,
235–6, 240–2, 282–3, 287

Pagans 22, 30, 47, 59, 68, 79, 82, 110–11,
134–5, 137–8, 140, 145, 151–4,
156, 159, 161–2, 166, 179, 195,
201, *see also* Animists
Palestine 120, 138
Pannonia 14, 19, 31, 53, 83, 124–6, 138
Patriarch of Constantinople 27, 34, 185,
193, 210, 227, 246, 282
Pechenegs 19, 53–4, 59–61, 71–3, 81–2,
88, 99–100, 103, 111–13, 124,
131, 149
Pereyaslavl 59, 61, 63, 102, 106, 111,
123–4, 160, 236
Pereyaslavl-Zalessky 122, 148, 173
Persia 7, 8, 11–12, 24–5, 34–5, 221, 259,
270
Poland, Kingdom of 2, 99, 106, 111,
124–5, 129, 131, 152, 155,
161–6, 184, 187, 193–6, 208,
227, 229–30, 237–8
Polish lands 125, 131, 137
Polish–Lithuanian Commonwealth 163,
166, 195, 210, 227–34, 236–40,
246, 253, 257–9, 263–4, 266–7,
269, 271, 274, 280, 282, 285,
287, 289, *see also* Rzeczpospolita

Polotsk   38, 59, 74, 79, 97, 103, 108,
   131–4, 136–7, 139, 140, 147,
   149–51
Polotsk, city and principality   38, 59, 74,
   79, 97, 103, 108, 131–4, 136–7,
   139–40, 147, 149–51
Polovtsians   82, 103–4, 109–11, 113, 116,
   121–4, 127–9, 138, 149, 154
Pope   93, 134, 137–8, 141, 159, 165, 189,
   210, 225–6, 228, 230, 284
prikazy (government offices)   200, 205,
   207, 212, 284
Primary Chronicle   24, 37, 46, 50, 52, 59,
   73, 75, 84–5, 87
Protestantism   195, 211, 215, 223–9,
   236–40, 286, 288
Prussia   211, 213, 237–8, 278, 286
Prussians   130–1, 133, 135, 137–9,
   144–6, 153, 155–6
Pskov   66, 133, 139, 141, 144–5, 147, 159,
   160, 193, 197, 199, 254, 261, 263

Qasim Khanate   183, 185, 187, 197–8,
   200, 205, 270
   khan of   184, 192, 203, 214
Qing Empire   219–22, 272, 277–80

Radimichis   47–8, 50–1, 55–6, 59
Radziwiłł, Janusz, Grand Hetman of
   Lithuania   235, 237
Radziwiłł, Janusz, Lithuanian
   magnate   229
Reconquista   194, 197, 213
Reformation   195, 223, 225–7, 230,
   237–8, 247, 271–2, 281, 284,
   288–9
religion   8, 10, 15–16, 18–23, 25–6, 68,
   81, 83–5, 89, 93, 110, 127, 134–
   5, 140, 153, 156–7, 163, 165–6,
   194–5, 221–3, 225, 227–9, 231,
   235, 237–8, 240, 246, 269, 272,
   282, 284
retinue   21, 38, 41–4, 46, 48, 52, 57–68,
   70–81, 85–8, 90, 95, 97–9,
   103–4, 110, 133, 144, 150–1,
   158, 171
Rhône   16, 29, 32
Rhos and Rhosia   45–6, 55–8, 60, 63–4,
   69, 76, 81, see also Varangians

Riga   49, 131, 134–41, 144, 159, 238
rokosz   229, 235, 238, 264
Rollo (Hrólfr, Robert)   29, 41
Romanov, Fyodor (Patriarch
   Filaret)   254–6, 259, 263, 267,
   270, 284
Rostov   38, 59, 82, 85, 99, 106–8, 157,
   173, 193
Rous' Lands   42–4, 49–68, 70–91, 93–8,
   101–3, 105–13, 118, 120–1,
   123–5, 127–31, 133–6, 139–41,
   143–4, 146–52, 154–6, 159–62,
   164, 166–7, 169, 171, 179,
   181–2, 184, 186–7, 189, 191–4,
   196, 202, 209–10, 217, 230, 256,
   282–3, 285–6
Rurik   38, 41–2, 44, 46–7, 52, 56, 58, 71,
   73–4, 82, 93, 96, 98, 129, 187
Rurikid princes   73, 98, 102–3, 105,
   107–10, 129–30, 140, 156, 158,
   250, 261
Ruthenian language (rus'ka mova)   193,
   238
Ruthenians (rus'kie)   91, 149, 152–3,
   162, 179, 186, 190, 193, 195–6,
   230, 232–5, 237–9, 270, 285–6,
   289
Ryazan   106, 121–2, 149, 164–5, 170–1,
   173–5, 193, 197, 199, 200, 261,
   266, 270
Rzeczpospolita   163, 195, 227, 236–41,
   257, 260, 262, 279–80, 285–9,
   see also Polish–Lithuanian
   Commonwealth

Safa Giray   202, 204
Safavid dynasty   221–3
Sahib Giray   198–9
Samanid Emirate   25–7, 52, 94
Samarkand   25
Samogitia and Samogitians   139–41, 151,
   153, 160, 163–4
Sarai   156, 205, see also New Sarai
Sarmatian
   myth   232
   population   48, 83, 285
Scandinavia   6, 9, 29, 39, 43, 45, 62, 70,
   76, 84, 89, 93–4, 130
Schism   283–5, 287, see also Old Belief

Index

Scythian
    Kingdom 11
    population 48, 73, 83, 232
Semender 15, 17
Semigallians 135–6, 140–1, 151, 153
service Tatars 192, 197, 203, 266
servitors 182, 185, 191, 193, 200, 206–7,
    212, 216, 249–55, 257–64,
    266–7, 269–73, 275–8, 280
Severians 48, 50–4, 56, 57, 59, 71, 81, 83
Shahghali (Shah-Ali) 199, 203, 205
Shaybanids 273–4
Shuisky, Vasily 256, 261–6, 269
Shvarn 151, 155
Siberia 3, 6, 7, 112, 114, 117, 121, 192,
    252–3, 259, 266, 270–81, 288–9
Siberian Khanate 180, 209, 252, 273–5
Sigismund III Vasa 227–9, 232, 237–8,
    257, 259, 264–7, 269
Silk Road 16, 40, 49, 72
Simeon Bikbulatovich (Sain Bulat) 205,
    214, 216, 249–50
Simeon the Proud 160–1, 167
slaves and slave trade 11, 14, 39, 58, 66,
    70, 73, 79, 84, 118, 175, 202, 234,
    236, 241–2, 247, 254, 262
Slavs 14, 18, 37–44, 46–8, 50, 54, 57–8,
    62, 65, 67, 74, 81–3, 86, 88, 90,
    96, 107, 110, 131, 136–7, 140,
    154, 187, 285
Slovenes 38–40, 42, 44, 47, 59, 61, 81, 83
Smolensk 47, 49, 56, 106–8, 122, 128–9,
    132–3, 139–40, 147, 150, 157,
    159, 170, 176, 186, 190, 200,
    238, 253, 257, 263, 266, 269, 271
sovereignty 1, 16, 49, 53, 74, 77–8,
    101, 162, 167, 171–2, 174, 179,
    181, 184–7, 190, 196–202, 206,
    208, 228, 240, 247, 251, 267,
    272, 284
statehood 62–3, 67, 73–4, 76, 95–6, 101,
    197, 200, 235
strel'tsy, *see* musketeers
Subutai 116, 123–5
Sui dynasty 7, 8, 114
Suzdal land 106–8, 121, 158, 168, 170,
    261, *see also* Vladimir-Suzdal
    principality
Sviatopolk Iziaslavich 106, 109

Sviatopolk Vladimirovich (the
    Accursed) 99–101
Sviatoslav 56, 67–73, 75–9, 81, 84–7,
    94, 97
Sviyazhsk 203–4
Sweden 29, 62, 108, 148, 165, 192, 208,
    223, 229–30, 236–8, 253, 257,
    264, 266
szlachta 140, 163, 193, 227–40, 256–7,
    259–60, 263–4, 269–70, 285, 288

Tang Empire 114–15
Tanguts 115–16
Tatars, Central Asian 115–16
Temuchin, *see* Chinggis Khan
Tengrism 15, 17, 19
Teutonic Order 111, 137–8, 141, 144–6,
    150–3, 155–6, 159–65
Thirty Years' War 227, 232, 234, 237,
    239, 242, 286
Timur (Tamerlane) 163, 169, 180, 220–1
Tmutarakan (Tamantarkhan) 87, 101,
    104
Tokhtamysh 163–4, 169–77, 179–81
Torks 87, 111–13, 124
Transylvania 53, 125, 138, 235
Treniota 153
tribute 11–12, 18–19, 22, 27–8, 40,
    46–51, 55, 57–62, 64–7, 70, 72,
    74, 87, 99, 113, 124, 129, 134,
    146–7, 149, 154, 157–8, 167–9,
    171, 176–7, 179, 180, 185–6,
    188–92, 198, 206, 209, 241,
    272–3, 276
tsar, as emperor's title 130, 173–4,
    189–93, 202–11, 213–17, 236,
    249–53, 268
Tsardom of Muscovy 202–16, 236–8,
    241–2, 246, 248–55, 257–8,
    260–73, 275, 277–81, 285–9
Tungus peoples and languages 113–15,
    117, 275, 277
Turkic Khaganate 11, 13, 14, 112, 114,
    117, 124

Uglich 122, 146, 203, 255, 262, 268
Ukrainian (Ruthenian) lands 229–31,
    234, 238, 241, 263, 286
Ulugh Muhammad 181–3, 185

298 *Index*

Uniate (Greek Catholic) Church 210, 228, 230
Union of Brest 210, 228, 238, 246
Union of Kreva 162–3
Union of Lublin 163, 195, 227, 230, 237
Ural Mountains 6, 14, 23–4, 38, 53, 72, 112, 118, 121, 124, 126, 143, 180, 191, 194, 205, 253, 270–4, 280, 288
Uyghur Khaganate 114, 121
Uzbek, khan 156–60, 167, 172, 176, 186

Varangians 37–8, 40–2, 46–7, 49, 56, 58–62, 65, 68, 73–4, 79–82, 84, 90, 95, 98–101, 108, 110, 131, 133, *see also* Vikings
Vasilko Romanovich 152, 155
Vasily I 164, 180, 186
Vasily II 164–5, 180–6, 197
Vasily III 198–202, 206, 211
veche 41, 76, 95–7, 99, 102–4, 107, 158, 182, 193, 199, 248
Vesians (Ves') 37–8, 47, 54
Vikings 28–30, 32–3, 37–48, 54, 62, 67, 69, 71, 81, 84, 93–4, 130, *see also* Varangians
Vladimir Monomakh 103–9, 186, 190–2, 209
Vladimir-Suzdal principality 110, 120–3, 129, 144–5, 147–52, 154, 158, 166–8, 174, 176, 179, 185–6, 193, 196
Vladimir Sviatoslavich 23, 68, 73, 75–6, 78–88, 94–102, 108, 111, 131, 186–7

Voishelk (Vaišelga) 153
Volga 6, 13, 15, 18–22, 37–40, 42–5, 49, 52–4, 58, 67, 70, 72, 81, 83, 87, 89, 112, 116, 118, 121–2, 126, 147, 165, 169, 172–5, 180, 182, 186, 199, 203, 205, 208, 253, 255, 259, 265–7, 270
Volga–Baltic trade route 39–42, 44–5, 49, 52, 54, 56, 58, 70, 72, 82, 87, 89, 98, 111, 131, 209
Volhynia 106, 111, 132, 139, 155, 161, 165, 195, 234, *see also* Galician-Volhynian principality
Volkhov 38–9, 42, 44
Vseslav of Polotsk 103, 132
Vyatichians 50–1, 70, 81, 87, 107
Vyshgorod (Vusegrad) 56, 66
Vytautas 162–6, 173, 175–6, 180–1, 186, 195

Xiongnu 9, 11, 114, 118

Yadegar Mokhammad 204–5
Yadigar 205–6, 271, 273–4
yarlyk (*Zarlig*) 129, 148–9, 154, 157–8, 167–8, 172, 174, 176, 181, 193
Yaropolk 75–80, 97, 99, 101
Yaroslav Vladimirovich 88, 99–104, 108, 131–2, 147
Yaroslav Vsevolodovich 122, 128–9, 147–8, 150
Yermak 273–4
Yotvingians 121, 139, 151, 155–6

Zaporozhian Sich 231, 234

Printed in the USA
CPSIA information can be obtained
at www.ICGtesting.com
LVHW020443040724
784649LV00003B/61